The Economics of Human Rights

Economics plays a key role in human rights issues as decision-makers weigh the incentives associated with choosing how to use scarce resources in the context of committing or escaping human rights violence. This textbook provides an introduction to the microeconomic analysis of human rights utilizing economics as a lens through which to examine social topics including capital punishment, violence against women, asylum seeking, terrorism, child abuse, genocide, and hate.

Whether analyzing the decisions made in capital punishment cases, the causes and consequences of genocide, or the impact of terrorist acts on domestic and international decision-making, the science of economics provides tools and a systematic method of analysis and policy recommendation. This key text presents a method for integrating the social sciences of economics and human rights to create new opportunities for the investigation of social issues. Within each chapter, readers gain a fundamental understanding of a specific human rights issue, the decision-makers and the decision-making process involved, and the benefits and costs leading to the decisions. Experts on each issue, drawn from a variety of fields, contribute to each chapter and present first-hand accounts and different perspectives on each issue. The detailed analyses and accounts provided also explore the potential incentives involved in the prevention and termination of human rights violations.

Aiming to further economic inquiry and enhance interdisciplinary research, this textbook serves as a multi-purpose guide for a range of readers. Students, researchers, and educators, as well as those working in organizations supporting victims of human rights violations and policy-makers facing human rights challenges, will find this book informative and engaging.

Elizabeth M. Wheaton is a senior lecturer in economics at Southern Methodist University, USA. She is also the founder and CEO of Equip the Saints, a nonprofit consultancy that works to strengthen nonprofit organizations worldwide and to equip world changers to fulfil their personal missions, and a researcher on the subjects of child labor and the economics of human rights. She believes that you don't need a title, unlimited time, or abundant resources to change the world.

The Economics of Human Rights

Elizabeth M. Wheaton

Routledge
Taylor & Francis Group

LONDON AND NEW YORK

First published 2019
by Routledge
2 Park Square, Milton Park, Abingdon, Oxon OX14 4RN

and by Routledge
711 Third Avenue, New York, NY 10017

Routledge is an imprint of the Taylor & Francis Group, an informa business

British Library Cataloguing-in-Publication Data
A catalogue record for this book is available from the British Library

Library of Congress Cataloging-in-Publication Data
A catalog record has been requested for this book

ISBN: 978-1-138-50015-0 (hbk)
ISBN: 978-1-138-50016-7 (pbk)
ISBN: 978-1-351-01299-7 (ebk)

Typeset in Minion Pro
by Apex CoVantage, LLC

Visit the eResources: www.routledge.com/9781138500167

All of the glory belongs to God (Romans 8.28). All of the mistakes are my own.

Contents

Detailed contents

Acknowledgments

- Dr. Rick Halperin – for talking me into writing this textbook, shared hugs and tears, never-ending information on human rights, and contributing to this textbook.
- Jonathan Walther – for brainstorming case studies, creating datasets, and performing the econometric analysis for many of the textbook chapters.
- My incredible team of editors at Routledge Publishing and copyeditor, Dr. Helen Renwick.
- My brilliant textbook contributors – Dr. V. Wolfe Mahfood, Dr. Dennis Longmire, Jonathan Walther, Hannah Schauer, Dr. Sarah Feuerbacher, Eleazar Javier Saldivia Flores, Mike Fullilove, Al "Jeep" Castorena, Sandy Storm, Dr. Molly Arnold, Ardis Lo, Dr. Megan Parker-Hoffman, Dr. Ben Voth, Dr. Celestin Musekura, Earl McClellan, and Officer Dan Russell.
- My incredible research assistants at Southern Methodist University: Jonathan Walther, Juliette Barnum, Konnor Kinnear, Rory Samuels, Michael Wilson, Nick Whitaker, Zach Thompson, Daniel Howard, Dr. Sanchari Choudhary, Dr. Manan Roy, and Eimon Akbari.
- My beloved mentors – Dr. Mike Leeds and Dr. Mohsen Fardmanesh
- My beautiful family for encouragement, edits, and prayer – Dr. Ed and Ila Schauer, Jake Schauer, Hannah Schauer, and Sarah Engel, and the rest who love me as their person and who call me Aunt Beth.
- My encouragers – Dr. Laura Storino, Dr. Tomi Grover, Gina Garcia, SMU Economics Department, Dr. James Quick, Shoreline City, Northwest Bible Church Hesed group, and so many others.
- My experts – Jason Kalow, Dr. Joshua Rovner, Walt Green, James Balthazar, Dr. Jason McKenna, and attorneys Tom Hartsell, Jim Jenkins, Cindy Hellstern, Michael Hartley, and Craig Washington.
- My students at Southern Methodist University, Temple University, and Grambling State University.
- God the Father, Jesus Christ, and the Holy Spirit who make all things possible.

Preface

Principal features of the textbook

Each chapter is built to provide a consistent, logical structure so that the economic skills learned through this textbook are translatable for use in other fields of research. The first chapter of the textbook introduces students to the economic study of human rights, describes the steps to using economics to study any social issue, and sets the structure that will be used for each chapter. Each chapter following this introduction of technique will focus on a specific human rights topic: Capital punishment, violence against women, seeking asylum, terrorism, child abuse, genocide, and hate. Section 1 of each chapter begins with a general introduction to the human rights topic plus perspective introductions by experts in each issue. Section 2 provides fundamentals of the human right including key terms and the different perspectives involved. Section 3 includes a short description of the national and international agreements and laws related to the issue as well as major controversies related to those agreements. This section closes with a "check yourself" box to allow students to write their initial thoughts and views about the topic being discussed. In this way, students will be able to determine the biases that they bring to the study of the social issue. Section 4 follows with a brief history of the human rights topic. Section 5 gives an introduction to some of the major experts on the social issue as well as relevant data sources. This section closes with another "check yourself" box to allow students to write their thoughts about the potential biases in published research, the ideas of experts, and the data. Section 6 discusses some of the economic aspects of human rights and includes costs, benefits, and inefficiencies present in the economic structure of the human right. Section 7 presents the student with the opportunity to do econometric analysis with real data from the human rights field. Section 8 gives recommendations for future economics research in the human right and discusses limitations on economic analyses in this topic. This section closes with the final "check yourself" box to allow students to discuss how their ideas have changed about the human rights topic after completing the reading and econometric analyses. Section 9 provides a complete bibliography for the chapter. Section 10 provides the student with a chapter summary, key terms, review questions, recommended readings, web links to relevant information, and for some chapters, analytical problems.

The human rights topics under discussion are placed in a particular order in this textbook. Capital punishment is the first topic due to the wide range of data available for analysis, the succinct terminology from criminal justice, and the existing formal legal procedure. This chapter allows students to see an existing structure, work with a large dataset, and analyze the topic with some level of depth. Violence against women is the second topic. This is a wide area of study and this textbook covers only a narrow portion of the research. This chapter allows a view of a large field of information, works with a specific dataset, and analyzes a particular piece of the entire topic. Seeking asylum is the third topic, yet it is not in itself a human rights violation. It is more difficult to get a grasp of this topic due to the wide range of definitions of seeking asylum from around the world and the areas where seeking asylum may lead to human rights violations. Refugees and asylum seekers are often thought of as one and the same, which complicates the research. This topic will allow students to dig into a field that is current, but imprecise. Terrorism is the fourth topic. Acts of terrorism and sometimes the actions of governments responding to terrorism lead to violations of human rights. Child abuse is the fifth topic. Many of the human rights violations discussed within the textbook have an adverse, and possibly magnified, effect on children. Genocide, the sixth topic, is not only a field of research in itself, but may include aspects of all of the other human rights topics. The economics of hate, an area with relatively vague definitions, is the final topic. There are few datasets on incidents of hate and the existing ones may be contested due to the fact that the data-gatherers created the specific definitions for their datasets. Working through the topics in this order allows students to move from studying more formal, defined topics to fluid areas of research that are currently being created.

While there are some step-by-step instructions, this textbook is mainly written as a guidebook to assist students in learning to analyze diverse topics through the lens of economics. There are few social issues that have been fully defined, identified, and quantified. Most problem statements depend upon the stakeholders in the issue. The economist's task is to obtain relevant information, interpret it in economics terms, analyze the issue using reliable data, and present it in a way that is logical and intuitive. This textbook provides readers with guidance on how to research and analyze human rights issues; make observations regarding background information, existing discussions about the issue, and the sources and reliability of data; apply deductive and inductive economic reasoning to interpret and model the complications of a specific contemporary issue; perform qualitative and quantitative data analysis and inference of patterns; think critically about the problem for the purpose of discerning whether a different problem than the one stated by stakeholders may exist; understand that different approaches may lead to different solutions; and provide possible policy recommendations.

Check yourself boxes

The three check yourself boxes in each chapter pose questions in relation to a different aspect of the chapter text, as follows:

Check yourself box 1: Personal biases
What are the student's biases toward the human rights topic? What are the sources of these
    biases? This personal activity allows students to discover and list personal biases that
    may be influencing their ideas and research methods.

Check yourself box 2: Research and data biases
Each of the topics is intense and has the potential to create opposing views. These views can
    translate into biases. This activity gives students the chance to identify potential biases
    in published research, organizational behavior, and datasets.

Check yourself box 3: Changes to bias
Some of the material in the chapter will be new to many students. In addition to provid-
    ing new information for decision-making, the material could change a person's initial
    biases, or create new biases. This final activity in each chapter presents a way for students
    to see how the process of gaining new insight has affected personal biases that can influ-
    ence their research.

Supplements

The textbook has online components to enhance the learning experience for students, faculty, and academic staff.

Each student will have access to the following resources:

- A personal journal that can be downloaded and saved to complete the three check yourself boxes in each chapter. These journals can be saved for personal access and for copying and pasting into class assignments.
- A guideline to government and nongovernment (nonprofit) organizations and resources associated with each of the human rights topics from the textbook.
- Quizzes and flashcards that can be downloaded, saved, and printed to facilitate study of the textbook material.

Each faculty or academic staff member will have access to the following resources:

- A guideline to using the check yourself boxes as class assignments.
- PowerPoint® slides highlighting key points and definitions for classroom presentations.
- Short-answer questions that can be used for exams, posted online for educational management, or emailed to students. Each assignment will include suggested answers. The questions can be used as practice or as graded assignments.
- Empirical data to accompany the econometric exercises will be available in the form of Excel® sheets. This data can be posted online for educational management or emailed to students for their use. Each assignment will include suggested answers to the empirical assignments. The analyses in the textbook utilize STATA®, but other data analysis software may be used.

The eResources can be found at: www.routledge.com/9781138500150

---

1 Economics of human rights

Contributor: Rick Halperin, Ph.D.

IT TAKES LITTLE time to open the news and read about the horrors going on around the world, some of which are too close for personal comfort. Many people put up a wall to protect themselves from these horrors, choosing to focus on protecting their own families and belongings. While one's own comfort can crowd out some of the discomforts of the world, there are other people who seek positive change in the world and are willing to put time, energy, and resources toward creating that change.

Change by itself does little good if the circumstances surrounding the present realities are unknown or not understood. When coupled with knowledge from other fields, economics provides a way to analyze the decision-making processes at work in social situations. Economics can help when a social scientist wants to know the consequences of a county deciding to try a murder case as a capital case in which the outcome may be the death penalty; when an international nonprofit organization is concerned about the likelihood of genocide occurring in one of its target areas; when a politician wonders how violence against women affects the viability of laws and voting outcomes; when a citizen ponders how much of the news about "hate crimes" is accurate; when a traveler considers the incidence of terrorism in a specific area; or when human rights organizations are interested in how human rights violations occur during asylum seeking. Each of these events relates to the decision-makers themselves, the costs and benefits they face, and the outcomes of those decisions. This process is called cost-benefit analysis and is one of the foundations of economics.

Economics is the study of choice when dealing with scarcity. Social issues are prime places to study scarcity and the choices being made on those landscapes. This textbook is for those who want to 1) understand how economic applications can address social issues and 2) understand how economics can be applied to any topic. Economics is one way to analyze the choices being made in each area of human rights and to pinpoint positive or negative incentives that can be used in policy-making to affect those choices.

This chapter provides a pathway through the basic structure of the textbook. Each chapter will mirror this structure to provide the clearest understanding of the process of approaching a human rights topic through the lens of economics. Economics takes the approach of observation to create hypotheses, collecting data related to these hypotheses, analyzing this data, reporting outcomes as well as whether the hypotheses were proven true or false, or not proven, and recommending which variables could change the incentives that affect decision-makers. The study of human rights also begins with observations. When those observations include violations of the agreed-upon human rights of a culture, the recommendation is that policy be used to prevent the human rights violations from occurring. In this regard, the study of human rights is a study of policy that reduces and obviates violations. Economics can be beneficial to this study as it takes existing hypotheses of the causes of the human rights violations, recommends what data should be collected or how to use existing data, analyzes this data in relation to existing hypotheses, and recommends variables that could change the incentives. Economics provides a set of tools that can help to identify and change incentives.

Economic decisions play several different roles in the area of human rights, but mainly focus on cost–benefit decisions of potential human rights violators and victims, and society. The textbook is written for upper-level economics undergraduate students and students in other disciplines studying human rights issues. Its primary audience is anyone who wants to gain a perspective on how to analyze diverse topics using economic theory and models, econometric tools, case studies, and data. The textbook is not meant to cover all human rights topics nor all the economics theory that pertains to each human rights topic. Rather, it is an opportunity for students to learn new information and analyze data in order to make informed decisions and contribute to quality research.

Section 1: Introduction to the economics of human rights

Unit 1: General introduction to human rights

Human rights studies and economics are social sciences that study interactions within society. There are economic foundations and implications at the heart of each violation of human rights, but "human rights" is not in itself a field of economics. On the other side, an economist must gain an understanding of the specific human rights topic in order to have an accurate perspective about the types of decisions, costs, and benefits that exist within that area. Both fields are needed to understand the dynamics of the economic decisions underlying human rights violations.

The term "human rights" elicits a wide range of responses – from strong emotion to stoicism, from curiosity to apathy. The study of human rights spans years, geography, and ideology. Human rights groups address issues such as the death penalty, women's rights, children's rights, human rights related to poverty, prisoners, people at risk, national security, countering terrorism, torture, refugee and migrant rights, censorship and free speech, human rights related to business, lesbian-gay-bisexual-transsexual (LGBT) rights, and human rights related to military, police, arms, and international justice. The most widely accepted definition comes from the 1948 United Nations Universal Declaration of Human Rights (UDHR).

Unit 2: Economics perspective

Elizabeth Wheaton, Ph.D.

As the founder-CEO of the nonprofit consulting organization Equip the Saints and senior lecturer at Southern Methodist University in Dallas, Texas, Dr. Beth Wheaton seeks ways to equip world changers. Her research, augmented by her multiple degrees in economics and international business, focuses on the economic decisions and incentives surrounding child labor, human trafficking, and human rights. As the lead author of this textbook, she had the pleasure of extending her work along with a team of subject experts.

If you are sitting in a room of 100 people, look around and imagine you are all under four years old. The World Bank reports that on average 42.5 out of 1,000 children worldwide die before the age of five, so 96 of the people around you in the room will therefore survive to five years old. The United Nations (U.N.) Children's Fund estimates that 150 million children (an average of 24% in developing countries) are engaged in child labor, some of it in the worst forms of child labor such as sex trafficking. Economic theory and modeling can be used in the fight against human rights violations, in conjunction with international data collection, expertise in each topic area, government and non-government organizations on the front lines, and people around the world with the passion to change the world.

Across the world there are calls for social justice, whether it is the rescue of orphans or animals, the saving of habitat or culture, or the protection of women's or children's rights. Social justice – the administration of the body of work that makes up human rights in a way that provides all people with equal economic, political, and social rights and opportunities – stems from human rights. Human rights is the codified body of work coming from the national and international agreements, laws, and protocols that represent the rights of all human beings. An educated study of the human rights behind each of the social justice movements is necessary to understand, and possibly change, the decision processes underlying each of the human rights violations.

Economics is the study of choice when dealing with scarcity and focuses on the decision-making process by examining the costs and benefits that lead to a choice by an individual or a group. While the heart of human rights is that all people should be treated equally and with dignity, economics focuses on efficiency or the allocation of resources in order to gain the best possible outcome for the most people. Despite this, economics interacts with human rights in a number of ways. For instance, violations of human rights do not seem rational, but someone is making the choices to commit those violations. It may be possible to discover incentives that can change that person's choices by changing the costs and benefits of making that decision.

Analyses of social situations such as human rights violations point to the fact that the solutions are complex and require the abilities and resources of a diverse group of people. The protection of human rights is affected by scarcity, because if there were unlimited resources available – money, the time of experts in areas such as the creation of laws, law enforcement, dispute resolution, etc. – the human rights violations may be prevented. There are current examples of human rights violations which have gone unchecked due to the lack of resources. If murder could be prevented, capital punishment would not be needed. If adequate discovery systems could be created to handle childhood trauma, anger management, and other psychological issues, violence against women would not occur. Similar assumptions could be made in other human rights issues like asylum seeking, terrorism, genocide, and incidents fueled by hate. A scarcity of monetary and nonmonetary resources may lead to a setting in which the violation is possible.

While economics is not the only tool that can be used to analyze human rights, human rights advocates are calling for more interdisciplinary research and work to find solutions for the human rights issues that occur around the world. Economists trained to step into an unfamiliar field will have more career and life opportunities as well as more tools to change the world.

Section 2: Fundamentals of human rights

Correctly defining terms is essential for valid research. Inaccurately defined goals lead to irrelevant research. For instance, some people confuse human smuggling with human trafficking. Human smuggling is the illegal movement of people across borders. While this is illegal, the term implies that the people being smuggled are moving across borders voluntarily.

Human trafficking, on the other hand, is a human rights violation. The U.N. Protocol to Prevent, Suppress and Punish Trafficking in Persons Especially Women and Children (2003), defines trafficking in persons as:

> . . .the recruitment, transportation, transfer, harbouring or receipt of persons, by means of the threat or use of force or other forms of coercion, of abduction, of fraud, of deception, of the abuse of power or of a position of vulnerability or of the giving or receiving of payments or benefits to achieve the consent of a person having control over another person, for the purpose of exploitation. Exploitation shall include, at a minimum, the exploitation of the prostitution of others or other forms of sexual exploi- tation, forced labour or services, slavery or practices similar to slavery, servitude or the removal of organs.

The terms human smuggling and human trafficking are therefore widely disparate and can- not be used synonymously.

Melanie Shepard and Ellen Pence (1999) list three criteria for collecting reliable data: "First, the data must be collected consistently. . . A second criterion relating to obtaining data is that information must be accurate. . . Finally, the information must reflect the experience of the people involved and not be so transformed by the need to make it institutionally read- able that it no longer tells us what is happening."

The goal of economics is to use economic theory and models and reliable data to complete the quality analysis necessary for policy-making decisions. It is important for the researcher to not only obtain a solid information basis, but also to identify personal biases and biases from other sources. Bias can cause inaccuracies in research method and analysis of results. Scientific research requires systematic observations, measurements, and experi- ments, and the formulation, testing, and modification of hypotheses. In accordance with this description, below are some of the major definitions used within this textbook. Other defini- tions are provided on a chapter-by-chapter basis.

The Office of the United Nations High Commissioner for Human Rights (OHCHR), which will be introduced later in the chapter, defines **human rights** as "rights inherent to all human beings, whatever our nationality, place of residence, sex, national or ethnic origin, colour, religion, language, or any other status. We are all equally entitled to our human rights without discrimination. These rights are all interrelated, interdependent and indivisible." There is no clear definition of a **human rights violation**, partly because a violation often depends upon the opinion of the person. The following chapters will include information on the controversies related to each human rights topic. In general, a human rights violation might be considered to be any violation of the 30 articles of the UDHR (discussed below), but not all nations have ratified this agreement.

According to the United States (U.S.) Office of Justice Programs Bureau of Justice Statistics (BJS), **capital punishment** "refers to the process of sentencing convicted offenders to death for the most serious crimes (capital crimes) and carrying out that sentence. The spe- cific offenses and circumstances which determine if a crime (usually murder) is eligible for a death sentence are defined by statute and are prescribed by Congress or any state legislature." The BJS also defines **death row** as "the area of a prison in which prisoners who were under a sentence of death were housed. Usage of the term continues despite the fact that many states do not maintain a separate unit or facility for condemned inmates."

The U.S. Department of Justice Office on Violence Against Women (OVW) was estab- lished in 1994 with the Violence Against Women Act (VAWA) "to provide federal leadership in developing the national capacity to reduce violence against women and administer justice for and strengthen services to victims of domestic violence, dating violence, sexual assault, and stalking." This will be the working definition of **violence against women** for this textbook.

According to the U.N. High Commissioner for Refugees (UNHCR), an **asylum seeker** is "someone whose request for sanctuary has yet to be processed" after that person has applied for asylum under the 1951 Refugee Convention on the Status of Refugees. The granting of asylum partially depends upon whether the asylum seeker has a well-founded fear of persecution because of race, religion, nationality, political belief, or membership of a particular social group if the person returns to their country of origin. Once the request for asylum has been granted, the person becomes a refugee. For the sake of contrast, an economic migrant is a person who leaves the country of origin to find employment in another country.

The U.S. Department of Defense defines **terrorism** as "the calculated use of unlawful violence or threat of unlawful violence to inculcate fear; intended to coerce or to intimidate governments or societies in the pursuit of goals that are generally political, religious, or ideological." Specific types of terrorism will be discussed in that chapter.

Child abuse as defined by the Federal Child Abuse Prevention and Treatment Act (2010) is "at a minimum, any recent act or failure to act on the part of a parent or caretaker which results in death, serious physical or emotional harm, sexual abuse or exploitation; or an act or failure to act which presents an imminent risk of serious harm." While many of the factors that affect the prevalence, severity, and impact of violence against women also affect children, a child has a lower level of self-determination than an adult, which can lead to increased harm.

According to Article II of the 1948 Convention on the Prevention and Punishment of the Crime of Genocide,

> . . .**genocide** means any of the following acts committed with intent to destroy, in whole or in part, a national, ethnical, racial or religious group:
>
> a)   Killing members of the group;
> b)   Causing serious bodily or mental harm to members of the group;
> c)   Deliberately inflicting on the group conditions of life calculated to bring about its physical destruction in whole or in part;
> d)   Imposing measures intended to prevent births within the group;
> e)   Forcibly transferring children of the group to another group.

Hate is defined in the *Merriam-Webster Collegiate Dictionary* (2004) as "intense hostility and aversion usually derived from fear, anger, or sense of injury." According to the Federal Bureau of Investigation (FBI) Civil Rights Program, a **hate crime** is a "criminal offense against a person or property motivated in whole or in part by an offender's bias against a race, religion, disability, sexual orientation, ethnicity, gender, or gender identity." A hate crime is thus a traditional crime such as murder or arson with an intentionality due to a component of deep, negative bias.

The chapters in this book are set up to take advantage of the most accessible definitions and data in the early chapters and then progress to those areas where this information is less available. Due to the legal background of capital punishment, there are well-defined definitions associated with the issue. Texas counties are "required" to provide certain data to the State of Texas; however, not all counties provide this information. This provides for a good, but not complete, dataset on capital punishment in Texas. Violence against women data is often of a medical nature and is therefore subject to the federal Family Educational Rights and Privacy Act (FERPA) law. This makes certain data unavailable to researchers. There are also issues with vague definitions and lack of or incorrect self-reporting. Definitions for seeking asylum vary between nations and international organizations. Many studies count all of these people as refugees, disregarding those who are seeking asylum and plan to return to their home countries when circumstances allow. Terrorism data is difficult due to the inherently secretive nature of terrorist organizations. Some terrorist acts may be created by an individual or a small group of people who state some affiliation with a certain terrorist organization, but it is difficult to know whether the terrorist act was actually planned and carried out *by* the terrorist organization. It is rare that a neutral party will be present during a time of genocide, so the information collected comes from participants or survivors of genocide and may be severely biased. Many of the components of violence against women will appear again in the child abuse research: The added element is the stark vulnerability of children in abusive situations. Genocide research is complex in that it incorporates pieces of all of the other human rights violations. Universal, cohesive definitions of "hate" do not yet exist; meaning that the data being collected is biased by the researcher's personal definition of hate. Later chapters in this book will discuss situations in which the definitions and data are unreliable or unavailable.

Section 3: Agreements behind human rights

Depending upon a person's perspective, a group of individuals may be considered terrorists or freedom fighters. One position says that a man has a right to discipline his wife; another defines physical or psychological control as violence against women. Some people believe that a woman should have complete rights over her body, including the right to have a legal abortion. Others believe that the unborn fetus has the right to life. These are topics that cause controversy, intense discussion, fearful arguments, the outpouring of funds to lobby for specific legislation, and the creation of new nonprofit organizations.

Before analyzing issues related to human rights, a foundation is needed upon which to do the analysis. National and international agreements and laws created by policy-makers determine whether something is a human rights violation. The job of the economist is to analyze the data and information surrounding human rights violations. Economics focuses on **positive statements** that describe "what is" or the facts rather than on **normative statements** describing "what should be" or opinions.

Each chapter of this textbook begins with a guide to the basic agreements and controversies surrounding the human rights topic. These are not inclusive lists as there are agreements at many different government and nongovernment levels. The agreements include national agreements in the United States as well as in some other countries for which there is case study analysis. International and multinational agreements are presented as international background, and major controversies are also discussed. The textbook is a resource that provides effective economics training that can be used to analyze human rights issues.

Unit 1: National agreements

Most countries have laws protecting the rights of citizens. In the United States, there are a number of laws and government departments that work to ensure human rights. The U.S. National

Archives and Records Administration (NARA) houses the Charters of Freedom, the three documents most important to the founding and philosophy of America. These include the U.S. Declaration of Independence, the Constitution, and the Bill of Rights.

The U.S. Department of State Bureau of Democracy, Human Rights and Labor is the main federal agency in charge of human rights work. The goal of this bureau is "Promoting freedom and democracy and protecting human rights around the world" as it is central to U.S. foreign policy. The U.S. Department of State also publishes reports on human rights practices by country and reports on international religious freedom, trafficking-in-persons, U.S. treaties, and advancing freedom and democracy.

The American Bar Association (ABA) established the Rule of Law Initiative in 2007. Its goal is to "promote justice, economic opportunity and human dignity" which codifies (places in specific order) the laws of a country. It states that "rule of law promotion is the most effective long-term antidote to the pressing problems facing the world community today, including poverty, economic stagnation, and conflict." In addition, the ABA's Section of Civil Rights and Social Justice has the goals of "raising and addressing often complex and difficult civil rights and civil liberties issues in a changing and diverse society; and ensuring that protection of individual rights remains a focus of legal and policy decisions." The program was established to "consolidate five overseas rule of law programs," the first of which was the Central European and Eurasian Law Initiative, created in 1990 after the fall of the Berlin Wall.

Unit 2: International agreements

The Universal Declaration of Human Rights (UDHR) is a milestone document in the history of human rights. Drafted by representatives with different legal and cultural backgrounds from all regions of the world, the declaration represents a common standard for all peoples and all nations. It sets out, for the first time, fundamental human rights to be universally protected.

The UDHR declares 30 articles (http://www.un.org/en/universal-declaration-human-rights) that demarcate the "equal and inalienable rights of all members of the human family." The U.N. General Assembly adopted the UDHR in Paris, France on December 10, 1948. Two covenants were added in 1966 (the International Covenant on Civil and Political Rights and the International Covenant on Economics, Social and Cultural Rights) and ratified in 1976 to become the International Bill of Human Rights. According to the articles in the UDHR, human rights include the aspects described in Table 1.1.

TABLE 1.1   Universal Declaration of Human Rights (UDHR, 1948)

Article 1	Freedom and equality in dignity and rights for all human beings.
Article 2	Rights and freedoms regardless of any distinction of the individual and geographic location.
Article 3	Right to life, freedom, and safety.
Article 4	Freedom from slavery and bondage.
Article 5	Freedom from torture and brutal or humiliating treatment and punishment.
Article 6	Right to be recognition as a person before a court of law.
Article 7	Freedom from discrimination before the law.

(Continued)

TABLE 1.1 (Continued)

Article 8	Right to action by a national tribunal for acts violating a person's fundamental rights.
Article 9	Freedom from arrest, confinement, or exile without legal purpose.
Article 10	Right to a non-prejudiced and public trial related to criminal charges against the person.
Article 11	1) The right to be considered innocent until proven guilty. 2) Freedom from being held guilty for an offense that was not a legal offense at the time it was committed.
Article 12	Freedom from attack on personal privacy, family, home, reputation, or correspondence.
Article 13	1) Freedom to travel within and live anywhere within a country. 2) Freedom to leave and return to any country.
Article 14	1) Right to seek asylum from persecution in other countries. 2) Freedom from asylum being revoked for non-political crimes.
Article 15	Right to hold a nationality and to change nationality.
Article 16	1) Freedom to marry, if person is of legal age. 2) Right to only marry under free consent by both spouses. 3) Right of the family to protection by society and the state.
Article 17	Right to own and keep personal property.
Article 18	Freedom of thought, personal moral code, and religion.
Article 19	Freedom of expression.
Article 20	1) Right to gather peacefully. 2) Freedom from being forced to join an association.
Article 21	1) Right to be part of government in own country. 2) Right to use public service in own country. 3) Right to genuine, periodic elections.
Article 22	Freedom to enjoy economic, cultural, and social rights.
Article 23	1) Right to work and choose employment. 2) Right to equal pay for equal work. 3) Right to financial assistance to ensure personal and family health. 4) Freedom to create and join trade unions.
Article 24	Right to leisure.
Article 25	1) Right to a standard of living that protects personal and family health and well-being. 2) Right of mothers and children to special assistance.
Article 26	Right to a sufficient education.
Article 27	1) Freedom to engage in cultural life. 2) Right to protect personal production of different forms of culture.
Article 28	Right to live in a way that engages all of the rights and freedoms in the Declaration.
Article 29	Responsibility of each person to uphold the rights in the Declaration.
Article 30	Freedom from destruction of any rights and freedoms set in the Declaration.

There are many other international human rights agreements, laws, and agencies. The African Charter on Human and Peoples' Rights was created in 1986 and was ratified by more than 40 African states. Its premise is "to promote human and peoples' rights and freedoms and taking into account the importance traditionally attached to these rights and freedoms in Africa..." The American Convention on Human Rights "Pact of San Jose, Costa Rica" was adopted in 1969 by 25 American states, but not including the United States or Canada, with the goal "to consolidate in this hemisphere, within the framework of democratic institutions, a system of personal liberty and social justice based on respect for the essential rights of man." One protocol was added in 1988, related to economic, social, and cultural rights, and a second protocol in 1990 called for states to abolish the death penalty.

The U.N. Secretariat has various offices handling different human rights issues. The Office of High Commissioner for Human Rights (OHCHR) was created in response to the Vienna Declaration and Programme of Action adopted in 1993 at the World Conference on Human Rights in Vienna, Austria. The OHCHR "represents the world's commitment to universal ideals of human dignity" and has "a unique mandate from the international community to promote and protect all human rights." The four divisions of the OHCHR are Research and Right to Development, Human Rights Treaties, Field Operations and Technical Cooperation, and Human Rights Council and Special Procedures. The four-part mission of the U.N. Office for the Coordination of Humanitarian Affairs (OCHA) is to mobilize and coordinate effective and principled humanitarian action in partnership with national and international actors in order to alleviate human suffering in disasters and emergencies; to advocate the rights of people in need; to promote preparedness and prevention; and to facilitate sustainable solutions. The mission of the United Nations High Commissioner for Refugees (UNHCR) is to protect the rights and well-being of refugees all over the world.

The World Health Organization (WHO) was established in 1946. The WHO Constitution was ratified in October 1947 and was the first international agreement to delineate health as a human right. It states, "The enjoyment of the highest attainable standard of health is one of the fundamental rights of every human being without distinction of race, political belief, economic, or social condition."

There are many more international human rights agreements. Some of the major conventions include the U.N. Convention on the Prevention and Punishment of the Crime of Genocide (1948), the Geneva Conventions (1949), the European Convention for the Protection of Human Rights and the Fundamental Freedoms (1950), the U.N. Convention on the Political Rights of Women (1953), the International Labour Organization's Abolition of Forced Labour Convention (1957), the U.N. International Convention on the Elimination of All Forms of Racial Discrimination (1965), the U.N. International Covenant on Economic, Social and Cultural Rights (1966), the U.N. International Covenant on Civil and Political Rights (1966), the International Conference on Human Rights' Proclamation of Teheran (1968), and the U.N. Convention against Torture and Other Cruel, Inhuman or Degrading Treatment or Punishment (1985).

There are six main venues for the enforcement of human rights law, and the enforceability of penalties depends in part on the agreement of the member nations to comply with the ruling of the international legal authority. The International Court of Justice (1945) is located in The Hague, the Netherlands, the only United Nations principle organization to be located outside of the United States. This court reviews legal disputes between states and legal questions from the United Nations. The mandate of the OHCHR is to promote human rights. The mission of the Organization of American States' Inter-American Commission on Human Rights (established in 1948) is to "promote the observance and protection of human rights" between member countries. The European Court of Human Rights (est. 1950) hears disputes between member states and makes sure the U.N. Development Programme (UNDP) is enforced in Europe. The European Court of Justice (est. 1951) is comprised of the General Court and the Court of Justice. It ensures that "EU law is interpreted and applied the same in every EU country; ensuring countries and EU institutions abide by EU law." The United Nations International Covenant on Civil and Political Rights (ICCPR) Human Rights Committee (est. 1966) monitors ICCPR obligations.

Unit 3: Controversies

This textbook analyzes the background of six human rights areas. Within each of those human rights fields, there are different points of view. For example, within capital punishment, there is the position that to take a life is a violation of a person's human rights. The opposing faction believes the punishment fits the crime and points to legislation that makes the death penalty a legal penalty. There are wide ranges of activities that are described as violence against women and child abuse. In large part, the culture of a population determines which behaviors related to women and children constitute illegal activities. In many countries, people who seek asylum do not have the same rights as legal residents of a country. Terrorist actions cause human rights violations through physical, mental, security, and resource damage. The international community is hesitant to call a nation's domestic crisis genocide, regardless of the number of people killed, raped, incarcerated, or put to flight. Some people believe that "hate crimes" are far worse than other crimes due to the motivation of the individual, while others view them as no worse than other crimes.

There are no limits to the controversies, but it is possible to build a foundation that allows researchers to analyze different human rights issues. In order to produce reliable research, economists must identify and acknowledge the personal biases that might affect their research, so that future researchers will be aware of those biases. This textbook works through a process that allows a person to build a foundation for understanding each human

CHECK YOURSELF BOX: PERSONAL BIASES ABOUT HUMAN RIGHTS

Statistically speaking, it is unlikely that you are a human rights major and even less likely that you are a human rights expert. If you are, we are glad you have taken time to read this textbook. If you are not, you probably have some strong reactions to human rights. You may find it a topic of interest, but you may have some troublesome thoughts about individual issues or the whole field of human rights. As we have discussed, doing research with biases will affect the integrity of your research and can make it unreliable for policy analysis. This is a great time to write down those biases and the source of each bias. Take some time to write down a full account of your reasons for and against human rights in general or in regard to specific issues. This is not to test your worth as a person. It is to help you determine your personal biases, separate your biases from the information presented, and look at the human rights issue in a scientific way so that you can do the best possible economics analysis. Keep this list of your biases, consider how your biases align with or go against others' biases, and see whether these biases change by the end of the chapter.

rights topic with good definitions applicable, national and international, a basic understanding of the history behind violations, and information about experts.

Section 4: History of human rights

The daily news provides a plethora of bad things that happen between human beings. Although these things may not happen in the same way, as George Santayana said in 1905, "Those who cannot remember the past are doomed to repeat it." Interest in human rights goes back a long way. The Cyrus Cylinder is the first known charter of human rights and was written in 539 B.C. Cyrus the Great, the first king of ancient Persia, conquered the city of Babylon and freed the slaves. He declared that all people had the right to choose their own religion and established racial equality. The first four articles of the UDHR parallel this ancient document. Many other human rights documents followed the Cyrus Cylinder, including the Magna Carta in 1215, the Petition of Right in 1628, the U.S. Constitution in 1787, the French Declaration of the Rights of Man and of the Citizen in 1789, and the U.S. Bill of Rights in 1791.

The first academic human rights program at a liberal arts college in the United States was established by Trinity College in Hartford, Connecticut in 1998. Its mission is to "foster critical debate about human rights problems, inter-disciplinary dialogue, and conversations that bridge the divide between local and global human rights concerns." By 2015, 20 degree courses in human rights existed in the United States, including 11 degree-granting programs. These included seven undergraduate and four graduate programs. The primary goals of these programs are to learn about human rights and to address concrete social and economic needs, such as poverty and discrimination, and political crises, such as war and political repression. Graduates from these programs work in the areas of international tribunals, intergovernmental bodies, government, academia, and non-governmental organizations such as the International Network for Economic, Social and Cultural Rights in New York.

TABLE 1.2   Human rights programs in the United States

Degree-granting human rights programs		Non-degree-granting human rights programs
Undergraduate	Graduate	
Bard College	Arizona State University	Boston College
Barnard College	Boston University	Colby College
Columbia College at Columbia University	Columbia University	
Pennsylvania State University	George Mason University	Duke University
Southern Methodist University	Harvard University	Emory University
	Indiana University Bloomington	
	New York University	
Trinity College	Notre Dame (Law)	Florida State University
University of Arizona	Trinity College	George Mason University
University of Chicago	Rutgers University	Johns Hopkins
University of Connecticut		

(Continued)

TABLE 1.2   (Continued)

Degree-granting human rights programs		Non-degree-granting human rights programs
Undergraduate	Graduate	
University of Dayton, Ohio	University of Denver	MIT
University of Texas at Austin	University of San Francisco	Stanford University
Webster University		
	University of Minnesota	University of California at Berkeley
	University of Washington	University of California at Davis
	Webster University	University of Cincinnati
		University of Iowa
		University of Nebraska
		Yale University

Source: http://hrlibrary.umn.edu/edumat/hreduseries/hrhandbook/part1c.html

Section 5: Meet the human rights experts

Economics by itself can do little to solve social problems; however, economics can be an effective tool when combined with the expertise and tools of other disciplines. Combining disciplines means adding new non-economic concepts and adapting economic concepts to new realities. Economics assumes that people think rationally: that is, that people make decisions by using all of the information they personally have at hand. Other disciplines can bring different perspectives into the models by introducing automatic thinking, social thinking, thinking with mental models, and framing (Allison Demeritt, Karla Hoff, and James Walsh, 2015). While including these variables complicates the model, it can also add greater understanding for policy-making.

Generally speaking, economists are not experts on human rights. The economist needs to have some detachment in order to gain a dispassionate view of the subject. The complexity of each human right is such that it takes years of experience and research to learn the facts behind the actions making up the human rights violation. This is the reason the authors of this textbook recommend working in an interdisciplinary fashion, so that the person who knows economics works closely with an expert on that particular human right, and possibly other experts too. In this way, the analysis is relevant from a range of perspectives.

There are many ways to learn about human rights topics, but an important first step is to do some general information-gathering. Reading peer-reviewed journal articles, listening to talks from experts, and watching documentaries about the topic can be informative. This process involves locating relevant, valuable information; making a note of the bias of each author, expert, or documentary maker; and creating a list of significant questions. The economist will rarely be an expert in the human rights field. This creates the need to talk to or read research from human rights experts to determine what has happened, what is being done, and what is needed in the particular human rights area. There are many experts on any given topic who are willing to talk with an open-minded individual with relevant questions. Different experts will provide different perspectives and some experts – such as people in nearby universities, government offices, and nonprofit organizations – are accessible for discussion via email or phone call. Patience and humility are characteristics that can help a researcher access useful and expert information.

Information and data may be gathered from universities (see Table 1.2 for a partial list of programs), research centers, nonprofit organizations, and federal agencies. Many of the major international policy centers, data collection facilities, and nongovernment or nonprofit organizations are located in cities throughout Europe and further abroad. Seeking experts in these areas provides a wider understanding of the implications of human rights abuses and the needs of policy-makers worldwide. Some of these human rights organizations are listed in Table 1.3. Each description is a quote from the specific human rights organization's website and websites are provided in the eResources. Relevant nonprofit organizations with specific human rights focuses will be discussed in subsequent chapters.

TABLE 1.3 Human rights organizations

Human rights organizations	Description
Amnesty International in London, England	"A worldwide movement of people who campaign for internationally recognized human rights for all . . . we work to improve human rights through campaigning and international solidarity."
Business & Human Rights Resource Centre in London, England	"We work with everyone to advance human right in business. We track over 8000 companies, and help the vulnerable eradicate abuse."
Center for Economic and Social Rights (CESR) in New York City, NY	"Works to promote social justice through human rights . . . seek to uphold the universal human rights of every human being"
Freedom House in Washington, D.C.	"An independent nongovernmental organization that supports the expansion of freedom in the world. Freedom is possible only in democratic political systems in which the governments are accountable to their own people; the rule of law prevails; and freedoms of expression, association, and belief, as well as respect for the rights of minorities and women, are guaranteed."
Human Rights First in New York City, NY	"Human Rights First promotes national security policies that respect human rights, focusing primarily on U.S. counterterrorism measures. The Law and Security program works to bring government counterterrorism and related national security efforts into compliance with international humanitarian law (armed conflict laws), human rights law."
Human Rights Internet (HRI) in Ottawa, Ontario	"Committed to social justice, good governance and conflict prevention . . . through human rights informed policy formation, knowledge transfer and development, promotion of dialogue, training, and information distribution. HRI works with governmental, intergovernmental and nongovernmental actors to disseminate information, empower marginalized groups, stimulate reflection, and initiate policy change and institutional development."

(Continued)

TABLE 1.3 (Continued)

Human rights organizations	Description
Human Rights Watch in New York City, NY	"Dedicated to protecting the human rights of people around the world. They stand with victims and activists to prevent discrimination, to uphold political freedom, to protect people from inhumane conduct in wartime, and to bring offenders to justice. They investigate and expose human rights violations and hold abusers accountable. They challenge governments and those who hold power to end abusive practices and respect international human rights law. They enlist the public and the international community to support the cause of human rights for all."
Human Rights without Frontiers in Brussels, Belgium	[Human Rights without Frontiers] "seeks to shape European and international policy in ways that strengthen democracy, uphold the rule of law and protect human rights globally."
International Committee of the Red Cross in Geneva, Switzerland	"An independent, neutral organization ensuring humanitarian protection and assistance for victims of war and armed violence."
International Women's Rights Action Watch (IWRAW) in Minneapolis, MN	"Organized at the Third World Conference on Women in Nairobi, Kenya, to promote recognition of women's human rights under the United Nation's Convention on the Elimination of All Forms of Discrimination against Women (the CEDAW Convention), an international human rights treaty."
Mental Disability Rights International (MDRI) in Washington, D.C.	"Dedicated to promoting the human rights and full participation in society of people with mental disabilities worldwide."
OSCE Legislation on Human Rights in Vienna, Austria	"Provides direct access to international norms and standards relating to specific human dimension issues as well as to domestic legislation and other documents of relevance to these issues . . . available from the site for lawmakers across the OSCE region."
UNICEF in New York City, NY	"UNICEF works in 190 countries and territories to save children's lives, to defend their rights, and to help them fulfil their potential."
U.S. Human Rights Network in Atlanta, GA	"The US Human Rights Network is a national network of organizations and individuals working to build and strengthen a people-centered human rights movement in the United States, where leadership is centered on those most directly affected by human rights violations, and the full range of diversity within communities is respected and embraced."
Vital Voices Global Partnership in Washington, D.C.	"Identifies, trains, and empowers emerging women leaders and social entrepreneurs around the globe, enabling them to create a better world for us all."
World Health Organization (WHO) in Geneva, Switzerland	"Primary role is to direct international human health within the United Nations' system and to lead partners in global health responses. . . The right to health is subject to progressive realization and acknowledges resource constraints. However, it also imposes on states various obligations which are of immediate effect, such as the guarantee that the right will be exercised without discrimination of any kind and the obligation to take deliberate, concrete and targeted steps towards its full realization."

Some of the U.S. federal agencies that work on different roles relating to human rights are listed in Table 1.IV.

TABLE 1.4 U.S. federal agencies involvement in human rights areas

Federal agency	Mission	National/ international	Role in counterterrorism	Role in seeking asylum	Role in violence against women	Role in hate crimes
Central Intelligence Agency (CIA) – www.cia.gov	To collect and analyze intelligence and conduct covert action to safeguard the U.S.	International	Counterterrorism Center (CTC) has both operational and analytic functions and works with other U.S. government agencies and foreign liaison partners to target terrorists.	None	None	None
Federal Bureau of Investigation (FBI) – www.fbi.gov	To protect the American people, provide leadership and criminal justice services, and uphold the Constitution of the United States.	International	Top investigative priority – to eliminate the risk of domestic and international terrorism to the United States and U.S. interests abroad.	None	Human trafficking initiatives.	Conduct investigations; support law enforcement, prosecution decisions, and public outreach and training; and produce yearly U.S. statistics.
Immigration and Customs Enforcement (ICE) – www.ice.gov	To ensure public safety and homeland security by providing enforcement of federal laws regarding border control, immigration, trade, and customs.	International	The Counterterrorism and Criminal Exploitation Unit, dedicated to preventing terrorists from leveraging America's immigration system to infiltrate the homeland.	Enforcement of immigration rules and regulations.	Human trafficking initiatives.	None

(Continued)

TABLE 1.4 (Continued)

Federal agency	Mission	National/ international	Role in counterterrorism	Role in seeking asylum	Role in violence against women	Role in hate crimes
Bureau of Alcohol, Tobacco, Firearms and Explosives (ATF) – www.atf.gov	To prevent federal offenses involving firearms, explosives, arson, bombings, and illegal alcohol and tobacco products.	Mainly national, but six foreign offices.	The ATF has no direct mission related to terrorism, other than preventing their illegal acquisition of firearms in a similar fashion to non-terrorists.	None	None	None
U.S. Marshals Service – www. usmarshals.gov	To protect, defend and enforce the American justice system.	Mainly national, but three foreign offices.	None	None	None	None
Customs and Border Protection – www. cbp.gov	To protect America's borders from dangerous people and materials.	National	None	None	Human trafficking initiatives.	None

CHECK YOURSELF BOX: HUMAN RIGHTS RESEARCH AND DATA BIASES

In the first check yourself box, you created a list of your personal biases about human rights. Now consider and write down possible biases of other persons and organizations. What is the researcher's background? What benefit does an individual researcher gain from doing this particular research: personal association with the topic, more publications, prestige, or something else? What benefit does an organization gain from being part of this conversation: the implementation of an organizational agenda, influence on or control of policy-making, increased donations? These biases are likely to impact what research is completed, the data gathered, and the material published. Understanding these biases will help the researcher to discern the different sides of an issue and how biases affect outcomes.

Section 6: Economic structure of human rights

Economics is the science of choice when dealing with scarcity, while **scarcity** is having inadequate resources to fulfill all of people's needs and wants. As noted previously, the economic structure of human rights focuses on the costs and benefits that lead to the choices made by the participants (whether voluntarily or involuntarily) in each of the human rights violations. It is not always a simple exercise to identify either the choices that are made or the people responsible for those choices.

Choices are part of each of the human rights violations discussed in this textbook. In capital punishment, there are many decisions being made: by law enforcement, by the courts, by the prosecution team, by the defense team, by the defendant, by the prison system and by the law-making entities. Violence against women and child abuse involve decisions by the perpetrator of the violence, by the women and children who are victims of violence, by the families and social groups surrounding these women and the perpetrators, by society (as it determines moral acceptability and unacceptability), by medical and other help-providing agencies, by nonprofit organizations, and by law-makers. When people seek asylum, choices are being made by the asylum seekers, by the people they travel with, by people who have some influence over the locations and regimes through which the asylum seekers travel, by local and national government agencies and nongovernment agencies, by law-makers, by international organizations, and by society, as individual views often lead to certain people being elected and thus policy decisions in relation to seeking asylum. Terrorism involves decisions by a terrorist organization, by its rivals (which may be terrorist organizations or other groups), by businesses that either support or oppose the terrorists, by local and national government agencies, by victims of terrorist acts, by citizens concerned about terrorist acts, by society's feelings about the terrorist organizations, and by international organizations that may support or oppose the terrorist organizations. Genocide is perpetuated by a small group of genocidaires. The decisions made by genocidaires – along with their allies, people caught up in the genocide violence (whether supporting, opposing, or remaining neutral), businesses in the area, local and national government and law enforcement agencies, and international organizations – are relevant, as is society's decision to pay attention to the fact that the violence is occurring or to ignore it, and whether to put forth effort to stop the genocide. This textbook uses the definition from the *Merriam-Webster Collegiate Dictionary* (2004), which states that a **hate crime** is "any of the various crimes when motivated by hostility of the victim as the member of a group, as based on color, creed, gender, or sexual orientation." Choices in the area of hate are made by perpetuators of hate and hate crimes, by their victims, by society's attention to and response to the crime, by law-creating organizations, by law enforcement, by courts, by legal prosecution and defense teams, and by incarceration entities.

Each human rights area is complex because there are varying incentives leading to the numerous decisions that may be taken by various people and organizations. The media also make their choice regarding what to report and how to report it. This coverage can affect society's response to a human rights violation.

Behavioral economics is the field most closely related to the economics of human rights as it analyzes the static and dynamic choices made by individuals and groups. In 1986 the Russell Sage Foundation and the Alfred P. Sloan Foundation launched the first behavioral economics program and opened it as a new field of economics. The mission of this field is to "work out how cognitive biases, mental rules of thumb, interpersonal relationships and social networks and norms can cause real-life economic decisions to deviate from the standards of rational, self-interested maximization" (russelsage.org/research/behavior-economics-detailed). This field includes areas such as inter-temporal choice (choosing based on more than one time period) and economic sociology. The economics of human rights will cross into this and other areas of economics.

Analysis is incomplete when decision-making is examined without considering the human costs in the same way that analysis of human rights is incomplete without considering the decisions that drive part of the human rights violations. According to the Death Penalty Information Center, there have been an average of 55 persons put to death annually by capital punishment in the United States over the past 20 years. There are numerous genocides happening around the world at any one time. The U.S. Department of Justice reports (2000) that "More than half of the surveyed women reported being physically assaulted by an adult caretaker as a child and/or as an adult by another adult, and nearly one-fifth reported being raped at some time in their lives." The UNHCR reports, "At least 1.66 million people submitted applications for asylum in 2014, the highest level ever recorded." The U.S. Department of State (n.d.) reports, "Although the number of terrorist attacks from 2006 to 2013 has decreased, there have been approximately 90,000 total terrorist attacks in this time period." Each of these acts is costly, not only in terms of human suffering and lost resources, but also in monetary terms. This means that effective solutions can lead to helping humans and may also assist in monetary and resource savings.

Instead of shrinking from the problem of the benefits of a particularly gruesome issue, the economist takes a step back and asks, "Who is benefitting from this action and what benefits and costs are they receiving?" Economic theory assumes people and organizations maximize the net benefit (equal to benefit minus cost) of their choices. For a person, this net benefit is economic well-being, while for a firm it is economic profit. For a person or organization to commit to an action, there must be a positive net benefit due to the benefits of the action outweighing the costs.

Economic efficiency is allocating resources to get the highest value for society. In general, a model of **static efficiency** is used to determine the efficient allocation in one period of time, as opposed to across time. This is different from **equity**, in which each person has the same allocation of resources, costs, or risks. Economic efficiency in human rights might make it look like the majority of people are protected from human rights violations, while some people are not protected. This will be disagreeable for those who strive for equity across all peoples and socioeconomic groups. It is illogical to believe that there will never be a time when everyone is safe from all human rights violation, unless crime, war, and hatred can all be extinguished. Perhaps a better way to look at efficiency is to ask the following questions related to human rights: 1) What resources are already in place and being used efficiently to eliminate human rights violations? 2) What resources are in place, but are not being used efficiently? 3) What resources are available that could be used, but are not currently being used? 4) In which areas are resources lacking that are needed to eliminate human rights violations? With these four questions, a well-defined structure of the government, legal, law enforcement, social services, societal, and other resources at work or available to combat a specific human rights violation can be established. It also suggests limits beyond which it is not economically beneficial to earmark resources for fighting against a certain human rights violation, due to lack of benefit or high cost.

Since resources that are used to fight and prevent human rights violations are limited and there are costs and benefits connected with decisions on resource allocation, economic cost–benefit analysis is used to analyze decision-making. Article 25 of the UDHR states, "Everyone has the right to a standard of living adequate for the health and well-being of himself and of his family, including food. . ." Imagine, then, that a person is suffering from a lack of food and has two choices that must be made repeatedly over a length of time, such as deciding whether to buy food or to steal it. Each time the person goes to a store or market, he has these two choices. Imagine further that the person does not have much money to buy food. A marginal choice is one in which the person does not go from paying for food all of the time to stealing food all the time, but instead is able to decide to pay for food some of the time and steal some of the time. The person does not decide to steal all of the time, but decides on the margin by determining his cost of buying the item versus the cost of getting caught stealing the food. These marginal choices will be analyzed in a cost–benefit model in each of the human rights topics analyzed in this textbook.

Unit 1: Costs of human rights violations

Within each human rights violation, there are multiple explicit (monetary) and implicit (nonmonetary) costs. When a county district attorney makes the decision to try a case as a capital crime, the county is liable for the cost of the capital case. An abuser weighs the costs to himself when he decides to abuse a woman in his life and what type of abuse to inflict. U.S. Citizenship and Immigration Services (USCIS) and similar organizations in other countries incur costs in the process of deciding which persons will be granted asylum within their national borders, while asylum seekers determine when and how to seek asylum. Terrorists decide on terrorism targets and the type of terrorist attacks, while nations decide if and how to retaliate against terrorist attacks. People participating in genocide make decisions about what actions to take or not take during the attacks. People who commit crimes based on hate are making the decision to let their inner feelings come outward into an attack against a person or people due to race, gender, religion, or other factors. Each of the violations of human rights is the culmination of choices, based in part on costs to the decision-maker.

Marginal cost (MC) is the cost of the last unit produced or chosen. Continuing with the example that a person makes the choice to buy food or steal it, the increasing marginal cost of stealing the food means that each time the person steals there is a higher probability that he will be caught. In many places, the number of times a person is convicted of a misdemeanor (a relatively minor illegal offense) can add up to equal a felony (a relatively serious illegal offense, usually punishable by imprisonment). The more times the person is caught, the less chance he will have to get a good job and put in place the things needed for survival in a community. This means that each time the person decides to steal, the marginal cost increases. Marginal cost is shown in Figure 1.1, with the cost on the vertical axis. The height of the marginal cost curve at each quantity indicates the marginal cost of stealing that particular unit of food. The horizontal axis is the number of times the person chooses to steal (N).

FIGURE 1.1   Marginal cost of stealing food

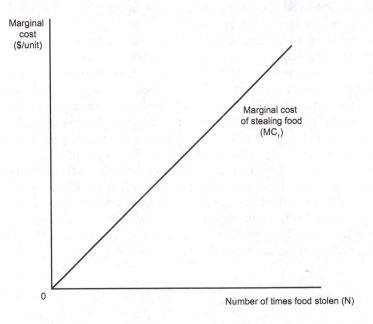

Unit 2: Benefits of human rights violations

Benefits will be analyzed from two angles. First, **net benefit** (equal to total benefit minus total cost) is considered from the standpoint of people or organizations that commit the acts that some deem human rights violations. It is important to identify the possible benefits people or organizations could be trying to gain from the action and the costs to the group associated with that action. Second, the net benefit to society of decreasing or eliminating the human rights violation is studied; for instance, the benefits to society of eliminating the specific actions of the violating group and the costs associated with actions that would eliminate the human rights violations.

  Marginal benefit (MB) is the benefit of the last unit consumed or chosen. Again, consider that a person chooses to either buy or steal food. The marginal benefit this person gets each time he steals a unit of food is the money that he does not have to pay to get the food plus the sustenance of consuming the food. Since the person only needs a certain amount of food, there is a decreased benefit from each unit of food he steals. The first few units stolen will sustain him. After that the food becomes increasingly less valuable to his survival. Figure 1.2 is a graph of marginal benefit showing the benefit on the vertical axis. As in Figure 1.1, the horizontal axis is the number of times the person chooses to steal (N). The height of the marginal benefit curve at each quantity indicates the marginal benefit of stealing the specific unit of food.

FIGURE 1.2   Marginal benefit of stealing food

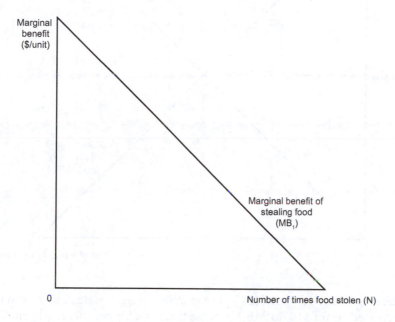

Once the marginal cost and marginal benefit curves associated with stealing food have been created, an equilibrium can be determined that predicts the number of times the person steals and the equilibrium where the marginal cost he is willing to pay to steal the last unit food is equal to the marginal benefit he receives from stealing the last unit of food. Figure 1.3 shows a graph of the marginal cost and marginal benefit on the vertical axis and the number of times the person chooses to steal. The equilibrium quantity (N_1) indicates the optimal number of times the person will steal food where the marginal cost of stealing food (MC_1) is equal to the marginal benefit of stealing food (MB_1).

Policy-makers in many countries have put laws in place to make theft illegal, even when the stolen item is food. If theft is increasing in an area, policy-makers may look for **incentives**, which are positive or negative motivations used to modify behavior. While the model in Figure 1.3 is simplified, it is important because an organization has choices to use incentives to change the outcome of the situation. Increasing the penalty for theft or finding new ways to catch someone stealing increase the cost of someone choosing whether to steal food. This is shown in Figure 1.4 as an upward shift in the marginal cost curve (from MC_1 to MC_2). Increasing the marginal cost for each time the person chooses to steal food leads to a lower number of decisions to steal. This is seen in Figure 1.4 when the number of times

FIGURE 1.3 Marginal cost and marginal benefit of stealing food

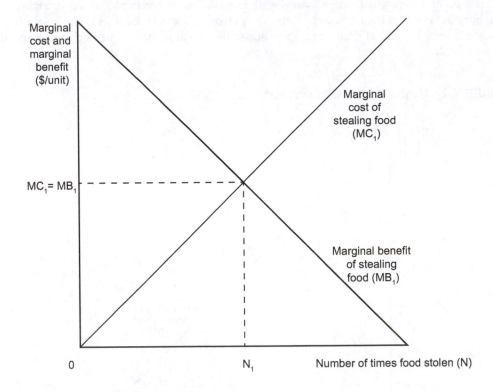

food is stolen is decreased from N_1 to N_2. The marginal benefit of stealing the last unit of food has also increased (from MB_1 to MB_2) because there is a higher marginal benefit at a lower quantity of food stolen.

To decrease theft, policy-makers could instead make changes to negatively affect the benefit of a theft. In this model, the benefit of stealing is the amount of money that does not have to be paid for food when it is stolen. Policy-makers can decrease the price of food, which results in a decrease in the marginal benefit of stealing a unit of food. This is illustrated in Figure 1.5 as a downward shift in the marginal benefit curve (MB_1 to MB_2). In this case, the person chooses to steal food fewer times (from N_1 to N_2) because it is now cheaper to buy a unit of food, so the marginal benefit of stealing each unit of food has decreased (MB_1 to MB_2). The marginal cost of stealing the last unit of food has also decreased (from MC_1 to MC_2) because there is lower marginal cost at a lower quantity of food stolen.

This relatively simple model is the basic structure of economic cost–benefit analysis. While this model demonstrates how economic cost–benefit analysis can be applied to a situation in which someone has to choose between buying and stealing food, later chapters will look at the costs and benefits of decision-makers who are associated with specific human rights violations.

Unit 3: Inefficiencies in economic structure of human rights

A **general equilibrium macroeconomic model** is one including all of the variables affecting decisions, including political, professional, personal, and monetary factors. Alternatively,

FIGURE 1.4 Increased marginal cost of stealing food

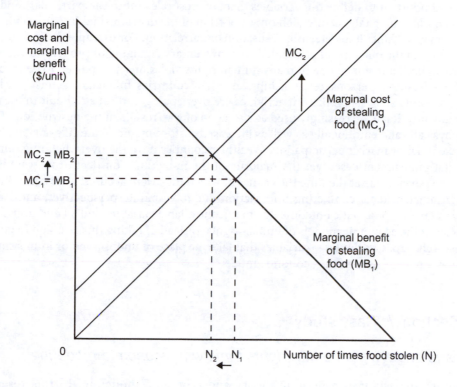

FIGURE 1.5 Decreased marginal benefit of stealing food

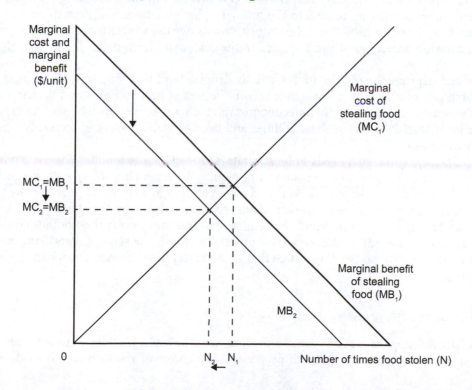

it will be important to define the variables that are most relevant to the particular model of partial equilibrium analysis, in which only a portion of the decision-making process is analyzed. It may be difficult to determine causation or correlation. For example, part of both the reason for and the outcome of genocide is the involuntary changing of property ownership. Terrorism, itself a major source of many human rights violations, is reported to be involved in politics, business, personal relationships, and many countries' financial systems. This leads to an economic analysis problem if activities are overlapping and thus difficult to measure independently. Rape, increasingly used as a weapon of war, results in the destruction of persons physically and emotionally as well as increased costs of medical care (if available) and a decrease in labor market participation. Wealthier counties have the overwhelming number of capital punishment cases, yet the majority of the individuals on death row were living below the poverty line at the time the crimes of which they were accused were committed.

Insufficient data, conflicting information due to disparate perspectives, and lack of ability to create a pragmatic outcome due to uncontrollable variables will all add to the inefficiencies of the economic models of human rights. Instead of taking this as a sign to give up the research, **proxy variables** – variables that take the place of unobserved or immeasurable variables – may be used in the economic model.

Section 7: Case study

Steps to analyzing a human rights topic with economic modeling

Economic analysis uses economic theory and economic modeling. In this research, points of interest are the main decision-makers involved in the human rights issue; the choices they are making related to the human rights violation; and how those choices interact to affect the situation. Next, positive and negative incentives associated with each decision are analyzed and included in the cost–benefit model of the human rights violation.

The steps presented here are not strictly defined, but this is one way to structure the research process. Economic research is rare in the area of human rights and therefore is a relatively untapped opportunity for economists and other practitioners who wish to expand their economic skills and analytic abilities and become viable parts of potentially world-changing teams.

Underlying research needs to be accurate, thorough, and scientific. The basic phases of the scientific method in this context will require the researcher to: 1) Ask an effective research question; 2) complete background research through a review of peer-reviewed literature and interviews; 3) use economic theory to analyze the issue; 4) test analysis through econometric methods; 5) interpret the results; and 6) communicate the findings. The following section expands on this important process to include the steps of identifying biases, talking with experts, and writing – steps that are necessary to the economics of human rights research.

Step 1: Ask an effective research question

Carefully defining the research topic is the first step. The topic provides a guide to research and it may be modified as research progresses. The choice of research area is made after reading published research, talking with experts, reviewing relevant data sources, and determining the parameters of the research. The research needs to be well-defined so that it is neither too broad nor too narrow. For example, within the topic of violence against women, research could be conducted on the victims, the perpetrators of violence, the circumstances that keep women in the cycle of violence, resources to combat violence, and a variety of other issues. Keeping notes of research reviewed, people interviewed, and data sources helps to refine the research and prepare for writing. This textbook provides access to an online journal that can be used for this purpose.

Step 2: Identify biases

Throughout this textbook, opportunities are presented to complete a personal electronic journal to record research, thoughts, and biases. Each person has bias from place of birth, upbringing, secular or religious views, experiences, travels, habits, and other influencers. A researcher's bias can drive the research in an unscientific manner that can make the outcomes unreliable for policy-making. It is important for the researcher to identify their own biases, determine how these biases may lead to regard or disregard for certain information, listen to the experts (even when the researcher does not agree), and write in a way that makes policy-makers aware of potential bias in the research.

Step 3: Complete background research through a review of peer-reviewed literature and interviews

Extensive research has been published on some topics, while other topics are not well documented. The researcher needs to read background information on the topic in question from sources such as peer-reviewed journal articles, conference papers, dissertations, interviews of subject matter experts, documentaries, and other scholarly information produced within the last five years or longer, depending upon the subject matter. These sources will provide information on current trends in research as well as a wealth of bibliographies of past publications that can be used in research. Secondary sources include recent (i.e. published during the last five years) newspaper articles, information from nonprofit organizations, and other sources. It is again important to note biases. For example, organizations may report statistics that are beneficial to their stances, shine the best light on their affairs, or help them raise funding. Notes should be made on the information discovered as this will become the foundation for research.

As stated above, one of the most important components of successful research is to get the definitions right. This means that the researcher has done enough reading, questioning, writing, and more questioning to decide the best definitions to use in the research.

Step 4: Identify important questions to ask the experts

During the research process, a researcher will want to make a note of people who are considered experts on the topic. These people may be found through their personal research, their appointments in different government agencies or nongovernment organizations, or through public speeches. When reading a peer-reviewed paper, it is helpful to review the citations to identify other possible experts in the subject area. Once the researcher has done background reading, it is possible to write down important questions to be answered by the research project.

Step 5: Ask the expert(s)

It is imperative that a person prepares for a face-to-face or phone interview with a subject expert since no one likes to waste time talking with someone who is not prepared to ask informed questions. Listening carefully, making notes, and asking follow-up questions will lead the researcher to valuable information and may open doorways to other experts, information, and data. With the consent of the expert, the researcher should take notes on what was said and impressions during the interview. It may be possible to record the interview. The expert should be assured that the researcher will not publish any part of the conversation before first getting that expert's authorization.

It is insightful to ask the expert to describe the process by which they became an expert and the training necessary to become an expert on the topic. This will provide insight into the expert's biases that may not be evident in the expert's published research. Finding out these biases can offer answers to problems faced later on in research.

Asking the expert for a list of must-read resources will provide another great source of information. For example, the author of this textbook was offered lists and even personal copies of papers and books by several experts. This information is a great gift that can save the researcher hours of research and uninformed wandering through the subject-matter landscape.

It is possible that the expert is willing to review and edit near-complete research papers. This can greatly increase the quality of research as long as the researcher is willing to be humble and consider the expert's advice, even if not all suggestions are used.

Step 6: Use economic theory to analyze the issue

The next step is brainstorming and listing potential decision-makers who affect, or are affected by, the situation, and recording the choices they make in regard to the topic of interest. Within the initial broad list, include sub-actors who may influence, or be influenced by, the choices made. The researcher's decision may be to focus on only a subset of the actors, but all should be kept in the list for future review and research.

Writing down the thoughts from the brainstorm can provide areas of interest to the researcher. For example, what are the choices each of the decision-makers in a human rights topic faces and what costs and benefits affect their choices? How do the parts fit together? Where are the gaps? The researcher should take these brainstormed thoughts and see if there is a possible structure to the issues. This will help determine the most effective means of applying economic theory and models to human rights data. This step will include translation of the human rights information into economics, determination of the most applicable ways to study each human rights area with economics theory and methods, and creation of a list of necessary expert information and data for analysis.

Step 7: Test analysis through econometric methods and interpret the results

Econometric analysis uses statistics and other mathematical applications to analyze economic situations. It requires not only an understanding of the economics, but also comprehension of statistical techniques and the interpretation of the resulting numbers back into economics. If the researcher is not familiar with some of these techniques, an expert in econometrics can provide valuable guidance.

Step 8: Write, revise, rewrite

With all of the information collected and data analyzed, it is now time to write. The researcher will continue to read new material as gaps in knowledge become apparent and then will write, revise, and rewrite until the structure takes shape.

Step 9: Submit writing to other researchers and experts for their review

Experts and editors add valuable information and insight as well as increased quality to a researcher's work. It is important to humbly listen to or read through comments and critiques and make objective decisions on whether the information is pertinent to the study.

Step 10: Revise, review, finish writing, and communicate the findings

The final stage is to consider the comments and critiques of experts and editors, use and discard the information as necessary, and revise the research if needed. The research should be reviewed a final time before submitting or presenting it.

Section 8: Recommendation for future research

This textbook is designed to build a foundation of knowledge about each of the human rights topic it covers. Once a general understanding of the topic is achieved, it is possible to move toward a more specific area of research. Each chapter provides recommendations for further study in the specific research areas. There are unlimited topics of interest beyond those presented that can be understood more fully with economics research. Some of these human rights topics include the economic components of conflict, disability, disappearances, disarmament, free expression, gay/lesbian/bisexuality/transsexuality rights, indigenous rights, landmines, reform through labor, microcredit, practices of multinational corporations, police brutality, political rights, religious freedom, torture, and war crimes.

CHECK YOURSELF BOX: CHANGES TO PERSONAL BIASES ABOUT HUMAN RIGHTS

The goal of this textbook is not to teach you *what* to think about human rights, but rather to show you a new *way* to think about human rights issues. Look back at the first check yourself box (personal biases about human rights). Take a few minutes to write down whether your ideas about human rights changed. If they did, what are the reasons for the change – new information, a new way of thinking, something else? If your ideas did not change, what are the reasons there was no change? Be honest with yourself. It is possible, but not statistically probable, that you already knew everything that was presented. If you learned new things, are biases blocking you from discovering new tools or ways to use the tools you already possess? This process will help you discover how to be more scientific and to gain valuable information that you may never have encountered.

Section 9: Bibliography

Demeritt, Allison; Hoff, Karla; and Walsh, James. (2015). *Behavioral development economics: A new approach to policy interventions.* Washington, D.C.: Center for Economic Policy Research.

Federal Bureau of Investigation. (2015). Hate crimes statistics. Retrieved from https://ucr.fbi.gov/hate-crime/2015

Merriam-Webster Collegiate Dictionary. (2004). Springfield: Merriam-Webster, Inc.

Shepard, Melanie and Pence, Ellen (Eds.). (1999). *Coordinating community responses to domestic violence: Lessons from Duluth and beyond.* Thousand Oaks: SAGE Publications Inc.

United Nations General Assembly. (2003). *The United Nations protocol to prevent, suppress and punish trafficking in persons especially women and children.*

U.S. Department of Justice. (2000). *Full report on the prevalence, incidence, and consequences of violence against women.* Retrieved from https://www.ncjrs.gov/pdffiles1/nij/183781.pdf

U.S. Department of State. (n.d.). *Number of terrorist attacks worldwide between 2006 and 2016.* In Statista - The Statistics Portal. Retrieved May 27, 2018, from https://www.statista.com/statistics/202864/number-of-terrorist-attacks-worldwide

Section 10: Resources

Unit 1: Summary

The economics of human rights is the observation and analysis of human rights issues and violations through the lens of economics. There is a codified system of laws and agreements that set the terms of individual human rights, although not all countries have signed these agreements and many controversies exist. There is a wide range of human rights topics and hundreds of organizations and experts involved in each topic. This textbook looks at the economics of capital punishment, violence against women, seeking asylum, terrorism, child abuse, genocide, and hate. For each of the topics, it is important to determine who makes the decisions as well as individual costs and benefits. Economic research of human rights topics involves a step-by-step process of information gathering, analysis, and reporting.

Unit 2: Key concepts

Asylum seeker: A person who has crossed or is at an international border and requests asylum.

Capital punishment: The U.S. Bureau of Justice Statistics defines capital punishment as "the process of sentencing convicted offenders to death for the most serious crimes (capital crimes) and carrying out that sentence. The specific offenses and circumstances which determine if a crime (usually murder) is eligible for a death sentence are defined by statute and are prescribed by Congress or any state legislature."

Child abuse: The Federal Child Abuse Prevention and Treatment Act (2010) defines child abuse as "at a minimum, any recent act or failure to act on the part of a parent or caretaker which results in death, serious physical or emotional harm, sexual abuse or exploitation; or an act or failure to act which presents an imminent risk of serious harm."

Choices: Voluntary or involuntary decisions made by decision-makers.

Death row: According to U.S. Office of Justice Programs Bureau of Justice Statistics, death row is "the area of a prison in which prisoners who were under a sentence of death were housed. Usage of the term continues despite the fact that many states do not maintain a separate unit or facility for condemned inmates."

Economics: The science of choice when dealing with scarcity.

Equity: A situation in which each person has the same allocation of resources, costs, or risks.

General equilibrium macroeconomic model: An economic model that includes all of the variables affecting decisions, including political, professional, personal, and monetary factors.

Genocide: The deliberate destruction of part or all of a group of people.

Hate: According to the *Merriam-Webster Collegiate Dictionary* (2004), hate is "intense hostility and aversion usually derived from fear, anger, or sense of injury."

Human rights: The codified body of work coming from national and international agreements, laws, and protocols that represent the rights of all human beings. The U.N. OHCHR defines human rights as "rights inherent to all human beings, whatever our nationality, place of residence, sex, national or ethnic origin, colour, religion, language, or any other status. We are all equally entitled to our human rights without discrimination. These rights are all interrelated, interdependent and indivisible."

Human rights violation: Any violation of the 30 articles of the UDHR.

Incentives: Positive or negative motivations used to modify behavior.

Marginal benefit (MB): The benefit received from the last unit of consumption.

Marginal cost (MC): The cost of the last unit of production.

Normative statements: Describe "what should be" or opinions.

Positive statements: Describe "what is" or the facts.

Proxy variables: Variables that take the place of unobserved or immeasurable variables in economic models.

Scarcity: Not having enough resources to fulfill all of people's needs and wants.

Social justice: The administration of the body of work that makes up human rights in a way that provides all people with equal economic, political, and social rights and opportunities. Social justice stems from human rights.

Terrorism: According to the U.S. Department of Defense, terrorism is "the calculated use of unlawful violence or threat of unlawful violence to inculcate fear; intended to coerce or to intimidate governments or societies in the pursuit of goals that are generally political, religious, or ideological."

Violence against women: The use of physical, verbal, emotional, sexual, or financial violence by a perpetrator against a female victim.

Unit 3: Review questions

1. How can economics inform human rights research?

2. How is "human rights" different than social justice?

3. What are some of the laws in the United States related to human rights?

4. What are some of the international agreements that make provision for human rights?

5. Why are there controversies about human rights?

6. Give a brief description in your own words of the following: Capital punishment, violence against women, seeking asylum, terrorism, child abuse, genocide, and hate.

7. How can economic efficiency be used to analyze a human rights topic?

8. What part does scarcity play in human rights violations?

9. How can creating incentives to change marginal cost and marginal benefit affect a person's decision?

10. Why may inefficiencies exist in the economic analysis of human rights?

11. Describe the steps to analyzing a human rights topic with economic modeling.

Unit 4: Recommended readings

Brownlie, Ian and Goodwin-Gill, Guy (Eds.). (2010). *Brownlie's Documents on Human Rights*, 6th ed. Oxford: Oxford University Press.

Haas, Michael. (2008). *International human rights: A comprehensive introduction*. Routledge: New York.

Hunt, Lynn. (2007). *Inventing human rights: A history*. New York: W. W. Norton & Company.

Laqueur, Walter and Rubin, Barry (Eds.). (1989). *Human rights reader*. New York: Meridian.

Pogge, Thomas (Ed.). (2007). *Freedom from poverty as a human right. Who owes what to the very poor?* Oxford: Oxford University Press.

Unit 5: Web links

Amnesty International: https://www.amnesty.org
Business & Human Rights Resource Centre: https://www.business-humanrights.org
Center for Economic and Social Rights: http://www.cesr.org
Freedom House: https://www.freedomhouse.org
Human Rights First: https://www.humanrightsfirst.org
Human Rights Internet: http://www.hri.ca
Human Rights Watch: https://www.hrw.org
Human Rights without Frontiers: http://www.hrwf.eu
Inter-American Commission on Human Rights: http://www.oas.org/en/iachr
International Committee of the Red Cross: https://www.icrc.org
International Women's Rights Action Watch: https://www.iwraw-ap.org
Mental Disability Rights International: http://www.globalmentalhealth.org
UNICEF: https://www.unicef.org
United Nations Human Rights Treaty System: https://www.ohchr.org/Documents/Publications/FactSheet30Rev1.pdf

U.S. Human Rights Network: https://www.ushrnetwork.org

United States Department of State Bureau of Democracy, Human Rights, and Labor: https://www.state.gov/j/drl

United States Government – promotion of human rights: https://www.humanrights.gov

Universal Declaration of Human Rights: https://www.un.org/en/universal-declaration-human-rights

Vital Voices Global Partnership: https://www.vitalvoices.org

World Health Organization: http://www.who.int

2 Economics of capital punishment

Contributors: V. Wolfe Mahfood, Ph.D., Dennis Longmire, Ph.D., Rick Halperin, Ph.D.

I N 1991, a single-family house in the small town of Corsicana, Texas went up in flames. The fire took the lives of three small children: a girl aged two and twins aged one. The father who was taking care of the children got out of the house alive. Two weeks after the fire, the father was arrested on charges of capital murder based on the evidence collected by a local certified arson inspector and one of the state's leading arson investigators. In 1992, the father of the three girls was convicted of capital murder and lived on death row in Texas until he was executed by lethal injection in 2004.

Section 1: Introduction to the economics of capital punishment

In economics, **capital** is defined as the resources used in the production of goods and services. This type of capital includes the machinery, equipment, buildings, and vehicles used in creating a firm's output. The study of capital in the human rights context goes back to the Latin word *caput*, meaning head. A **capital offense** is a criminal charge punishable by the death penalty or "losing one's head." It is a crime such as murder or betrayal of one's country that is determined to be so serious that the death penalty is considered an appropriate punishment. The **death penalty** is the punishment of execution given to a person who has been convicted of a capital offense by a court of law, although there may be reasons that the punishment is never administered. A **capital trial** is the process of trying a person for a capital offense and, if convicting, administering the death penalty. **Capital punishment** is the legal killing of a person as punishment for a capital offense. The terms death penalty and capital punishment are sometimes used interchangeably, but a person convicted of the death penalty may never be executed (i.e. capital punishment may never be enacted). This textbook will focus on the capital punishment system in the U.S. as administered by the appropriate government authorities.

Richard Dieter (2005) observes that "in broad terms, the death penalty is about a search for justice and the safety of the community." However, capital punishment has been more narrowly defined as "a practice whereby a properly constituted authority puts to death a convicted offender in punishment for a crime" (David Garland, 2010). Capital punishment is a widely contested human rights topic. Populations are divided across the two main positions – that of the death penalty being cruel, inhumane, and degrading, and that of the death penalty being an acceptable form of punishment for the worst criminal violations and legal under state and federal law. A person's position on this topic can affect the probability of their election to public office, their standing in a community, and their eligibility for sitting on the jury of a capital murder trial. Both death penalty advocates and abolitionists have vehemently argued the morality, along with the constitutionality, of the death penalty since the inception of America's criminal justice system (Hashem Dezhbakhsh and Joanna Shepherd, 2003; Margaret Farnworth et al., 1998). Broadly speaking, there are only two sides to the capital coin: Societies that support the use of capital sanctions and those that oppose it. Nonetheless, there are extensive conflicting views within the death penalty debate, such that "Proponents and opponents of capital punishment engage a dizzying array of issues, marshal idiosyncratic arguments, draw support whence available – be it science or faith, data or rhetoric – and arrive, as often as not, at diametrically contrasting conclusions" (James Acker, 2008).

Currently, 31 states, the federal government, and the U.S. military have capital punishment infrastructures (Death Penalty Information Center, 2017). At the end of 2016, the Death Penalty Information Center in the U.S. reported 31 states with the death penalty and 19 states without the death penalty. The highest number of executions in the U.S. was 98 in 1999 and the lowest in the last 20 years was 11 in 1988. Since 1976, Texas has had the most executions (538), followed by Oklahoma with 112, Virginia with 111, Florida with 92, and Missouri with 87. Of those executed, lethal injection was used in 1,267 cases, electrocution in 158 cases, gas chamber in 11 cases, hanging in three cases, and firing squad in three cases. Table 2.1 provides a look at numbers related to the capital punishment process.

TABLE 2.1 Capital punishment statistics by state

State	Year death penalty re-enacted	Current death row population	Women on death row	Murder rate (per 100,000)	Method	How sentence determined
Alabama	1976	191	5	8.4	Injection or electrocution	Jury, but judge can override jury's recommendation
Arizona	1973	124	3	5.4	Injection or gas	Jury
Arkansas	1973	32	0	7.2	Injection or electrocution	Jury
California	1973	746	22	4.9	Injection or gas	Jury
Colorado	1975	3	0	3.7	Injection	Jury
Delaware	1947	17	0	4.2	Injection or hanging	Jury, but judge can override jury's decision
Florida	1972	374	3	5.4	Injection or electrocution	Jury, but judge can override jury's recommendation
Georgia	1973	61	0	6.6	Injection	Jury
Idaho	1973	8	1	2.9	Injection	Jury
Indiana	1973	12	1	6.6	Injection	
Kansas	1994	10	0	3.8	Injection	

(Continued)

TABLE 2.1   (Continued)

State	Year death penalty re-enacted	Current death row population	Women on death row	Murder rate (per 100,000)	Method	How sentence determined
Kentucky	1975	33	1	5.9	Injection or electrocution	Jury
Louisiana	1973	73	2	11.5	Injection	Jury
Mississippi	1974	48	2	8.0	Injection	Jury
Missouri	1975	24	0	8.8	Injection or gas	Jury
Montana	1974	2	2	3.5	Injection	Jury decides on aggravators; Judge decides sentence
Nevada	1973	82	0	7.6	Injection	Jury
New Hampshire	1991	1	0	1.7	Injection or hanging	Jury
North Carolina	1977	152	3	6.7	Injection	Jury
Ohio	1973	144	1	5.6	Injection – one drug protocol	Jury
Oklahoma	1973	47	1	6.2	Injection, electrocution, firing squad	Jury
Oregon	1978	33	1	2.8	Injection	Jury
Pennsylvania	1974	169	2	5.2	Injection	Jury
South Carolina	1974	41	0	7.4	Injection or electrocution	Jury
South Dakota	1978	3	0	3.1	Injection	Jury
Tennessee	1974	62	1	7.3	Injection or electrocution	Jury
Texas	1973	243	6	5.3	Injection	Jury
Utah	1973	9	0	2.4	Injection or firing squad	Jury
Virginia	1975	5	0	5.8	Injection or electrocution	Jury
Washington	1975	8	0	2.7	Injection or hanging	Jury
Wyoming	1977	1	0	3.4	Injection or gas	Jury

Death Penalty Information Center, 2018

TABLE 2.2   Countries with legalized death penalty

Currently in use		Not used in last ten years
Afghanistan	Lesotho	Algeria
Antigua and Barbuda	Libya	Benin
Bahamas	Malaysia	Brunei Darussalam
Bahrain	Nigeria	Burkina Faso
Bangladesh	Oman	Cameroon
Barbados	Pakistan	Central African Republic
Belarus	Palestinian authority	Eritrea
Belize	Qatar	Ghana
Botswana	Saint Kitts & Nevis	Grenada
Chad	Saint Lucia	Kenya
China	Saint Vincent & Grenadines	Korea (South)
Comoros	Saudi Arabia	Laos
Congo (Democratic Republic)	Singapore	Liberia
Cuba	Somalia	Malawi
Dominica	South Sudan	Maldives
Egypt	Sudan	Mali
Equatorial Guinea	Syria	Mauritania
Ethiopia	Taiwan	Mongolia
Gambia	Thailand	Morocco
Guatemala	Trinidad and Tobago	Myanmar
Guinea	Uganda	Nauru
Guyana	United Arab Emirates	Niger
India	United States of America	Papua New Guinea
Indonesia	Vietnam	Russian Federation
Iran	Yemen	Sierra Leone
Iraq	Zimbabwe	Sri Lanka
Jamaica		Swaziland
Japan		Tajikistan
Jordan		Tanzania
Korea (North)		Tonga
Kuwait		Tunisia
Lebanon		Zambia

Internationally, there are 95 countries that have legalized the death penalty, 63 of which have administered the death penalty within the last 10 years. Table 2.2 presents a listing of these countries as of January 2017.

While this textbook discusses capital punishment worldwide, it focuses upon capital punishment in Texas. Texas has the largest death row population after California and the most executions of any U.S. state. The case study for this chapter is based on data from counties in Texas. Note that extrajudicial executions carried out without due process of law, as when a person or group of persons executes another person or persons, are not considered capital punishment. This type of execution will be discussed in the economics of hate chapter.

This chapter provides introductions to the perspectives of human rights and capital punishment, relevant definitions, and a brief history of capital punishment in the United States, which is necessary to understand the process of capital punishment. A brief outline of the murder arraignment process is set out. The case study uses multiple regression to analyze the economic costs of the capital punishment system in Texas between 2005 and 2007. This partial equilibrium analysis incorporates cross sectional data. Finally, the chapter will provide some discussion of the limitations on research and recommendations for further research.

The chapter presents the writing of two scholars who represent divergent stances on capital punishment. These statements are meant to introduce students to the wide range of, and often conflicting, ideas on a specific subject.

Unit 1: Human rights perspective

Rick Halperin, Ph.D.

Rick Halperin is director of the Embrey Human Rights Program at Southern Methodist University in Dallas, Texas. He has a Ph.D. in history from Auburn University. Dr. Halperin teaches courses in the History Department and leads human rights educational journeys to places such as Argentina, Bosnia, Cambodia, El Salvador, Germany, Poland, Rwanda, South Africa, and the United States. He has served on the board of Amnesty International USA and as a member of the National Death Penalty Advisory Committee, the National Coalition to Abolish the Death Penalty, and the Texas Coalition to Abolish the Death Penalty. He is a runner and owns five Siberian Huskies.

On April 29, 1998, I witnessed the execution of a man by lethal injection. I walked into the death chamber viewing room with the man's mother and spiritual advisor to see him strapped onto a gurney with leather restraints at his ankles, shins, waist, and chest. He wore a navy prison one-piece jumpsuit, white socks, and tennis shoes. His hands were taped with bandages so that his hands and fingers were entirely hidden. A needle was inserted into each forearm and connected to a tube of clear solution. A towel folded in thirds served as a pillow.

I had been corresponding with the man, who steadfastly maintained his innocence of the 1988 death of a lady who had been raped and stabbed by two men. With the impending execution date, the man hoped to be granted an evidentiary hearing that he and his lawyer felt would cast serious doubts upon his conviction, a hope that was dashed on April 28, 1998 as the courts rejected the man's request. When I spoke in person with the man, he spoke of the psychological and physical torture he endured for 10 years on death row. He would often come back to his cell from a visit with his family to find the guards had destroyed his personal belongings and he talked of the common physical torture he experienced at being handcuffed as five or six guards beat, kicked, and punched him. He stated, "we are the condemned . . . no one cares about us . . . we have no one to complain to . . . they look at us like we are animals, and they treat us worse. If they kill me Wednesday night, it will only mean that I am going home, going to the land of my ancestors. I will be free from here."

A microphone was lowered down to the man strapped to the gurney. With his eyes closed, the man made a statement claiming his innocence and telling his mother he loved her. With the statement completed, the medical technician started the flow of the lethal injection. The man's chest rose and fell a few times. Within moments the man appeared to be in a deep sleep, and then, suddenly, he let out a long exhalation, making a coughing-gurgling noise. His chest stopped moving and he lay perfectly still with no expression on his face. "Death is at 6:27."

Dr. Karl Brandt, the personal physician of Adolf Hitler, devised lethal injection as a planned method of killing in 1939. It was initially designed to be used to kill children and later adults and was incorporated into the 1939 "Fuhrer decree," a program of euthanasia designed to eliminate "life unworthy of life."

The significance of human rights is precisely that some means may NEVER be used to protect society because their use violates the very values that make society worth protecting. The death penalty is the ultimate human rights violation. It has no power to prevent crime and is a particularly calculated, cruel, cold-blooded form of killing. It is the ultimate inhuman and degrading punishment. When inflicted for criminal offenses, it represents nothing more than a judicial lottery. The sad truth is that America's judicial system, especially when concerned with capital cases, is stained with racism, hatred, and dishonor.

The fact that the United States has executed over 1,400 individuals since 1977 is shocking enough. But the circumstances under which some of them are being put to death – and the lack of public outrage – make a chilling statement about the American notion of justice. The condemned in America today are constantly dehumanized and labeled as "filth," "garbage," "scum," "monsters," and "evil," people whose extermination is deemed "necessary" and "deserved." The acceptance and practice of the death penalty represent nothing more than a Nazi-like mentality which is designed to declare some persons as "life unworthy of life" and then to exterminate them in the name of the law.

U.S. politicians and national leaders of both genders and both major political parties still believe they can solve urgent social and political problems by executing prisoners and that the answer to solving the national crime problem is to be found in continually meting out death sentences. Over 3,000 people currently languish on America's death rows, including over 50 women and many others who are profoundly mentally ill and/or innocent.

Are we as a nation going to accept America's bloodshed, both in the streets and in the death houses, or are we ready to stand up and do what is right? When will we, as a nation, have the moral courage to say "enough?" We can change the direction in which our nation is headed; we can prevent this decade from becoming bloodier than the last. Let us send a signal to our leaders that we demand action to solve our national social problems, and that we are tired of excuses and state-sanctioned premeditated murder.

Unit 2: Criminal justice perspective

V. Wolfe Mahfood, Ph.D.

Dr. V. Wolfe Mahfood is a Law Librarian III for the Texas Department of Criminal Justice, for whom she was previously an investigator and a correctional officer. Dr. Mahfood has a Ph.D. in criminal justice from Sam Houston State University and an MBA from Lamar University. She has extensive criminal justice training and is a former four-time world super middleweight and light heavyweight boxing champion.

As applied within the United States, capital punishment is not a violation of human rights. Rather, it is a legal sanction authorized under due process of law that, in fact, falls perfectly within the minimum guidelines set forth by the United Nations in advocating the advancement of human rights via governmental systems. Specifically, as declared within the Universal Declaration of Human Rights (1948), governmental systems are just, in so long as they reflect "the will of the people" (Article 21, Section 3). Regarding criminal justice processes, advancing human rights demands that individuals are not "subjected to arbitrary arrest, detention, or exile" (Article 9). If charged with a criminal offense, individuals are "entitled in full equality to a fair and public hearing by an independent and impartial tribunal" (Article 10), whereas a man is "presumed innocent until proved guilty according to law in a public trial at which he has had all the guarantees necessary for his defense" (Article 11). Lastly, governments must ensure that all persons, especially those within their correctional systems, are not "subjected to torture or to cruel, inhuman or degrading treatment or punishment" (Article 5).

Given that the U.S. Supreme Court has assured every one of the aforementioned conditions attach to all capital prosecutions, the right of democratically-elected governments to enforce the will of their people via capital punishment is absolutely above reproach. Enforcing the death penalty is not a human rights issue. It is, however, a tremendously contested political matter, in which detractors often frame their agenda as human rights concerns in a misguided attempt to isolate capital prosecutions from the whole of the criminal justice process.

Obviously, capital prosecutions cannot exist outside of criminal justice systems. Hence, highlighting capital prosecutions without questioning the remainder of the process is a backhanded ploy to push a narrowly-focused political agenda without having to address the plethora of systemic concerns that would necessarily surround the entire criminal justice process if such conditions were found rampant within any single part of it. In other words, if the capital prosecution process is corrupt and requires changing, then the entire criminal justice system requires the same changes. Alternatively, arguing capital punishment as a violation of human rights is certainly more appealing to the voting public than arguing for savage murderers to retain the absolute value of their lives in spite of the wretched disregard these criminals have demonstrated for the rights and lives of their innocent victims.

Either way, arguing capital punishment as a human rights concern provides detractors an easy opportunity to advance their agenda without having to address an actual matter of government – specifically, the will of the people. Not only does this approach hijack democracy, but it works to lessen the importance of legitimate human rights concerns. This understood, as a matter of effective and efficient government, it is still necessary to study capital prosecution processes as well as their subsequent effects on other policy matters. It is not, however, necessary to continue debating the humanity of capital punishment, its constitutionality, or other arguments related to routine arbitrariness, discrimination, socioeconomic prejudice, ineffective counsel, corrupt officials, as well as simple questions of deterrence, retribution, reformation, incapacitation, and innocence. As for each of these ideas, there are literally countless, well-supported arguments available to validate whichever side of the coin individuals wish to call. Of course, regardless of which side that may be, the Supreme Court has already and unequivocally established capital punishment as a legal, humane sanction within America's criminal justice systems.

I personally support the death penalty. In fact, having worked in corrections for almost 25 years, I believe that death row is heavily under-populated. But governments should not operate on personal beliefs. Instead, rational administrations must concern themselves with all aspects of society, to include the social welfare and economic consequences of capital prosecutions. Given the limited funding sources of government, it would be naive to suggest that a price tag should not be placed on justice. It would be equally absurd to assume that all persons within a society would agree upon the cost of justice, especially when the effects of that cost are not equally distributed across all members of society.

Accordingly, elected officials must determine what policies best support their community needs, as well as citizen preferences. As a practical matter, governments must also finance these policies. Needless to say, compromise is a certainty. As such, in determining affordable costs for governmental goods and services, administrators must engage the will of the people lest those managers risk reelection. If the public fails to find that capital prosecution costs add value to their communities, then governments should refrain from such expenditures. If, however, societies find value in capital prosecutions in spite of their excess costs, then in accordance with the Tenth Amendment, those communities are entirely within their authority to fund capital trials in lieu of other government services. In the end, both administrators and the people must understand the benefits, costs, and social welfare consequences of capital prosecutions, as opposed to other prosecutorial options, in order to pursue the most informed and rational criminal justice policies.

Section 2: Fundamentals of capital punishment

Terms and trial process stages

Analyzing a market requires a firm understanding of actors involved, the costs and benefits of each actor, and the structure of the market. In a similar way, the economist who analyzes capital punishment needs to understand the foundation of the death penalty, including the persons who make decisions, the costs and benefits to those persons, and the structure of the capital trial process. Capital punishment and human rights expert Rick Halperin states, "The death penalty is a process, not an act."

In addressing more serious criminal violations, law enforcement agencies throughout the United States have codified legally acceptable sanctions. Governments may impose capital punishment, also known as the death penalty, for capital offenses such as evidence of multiple murders, a murder while committing a felony, torture, lying in wait to kill someone, or killing a peace officer. Capital punishment makes no attempt to rehabilitate offenders, but invokes isolation. According to Roy Adler (2008), "the purposes of capital punishment are threefold: 1) to prevent the murderer from killing again either inside or outside of prison, 2) to demonstrate that murder is a crime like no other for which society reserves a punishment like no other, and 3) to dissuade others from murdering."

After the Supreme Court ruling on *Furman v. Georgia*, each state had to find a way to meet the new Supreme Court capital punishment statutes, but was allowed the discretion of determining how to fulfill those requirements. Some states followed the procedures put in place by Georgia in which the judge or the jury must consider all mitigating or aggravating circumstances authorized by law and weigh them against any of the listed aggravating circumstances supported by evidence. **Mitigating circumstances** are evidence that the defense provides during the sentencing phase to explain why the defendant should not receive the death penalty. The evidence, such as prior criminal record, abusive childhood, mental problems, or age, is meant to reduce the culpability or blame of the defendant for the criminal act. **Aggravating circumstances** are facts that increase the culpability for the criminal act. The evidence could be in relation to circumstances of the crime, prior criminal record, evidence about the victim and the victim's family, or the future dangerousness of the defendant. This process is to determine guilt by balancing the aggravating factors against a list of mitigating factors.

Texas chose an alternate type of capital punishment statute that uses a bifurcated trial process in which the trial is divided into two trial phases: The guilt phase and the penalty phase. During the **guilt phase**, the jury must decide whether a person is guilty "beyond a reasonable doubt." If the jury's decision is "guilty," the trial moves to the **penalty phase,** in which the jury reviews the evidence of aggravating and mitigating evidence to determine whether the punishment for the capital offense will be the death penalty or life without parole. If the verdict is the death penalty, the defendant is automatically given the right to appeal the decision to the Texas Court of Criminal Appeals, one of Texas' two supreme courts. The complex bifurcated capital punishment trial process in Texas will be described further below, along with important terminology.

Stage I: Investigation stage

Once a murder has been committed, law enforcement work to create a strategy to gather evidence surrounding the crime. This involves a complex method of brainstorming, searching for and analyzing evidence, following evidence leads, interviews, and documentation. For a capital case, this is called the **investigation stage**. A warrant may be issued for the arrest of a suspected individual, or multiple warrants if there are multiple suspects. Once the warrant(s) has been issued and the suspect(s) apprehended, law enforcement officers place the suspected individual(s) under arrest and in isolation. **Isolation**, commonly called incapacitation, suggests that the offender poses risks to society and must be isolated from society. If the person suspected of murder has fled to a place outside of the law enforcement's jurisdiction, the **extradition process** might be used, in which law enforcement across regions work together to bring the person back to the area where the crime happened in order to stand trial. Once the person is in law enforcement custody, a **bond hearing** is held to determine the bond amount necessary to let the person go until the trial, or the person may be held without a bond. A bond may not be granted due to the seriousness of the accusation against the person under arrest. Law enforcement will continue the investigation stage by collecting physical and verbal evidence surrounding the crime to be used in the prosecution of the suspect(s).

If the decision is for capital punishment, the accused person is the impending defendant in a capital murder trial. At this point, the case against the suspected person may go forward to the **indictment stage**, or it may be dropped. If the prosecution team in a murder trial determines to try the suspect for **capital murder**, which is murder for which death penalty may be imposed, the process proceeds in multiple stages. In Texas, the district attorney or the assistant district attorney makes the decision to prosecute the accused (who is now referred to as "the impending defendant") for a **capital offense**, a crime warranting the death penalty. There are many decisions made within each of these stages as the courts follow established rules and principles in legal proceedings in order to protect and enforce private rights, called **due process of law**.

Stage II: Indictment stage

The **indictment stage** encompasses the guilt phase of the bifurcated trial process in which the court gathers a group of citizens to be members of the jury. This jury is sometimes called a **death-qualifying jury** because each jurist must be able to decide for a sentence of the death penalty or life without parole as possible punishments. The impending defendant is **capital eligible**, meaning that specific determinants are present so that the impending defendant may be given the death penalty.

Stage III: Pretrial stage

In the **pretrial stage**, the judge may decide to dismiss the case. If not dismissed, the defense and prosecution teams meet to determine whether they can reach a plea bargain for lesser charges. If no plea bargain is made, the prosecution will seek the death penalty once there is a determination of competency to stand trial for capital murder. If it is determined that the suspect is competent to stand trial, a capital murder trial is held.

Stage IV: Trial stage

Once the capital trial reaches the **trial stage**, also called the **guilt phase**, the accused person is called "the defendant." A **defendant** is a person accused of a crime in a court of law. During this phase, attorneys for the prosecution present evidence of aggravating circumstances. The attorneys for the defense may choose to present evidence of mitigating circumstances. There are three possible outcomes to this trial for the defendant: 1) A finding of "not guilty," 2) conviction of a non-capital offense, or 3) conviction of a capital offense. If the outcome of this trial is a verdict of guilt, the trial process moves to the sentencing stage.

Stage V: Sentencing stage

The **sentencing stage**, also called the **punishment phase**, encompasses the penalty phase of the capital punishment process. With the sentence of capital murder in the trial stage, the jury must then determine whether the punishment for the crime is **life without parole** (imprisonment for life) or the **death penalty** (execution).

Stage VI: Appeals stage

If the sentencing stage ends with a conviction and sentence of death, the **appeals stage** occurs automatically. In Texas, the defendant lives on **death row** – prison sections set aside for prisoners sentenced to death located in the Texas Department of Criminal Justice – during the appeals stage. Male death row inmates are housed in the Polunsky Unit and females are housed in the Mountain View Unit. There is a mandatory appeal to the conviction, but the person must get representation before the appeal becomes active and is heard by the Texas Court of Criminal Appeals.

The convicted person may lose the original trial lawyer, is not automatically assigned another lawyer, and may wait years while living on death row to have a lawyer assigned so that the appeal may be heard. Once a lawyer has been assigned, the lawyer has approximately one month to gather all evidence for the appeal. The lawyer may apply for an extension of time to collect evidence, but it is not automatically granted. DNA evidence may be admitted as evidence at any time due to its being indisputable. However, the DNA lab testing process may be flawed and test results may be delayed.

During this stage, state and then federal supreme courts rigorously review the case in a method called "super due process." In review of the trial, the Supreme Court may find harmless errors that do not affect the outcome of the trial, or it may find harmful errors. If the latter type of error is found, the entire trial can be thrown out and the defendant retried to correct for errors. The U.S. Office of the Attorney General represents the prosecution during this stage. Once the defense has presented all appeals to the state Supreme Court, it has the option of appealing to a Federal Court. In a similar way, if a state Supreme Court disagrees and reverses the decision of the lower courts, the prosecution can appeal the decision to the Federal Court. This is a rigorous process. A Texas defendant spends an average of 10.87 years on death row (Texas Department of Criminal Justice, 2014). The

2015 national appellant average for a death row offender was 15.8 years (Death Penalty Information Center, 2017).

Stage VII: Clemency stage

In the **clemency stage**, the governor of a state may temporarily or permanently halt the execution of a defendant given the death penalty. The reasons may be due to such factors as new or better evidence (such as DNA evidence) or the mental state of the convicted person.

Stage VIII: Execution

The final stage of the capital punishment process is **execution** or the carrying out of the death penalty. Texas, like the majority of states, uses lethal injection as its instrument of execution. Table 2.1 above gave the methods of execution used by different states, which include not only lethal injection, but also death by gas, electrocution, hanging, and firing squad.

Section 3: Capital punishment as a violation of human rights

Unit 1: National agreements

U.S. Supreme Court rulings concern violation of the Eighth Amendment: "Excessive bail shall not be required, nor excessive fines imposed, nor cruel and unusual punishments inflicted." Most of the U.S. Supreme Court rulings deal with examining whether or not the use of capital punishment in the case violates the rights granted by the Eighth Amendment, in that they are either unduly cruel or the punishment of death is disproportional to the crime.

U.S. Supreme Court decisions on capital punishment center upon four key issues: 1) The proportionality requirement (the punishment fits the crime), 2) the principle of individualized sentencing, 3) the method of execution, and 4) the classes of persons not eligible for the death penalty.

The proportionality requirement came about with the 1972 *Furman v. Georgia* decision (408 U.S. 238) that made the existing death penalty law unconstitutional. It was determined that the laws were in violation of the Eighth Amendment due to discrimination against poor and minorities, and that the death penalty made only minor contributions to society. Decision *Gregg v. Georgia* (428 U.S. 153) reinstated the death penalty in 1976. It was determined that the death penalty was not unconstitutional in all cases, due to the new procedures set in placed by Georgia's trial procedure.

The 1977 Supreme Court decision *Coker v. Georgia* (433 U.S. 584) limited the death penalty to capital offenses and stipulated that it did not apply to the crime of rape of an adult woman. The Supreme Court later determined that the death penalty was not a constitutional punishment for the crime of rape of a child, unless the child died from the effects of the rape (*Kennedy v. Louisiana*, 554 U.S. 407, 2008).

During the appeals process in the 1988 *McClesky v. Kemp* trial (753 U.S. 877), the defendant brought forth evidence of mitigating circumstances based on the Baldus study (David Baldus, Charles Pulaski, and George Woodworth, 1983). The study showed evidence of racial bias in the sentencing of black men convicted of killing white police officers in Georgia in the 1970s. The Supreme Court decision favored the prosecution.

The principle of individualized sentencing was established with the 2002 Supreme Court decision *Ring v. Arizona* (536 U.S. 584) with the determination that a defendant being prosecuted for a capital crime has the right to a jury trial. This means that the sentencing judge cannot make the decision to impose the death penalty without a jury decision. In 2006, the Supreme Court *Brown v. Sanders* decision (546 U.S. 212) found that the death sentence is unconstitutional if a jury decision was made based upon invalid aggravating factors, unless there are other aggravating factors present that contain the same facts and circumstances as the invalid factors. *Kansas v. Marsh* (548 U.S. 163) is the 2006 Supreme Court decision which found that a life sentence must be imposed for three reasons: If the State cannot prove beyond a reasonable doubt that the aggravating circumstances exist, or that aggravating circumstances outweigh the mitigating circumstances, or if the jury is not able to make a unanimous decision.

The 1988 Supreme Court decision *Thompson v. Oklahoma* (724 U.S. 780) was to uphold a sentence of death for the defendant, who had been 15 years of age at the time of the crime. This was overturned with the 2005 *Roper v. Simmons* decision. The decision to uphold a capital murder conviction for a person with mental retardation was made in the 1989 *Penry v. Lynaugh* case (832 U.S. 915). This decision was overturned in the 2002 *Atkins v. Virginia* decision. The 1993 Supreme Court decision *Herrera v. Collins* (506 U.S. 390) did not allow a stay of execution for the purpose of providing new evidence of innocence.

In 2002, the first case came before the Supreme Court in regard to persons who are not eligible for the death penalty. The *Atkins v. Virginia* (536 U.S. 304) decision stated that persons who are mentally retarded are not eligible for the death penalty because the severity of the crime is diminished due to the mental handicap. The Supreme Court decision *Bobby v. Bies* (556 U.S. 825) in 2009 made it possible for courts to reconsider the mental capacity of death row inmates who had been labeled mentally retarded when they were convicted before the 2002 *Atkins v. Virginia* decision. *Roper v. Simmons* (543 U.S. 551) is the Supreme Court's 2005 decision that made it unconstitutional to sentence juveniles to death.

The 2008 Supreme Court decision *Baze v. Rees* (553 U.S 35) found it constitutional to use lethal injection as a method of execution. A main concern was evidence that the three-drug combination used for lethal injection may not alleviate pain and may cause paralysis, so that the convicted criminal cannot signal that the pain is occurring.

Unit 2: International agreements

There are a number of international human rights agreements relating to capital punishment. The U.N. Universal Declaration of Human Rights, as discussed in Chapter 1, includes Article 3 which says, "Everyone has the right to life, liberty and security of person," and Article 5 which states, "No one shall be subjected to torture or to cruel, inhuman or degrading treatment or punishment." Several other articles relate as a whole or in part to the trial system or to other aspects of the capital punishment system.

The U.N. International Covenant on Civil and Political Rights (ICCPR) includes Article 6, which states the United Nation's stance on the death penalty. The ICCPR says that capital punishment is a human rights violation if assigned by an incompetent court, if execution takes places prior to the proper appellate process, if used in the case of genocide, and if assigned to persons under 18 years of age or pregnant women. The Second Optional Protocol of this covenant is aimed at phasing out and abolishing the death penalty. The only time member states can use the death penalty is in times of war, which can only be used if the member state declares that they reserved this tool at the time that they signed the protocol. It also requires signatories to provide some proof of their efforts to get rid of the death penalty.

The purpose of the U.N. Convention Against Torture and Other Cruel, Inhuman or Degrading Treatment or Punishment (the U.N. Torture Convention) is to prevent states from intentionally inflicting severe pain or suffering on people. This convention relates to the way the death penalty is conducted.

The Inter-American Commission on Human Rights created the American Convention on Human Rights, which includes Article 4 as a right to life statement. It defines capital punishment as a human rights violation when used in each of the following cases: 1) To punish political offenses, 2) for minors, persons 70 years or older, or pregnant women, and 3) prior to the convicted person exhausting their applications for amnesty, pardon, and commutation of sentence.

The European Council's Convention for the Protection of Human Rights and Fundamental Freedoms created Protocol No. 6 calling for the abolition of the death penalty except for exceptional crimes during wartime, and Protocol No. 13 concerning the abolition of the death penalty in all circumstances. Protocol No. 13 is the first legally binding international treaty to entirely abolish the death penalty.

Unit 3: Controversies

As seen in the two perspectives introduced at the beginning of the chapter, there is a wide gap between those who do and those who do not believe that capital punishment is a human rights violation. On the human rights side, there are arguments that the death penalty is cruel, inhumane, and degrading and is considered a violation of a person's rights because of the taking of a life; the poor quality of evidence against the accused; discrimination and/ or lack of due process during the trials; the bias of choosing capital-eligible jurors; the time limits on appeals; the treatment and possible solitary confinement of the accused on death row; the cost to society and counties of the trials and mandatory appeals process; and the cost and efficiency of the death instrument.

A major argument by human rights advocates has been based on evolving standards of decency. According to Chief Justice Warren, the Eighth Amendment "must draw its meaning from the evolving standards of decency that mark the progress of a maturing society" (*Trop v. Dulles*, 356 U.S. 86, 101 (1958)). There are a number of issues that can be classified as evolving standards of decency. In 1986 (*Ford v. Wainwright*, 477 U.S. 399) the U.S. Supreme Court banned the execution of persons who had been declared mentally incompetent or insane, but it took until 2002 in *Atkins v. Virginia* (536 U.S. 304) for this to take effect in cases of mental retardation under the "cruel and unusual" clause of the Eighth Amendment. Several groups, including the American Psychiatric Association, the American Psychological Association, the National Alliance for the Mentally Ill, and the American Bar Association, have called for exemption of defendants with severe mental illness. The American Civil Liberties Union (ACLU, 2012) argues that government does not possess the right to terminate life, regardless of its legal authority to do so. They present religious and moral oppositions. The ACLU notes the ethical conundrums associated with capital punishment, particularly the hypocrisy of state-sanctioned executions as retribution for private acts of murder (ACLU, 2012). Equally contested is the brutalization effect: "This theory postulates that executions may coarsen attitudes, implicitly sanction lethal violence, and thus unwittingly inspire the commission of more instead of fewer murders" (James Acker, 2003). In the *Roper v. Simmons* case in March

2005, the U.S. Supreme Court declared it unconstitutional to execute defendants who had committed the crimes while they were juveniles.

Advocates of the death penalty do not consider capital punishment a human rights violation and approve of the process because it is legal under federal and some state law; because it is unbiased due to two defense lawyers being assigned to the accused and the fact that there is an automatic appeal when a death sentence is rendered; because it makes society safer by getting the "worst" criminals off the streets; and because it makes perpetrators pay for their crimes. The U.S. Constitution allows the use of capital sanctions as long as the accused are provided due process of law. At the same time, the Constitution is a "living, breathing document" that evolves with the social standards of the people it governs. As such, constitutional opposition to capital sanctions is often rooted in its prohibition of cruel and unusual punishment as well as the Equal Protection Clause, both of which are routinely cited when arguing disparities in capital charging policies across states and their local jurisdictions (Michael Mello, 2008). By intended design, however, the public policies of one state do not inherently bind those persons residing in another. Rather, the Reserve Clause (Tenth Amendment) authorizes states, and by extension local districts within states, to legislate and subsequently enforce public policy within their respective governments as seen fit by the people they serve.

Life without parole is often viewed as an alternative to capital punishment. Given "doubts about the death penalty's fairness, a heightened concern about the risk of executing innocent people," and the excessive financial burden created by way of capital prosecutions, the use of lifetime imprisonment rather than death is causing "many more Americans to have second thoughts about capital punishment" (James Acker, 2003). Life without parole suggests that once offenders are sentenced for criminal acts, they will spend the remainder of their lives incarcerated in state or federal penal institutions. This permanent loss of liberty protects society from dangerous criminals while theoretically serving as adequate compensation for social wrongs.

Life without parole inside a maximum-security institution creates incapacitation effects that are similar to execution, although incarceration does not eliminate an offender's ability to seriously hurt or kill other inmates and staff while confined (Acker, 2003). Life without parole does not prevent murderers from enjoying their own lives, despite being incarcerated. Nor does it eliminate the possibility of offender escapes.

As a matter of social indignation, opponents argue that capping criminal consequences at the lower standard of life without parole would subsequently reduce public sensitivity to extreme and vile acts of murder: "In other words, one life taken or ten lives taken, the penalty would be life or life without parole, thus lessening the reaction of society to individual outrageous acts" (James Ardaiz, 2008). Ardaiz also claimed that life without parole fails to provide adequate means of retribution. Rather, by assigning the death penalty, society has expressed social outrage toward the horrifying nature of particularly dreadful crimes. By invoking death, Ardaiz contends that "society rejects the argument that a guilty life merits the same protection from loss as an innocent life."

Life without parole is a sentencing determination wherein the government indefinitely confiscates offenders' liberties by isolating them from society for the remainder of their lives. Once incarcerated, offenders have no legal opportunity for furlough, parole, or discharge. "Such a severe punishment is imposed because the crime is so egregious . . . that society elects to separate the perpetrator from their fellows and exact the most severe retribution available short of death" (Ardaiz, 2008). Because life without parole suggests offenders are permanently exiled, thus negating suspicions regarding their future threat to society, governments often utilize this sentencing option in lieu of capital sanctions. "It is also a sufficiently harsh sanction to satisfy many people's notions of just deserts" (James Acker, 2008).

Though many argue the capital punishment process is too lengthy, appeals are afforded rigorous scrutiny. If the appellant process were significantly reduced beyond that of the current federal guidelines set forth under the Anti-Terrorism and Effective Death Penalty Act (1996), it is likely that legally innocent persons would be executed.

Another controversial issue has to do with obtaining drugs for capital punishment by lethal injections. Since 2012, the United States has no longer been able to obtain the drugs traditionally used for lethal injection from European pharmacies. These drugs cost around $1,000 per dose. The United States has resorted to using U.S. compound pharmacies. The cost of the drugs is now around $663,000 and there have been several incidents where the drugs did not cause immediate death. In the 2008 *Baze v. Rees* case, the U.S. Supreme Court upheld the constitutionality of lethal injection even if the drugs ran the risk of inflicting pain during the death process. Although the majority of the U.S. Supreme Court is pro-capital punishment, Justice Stephen Breyer has heavily criticized the U.S. capital punishment system, saying that it is "unreliable, arbitrary, and shot through with racism."

Texas has the dubious distinction of having the third-largest death row population (286) and the most executions (538 since 1982) anywhere in the Western free world. Executions in this state are carried out by lethal injection, but elsewhere in the country inmates are killed by firing squad, hanging, electrocution, and lethal cyanide gas.

These are a few of the controversial topics related to capital punishment. Other issues will be discussed in the section "Inefficiencies in the economic structure of capital punishment."

CHECK YOURSELF BOX: PERSONAL BIASES ABOUT CAPITAL PUNISHMENT

As we saw in the individual perspectives set out at the opening of this chapter, different people hold strong opinions for and against capital punishment. You may have known a little or a lot about capital punishment before starting this chapter. What are your thoughts on capital punishment? Do you tend to side for or against capital punishment? Have you had any experiences related to capital punishment? What have you read? Who have you met? And what impressions do you have that lead you to choose one side or the other? Discovery of your personal biases and the elements that helped to create your outlook on capital punishment will help you discern when your biases are coloring your research.

Section 4: History of capital punishment in Texas

This textbook focuses on capital punishment in Texas. Texas has by far the highest number of executions in the United States, accounting for one-third of all executions in the country (Guy Goldberg and Gena Bunn, 2000).

As with most frontier societies, when the United States was founded, it did not have a formal prison system. Until the late 1700s, individual townships regulated justice for criminal acts. While punishment for minor or first-time offenders could be addressed at the local level through monetary fines or corporal punishment, "capital punishment was the criminal law's principal defense against repeat offenders and other criminals who threatened individual safety and the social order" (James Acker, 2003).

The development of state-sponsored prisons reduced America's reliance on capital sanctions to ensure safer societies. By the mid-1800s, many northern states had seriously restricted their use of the death penalty and by 1860, only persons found guilty of murder and treason would be subject to execution in the north (Acker, 2003). The south, however, had made only minor decreases in the use of the death penalty. Over the last one hundred years, public support for the death penalty in America waned.

There are three main eras in the history of capital punishment in Texas. The first stage is the "hanging era" (Guy Goldberg and Gena Bunn, 2000). Before the twentieth century there were no centralized administrations to carry out the death penalty and courts handled a murder case in much the same manner as theft or other criminal cases. Jonathan Sorenson and Rocky Pilgrim (2006) depict the costs of the death sentence at this time as varied, depending upon the costs of the rope (unless one could be borrowed), the building of a gallows if a strong tree was not available, and the payment to the executioner (sometimes performed by local law enforcement).

The invention of the electric chair in 1924 began the second era of capital punishment in Texas. This changed the way in which executions were administered as the state prison in Huntsville, Texas housed the state's single electric chair (Sorenson and Pilgrim, 2006). This centralized the death penalty in Texas, brought about new ideas in addressing capital punishment, and impacted the judicial system in Texas.

Capital punishment in Texas saw a dramatic change in 1972 as a result of the Supreme Court case *Furman v. Georgia*. By a 5–4 vote, *Furman v. Georgia* declared that "although the use of execution by the states is not per se unconstitutional, the process by which it was being carried out violated the EighthAmendment's prohibition of cruel and unusual punishment" (Raymond Paternoster, 1984). This landmark case had the largest and most detrimental systemic impact on the Texas judicial system's handling of capital eligible cases. This court case ruled that the death penalty was unconstitutional and led to the bifurcating of capital trials to deal with the arbitrary and possibly discriminatory practices under the prevailing statutes (Elizabeth Vartkessian, 2012). Post-*Furman*, Texas Legislature had to find ways to make sure the Texas capital punishment system fit the Supreme Court statutes to avoid discriminating factors that could influence death penalty cases. In addition, there were other variables that state legislatures had to address, such as the possible future danger to society of the plaintiff. In 1976, the Supreme Court ruled in *Gregg v. Georgia* to once again allow states to enforce capital sanctions.

In addressing the Supreme Court decision, Texas adopted a system in which jurors are polled to determine their effectiveness in the courtroom decisions in determining "special" cases, mitigating circumstances, and discriminatory factors. Texas adopted a policy that set a mandatory review of the death sentence by the Texas Court of Criminal Appeals if a plaintiff was given the death penalty. In addition, Texas began the use of lethal injection in carrying out death sentences (Guy Goldberg and Gena Bunn, 2000). Since 1976, the Supreme Court has further qualified death-eligible individuals, including exemptions for mentally retarded and juvenile offenders, as discussed previously.

December 1982 saw the first post-*Furman* execution and started the third stage of capital punishment in Texas, which Jonathan Sorenson and Rocky Pilgrim (2006) called the Lethal Injection Era. This stage is characterized by increases in court time, court administrations, court employment, jail time, overturned cases, and costs to the court. During this stage, capital eligible cases were split into two phases: The capital eligible trial to determine the plaintiff's guilt, and the sentencing trial. The defendant's lawyers would argue the determination of guilt, and if found guilty, would argue for a lesser punishment than death.

Since 1998, the national rate of death sentences has declined by almost 83% (Death Penalty Information Center, 2017). Of these, the majority of executions occur in southern states, with the State of Texas executing more offenders than any other state (James Ackers, 2003).

■ Section 5: Meet the capital punishment experts

Capital punishment is a complicated process involving experts in a variety of fields. A researcher may decide to contact experts who can answer specific questions. Some of the areas where experts on capital punishment can be found are listed in Table 2.3.

Table 2.4 presents some of the major nonprofit organizations involved in work regarding capital punishment. The majority of these are anti-capital punishment nonprofit organizations.

TABLE 2.3   Areas and fields of expertise related to capital punishment

Area of expertise	Field of expertise	Description
Research and possible sources of data	Criminal justice	The study of the systems in place to provide sound criminal justice policy.
	Criminology	The study of criminals.
	Sociology	The systematic study of human society.
	Human rights	The study of national and international law to ensure the rights of all human beings.
	Psychology	The study of mental processes and behavior.
Criminal justice institutions	Law enforcement	Local, state, and federal police.
	Law	Lawyers specializing in capital punishment, district attorneys, assistant district attorneys, law schools, the U.S. Department of Justice.
	State, federal, and supreme courts	The judicial system.
	Corrections	Prison officials and those with knowledge of means of incarcerating criminals.
Expert witnesses	Experts in investigations, ballistics, psychology, etc.	Sources of evidence regarding aggravating circumstances for the prosecution.
	Experts in social work, investigations, etc.	Sources of evidence regarding mitigating circumstances for the defense.
Activism	Human rights experts	Knowledge of circumstances surrounding the violation of human rights law.

Area of expertise	Field of expertise	Description
	Persons exonerated from sentence of capital punishment	Knowledge of living on death row as a convicted criminal.
Medical	Lethal injection experts	Knowledge of drugs used for lethal injection, efficiency of the drugs, and the side affects.

TABLE 2.4 Nonprofit organizations working in the area of capital punishment

Amnesty International	www.amnesty.org
Amnesty International USA	www.aiusa.org
Death Penalty Information Center (DPIC)	www.deathpenaltyinfo.org
Innocence Project	www.innocenceproject.org
Journey of Hope	www.journeyofhope.org
Murder Victims Families for Human Rights (MVFHR)	www.mvfhr.org
NAACP Legal Defense Fund (LDF)	www.naacplldf.org
National Coalition to Abolish the Death Penalty (NCADP)	www.ncadp.org
Texas Defender Service	www.texasdefender.org
Witness to Innocence	www.witnesstoinnocence.org

CHECK YOURSELF BOX: CAPITAL PUNISHMENT RESEARCH AND DATA BIASES

Before looking at the economic structure of capital punishment, take some time to think about the biases that you may encounter in researchers, prosecuting and defense attorneys, judges, nonprofit organizations involved in the issue of capital punishment, and citizens who sit on juries. Why is each group a part of the capital punishment discussion? How would they benefit personally from abolishing capital punishment or maintaining the system? What are these people's opinions of a person on death row? Who is collecting the capital punishment data and how might their backgrounds and goals bias the data? Your research in capital punishment will be limited by the background information and data provided by others, so it is important to understand how their biases may translate into variances in published research and databases.

Section 6: Economic structure of capital punishment

Chapter 1 introduced **economic efficiency** as the highest value to society from resource allocation and analysis of the costs and benefits associated with decisions. Applying analysis to the area of capital punishment, a network of choices is revealed that leads to the trial verdict. Each step of the capital murder trial process contains decisions by one or more groups of individuals. The costs and benefits associated with each of those decisions lend direction to the outcome of the trial. Each choice can lead to a different branch along the capital trial path.

Historically, cost-benefit analyses of most social programs have been performed at the microeconomic level, meaning that the costs and benefits are expressed in terms of individual participants (John Roman, 2004). **Public policy**, defined as the government laws and regulations created to safeguard society, is concerned with "the principle that a person should not be allowed to do anything that would tend to injure the public at large" (*Black's Law Dictionary*, 2009). The difficulty in applying traditional cost–benefit analysis to public policy is in translating "expected costs and expected benefits into statements that are meaningful to consumers of cost–benefit analyses" (Roman, 2004). Public policy, as in the case of capital punishment, requires cost–benefit analysis at a community level. "The effects of a policy change on society are no more or no less than the aggregate of the effects on the individuals who constitute society" (Paul Portney, 2008). Better quality cost–benefit analysis of social policy exists at the community, rather than the individual level. Effective public policy evaluations weigh both the monetary costs of programs as well as their ensuing effects, as realized at the community level. Addressing the efficiency of community actions requires accountability in the distribution and equity of county funds (Tosihiro Oka, 2003). Effective public policy evaluations weigh both the monetary costs of programs and their ensuing effects at the community level.

Evaluations of public policies must consider how regulations affect all persons within society instead of solely their effect on governments' net assets (Paul Nutt, 2005). Additionally, governments generally operate as collateral systems where the policies of one agency often require the uncompensated resources of another. Alternatively, the risks assumed by one agency may result in unearned benefits being realized by differing agencies. As such, when evaluating public policy such as capital punishment, there is often no clearly identifiable benchmark to determine the policy's ultimate value to any given government (the Civic Federation, 1997).

Decisions that affect the outcome of a capital murder trial are being made throughout the capital punishment process. A reasonable goal in terms of capital punishment is to prosecute a person for capital murder when the evidence is sufficient beyond a reasonable doubt that the person committed the crime. Texas has specific systems in place with the intent of providing a suspect with a fair trial: These include the law enforcement, legal, and judicial systems. The areas lacking in resources to eliminate the possibility of trying and convicting a person wrongfully accused are within the same area in which systems are in place to handle the fair trial. The following pages will briefly discuss the capital trial phases to determine some of the major choices being made by law enforcement, jurors, judges, the courts, the prosecution legal team, the defendant, and the defense legal team.

During the investigation stage, law enforcement has many decisions to make before placing a suspect under arrest. This includes the number of officers to assign to the case, time spent on the case, thoroughness in seeking evidence, and the resources to dedicate to searching for suspects. It is not only the complexity of the crime but also the diligence of law enforcement that determines who is arrested and what evidence is gathered. In Texas, the district attorney has the task of deciding whether the person will be charged with capital murder, non-capital murder, or a lesser charge, or will be released.

The choices of the accused and the way in which they respond to the actions of others during the investigation stage have an important bearing on the outcome of a trial. One of most important decisions will be whether the accused person asks to see a lawyer. Under the mirandizing process, all questions from law enforcement must cease until a lawyer arrives to represent the accused person. Other decisions the accused must make include the response to questioning by law enforcement and compliance during the arrest and while being processed within the law enforcement system.

If the district attorney charges the accused person with a capital crime, the impending defendant (as the accused is now called) must decide whether to accept the representation of a court-appointed qualified capital defense attorney or to be "pro se," which means to defend oneself. If the choice is defending self, the court appoints a qualified capital defense attorney to serve as an advisor throughout the pretrial and trial stages. If the choice is to accept the representation of a defense lawyer, the impending defendant has the right to dismiss the attorney at any time, but this dismissal process cannot continue long-term in a way that delays the capital murder trial.

Choices during the indictment stage include the choosing of a competent death-qualifying jury and the jury's decision on whether to charge and on what charge to try the suspect. If the jury's decision is a verdict of capital eligible, then two defense lawyers are assigned by the State to represent the suspect. The pay of capital defense lawyers is very low and a capital case is time-consuming, which can lead to the question of how diligent defense lawyers are willing to be in defending a person in a capital murder trial.

The impending defendant must decide how to act in court and whether and how to work with the defense lawyers. Questions asked by lawyers may lead to mitigating evidence that affects the outcome of the trial. Disruption in court can lead to removal from court and the trial continues without the impending defendant present. In the case of a defendant who has shown signs of violence, it is possible that the person will be wearing a stun belt that is controlled by the judge. Both behavior and action (or inaction) may have consequences that affect others' decisions.

The judge in the pretrial stage has to decide whether the jury's verdict is accurate, and whether to uphold the decision or dismiss the case. If the case is not dismissed, the prosecuting and defense attorneys come together to plea bargain. The prosecution may use the death penalty as a bargaining tool to get the impending defendant to plead guilty in exchange for a life sentence. Whether the plea bargain happens, and the stipulations of the plea bargain, depend upon the choices made by the different law teams. If no plea bargain is reached because one or both sides refuse to accept the terms of the plea bargain, the case moves to trial.

The actions and behaviors of the impending defendant may have a direct impact on the likelihood of a plea bargain and the form this agreement takes. If the death penalty is definitely on the bargaining table, the defendant could plead guilty and receive a sentence of life without parole. Ultimately the accused decides whether to accept the plea bargain. If no plea bargain is reached, the accused is now called the defendant in the case.

The trial stage contains many decisions. The prosecuting team presents aggravating circumstances that have been collected by law enforcement and the testimony of expert witnesses. The defense team hire their own investigators and expert witnesses and may present evidence of mitigating circumstances. Choices are made about whether to spend the time and money to collect each of these pieces of evidence. The jury must then decide, based on the evidence, whether the person is guilty of capital murder, guilty of a lesser crime, or not guilty. If the verdict is guilty, the case moves to the sentencing stage.

During the trial stage, the defendant may choose to testify on their own behalf, with or against the advice of the representing attorney. The defendant's ability to work with the defense attorneys may have a direct bearing on the case.

During the sentencing stage, the jury must decide whether the defendant should be punished by life in prison (life without parole) or by execution (death penalty). If the verdict is life without parole, the prison system must determine where to house the sentenced person for the rest of their life. If the decision is for the death penalty, the case automatically goes into appeals.

If the defendant is found guilty of capital murder, they must then go through the sentencing stage. The manner in which the defendant has presented themselves may influence the punishment determined by the jury. The defense lawyers may choose to present mitigating evidence at this point if it did not come out during the trial. At this point, the defendant has few, if any, choices.

During the appeals stage, the Supreme Court reviews the case. This is a concentrated process in which all of the evidence is reviewed along with existing legislation affecting the case. The defense presents any mitigating evidence that may have some bearing on the case. The defense lawyers again have the choice of how hard to seek evidence to support the defendant's innocence. After review, the Supreme Court chooses to either uphold or reverse the verdict.

If the Supreme Court has upheld the verdict of the death penalty, the defendant lives on death row until execution. The governor of Texas has the option of temporarily or permanently stopping an execution in the clemency stage.

If no clemency is given, the person is executed. State legislature and officials decide which form the death penalty will take. Within legal guidelines, the defendant has the choice to meet with certain people before the execution and to continue to appeal to the Supreme Court. Before execution, the defendant has the right to make a statement.

As stated, economic efficiency requires that all costs and all benefits be considered in the cost–benefit analysis to determine maximum net benefit. As can be seen by the complex decision-making structure within capital punishment, it is difficult to determine economic efficiency.

There have been two main types of research relating to the economics of capital punishment. The first type is cost studies that analyze the cost of the capital punishment procedure. While there are many fiscal costs of capital punishment, there are some costs that cannot be monetized. The second type of research is the analysis of capital punishment as a deterrent, in which a person is deterred from committing murder due to the possibility of being tried for capital murder and receiving the death penalty. It would be a benefit to society if capital punishment were a deterrent to murder, but it is difficult to monetize the benefits, or perceived benefits, of the death penalty. These issues are discussed in the next two sections.

Unit 1: Costs of capital punishment

In 2016 the U.S. Government had a budget deficit of -$3.3% of GDP (GDP of $16.5 trillion) with total receipts of $2.99 trillion and total outlays of $3.54 trillion. Texas approved a budget of $209.4 billion for 2016–2017, including $11.5 billion (an increase of $2.3 billion from 2015–2016) for the Texas Department of Public Safety ($750 million) and the Texas Department of Criminal Justice. Careful fiscal (government spending) policy is important in the short- and long-term. National, state, and local bureaucracy controls most areas of importance in terms of justice under their authorities. Because the criminal justice system is extensive and expensive, there is often a tradeoff between justice and fiscal survival. The cost studies reviewed below and the case study concentrate on the implicit fiscal costs of capital prosecution, but the implicit (nonmonetary) costs of trying a person for capital murder will also be discussed.

As previously stated, 31 states, the federal government, and the U.S. military have capital punishment infrastructures (DPIC, 2017). Texas is one of the states that utilize capital sanctions as part of their criminal justice systems. Professor Corinna Lain, associate dean of faculty development at the University of Richmond and renowned for her writings in the areas of constitutional theory and the death penalty, stated that Texas is "the capital of capital punishment" since it "sends more people to death row than any other state and it executes them far faster" (Adam Gershowitz, 2009). In fact, since the 1976 *Furman* decision reinstating capital punishment as a legitimate criminal sanction, Texas has carried out over one-third of all capital sentences within the United States. (DPIC, 2017). Chapter 1 introduced **marginal cost** (MC), which is the additional cost of the last unit of production or choice. For example, each time a murder is committed in a Texas county, the district attorney chooses whether to try the person for capital murder. This is not a cheap choice: each capital murder trial is expensive to the tune of hundreds of thousands of dollars. In Texas, the average capital trial costs $2.5 million.

In Texas, 62% of all felony defendants are **indigent** (Texas Task Force on Indigent Defense, 2008), lacking the funds to bear the financial burden of defense costs. Since "almost all the accused persons Texas seeks to execute lack the financial means to retain counsel" (Texas Appleseed Fair Defense Project, 2000), ultimately county governments must bear the remaining financial burden for both defending and prosecuting most capital cases. In 2005, the State of Texas assumed only 11.3% of the total indigent expense related to those defendants (Jennifer Saubermann and Robert Spangenberg, 2006). More precisely, as provided by the Texas Code of Criminal Procedure, Article 11.071, except for a maximum of $25,000 in state-funded reimbursement for writs of habeas corpus, the originating jurisdiction must bear the entire prosecution costs of capital trials. The elevated price of capital trials means that local governments are undeniably affected by the fiscal distress of these expensive prosecutions (Katherine Baicker, 2004).

A number of capital punishment cost studies have been published. In 2006, Jonathan Sorenson and Rocky Pilgrim stated that the capital punishment cost studies to that date overstated the findings, such that "historically capital punishment is at least as cost effective as life imprisonment and probably even more so." Looking at the post-*Furman* period, Sorenson further critiques the studies because of inefficiency, lack of data, and unreliability of estimates, especially as they relate to the alternative sentence of life without parole. According to Sorenson and Pilgrim (2006), "The stronger studies are usually completed by economists rather than newspaper reporters," due to large pools of recent data, analysis against the alternative life sentence, and "multiple estimates based on varying assumptions about the future rate of reversals in death-penalty cases." At the time, Sorenson encouraged researchers to follow the "ideal" methodology of the National Center of State Courts.

The following tables provide a review of the main capital punishment cost studies. Table 2.5 presents the main academic studies. Table 2.6 presents the state and federal analyses. Table 2.7 presents capital punishment reports by non-government organizations. Table 2.8 presents news articles regarding the cost of capital punishment.

TABLE 2.5 Academic cost studies of capital punishment

Year	State	Main findings	Source
1982	New York	Death penalty cost = $1.8 million per case	Gradess, Jonathan. (1982, April 1). *Capital Losses: The price of the death penalty for New York State*. NY State Defenders Assn.
1992	Texas	Death penalty cost = $2.3 million per case	Hoppe, Christy. (1992, March 8). Executions cost Texas millions: Study finds it's cheaper to jail killers for life. *Dallas Morning News*.
2009	North Carolina	Death penalty costs $11 million per year	Cook, Phillip. (2009, December 11). Potential savings from abolition of the death penalty in North Carolina. *American Law and Economics Review*.

(Continued)

TABLE 2.5 (Continued)

Year	State	Main findings	Source
2012	Nevada	Death penalty cases cost $170,000-$212,000 more than non-capital cases	Miethe, Terance. (2012, February 21). *Estimates of time spent in capital and non-capital murder cases: A statistical analysis of survey data from Clark County defense attorneys.* Department of Criminal Justice, University of Nevada, Las Vegas.
2013	Colorado	Death penalty case cost six times non-capital cases	Marceau, Justin and Whitson, Hollis. (2013). The cost of Colorado's death penalty. *University of Denver Criminal Law Review, 3*(145).
2015	Washington	Capital cases cost $1 million more for prosecution	Collins, Peter; Boruchowitz, Robert; Hickman, Matthew; and Larranaga, Mark. (2015, January 1). *An analysis of the economic costs of seeking the death penalty in Washington State.* Seattle University.
2013, 2016	Oregon	Death penalty 50-500% more expensive than life without parole	Kaplan, Aliza; Collins, Peter; and Mayhew, Venetia. (2016, November 16). *Oregon's Death Penalty: A Cost Analysis.* Seattle University. Kaplan, Aliza. (2013). Oregon's death penalty: The practical reality. *Lewis & Clark Law Review, 1*(36).
2016	Nebraska	$14.6 million to maintain capital punishment system	Goss, Ernie; Strain, Scott; and Blalock, Jackson. (2016, August 15). *The economic impact of the death penalty on the State of Nebraska: A taxpayer burden?* Goss & Associates Economic Solutions.

TABLE 2.6 State and federal capital punishment analyses

Year	State	Main findings	Source
2002	Indiana	Death penalty costs 38% more than life without parole.	Indiana Criminal Law Study Commission (2002, January 10). Commission report on capital sentencing.
2003	Kansas	Death penalty costs $1.26 million per case.	Kansas Legislative Division of Post Audit. (2003, December). *Performance Audit Report: Costs incurred for death penalty cases: A K-GOAL.* Audit of the Department of Corrections.

Year	State	Main findings	Source
2004	Tennessee	Death penalty costs 48% more than non-capital.	The Tennessee Comptroller of the Treasury Office of Research's Report. (2004). *Tennessee's death penalty: Costs and consequences.*
2008, 2010	Federal	Federal death penalty case costs eight times cost of other cases.	Gould, Jon and Greenman, Lisa. (2008, June). *Update on cost, quality, and availability of defense representation in federal death penalty cases.* Office of Defender Services of the Administrative Office of the U.S. Courts. Gould, Jon and Greenman, Lisa. (2010, September). *Report to the Committee on Defender Services Judicial Conference of the United States.*
2008, 2011, 2012	California	Would save $170 million per year if commuted to non-capital cases.	Alarcon, Arthur and Mitchell, Paula. (2011, updated 2012). *Assessment of costs.* Commission on the Fair Administration of Justice.
2014	Idaho	Capital cases take more time to resolve than non-capital cases at most trial stages.	Office of Performance Evaluations, Idaho Legislature. (2014, March 17). *Financial costs of the death penalty.*
2014	Kansas	Capital case costs four times non-capital case.	Judicial Council. (2014, February 13). *Report of the Judicial Council Death Penalty Advisory Committee.* Kansas Legislature.
2015	Nevada	Death penalty cost = $1.03–1.3 million per case.	Lochhead, Colton. (2014, December 2). Audit: Death penalty nearly doubles cost of Nevada murder cases. *Las Vegas Review.* Legislative Auditor. (2014, November 17). *Performance Audit: Fiscal costs of the death penalty.* State of Nevada.
(April and May) 2015	Indiana	Death penalty costs 4.25 non-capital case.	Two state assessments.

Phillip Cook (2009) notes two kinds of trial costs: Cash costs and in-kind costs. Cash costs are monetary payments used to finance death penalty investigations and their related trials. These include, but are not limited to, expenses such as attorney fees for indigent offenders, court officer costs, expert witnesses, and jury allowances. In-kind costs, such as the time used by criminal investigators and the district attorney's office to prepare for capital trials, are more concerned with the effects of non-monetary expenses on the efficiency of other government programs. In economics, these in-kind costs are called **opportunity costs** – what must be given up to get something else. In public policy, opportunity costs reflect how resources consumed by one program directly impact the functioning of other programs. There are underlying relationships between funding capital prosecutions and subsequent

TABLE 2.7   Non-government organization capital punishment reports

Year	State	Main findings	Source
2005	New Jersey	Death penalty costs state $11 million per year.	New Jerseyans for alternatives to the death penalty. (2005, November 21). *New Jersey Policy Perspectives Report*. Press Release.
2006	Washington	Death penalty costs extra $470,000 per case.	Washington State Bar Association. (2006, December). *Final Report of the Death Penalty Subcommittee on Public Defense*.

TABLE 2.8   Non-government organization capital punishment reports

Year	State	Main findings	Citation
1988	Florida	Death penalty costs state $51 million a year more than non-capital cases.	Dieter, Richard. (1988, July 10). Bottom line: Life in prison one-sixth as expensive. *Miami Herald*. *Palm Beach Post*. (2000, January 4). The high price of killing killers.
1988, 2004, 2005	California	Death penalty costs state $90–114 million per year.	*Sacramento Bee*. (1988, March 28). Closing death row would save State $90 million a year. *New York Times*. (2004, December 18). San Quentin debate: Death row vs. Bay views. *Los Angeles Times*. (2005, March 6). Death row often means a long life.
1992	Texas	Death penalty costs average $2.3 million.	*Dallas Morning News*. (1992, March 8). Executions cost Texas millions.
2008	Maryland	Death penalty costs average $1.9–3 million.	McMenamin, Jennifer. Death penalty costs Maryland more than life term. *Baltimore Sun*.
2016	Pennsylvania	$272 million spent per execution.	Brambila, Nicole. (2016, June 17). Executing justice: Pennsylvania's death penalty system costs $816 million. *The Reading Eagle*.

resources available to local governments (Cook, 2009). If jurisdictions choose to spend government funds prosecuting capital cases, then they are necessarily doing so at the expense of other funded programs. These reductions in resources or services, which create differing effects within subsets of the population, are known as the opportunity costs associated with capital punishment.

According to the U.S. General Accounting Office (1989), there are ten stages where capital trials may incur costs. Compared to other felony prosecutions, capital trials have only one additional cost point: Execution. Although there is approximately the same number of stages regardless of a trial's classification, each stage related to capital prosecution carries a significantly greater price tag than adjudicating non-capital crimes. The ten possible cost stages of capital prosecutions are 1) criminal investigations, 2) indictment, 3) pre-trial motions and investigations, 4) trials, 5) sentencing, 6) incarceration, 7) appeals (the number of appeals differs by state of conviction, with ten levels of appeal being the greatest allowance of any state), 8) post-conviction petitions, 9) clemency requests, and 10) execution.

In capital trials, defendants are guaranteed the maximum level of due process protection. "This especial concern is a natural consequence of the knowledge that execution is the most irremediable and unfathomable of penalties; that death is different" (Justice Marshall, *Ford v. Wainwright* (1986), 477 U.S. 399). Subsequently, in comparison to other serious

TABLE 2.9 Costs of capital punishment

Branch	Costs
Law enforcement	Opportunity and overtime cost of officers and investigators
	Criminal processing costs
	Incarceration costs
Legal – prosecution	Opportunity and overtime cost of prosecution team
	Cost of plea bargain process
	Cost of expert witness
Legal – defense	Opportunity and business expenses of defense team
	Investigation expenses
	Cost of expert witnesses
Court	Opportunity of judge's time
	Cost of search for capital-eligible jurors
	Cost to pay, and sometimes house and feed, jurors to sit for case
	Opportunity cost of court staff's time
	Opportunity cost of federal and supreme court appellant reviews
Corrections	Incarceration costs
	Inmate transportation costs
	Security cost of keeping inmate safe from other inmates, visitors, and guards
	Execution costs – personnel on hand, lethal injection, funeral arrangements
Overall costs	Opportunity cost of using state and federal funds to try a capital case

murder trials involving life without parole, litigation and appeals processes of capital trials require greater attention to procedural rights (Philip Cook, Donna Slawson, and Lori Gries, 1993). The accumulative effect of this attention necessitates that the due process protections afforded in capital trials are more expensive than those required of non-capital trials (Mark Larranaga, 2004; Rich Woodward, 2009).

Regardless of jurisdiction, capital trials require defendants to be represented by two attorneys, as opposed to only one being required for non-capital cases (Jonathan Gradess, 2008). Generally, attorneys involved in capital trials introduce more pre-trial motions than would be utilized in non-capital cases. Accompanying this significant increase in pre-trial time, capital defense lawyers bill at a higher per hour rate than those involved in non-capital cases (Phillip Cook, 2009; Robert Spangenberg and Elizabeth Walsh, 1989).

Prior to jury selection for capital trials, prospective jurors must be "death qualified" (David Garland, 2007). Mary Forsberg (2005) argues that death qualification implies that the juror "neither adamantly opposes or favors the death penalty and would be willing under some circumstances to vote to sentence someone to death." The capital **voir dire** process (the preliminary examination of a witness or juror to determine their competency to give or hear evidence) has been known to take months (Richard Dieter, 2009) and requires that jury pools for capital trials are necessarily larger than non-capital trials (Jonathan Gradess, 2008).

Capital litigation requires more effort and significantly more time to prepare. Prosecutors must spend time considering all possible evidence, regardless of how insignificant it may appear. Additionally, defense attorneys must also develop their own explanations of the crime. Often, this obliges them to retain criminal investigators and expert witnesses (Mark Larranaga, 2004). The hourly fee for these specialists is often higher in capital trials than for non-capital court appearances (Robert Spangenberg and Elizabeth Walsh, 1989).

During capital litigation, prosecutors and defense attorneys must present aggravating or mitigating factors to the crime. This, of course, requires significant evidence to be obtained by law enforcement and then reviewed by other officers of the court. Afterward, each side of the process again wields more expert witnesses to interpret this evidence. On average, this extends the amount of court time needed. Pending trial completion, which in general takes three to five times longer in capital cases than in non-capital cases, jurors are often sequestered (Jonathan Gradess, 2008) to prevent undue media or social bias from affecting their judgment. When doing so, the county pays for juror hotel rooms and meals.

If the jury finds the defendant guilty, an additional sentencing trial is conducted. In Texas, this bifurcated system requires defense counsel to extensively search for mitigating factors in the defendant's life that might suggest a reason to assign a lesser sanction than death (David Garland, 2007; Jonathan Gradess, 2008; Joseph Lentol, Helene Weinstein, and Aubry Jeffrion, 2005). This two-part process consumes a tremendous amount of time, resources, and money. On average, Mark Larranaga (2004) finds death penalty trials lasted approximately 25 months, whereas non-capital trials took an average of 15 months to conclude.

From a fiscal perspective, the extra time required for capital prosecutions reflects not only monetary costs, but also opportunity costs. Government officials, regardless of their role in the criminal justice system, are generally salaried employees who will be paid regardless of their case assignment, "But it would be misguided not to include the extra time that pursuing the death penalty takes compared to cases prosecuted without the death penalty in calculating costs" (Richard Dieter, 2009).

Criminals assigned to death row must be maintained in the most secure of environments which maintain higher staff to offender ratios than general population facilities. These inmates are generally assigned to single cells and require at least a two-officer escort when leaving their cells. They also require more frequent observation periods so as to significantly reduce imminent security threats, particularly in regard to violence against staff or other offenders. These enhanced security procedures are costly. For example, the Kansas Judicial Council (2014) finds the cost of housing a death row offender was $49,380 annually, as opposed to $24,690 for a general population offender.

A lesser-explored cost of all prosecutions is the financial burden imposed against governments in the case of wrongful imprisonment. In fact, the possibility of wrongful convictions is so prominent in judicial hearings that the federal government, the District of Columbia, and 32 states have all passed wrongful conviction statutes establishing an award rate per year of false imprisonment (with false imprisonment generally being established as actual innocence wherein the offender did not contribute to his own conviction, such as falsely confessing). Generally speaking, offenders relieved of death row due to wrongful convictions are awarded significant settlements, especially compared to wrongful conviction suits for non-capital cases. In 2004, President George W. Bush endorsed the Innocence Protection Act to award persons wrongly sentenced to the Bureau of Prisons a $50,000 per year false imprisonment stipend and, if appropriate, an additional $50,000 per year death row stipend (Innocence Project, 2009).

There are five methods of execution currently considered within the United States that do not violate the Eighth Amendment, as set out in Table 2.1: Lethal injection, lethal gas, firing squad, hanging, and the electric chair. Of these, legal injection is the primary method of execution within the United States. In fact, the majority of states that utilize capital punishment maintain legal injection as their sole means of execution (*Baze v. Rees*, 2008).

In *Baze v. Rees* (2008), the Supreme Court notes that at least 80% of states employing legal injection, as well the federal government, used the same drug combination of sodium thiopental, pancuronium bromide, and potassium chloride to cause death. Sodium thiopental is a fast-acting sedative used to prevent pain. Pancuronium bromide then paralyzes the body while potassium chloride induces cardiac arrest. Since 2009, however, a pharmaceutically induced shortage of this "death cocktail" has forced states to switch to a one-drug injection. Texas, along with many other states, chose pentobarbital. This is a barbiturate that slows the activity of the brain and nervous system. It is known to bring about a peaceful death and is often the drug of choice for assisted suicides (Oregon Health Authority, 2017). Prior to the shortage, Michelle Lyons, spokeswoman for the Texas Department of Criminal Justice, stated the cost of the lethal injection drugs was $83.35 per execution. Now using only pentobarbital, the State of Texas pays $1,286.86 per lethal injection (Death Penalty Information Center, 2012).

Staffing-related concerns, as well as increased security measures, create the largest execution-day costs. For example, in 2010, the State of Washington spent $97,814 on execution day. Of this, only $862 went to purchase sodium thiopental (Daniel Nasaw, 2012).The remaining funds were spent on additional security staff, along with food and counseling for said staff. Washington State also spent significant money to pitch media tents, as well as to provide additional fencing and lighting for demonstrators camped outside of the execution site (Nasaw, 2012).

The defendant in a capital murder trial has many monetary and nonmonetary costs. The main monetary expenses come from the payment of legal fees, if the defendant can afford to pay for legal counsel. Nonmonetary costs can be more significant and include physical and mental treatment during the trial process in the courtroom, by the defense lawyers, and while incarcerated (including the possibility of experiencing solitary confinement); loss of liberty during incarceration; loss of ability to earn an income due to incarceration; loss of a sense of security due to being in a prison setting; and anxiety regarding time limits on appeals, the diligence of defense attorneys, and the effect of the trial on family members (Susan Sharp, 2005); and the possible loss of life. A lack of knowledge of how the process works and the rights of the accused may result in the accused person's decision-making process being hampered during the trial process. This too can add to the accused person's costs.

One of the decisions affecting the system of capital punishment is the decision of state prosecutors regarding how many accused persons to try for murder and how many for capital murder. Individual states have limited resources for murder trials and the designation of capital murder increases the cost of the trial by hundreds of thousands of dollars. The following model illustrates how states that allow capital punishment for murder trials divide scarce resources between non-capital and capital-eligible cases.

The cost of non-capital-eligible murder trials is shown in Figure 2.1. The cost of each new unit, called **marginal cost** (MC), of resources allocated to these trials increases due to scarcity to time and funding. The cost of regular murder trials is quite a bit less than that of capital murder trials, so the marginal cost curve is relatively flatter for non-capital-eligible murder trials (MC_N).

FIGURE 2.1   Cost of non-capital murder trials

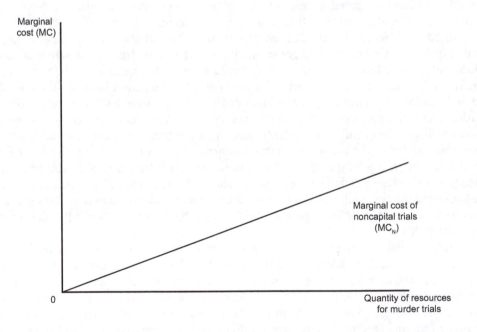

Not only are capital murder trials more expensive than murder trials, but costs of prosecuting a person for capital murder increase as the trial continues. At each stage, the capital trial cost increases due to more time commitment and resources of law enforcement, expert witnesses, the judicial system, lawyers, prison officials, jurors, and other relevant personnel. The cost of a capital-eligible murder trial is illustrated in Figure 2.2. The marginal cost curve for capital-eligible murder trials (MC_C) is relatively steeper than for murder alone.

FIGURE 2.2   Cost of capital eligible murder trials

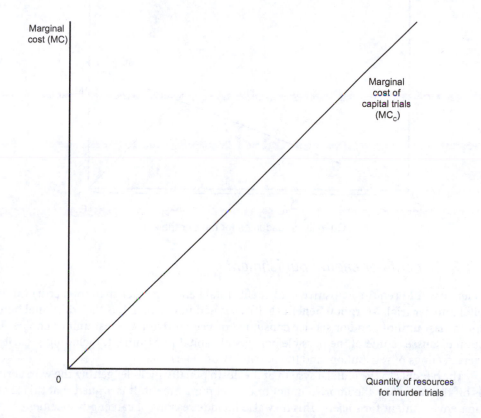

Once the costs of murder trials and the costs of capital murder trials have been ascertained, the state can determine the efficient allocation of scarce resources between murder trials and capital murder trials. In economics, this is done on a dynamic graph with two vertical axes, one for each of the marginal costs, as shown in Figure 2.3. In this model, the horizontal axis measures the total quantity of resources that are available for murder trials (Q_T) that is allocated between non-capital-eligible murder trials (Q_N) and capital-eligible murder trials (Q_C). Efficiency occurs when the marginal cost of the last non-capital-eligible murder trial (MC_{N1}) is equal to the marginal cost of the last capital-eligible murder trials (MC_{C1}). It is clear that if relative cost of trials is a deciding factor, states will choose to allocate far more resources for non-capital-eligible murder trials (Q_{N1}) than for capital-eligible murder trials (Q_{C1}).

FIGURE 2.3 Allocation of scarce resources between non-capital and capital eligible murder trials

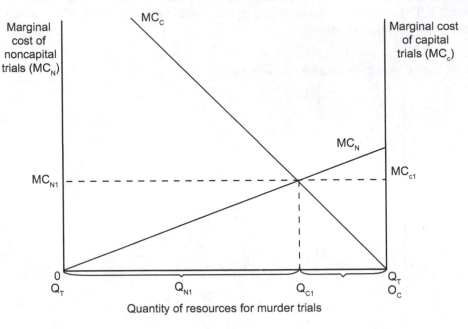

Quantity of resources for murder trials

Unit 2: Benefits of capital punishment

Efficiency would require a positive net benefit (total benefit greater than total cost) for each capital murder trial. **Marginal benefit** (MB), as stated in Chapter 1, is the additional benefit from the last unit of good or service consumed or used or from the last unit of choice. This section discusses some of the possible benefits of capital punishment, including security to society, feelings of retribution, and the possibility of deterrence.

The benefits to the judicial system of the death penalty include "getting the worst criminals off the street" by life imprisonment or capital punishment. It is argued that this creates a safer environment for society. This may also include reasons of career advancement on the part of officials within the capital punishment process by means of being "hard on criminals" (Mark Fuhrman, 2003). Stuart Banner (2002) states, "Whether a defendant was charged with capital or non-capital murder depended largely on whether the prosecutor was up for reelection." In addition, there has been some research into whether the capital punishment process of assigning defense lawyers to capital defendants depends partly upon the election of judges (Stephen Bright, 2000; Gerald Uelmen, 1998).

One arguable benefit to imposing the death penalty would be ensuring the greatest level of retribution. It embodies an attitude of being "tough on crime." Embracing that attitude is what allows most supporters of capital punishment to "report that they would continue to do so even if they were persuaded that life imprisonment is an equally effective deterrent to murder" (James Acker, 2003). According to Acker (2003), "Imposing a severe punishment allows society to express moral outrage at the offender's breach and simultaneously helps reinforce a shared sense of commitment to the violated norm." The concept of retribution validates certain traditional, religious, and cultural values within society (David Garland, 2007).

In 2016, a nationally conducted Gallop Poll indicated that 60% of the American public still favored the death penalty for a person convicted of murder. Testifying before a Maryland death penalty commission study, Joseph Cassilly noted that "Justice is not a cost–benefit analysis. Justice is doing the right thing, no matter how much it costs" (Arthur Alarcon and Paula Mitchell, 2011). According to David Garland (2005), society's willingness to "do the right thing" is "held in place chiefly by emotionally-charged political considerations rather than more instrumental concerns."

One potential benefit of capital punishment would be realized if capital murder had a deterrent effect – i.e. if the probability of being tried, convicted, and executed would deter a person from committing a murder. In the most heinous of cases, many have argued that "to fight and deter crime effectively, individuals must have every tool government can afford them, including the death penalty" (George Pataki, 1997). It is arguable, however, whether capital punishment represents a general deterrent to murder. There is, indeed, a specific deterrent (Michael Mello, 2008), though technically this should be considered to be incapacitation rather than deterrence (Dennis Longmire, personal communication, March 13, 2014). In measuring deterrence, William Tucker (2002) compared national murder rates to execution rates from 1930 through 2000. He found that between the 1930s and 1963, when the death penalty was earnestly applied, there was a continuous reduction in the national murder rate. However, as the United States lessened its use of capital punishment through the 1970s and 1980s, the murder rate per capita significantly increased. It was not until the early 1990s that capital sanctions returned to 1960s rates. At that point, the national murder rate then fell to corresponding 1960s levels. Consequently, Tucker (2002) claims that over 100,000 American people would not have been murdered had the United States maintained the level of capital sanctions through the 1970s and 1980s.

In a national study regarding deterrence, Richard Berk (2005) found that the State of Texas created an interesting abnormality. Berk performed a cross-section time series analysis using the execution and homicide rates of the 50 states over a 21-year period (1977–1997). With 1,050 observations, Berk notes that most states failed to execute anyone during most years. Some states executed more than five offenders within a year, with the State of Texas enacting comparably higher and more consistent levels of executions. Including Texas in his results, Berk noted that a deterrent effect was present across the nation. However, once Texas was removed from consideration, the deterrent effect was lost. Subsequently, Berk concluded that throughout the United States, the deterrent effect is only evident in the State of Texas and cautioned against the generalization of the state's results to the entire nation or in crediting the deterrent effect theory itself.

Ernie Thomson (1999) finds short-lived deterrent effects immediately following an execution; however, he also recorded evidence of long-term brutalization effects that created an eventual and overall increase in homicides. Michael Mello (2008) argued that "capital punishment does indeed deter crime, but so does life imprisonment." As such, the real question is not whether it deters crime, "but rather whether it deters crime any more significantly than does life imprisonment" (Mello, 2008).

In light of competing policy options, namely life without parole, is capital punishment the most cost-effective and efficient form of deterrence? The National Research Council of the National Academies (Daniel Nagin and John Pepper, 2012) states, "The committee concludes that research to date on the effect of capital punishment on homicide is not informative about whether capital punishment decreases, increases, or has no effect on homicide rates." This means that the research done to-date is not strong enough for the Council to conclude whether capital punishment has a deterrent effect – i.e. decreases the number of murders due to the penalty if convicted. The Council further states that the existing studies should not be used to inform capital punishment policy due to the flaws of incomplete models, non-credible assumptions, and ignoring the effects of noncapital punishments, such as life without parole.

The tables below highlight findings of the capital-punishment-as-deterrence studies. Table 2.10 looks at recent studies that have found that capital punishment had a deterrent effect.

TABLE 2.10 Capital punishment as a deterrent

Date	Author(s)	Source	Major finding(s)
2011	Dezhbakhsh, Hashem and Rubin, Paul.	From the "econometrics of capital punishment" to the "capital punishment" of econometrics: on the use and abuse of sensitivity analysis. *Applied Economics, 43(25).*	Scope of Donohue and Wolfers study is too narrow and reporting is selective.
2009	Cloninger, Dale and Marchesini, Roberto.	Reflections on a critique. *Applied Economics Letters, 16(17).*	Critique did not go through blind peer review process and findings do not justify modifying original results.
2009	Land, Kenneth; Teske, Raymond; and Zheng, Hui.	The short-term effects of executions on homicides: Deterrence, displacement, or both? *Criminology, 47(4).*	Models contradict each other, so definite ruling requires additional research and future analysis and replication.
2009	Zimmerman, Paul.	Statistical variability and the deterrent effect of the death penalty. *American Law and Economics Review, 11(2).*	Alternative model provides evidence supporting a deterrent effect in addition to the one critiqued by Donohue and Wolfers.
2009	Frakes, Michael and Harding, Matthew.	The deterrent effect of death penalty eligibility: Evidence from the adoption of child murder eligibility factors. *American Law and Economics Review, 11(2).*	Eligibility expansions enhance deterrence especially because they provide prosecutors with greater leverage to secure enhanced noncapital sentences.
2009	Hjalmarsson, Randi.	Does capital punishment have a "Local" deterrent effect on homicides? *American Law and Economics Review, 11(2).*	Disaggregated data finds little consistent evidence that Texas executions deter homicides.
2009	Donohue, John and Wolfers, Justin.	Estimating the impact of the death penalty on murder. *American Law and Economics Review, 11(2).*	2SLS studies use a problematic structure that is designed to capture the key deterrence elements.
2008	Cohen-Cole, Ethan; Durlauf, Steven; Fagan, Jeffrey; and Nagin, Daniel.	Model uncertainty and the deterrent effect of capital punishment. *American Law and Economics Review, 11(2).*	Deterrence literature plagued by model uncertainty and describes methods for addressing the uncertainty.
2008	Yang, Bijou and Lester, David.	The deterrent effect of executions: A meta-analysis thirty years after Ehrlich. *Journal of Criminal Justice, 36(5).*	Meta-analysis supports deterrent effect of executions, but depends on type of study carried out.
2006	Keckle, Charles.	Life v. death: Who should capital punishment marginally deter? *Journal of Law, Economics and Policy, 2(1).*	Marginal deterrence effect shown to be a direct negative function of prison conditions as they are anticipated by the potential offender.

Year	Author	Title	Description
2006	Zimmerman, Paul.	Estimates of the Deterrent Effect of the Alternative Execution Methods in the United States: 1978–2000. *American Journal of Economics and Sociology, 65(4).*	Panel of state-level data from 1978–2000 suggests that the deterrent effect of capital punishment is driven primarily by executions conducted by electrocution.
2006	Narayan, Paresh Kumar and Smyth, Russell.	Dead man walking: An empirical reassessment of the deterrent effect of capital punishment using the bounds testing approach to cointegration. *Applied Economics, 38(17).*	Murder supply equation suggests that support for deterrence is affected by gun violence and other crimes.
2006	Dezhbakhsh, Hashem and Shepherd, Joanna.	The deterrent effect of capital punishment: Evidence from a "Judicial Experiment." *Economic Enquiry, 44(3).*	Executions have a distinct effect that compounds the deterrent effect of reinstating the death penalty, robust across 96 regression models.
2005	Berk, Richard.	New claims about execution and general deterrence: Déjà vu all over again? *Journal of Empirical Legal Studies, 2(2).*	Claims of deterrence are a statistical artifact from the outlying states that execute more than five individuals in some years.
2006	Cloninger, Dale and Marchesini, Roberto.	Execution moratoriums, commutations, and deterrence: the case of Illinois. *Applied Economics, 38(9).*	Increased risk of homicide incurred after Illinois governor commuted the death sentences of all those who occupied death row in 2003.
2005	Weisberg, Robert.	The death penalty meets social science: Deterrence and jury behavior under new scrutiny. *Annual Review of Law and Social Science, 1.*	New econometric studies, using panel data techniques, report striking findings of marginal deterrence: up to 18 lives saved per execution.
2004	Shepherd, Joanna.	Murders of passion, execution delays, and the deterrence of capital punishment. *Journal of Legal Studies, 33(2).*	Longer waits on death row before execution lessen the deterrence. One less murder is committed for every 2.75-year reduction in death row waits.
2004	Zimmerman, Paul.	State executions, deterrence and the incidence of murder. *Journal of Applied Economics, 7(1).*	Structural estimates of the deterrent effect of capital punishment suggest that a state execution deters about 14 murders per year and the mechanism is the announcement effect, not the existence of a death penalty.
2004	Liu, Zhiqiang.	Capital punishment and the deterrence hypothesis: Some new insights and empirical evidence. *Eastern Economic Journal, 30(2).*	An average of eight murder victims might have been saved as a result of one execution for the sample period 1933–67.
2003	Mocan, H. Naci and Gittings, R. Kaj.	Getting off death row: Commuted sentences and the deterrent effect of capital punishment. *Journal of Law and Economics, 46(2).*	Each additional execution decreases homicides by about five and an additional removal from death row generates one additional murder.

(Continued)

TABLE 2.10 (Continued)

Date	Author(s)	Source	Major finding(s)
2003	Dezhbakhsh, Hashem; Rubin, Paul; and Shepherd, Joanna.	Does capital punishment have a deterrent effect? New evidence from postmoratorium panel data. *American Law and Economics Review, 5*(2).	Each execution results in 18 fewer murders with a margin of error of plus or minus ten. Results are not driven by tougher sentencing laws, and are also robust to many alternative specifications.
2003	Katz, Lawrence; Levitt, Steven; and Shustorovich, Ellen.	Prison conditions, capital punishment, and deterrence. *American Law and Economics Review, 5*(2).	Death rate among prisoners is negatively correlated with crime rates, consistent with deterrence.
2002	Yunker, James.	A new statistical analysis of capital punishment incorporating U.S. postmoratorium data. *Social Science Quarterly, 82*(2).	National time series data from 1930 to 1997 supports the deterrence hypothesis, but the same time series regression from 1930 to 1976 does not support the hypothesis.
2001	Cloninger, Dale and Marchesini, Roberto.	Execution and deterrence: A quasicontrolled group experiment. *Applied Economics, 33*(5).	Changes in the number of homicides in Texas and throughout the U.S. were negative, consistent with the deterrence hypothesis.
1999	Sorenson, Jonathan; Wrinkle, Robert; Brewer, Victoria; and Marquart, James.	Capital punishment and deterrence: Examining the effect of executions on murder in Texas. *Crime and Delinquency, 45*(4).	Initial results showed a relationship between executions and murder rates, but this relationship was proven to be false when control variables were included.
1999	Ehrlich, Isaac and Liu, Zhiqiang.	Sensitivity analysis of the deterrence hypothesis: Let's keep the econ in econometrics. *Journal of Law and Economics, 42*(1).	Leamer and McManus's inferences about deterrence are based on a flawed methodology, so Ehrlich and Liu offered a theory based sensitivity analysis that supports the deterrence hypothesis.
1996	Brumm, Harold and Cloninger, Dale.	Perceived risk of punishment and the commission of homicides: A covariance structure analysis. *Journal of Economic Behavior and Organization, 31*(1).	Homicide commission rate is negatively correlated with the perceived risk of punishment, supporting the deterrence hypothesis. The perceived risk of punishment is negatively correlated with the homicide commission rate, and positively correlated with police presence, supporting the resource saturation hypothesis.

TABLE 2.11   Capital punishment not a deterrent

Date	Author(s)	Source	Major finding(s)
2006	Fagan, Jeffrey.	Death and deterrence redux: Science, law and causal reasoning on capital punishment. *Ohio State Journal of Criminal Law, 255*(4).	Lack of reliability of studies due to errors and non-rigorous research techniques.
2006	Donahue, John and Wolfers, Justin.	The death penalty: No evidence for deterrence. *The Economists' Voice*, April.	Lack of credibility of estimates in statistical studies of deterrence.
2005	Donahue, John and Wolfers, Justin.	The uses and abuses of empirical evidence in the death penalty debate. *Stanford Law Review, 791*(58).	Comparison tests find lack of statistical evidence for deterrence of death penalty.
2005	Weisberg, Robert.	The death penalty meets social science: Deterrence and jury behavior under new scrutiny. *Annual Review of Law and Social Science, 151*(1).	Omitted variables make studies non-legitimate. High-execution states may have a distorting effect on deterrence.
2005	Fagan, Jeffrey.	Public policy choice on deterrence and the death penalty: A critical review of new evidence. Testimony before the Joint Committee on the Judiciary of the Massachusetts Legislature on House Bill 3934.	Incorrect statistical analysis, missing variables, and other deficiencies make the studies unreliable.
2004	Berk, Richard.	New claims about executions and general deterrence: Déjà vu all over again? University of California, Los Angeles..	Finds studies unreliable due to statistical errors and small data sets.

Table 2.11 reviews recent studies that have refuted the claim that the death penalty is a deterrent of capital murder.

While it is hard to imagine a benefit to a person being tried for capital murder, there have been cases in which the defendant chooses to defend himself during the trial to ensure that he receives the death penalty. If the defendant did indeed commit the murder, they may have gained some mental/emotional comfort from having committed that act.

Death penalty abolitionists are interested in policy-making that decreases, and ultimately eliminates, capital punishment. An analysis of the costs and benefits of the capital trial process can uncover incentives that would increase the cost or decrease the benefit of capital trials, thus affecting the number of capital trials.

Unit 3: Inefficiencies in economic structure of capital punishment

Concerns such as individual rights, distributive justice, and humanity are at the forefront of government action (Aidan Vining and David Weimer, 2009). However, research has shown "unequal political representation . . . across income groups and social classes . . . provides greater opportunity for powerful economic interests to dominate the legislative process and bias policy responsiveness toward the opinions of the wealthy" (Patrick Flavin, 2012). This means that the opinions of the poor are not of paramount importance to public policy when those opinions oppose the interests of middle class and affluent citizens.

In determining the cost-effectiveness of capital prosecutions, the death penalty is often compared to the closest alternative policy option providing a similar effect - namely life without parole. Both capital punishment and life without parole preserve societal objectives of deterrence, retribution, and isolation. In this regard, both sentences advance criminal justice (David Johnson, 2011). Human rights activists suggest that there is inefficiency in the choice to use the death sentence because the monetary costs are greater than the benefit to society. In accordance with what most research demonstrates, the Spangenberg Group (1993) concludes that "the death penalty is not now, nor has it ever been, a more economical alternative to life imprisonment."

Inefficiency means that a choice is being made that does not maximize net benefit (total benefit minus total cost). Sources of inefficiency in the modeling of capital punishment may come from missing data, gaps in understanding the process of capital cases, sections of Texas Law that do not allow for economically-efficient decisions, gaps in services to persons who are tried in capital cases, extenuating circumstances that are not cleared before the end of the capital trial, and the possible effect of politics.

Frank Baumgartner and Anna Dietrich (2015) assert that executions are "the third most likely outcome following a death sentence. Much more likely is it for the inmate to have their sentence reversed, or to remain for decades on death row." Baumgartner and Dietrich found that from 1973 to 2013 roughly 8,466 persons were sentenced to death in the United States. Of those, just 1,359 offenders, or approximately 16%, were actually executed. Even if all the offenders currently sitting on death row awaiting appellate dispositions were suddenly executed, execution rates would still only increase to about 24%. A large number of death row offenders (3,194, or almost 38%) have had their convictions overturned. In this event, local governments must then finance a new capital trial/sentencing hearing or accept lesser and less costly sentencing options, and "The frequent reversals mean that many more costs have fruitlessly been incurred without any payoff in the form of executions" (James Acker, 2003). Considering this, "the death penalty without executions is a very expensive form of life without parole" (Richard Dieter, 2009).

David Garland (2007) suggests that citizens elect representatives who express and produce government action that reflects the overall will of citizens. "The local ties and electoral accountability of the key criminal justice decision-makers give the American capital punishment process a highly politicized character and connect it directly to local politics and popular sentiment." Many agents within the judicial system are elected officials who must seek justice not only in the eyes of the law, but also in the hearts of their electoral bases. Accordingly, district attorneys vying for votes may use criminal sanctions to be seen as acting as agents of citizens (Raymond Paternoster, 1984; Gregory Totten, 2008).

There is considerable evidence to indicate that if additional time and money used on capital prosecutions, for example, were channeled into either police programs or community infrastructures, it would create a significant reduction in violent crime (Ling Ren, Jihong Zhao, and Nicholas Lovrich, 2008). In studying several U.S. cities during the 1980s, the National Research Council (2004) notes that failed community infrastructures were the causes of social disorder. More recent research has followed this line of reasoning to find that a "lack of economic development also impeded social integration and collective efficacy at both the community and the neighborhood level [and as such] resulted in a noteworthy increase in fear of crime among community residents" (Ling Ren, Jihong Zhao, and Nicholas Lovrich, 2008).

When public policies are maintained despite economic inefficiency, government officials may be called on to present evidence to support their continued use. In doing so, policy-makers are obligated to demonstrate how the use of inefficient programs ultimately benefits society. It may happen that administrators claim program-related benefits might not be immediately realized, but are forthcoming at some time in the future. The government may argue that the reduction of future social costs is a benefit to citizens, so that inefficient programs may be justified via the "purchase (of) social stability" (Takis Venetoklis, 2002).

Section 7: Case study

Cost of capital punishment in Texas

V. Wolfe Mahfood, Ph.D. and Dennis R. Longmire, Ph.D.

Dr. V. Wolfe Mahfood was introduced in Unit 2: Criminal justice perspective.
Dr. Dennis R. Longmire is a full professor and the director of practice development for the College of Criminal Justice and Criminology at Sam Houston State University. He has a Ph.D. in criminology and sociology from the University of Maryland. His areas of expertise and publications are in the areas of capital punishment, public attitudes toward crime and justice, crime rates and trends, competency to stand trial, and substance abuse and treatment.

This model examines the costs of capital punishment in Texas between 2005 and 2007 using multiple regression to do a partial equilibrium analysis with cross-sectional data created by Drs. Mahfood and Longmire. **Multiple regression** is the use of statistical analysis to predict the value of one dependent variable based on the values of two or more independent variables. **Partial equilibrium analysis** means analyzing only a part of an economic situation. The model does this by specifically studying the current situation and costs of capital punishment in Texas, without looking at the effects on the Texas economy as a whole. This type of analysis suggests the cost of one operation does not influence the cost of other operations. This is true for government service costs.

This study involves a two-part assessment of social welfare concerns. First, a general review of specific social concerns will be performed for 248 of the 254 counties in Texas. Next, a partial equilibrium analysis of government expenditures for 120 Texas counties, both those having capital prosecutions and those lacking such, is used to better understand the opportunity costs associated with capital trials. A partial equilibrium analysis requires a limited range of data where the cost of one item – capital trials – is a variable, whereas all other county expenses are assumed to be fixed. Multiple regression is then employed to help determine if capital prosecutions are the most efficient means of managing capital crimes.

Main findings of the study

In the long run, capital prosecutions did not affect other judicial efforts, sales tax rates, unemployment, or per capita income rates. In the short run, the costs of capital punishment did not lead to decreases in murder, or in violent or property crime rates. In the counties with capital trials, there was a reduction in police efficiency, as capital trials require a large quantity of police time.

Data

The data for general review comes from 248 Texas counties for the years 2005–2007. The data for the partial equilibrium analysis was collected from the financial records of 120 Texas counties during this time. These records suggest that capital trials led to funds shifting from one spending category to another. Facilities and finance funds were often transferred to finance capital trials, and there was an increase in health and welfare spending.

While most of these governments finance their operations in similar fashion, six of the largest Texas counties operate as business-like ventures. These enterprises generate enough funds to reduce or eliminate the need for county-based property taxes to subsidize many operations. As such, these counties will be removed from the study. They are Bexar, Dallas, El Paso, Harris, Tarrant, and Travis. Social welfare factors related to the remaining 248 Texas counties, namely the effective and efficient nature of district courts, police systems, and governments in the remaining 248 Texas counties will be examined. The second part of this project involves the annual financial reports from 120 county governments. These financial reports provide detailed accounts of revenue and fund expenditures for each county's primary government.

It should be noted that significant attempts to gather financial information from all 254 Texas counties were made. Despite the Transparency in Government reporting expectations of the Texas Comptroller of Public Accounts, less than ten percent of Texas counties had the necessary financial information readily available for public inspection on either state or county-based websites. As such, per the Texas Open Records Act, proper legal notice requesting said information was sent to all remaining counties. Though state law requires governments to respond to Open Records Requests within a reasonable time period, usually thought of as ten business days, the vast majority of county governments failed to comply with initial requests. Subsequently, two more rounds of Open Records Requests were submitted. However, despite having sent some counties up to three separate requests for information, only 126 counties made their financial information available. As previously noted, six of those counties have been excluded from this study due to their operating significant business ventures.

Reasons for the study

Before policy costs and values can be considered, it is important to understand why policies exist and how those policies help to manage social concerns. For this, law-makers consider three key aspects: 1) the problem, 2) members of society who are affected by the problem, and 3) the best possible means by which to address their concerns (Aidan Vining and David Weimer, 2009). Ideally, this best possible means then becomes public policy. Of course, despite the best of attempts, whenever strategies are designed to address the needs of society at large, they almost always create unintended side effects for various subsets within that society. For this reason, public policies should be routinely examined to ensure the manner by which government addresses social concerns is the best available option for the greatest number of citizens (Takis Venetoklis, 2002). For example, a government organization decides whether to execute a person convicted of the death penalty on a person-by-person basis based partly on the cost of the capital punishment process and the perceived cost to society of not executing the person. In Texas, the average cost of $2.3 million per capital murder trial (Richard Dieter, 1994). In Texas, the counties are responsible for financing many social services, including the burden of capital prosecutions, which causes financial distress for counties that prosecute capital cases. The question remains whether capital prosecutions are an effective means to address concerns of public safety in light of their opportunity costs, especially in comparison to the less expensive sentencing alternative of "life without parole."

Drs. Mahfood and Longmire's research examined the effect of the presence of capital trials on six different variables. They investigated whether the presence of capital trials affected:

1)   Felony docket clearance rates for district courts,
2)   Police clearance rates for felony offenses,
3)   Felony crime rates,
4)   County tax rates, including property, sales, and other taxes,
5)   Local unemployment and per capital income rates,
6)   Funding decisions and social goods.

Variables

To answer the research questions, specific information was needed. Every incidence of capital prosecution across the entire State of Texas between 2005 and 2007 was required, as well as the duration of the prosecution. To determine if capital prosecutions created delays in the processing of felony trials, it was also necessary to record every instance of felony prosecution for all trials. All trials involving murder (all instances of murder, regardless of statutory degree), violent crimes (aggravated assault, rape, and robbery), and property crimes (burglary, larceny, and auto theft) appeared in docket clearance rate indexes for all district courts throughout all Texas counties. The Texas Office of Court Administration was the source of the raw data for these trials and indexes.

Crime rates have long served as performance measures for local governments. To determine effective, even if not efficient, crime policy in light of capital prosecutions, data on all murder (regardless of statutory degree) plus victimization claims, both violent (aggravated assault, rape, and robbery), and property-related (burglary, larceny, and auto theft) crimes reported to all law enforcement agencies within all counties was needed. Raw crime data for these indexes was obtained from the Texas Department of Public Safety, Uniform Crime Report. To develop crime rate indexes for each county, their area populations were also necessary. In standard measure, local crime rates were developed per 100,000 people. As the Texas Office of Court Administration updates county populations annually based on citizen records maintained by each county courthouse, this source provides the most accurate census data.

Crime clearance rates are defined as the percentage of alleged crimes subsequently resolved by law enforcement agencies within the same year that the crime was reported. Though this figure does not include the presence or resolution of backlogged cases, it is generally considered "the most common measure of investigative effectiveness" expressed by law enforcement (Gary Cordner, 1989). Hence, to determine if the investigation of capital cases alters productivity levels in local police departments, crime clearance index rates for each county were developed. All instances of murder (all instances of murder, regardless of statutory degree), violent crimes (aggravated assault, rape, and robbery), and property crimes (burglary, larceny, and auto theft) reported to all law enforcement agencies within any county jurisdiction were used to develop crime clearance rates. These rates reflect the average of all clearance rates reported by all local law enforcement agencies within a single county. Raw data for these indexes was obtained from the Texas Department of Public Safety, Uniform Crime Report.

To determine if capital trials affect county employment or per capita income rates, the Texas Workforce Commission (TWC) provided relevant data for the study time frame. In particular, the TWC produced the annual unadjusted, unemployment rate, the per capita income per county, as well as the state averages for the aforementioned measures. Unemployment was defined as persons who are currently out of work, but actively seeking work. Unemployment rates were calculated by dividing the number of unemployed persons by the number of persons presently in the labor force. Per capita income was defined as the total aggregated income earned within a jurisdiction divided by that district's total population.

Traditionally, per capita income has been used as an evaluation tool in judging the quality of life seemingly available to residents of a particular area (United Nations, 2006). Research has shown that the increased costs associated with death penalty trial procedures lead to reduced expenditure in areas of public safety and also in capital projects such as road construction (Katherine Baicker, 2004). Since government is often a major employer for many small counties, it is possible that the reallocation of funds from local projects to death penalty trial procedures would increase unemployment rates (possibly decreasing per capita income values) for not only agency personnel, but also government contracted businesses. Should this occur, ample evidence suggests that it could affect property crime rates (Duha Altindag, 2012; Douglas Yearwood and Gerry Koinis, 2012). In particular, the system activity effect suggests criminal motivation increases "as deteriorating economic conditions affect social strain and social control" (Julie Anne Phillips and Kenneth Land, 2012). Alternatively, property crime rates could decline as more people remain home due to unemployment (Martin Andresen, 2012).

To determine if capital trials affect local revenue sources, namely property tax rates, each individual county appraisal district provided property tax rates for the years in question. To determine if capital trials affect other sources of local revenue, the Texas Comptroller's Office provided county-based local and sales tax rates, as well as information regarding the presence of other county tax rates. Annual financial reports demonstrate a county's financial stability, which, in turn, substantiates its ability to retain current fiscal policies (the Civic Federation, 1997). Thus, to determine if capital trials affect government-funding decisions and subsequent social goods, the AFRs for the relevant time period were obtained from the appropriate Office of Retention for each county. To help standardize the impact of capital prosecutions on fund expenditures throughout the study time frame, the percentage of funds allocated to each of the various fund types (as related to the total value of all expensed funds) was used as the basis for statistical analysis.

Katherine Baicker (2004) finds that the presence of capital prosecutions raised property taxes by 1.6% while decreasing fund expenditures for police and capital assets. If this is the case in Texas, it is expected that capital trials resulted in delayed improvements to land, buildings, and other material assets. Also, it is expected that reduced funding will manifest as a decrease in police expenditures, possibly resulting in reduced police effectiveness. In fact, police chiefs from around the country claim that reduced law enforcement expenditures not only extend police response times, but also create an increase in unresolved crimes (U.S.

Department of Justice, 2011). Conversely, Ben Shoesmith (2011) claims that "evidence suggests that an increase in police expenditures per capita does positively influence arrest rates."

Data analysis

The efficient and effective nature of local governments was examined on two levels. First, standard multiple regression was used to determine if the presence of capital trials created a significant effect on various operational standards associated with county governments. More specifically, regression models were run using death penalty trials in 2005 to predict possible outcomes (tax changes, etc.) in 2007, while controlling for other social factors such as unemployment. The time lag of 2005 to 2007 was used for several reasons: First, in order to ensure that the cause came before the effect, it was necessary to use predictors from an earlier wave to predict outcomes from a latter waves; second, this lag allowed government sufficient time to enact changes in fiscal policy as a result of the increased costs, or expected costs, associated with capital trials. 2005 and 2007 were selected as opposed to later years in order to avoid the outside influence of the massive federal funding (FEMA) awarded to many Texas counties in the wake of Hurricanes Katrina, Rita, and Ike. Finally, the years in question existed within the same election cycle for most Texas politicians and for all Texas district attorneys. Hence, using the years inside of a single election term helped to control for politically charged social influences.

Linear regression was appropriate as the outcome variables are continuous in nature (William Berry and Stanley Feldman, 1985). Probability or p-values associated with the chi-square model were used to determine the model's statistical significance, whereas the R2 model was used to determine the model's substantive significance. The impact of the individual predictors were measured using the p-values associated with each (statistical significance) and the standardized regression coefficients or beta (substantive significance).

Under the economic assumption of partial equilibrium analysis, opportunity costs associated with capital prosecutions were explored. *Black's Law Dictionary* (2004) defines this economic principle as an "analysis which treats a certain sector of the economy as though it is operating in complete isolation from the other sectors within the economy."

Univariate analysis

Below is the summary of the univariate analysis, which is an analysis that looks for patterns in the data. These results are presented in the order of the research questions. Ultimately, these results provide evidence that the presence of a death penalty trial only has a statistically significant effect on murder clearance rates and the percentage of monies distributed to funds that cover a county's financial tasks and facilities processes as well as health and welfare funds.

Death penalty trials

The six largest counties in Texas were removed from this study due to those counties having multiple business-like operations that significantly influenced each county's dependence on property tax revenue. Of the remaining 248 counties, 136 (54.8%) did not engage in death penalty trials during 2005, whereas 112 (45.2%) did report such trials. Table 2.12 summarizes the prevalence of death penalty trials.

TABLE 2.12   Death penalty trials

	Frequency	Percent
Counties with no death penalty trials	136	54.8
Counties with death penalty trials	112	45.2
Total	248	100.0

TABLE 2.13   Docket clearance rate ranges

	2005	2007
Murder trial docket	0 (44.8%) – 100 (8.5%)	0 (52%) – 100 (7.3%)
Violent trial docket	0 (9.3%) – 100 (1.2%)	0 (7.7%) – 100 (1.6%)
Property trial docket	0 (3.6%) – 100 (2%)	0 (1.6%) – 100 (2.4%)

Note: Percentages represent the number of counties that reported each clearance rate; however, not all counties prosecuted felony trials for the years of 2005 and 2007.

Felony docket clearance rates

Felony docket clearance rates were categorized as murder trial dockets, violent trial dockets, and property trial dockets. Docket clearance rates were categorized in this fashion to help determine if the processing of capital trials delayed or otherwise obstructed the general clearance rates of other felony trials. In particular, did the processing of capital trials hinder the processing of other murder, violent, or property crime trials? Docket clearance rates are presented in Table 2.13 for the years 2005 and 2007. The 2005 variables were used as predictors in some models with the 2007 variables being used as dependent variables.

Murder trial docket clearance rates in 2005 ranged from zero (111 or 44.8% of counties) to 100 (21 or 8.5% of counties). Approximately 90% of counties had a murder docket clearance rate of 80 or less. Violent trial docket clearance rates also ranged from zero (23 or 9.3% of counties) to 100 (3 or 1.2% of counties). Approximately 90% of the counties had a docket clearance rate of 71.4 or lower. Nine counties (3.6%) reported zero as their property trial docket clearance rate for 2005, while five counties (2%) reported 100 as their property trial docket clearance rate. Just over 90% of counties had a property trial docket clearance rate of 72.9 or lower.

In 2007, murder trial docket clearance rates ranged from zero (129 or 52% of counties) to 100 (18 or 7.3% of counties). Approximately 90% of counties had a murder docket clearance rate of 75 or less. Violent trial docket clearance rates also ranged from zero (19 or 7.7% of counties) to 100 (4 or 1.6% of counties). Approximately 90% of the counties had a violent trial docket clearance rate of 70 or lower. Four counties (1.6%) reported zero as their property trial docket clearance rate for 2007, while six counties (2.4%) reported 100 as their property trial docket clearance rate. Just over 90% of counties had a property trial docket clearance rate of 71.9 or lower.

Police effectiveness

Police effectiveness was measured in three ways: Murder crime clearance rates, violent crime clearance rates, and property crime clearance rates. In 2005, murder crime clearance rates ranged from zero (142 or 57.3% of the counties) to 300 (reported by a single county) cleared cases per 100,000 offenders. Ninety-six percent of counties had a murder clearance rate of 100 cases per 100,000 offenders or lower. Violent crime clearance rates ranged from zero (19 or 7.7% of counties) to 123.2 (reported by a single county) cleared cases per 100,000 offenders. Approximately 90% of counties had a violent crime clearance rate of 93.3 or lower per 100,000 offenders. Property crime clearance rates ranged from zero (five counties) to 100 (one county) cleared cases per 100,000 offenders. Approximately 90% of counties had a property crime clearance rate of 47.5 or lower cases per 100,000 offenders.

In 2007, murder clearance rates ranged from zero (151 or 60.9% of the counties) to 200 (two counties) cleared cases per 100,000 offenders. As in 2005, 96% of counties had a murder clearance rate of 100 cases or lower per 100,000 offenders. Violent crime clearance rates ranged from zero (17 or 6.9% of counties) to 229.3 (reported by a single county) cleared cases per 100,000 people. 97.6% of counties had a violent crime clearance rate of 100 cleared cases per 100,000 people or lower. Property crime clearance rates ranged from zero (ten counties) to 100 (four counties) cases per 100,000 people. As summarized in Table 2.14, approximately 90% of counties had a property crime clearance rate of 44 or lower cases per 100,000 offenders.

Crime rates

Crime rates were divided into murder, violent crime, and property crime. As with previous variables, crime rates are presented for both 2005 and 2007. In 2005, murder rates ranged from zero (130 or 52.4% of the counties) to 33.64 (reported by a single county) offenses per 100,000 offenders. Approximately 90% of counties had a murder offense rate of 9.62 or lower per 100,000 offenders. Violent crime rates ranged from zero (14 or 5.6% of counties) to 1,303.1 (reported by a single county) offenses per 100,000 offenders. Approximately 90% of counties had a violent crime offense clearance rate of 491.4 or lower per 100,000 offenders. Property crime rates ranged from zero (three counties) to 38,545.6 (one county) offenses per 100,000 people. Approximately 90% of counties had a property crime rate of 4,554.16 offenses per 100,000 people or lower.

In 2007, murder rates ranged from zero (136 or 54.8% of the counties) to 109.53 (reported by a single county) offenses per 100,000 people. Approximately 90% of counties had a murder rate of 7.93 or lower offenses per 100,000 offenders. Violent crime rates ranged from

TABLE 2.14 Crime clearance rate ranges

	2005	2007
Murder	0 (57.3%) – 300 (.4%)	0 (60.9%) – 200 (.8%)
Violent crime	0 (7.7%) – 123.2 (.4%)	0 (6.9%) – 229.3 (.4%)
Property crime	0 (2%) – 100 (.4%)	0 (4%) – 100 (1.6%)

Note: Percentages represent the number of counties that reported each crime clearance rate.

TABLE 2.15   Crime rate ranges

	2005	2007
Murder	0 (52.4%) – 33.64 (.4%)	0 (54.8%) – 109.53 (.4%)
Violent crime	0 (5.6%) – 1303.1 (.4%)	0 (5.2%) – 1666.67 (.4%)
Property crime	0 (1.2%) – 38545.6 (.4%)	0 (.8%) – 31666.67 (.4%)

Note: Percentages represent the number of counties that reported each crime rate range.

TABLE 2.16   County revenue sources

	2005	2007
Property tax reliance	19.21 (.4%) – 83.69 (.4%)	24.28 (.4% – 80.94 (.4%)
Property tax revenue (state average)	.31 (.4%) – 7.22 (.4%)	.31 (.4%) – 7.44 (.4%)
Sales tax	0 (53.6%) – .015 (.4%)	0 (53.2%) – 0.15 (.4%)
Other tax	0 (89.5%) – 1 (10.5%)	0 (89%) – 1 (10.9%)

Note: Percentages represent the number of counties that reported each revenue source.

zero (13 or 5.2% of counties) to 1,666.67 (reported by a single county) offenses per 100,000 people. Approximately 90% of counties had a violent crime rate of 522 offenses of lower per 100,000 offenders. Finally, property crime rates ranged from zero (two counties) to 31,666.67 (one county) offenses per 100,000 offenders. As summarized in Table 2.15, roughly 90% of counties had a property crime rate of 4,091.72 or lower per 100,000 offenders.

County revenue sources

County revenue sources were measured as the property tax reliance, percent of the total overall state average property tax revenue, sales tax rates, and other county tax rates. Notably, only the counties that provided financial data were examined in terms of property tax reliance (112 counties) and revenue values (110 counties). Historically, county governments have relied on property taxes as their main component of own-source revenue. Property tax reliance revenue value helps to determine if the overall property tax revenue of one county has changed in comparison to neighboring counties. Accordingly, the results of all percentages discussed herein reflect these adjusted base numbers and are summarized in Table 2.16. Again, all variables are presented for both 2005 and 2007 in order to reflect their use as predictor and outcome variables in the different models.

In 2005, property tax reliance rates ranged from 19.21 (reported by one county) to 83.69 (also one county). Approximately 90% of the counties had a property tax reliance rate of 74.29 or less. Percentage of property tax revenue values ranged from .31% to 7.22% (reported by one county each). Ninety percent of the counties had a percentage of property tax revenue value of 1.83% or less. Sales tax rates ranged from zero (133 or

53.6% of counties) to .015 (reported by one county). With the exception of one county, all others had a sales tax rate of .005 or lower. Other tax rates ranged from zero (222 or 89.5% of counties) to one (26 or 10.5% of counties). All counties fell into one of these two other tax rates.

In 2007, property tax reliance rates ranged from 24.28 (reported by one county) to 80.94 (also one county). Approximately 90% of the counties had a property tax reliance rate of 75.24 or less. Percentage of property tax revenue values ranged from .31% to 7.44% (reported by one county each). Ninety percent of counties had a percentage of property tax revenue value of 1.81% or less. Sales tax rates ranged from zero (132 or 53.2% of counties) to .015 (reported by one county). All but two counties had a sales tax rate of .005 or lower. Other tax rates ranged from zero (221 or 89.1% of counties) to one (27 or 10.9% of counties). All counties fell into one of these two other tax rates.

Unemployment and per capita income rates

In 2005, unemployment rates across Texas counties ranged from .024 (reported by one county) to .133 (reported by one county). Approximately 90% of counties had an unemployment rate of .066 or less. Per capita income rates in 2005 ranged from .390 to 2.562 (both rates reported by only one county). Approximately 90% of counties had a per capita income rate of 1.032 or less.

In 2007, unemployment rates across Texas counties ranged from .021 to .115 (both reported by one county). Approximately 90% of counties had an unemployment rate of .054 or less. Per capita income rates in 2007 ranged from .072 to 2.833 (reported by one county each). As summarized in Table 2.17, approximately 90% of counties had a per capita income rate of 1.051 or less.

Government funding

Government funding was measured as the percentage of total county spending that was distributed to 11 different areas: the general fund, the judicial fund, the financial fund, the facilities fund, the public works fund, the public safety fund, the transportation fund, the health and welfare fund, the capital outlay fund, the debt service fund, and the intra-governmental fund. These 11 categories were generally funded by all 126 reporting counties. In instances where funds were not reported in these specific categories, but were subdivided into greater detail (usually occurring in smaller counties), expenditures were then placed into the greater appropriate fund. As with all other variables, these are presented for both 2005 and 2007 in order to indicate their use as both predictor and outcome variables. As noted, data for government funding were collected for only 126 counties, with six of those counties then

TABLE 2.17 Unemployment and per capita income rate ranges

	2005	2007
Unemployment	.024 (.4%) – 133 (.4%)	.021 (1.2%) – .115 (.4%)
Per capita income	.390 (.4%) – 2.562 (.4%)	.072(.4%) – 2.833 (.4%)

Note: Percentages represent the numtber of counties that reported each rate.

being excluded from consideration due to their business-like revenue operations. Therefore, all percentages represented in Table 2.18 reflect this reduced sample size. As with all other variables, these are presented for both 2005 and 2007 in order to indicate their use as both predictor and outcome variables.

TABLE 2.18 Government funding decisions (as a percentage of total county spending)

	2005	2007
General fund	.0371 (.4%) – .5500 (.4%)	.0301 (.4% – .5790 (.4%)
Judicial fund	.0000 (.4% – .4072 (.4%)	.0000 (.4%) – .3695 (.4%)
Financial fund	.0000 (20.2%) – .3895 (.4%)	.0000 (19.4%) – .1392 (.4%)
Facilities fund	.0000 (10.5% – .3022 (.4%)	.0000 (8.9%) – 3831 (.4%)
Public works fund	.0000 (21.4%) – .2771 (.4%)	.0000 (19.8%) – .2551 (.4%)
Public safety fund	.0000 (1.6%) – .6183 (.4%)	.0000 (.8%) – .5205 (.4%)
Transportation fund	.0000 (4.4%) – .3794 (.4%)	.0000 (4%) – .4133 (.4%)
Health & welfare fund	.0000 (3.2%) – .4590 (.4%)	.0000 (2.4%) – .3495 (.4%)
Capital outlay fund	.0000 (16.5%) – .3579 (.4%)	.0000 (12.1%) – .3455 (.4%)
Debt service fund	.0000 (8.5%) – .8000 (.4%)	.0000 (6.9%) – .9340 (.4%)
Intra-governmental fund	.0000 (43.1%) – .2262 (.4%)	.0000 (43.1%) – .2242(.4%)

Note: Percentages represent the number of counties that reported each rate.

In 2005, the percentage of overall funding distributed to the general fund ranged from 3.71% to 55% (each reported by one county). Ninety percent of counties concentrated 36.47% or less of their total county spending to the general fund. The percentage of funding that each county distributed to the judicial fund ranged from zero (11 counties or 4.4%) to 40.72% (one county). Ninety percent of counties concentrated 18.55% or less of their overall county spending on the judicial fund. The percentage of county funding spent on the financial fund ranged from zero (50 counties or 20.0%) to 38.05% (one county). Ninety percent of counties spent 6.96% or less budgets on the financial fund. The percentage of overall funding that each county distributed to the facilities fund ranged from zero (10.5% or 26 counties) to 30.22% (reported by only one county). Ninety percent of counties concentrated 13.05% or less of their overall county spending on the facilities fund. The percentage of county spending dedicated to public works ranged from zero (21.4% or 53 counties) to 27.71% (reported by one county). Ninety percent of counties spent 4.72% or less on public works in 2005. In that same year, four counties (1.6%) spent no money on public safety; whereas one county distributed 61.83% of the total county spending to the public safety fund. Ninety percent of counties concentrated 38.19% or less of their overall county spending on the public safety fund.

The percentage of overall funding that each county distributed to the transportation fund ranged from zero (11 or 4.4% of counties) to 37.94% (one county). Ninety percent of counties set aside 29.26% or less of their overall spending into a transportation fund. The percentage of spending dedicated to the health and welfare fund ranged from zero (eight counties or 3.2%) to 45.9% (one county). Ninety percent of counties dedicated 11.29% or less of their overall spending to a health and welfare fund. The percentage of spending dedicated to the capital outlay fund ranged from zero (41 counties or 16.5%) to 35.7% (one county), with 90% of counties dedicating 14.34% or less of their overall spending to this fund. The percentage of overall funding that each county distributed to the debt service fund ranged from zero (21 counties or 8.5%) to 80% (one county), with 90% of counties dedicating 9.54% or less of their overall spending to this fund. Finally, the percentage of spending dedicated to the intra-governmental fund ranged from zero (107 counties or 43.1%) to 22.62% (one county) in 2005, with 90% of counties dedicating less than one percent of their overall spending to this fund.

In 2007, the percentage of overall funding that each county distributed to the general fund ranged from 3.01% to 57.9% (each reported by one county). Ninety percent of counties concentrated 32.01% or less of their total county spending on the general fund. The percentage of funding that each county distributed to the judicial fund ranged from zero (10 counties or 4%) to 36.95% (one county). Ninety percent of counties concentrated 19.27% or less of their overall county spending on the judicial fund. The percentage of county funding spent on the financial fund ranged from zero (48 counties or 19.4%) to 13.92% (one county). Ninety percent of counties spent 6.63% or less of their budgets on the financial fund. The percentage of overall funding that each county distributed to the facilities fund ranged from zero (8.9% or 22 counties) to 38.31% (reported by just one county). Ninety percent of counties concentrated 11.01% or less of their overall county spending on the facilities fund. The percentage of county spending on public works ranged from zero (19.8% or 49 counties) to 25.51% (reported by one county). Ninety percent of counties spent 3.98% or less on public works in 2007. In that same year, two counties (.8%) spent no money on public safety, while one county distributed 52.05% of the total county spending to the public safety fund. Ninety percent of counties concentrated 39.02% or less of their overall the public safety fund spending.

The percentage of overall funding that each county distributed to the transportation fund ranged from zero (10 or 4% of counties) to 41.33% (one county) in which 90% of the counties placed 27.48% or less of their overall spending into this fund. The percentage of spending dedicated to the health and welfare fund ranged from zero (six counties or 2.4%) to 34.95% (one county) in which 90% of the counties dedicated 13.68% or less of their overall spending to this fund. The percentage of spending dedicated to the capital outlay fund ranged from zero (30 counties or 12.1%) to 34.55% (one county), with 90% of counties dedicating 15.99% or less of their overall spending to this fund. The percentage of overall funding that each county distributed to the debt service fund ranged from zero (17 counties or 6.9%) to 93.4% (one county), with 90% of counties dedicating 9.61% or less of their overall spending to this fund. Finally, in 2007, the percentage of spending dedicated to the intra-governmental fund ranged from zero (107 counties or 43.1%) to 22.42% (one county), with 90% of counties dedicating less than one percent of their overall spending to this fund. The descriptive statistics for each previously discussed individual variable are summarized in Table 2.19.

Bivariate results

Bivariate correlations reveal the statistical relationships between two variables without considering the influence of any other variable. Notably, the presence of a death penalty trial was examined as an independent variable in order to ascertain the effect of this type of trial on

TABLE 2.19 Descriptive statistics

	2005			2007		
	Number	Mean	Standard deviation	Number	Mean	Standard deviation
Death penalty trial	248	.50	.501	248	.45	.499
Murder trial docket clearance	248	24.875	32.1447	248	28.206	32.9753
Violent trial docket clearance	248	42.994	22.1347	248	45.781	23.1895
Property trial docket clearance	248	48.086	19.9502	248	47.878	21.2812
Murder crime clearance rate	248	35.329	47.8525	248	39.550	50.8578
Violent crime clearance rate	248	58.197	31.5157	248	57.885	27.0905
Property crime clearance rate	248	27.074	17.1764	248	28.657	15.9295
Murder rate	248	3.5604	10.22860	248	3.4381	5.57779
Violent crime rate	248	290.9004	233.83181	248	263.6154	196.39670
Property crime rate	248	2309.8947	2346.77993	248	2533.0721	2840.43559
Property tax reliance	112	60.5194	12.07592	112	60.4129	13.21393
Property tax revenue	110	1.0245	1.03773	110	1.0221	1.00757
Sales tax	248	.00240	.002660	248	.00236	.002620
Other tax	248	.1089	.31211	248	.1048	.30696
Unemployment	248	.04272	.012254	248	.05182	.015106
Per capita income rate	248	.83189	.195035	248	.83589	.220858
% General fund	120	.183689	.1118167	120	.193215	.1115900
% Judicial fund	120	.117167	.0641334	120	.114149	.0678793
% Financial fund	120	.031623	.0298072	120	.034841	.0469331
% Facilities fund	120	.048152	.0546479	120	.048780	.0553792
% Public works fund	120	.016407	.0350599	120	.018178	.0398737
% Public safety fund	120	.272587	.0870689	120	.265093	.1032620
% Transportation fund	120	.152236	.0925647	120	.152229	.0946274
% Health % welfare fund	120	.054484	.0578757	120	.057740	.0663429
% Capital outlay fund	120	.067296	.0785530	120	.054571	.0734028
% Debt service fund	120	.051608	.0892255	120	.053487	.0824605
% Intra-governmental fund	120	.005193	.0241488	120	.006081	.0266782

TABLE 2.20 Bivariate correlations associated with presence of 2005 death penalty trials

	2005 Trial Pearson's Correlation	Significance
2007 Murder trial docket clearance	.165	.009
2007 Violent trial docket clearance	.135	.034
2007 Property trial docket clearance	.065	.306
2007 Murder crime clearance rate	.334	.000
2007 Violent crime clearance rate	-.065	.310
2007 Property crime clearance rate	-.141	.026
2007 Murder rate	-.016	.797
2007 Violent crime rate	.234	.000
2007 Property crime rate	.204	.001
2007 Property tax reliance	-.013	.891
2007 Property tax revenue	-.156	.105
2007 Sales tax	.111	.082
2007 Other tax	.021	.742
2007 Unemployment	.186	.003
2007 Per capita income rate	-.113	.075
2007 Percent general fund	-.219	.016
2007 Percent judicial fund	.054	.558

other county processes. The correlations between death penalty trials in 2005 and all other variables in 2007 are summarized in Table 2.20.

As shown, the presence of a death penalty trial in 2005 had a statistically significant relationship with property trial docket clearance rates (p =.306), violent crime clearance rates (p = .310), murder rate (p = .797), property tax reliance (p = .891), property tax revenue (p = .105), sales tax (p = .082), other tax (p = .742), per capital income rates (p = .075), and percent of judicial fund expenditures (p = .558). The direction of the relationships suggests that the presence of death penalty trials in 2005 were correlated with an increase in property trial docket clearance rates, sales tax, other tax, and percent of judicial fund expenditures in 2007. The presence of death penalty trials in 2005 was also correlated with a decrease in violent crime clearance rate, murder rate, property tax reliance, and per capital income rate in 2007.

Multivariate analysis is provided in the eResources associated with this textbook. There are 25 models provided in this unit, although none was considered statistically significant.

Discussion of the results

This research involved a cross-sectional analysis of the financial and bureaucratic effects of capital punishment. While a longitudinal study would have been preferred, and would possibly have provided more definitive answers, the current undertaking did yield an initial starting point for the understanding of financially-orientated opportunity costs associated with capital punishment policy evaluations. With this analysis, the six questions about effects of capital punishment expenditures on other government policies can be answered.

First, using a two-year time lag, results show that the presence of capital trials in year one has no effect on the processing of other felony trials two years later. It is unreasonable to imagine that the presence of a capital trial in year one would continue to affect the productivity levels of judicial processes two years after the fact, and yet a capital trial may slow down other judicial production levels. If this death penalty trial continued to occupy the criminal docket two years later, it would, of course, have the same continued effect on those production levels. Because of the unknown and/or prolonged processing times of capital trials, a cross-sectional analysis does not consider enough information to confidently address this long-term question.

Second, law enforcement officials often claim that the considerable manpower and hours required to investigate capital crimes place an undue burden on otherwise effective police investigations, thus decreasing the effectiveness of police. Since police investigations have a much shorter processing time than their related prosecutions, a cross-sectional analysis was appropriate. Regarding such, research finds that investigating capital crimes, which initiates capital prosecutions in year one, does create an increase in murder crime clearance rates two years later. Capital trials do not, however, have any effect on crime clearance rates pertaining to other felony charges.

Police investigations into felony crimes are distinguished by their nature, i.e. whether they are property crimes or violent crimes. Many times violent crimes are further dissected by their case style, with offenses of murder being processed by singularly-purposed homicide departments. Crime-appropriate staff generally conduct investigations into other felony crimes. Accordingly, other departmental squads are not inherently affected by capital investigations, so that neither the staff nor the resources associated with crimes unrelated to murder are directly affected by the political urgency of capital crimes. Hence, there is no general reason for capital investigations to alter the productivity levels of investigations into other violent or property crimes.

Since murder is a crime without a statute of limitations, homicide departments have the luxury of postponing some murder investigations in favor of more politically charged ones. As such, it is not unreasonable to expect that police investigations into capital crimes do, in fact, temporarily reduce productively levels of other less publicized homicide investigations. Subsequently, following the close of capital investigations, homicide detectives once again have the available time and resources to continue in pursuit of prior unsolved murder investigations.

Third, advocates for capital punishment have successfully argued many benefits of the process. Of great importance to these collective arguments is the matter of deterrence, as previously discussed. The current research does not support any claims of deterrence. Rather, results for this research indicated that capital prosecutions had no effect on property, violent, or murder crime rates.

Fourth, study results did not reflect an increase in property, sales, or other taxes as a consequence of capital prosecutions. Increases in county fees as a result of capital prosecutions were not considered in this research. County sales and other taxes were examined and found to be unaffected by the presence of capital prosecutions. Additionally, property taxes were unaffected by capital prosecutions. When considering property taxes, however, caution must be applied. It is important to understand that the tax rate alone does not determine a county's property tax revenue, which is the primary funding source for most counties. Rather, to determine the monetary value of a particular property tax rate, governments most also consider the assessed property value, along with the taxed percentage of that assessed value. The latter two factors are not considered in the present research.

Fifth, government is a major source of employment for many counties, especially smaller communities, so funding capital trials may have related spillover effects on local economies. With regard to the results from this study, capital prosecutions did not affect unemployment or per capita income rates of affected jurisdictions. Hence, while governments must change their spending patterns to finance capital trials, alterations do not force widespread or systemic income changes across local economies.

Finally, this study was also designed to identify whether financing capital trials influences other governmental funding decisions and subsequent social goods. Although a simple cross-sectional analysis does not provide sufficient information to determine spending patterns over time, it does confirm the obvious: To finance capital trials, sacrifices in other government programs must be made with the hope of reconciling those expenditures over time. Study results suggest that the initial financing of capital trials created subsequent shortages in financial and facility fund categories as well as increases in the health and welfare fund category.

The government depends on financial departments such as the county auditors, tax assessors, and appraisal districts for the imposition and collection of public taxes and fees to provide most social goods. Funding capital trials at the expense of financial departments puts a government at risk due to the future ability to operate effective revenue-receiving departments. This is also true of facilities funds, which generally allow for the upkeep and operation of all government properties that include permanent assets, such as buildings and land, and the development of new properties, such as public parks or county-owned entertainment venues.

Funding of capital trials creates a subsequent increase in cash flow for the health and welfare fund. Texas counties generally limit their total health and welfare expenditures to less than 6% of their total funds. In manipulating their available monies following capital prosecutions, governments may find themselves with insufficient amounts to adequately cover many aspects of their normal operations. To avoid political discontent, governments may channel remaining monies, even in insufficient values when compared to other fund usage, into the health and welfare fund.

Conclusions

Like many states, Texas manages the cost of capital prosecutions at the county level. In doing so, results from this study indicate that capital trials reduce the overall efficiency of local governments. In particular, the time and resources that police departments commit to capital murder investigations reduce their effective nature in investigating other simultaneously occurring felony murders. In addition, neither active police investigations into capital crimes nor the public processing of capital trials create a deterrent effect in county-based murder or other crime rates.

In this study, no changes in unemployment or per capita income rates were found as a result of capital prosecutions. Additionally, there were no changes in property or sales tax rates following capital trials. Again, however, it should be stressed that property tax rates are only one of three ways to alter revenues generated by any particular county.

Finally, results indicated that local governments manipulate their available funds to accommodate the large costs of processing capital trials. In particular, counties remove monies from both financial and facility funds in order to compensate for the immediate cost of capital trials. By doing so, local economies disconnect from future and/or potential revenue streams. Assuming there are then insufficient funds remaining to finance major government operations or significant potential revenue projects, governments then make the best out of a bad situation by increasing health and welfare funding.

Results from this study suggest that capital prosecutions create a financial liability to the people and the subsequent health of their governments. In return, capital trials offer no deterrent effect or other readily realized social benefits. If, in order to finance capital prosecutions, counties must forgo services and programs beneficial to improving government efficiency and yet receive no social benefit in the process, then capital trials are not cost effective.

Limitations on the research

This research does not allow for long-term effects of spending on capital cases. The use of longitudinal data would allow for research into the use of financing capital trials with new debt or postponing government projects.

While the annual fiscal reports under review belong solely to counties within the State of Texas, the generalizability of these findings is still quite broad. Since most governments within the United States operate in similar fashion, findings in Texas should be representative of those in other states. The applicability of these findings may be limited, however, by the sample size. Though all 254 Texas counties were asked to participate in this study, only 126 counties complied with that request. Of those 126 counties, six counties were subsequently removed from the study due to their governments generating significant revenues via business-like operations. As a result, the absolute influence of all capital prosecutions within a single state jurisdiction will not be completely captured.

Also, the available financial data presents several limitations, all of which focus around the autonomy of county governments: Therefore, they cannot be corrected. Despite county governments being a function of state governance, they are still granted large measures of discretion to act in accordance with their uniquely developed policies. For example, while the GASB Statement No. 34 mandates a degree of uniformity in accounting standards for AFRs, local governments are not required to subcategorize their budget expenditures in identical formats. Hence, while most counties itemize expenses according to purpose, there is still no unified consistency in reporting such. As a case in point, county-funded fire departments help to maintain public safety. As such, most counties assign those departmental expenses to their public safety funds. At their individual discretion, however, some smaller counties may assign these expenses to the general fund. As another example, corrections are generally considered a matter of public safety. Nonetheless, some counties may still expense related costs to their judicial funds.

Lastly, there are reporting differences in the fiscal and calendar years used by various state and county agencies. The Texas Local Government Code, Section 112.010, authorizes a county's fiscal year as the calendar year (used by 24.1% of counties). Counties may, however, adopt an October 1 fiscal year (used by 75.6% of counties). Counties with over 3.3 million residents may adopt either an October 1 or March 1 fiscal year (only Harris County qualifies and does use the March 1 date). Aligning with the reporting years of most Texas counties, the Texas Office of Court Administration uses the October 1 fiscal year. However, other reporting agencies associated with the State of Texas, such as the Texas Department of Public Safety, use a fiscal year beginning on September 1. Finally, it should be noted that while the Texas Department of Criminal Justice uses a fiscal year of September 1, reporting information concerning death row offenders is based on the calendar year.

Section 8: Recommendation for future economics of capital punishment research

This chapter provided a brief foundation for research on the topic of capital punishment. There are multiple areas within capital punishment that can be explored using economic analysis. For example, a major human rights question relates to the socioeconomic status of individuals on death row. In Texas, 62% of all felony defendants do not have the funds to hire their own defense attorneys. Reviewing crime rates leads to the discovery of areas with high poverty. Questions may arise as to whether murders that are potentially capital-eligible are happening at an increased rate in areas of poverty and whether there are other variables affecting the high rate of indigents on death row.

Socioeconomics is also a consideration in determining which counties prosecute capital cases. Considerations could include determination of when a county has enough money for a capital trial, the socioeconomics of those counties that have a high capital punishment rate, and when a sentence of life without parole is more cost-effective. The case study by Drs. Mahfood and Longmire excluded the six largest counties in Texas. These larger counties have more resources at their disposal due to their population, tax base, and other measures of local economy. Furthermore, larger counties have more diverse means by which to finance their operations. As such, simultaneously evaluating all available counties in Texas may allow larger counties to cancel out important effects felt by smaller ones. Keeping this in mind, future researchers may wish to distinguish counties by their population size.

There are many questions regarding the use of resources by law enforcement. The necessity to extradite a suspect is costly in terms of officer and staff time as well as transportation and other expenses for two or more agencies. Because it is expensive to search for suspects and evidence, a decision may be made to arrest the most likely suspect and close the investigation.

Aggravating circumstances and mitigating circumstances were previously discussed. The investigation, gathering of expert witnesses, and preparation for trial of this information are decisions for both the prosecution and the defense. There is also the question of effectiveness of assistance by the defense lawyers to the defendant and the time it takes a defendant on death row to get a defense lawyer for representation in the appellate court.

As seen, politics may play a part in the decisions to try a defendant on capital charges. Mark Fuhrman (2003) relates the account of a prosecutor who, for political reasons, was accused of choosing certain suspects to convict of the death penalty.

There are many issues related to the review of cases from lower courts by the federal and supreme courts. For example, there is a document called a "certiorari" that an appellate court can issue that states that they intend to review certain cases. Reviewing cases takes time and resources, which equates to benefits and costs to the federal or supreme court doing the review.

Governors have the right to grant clemency at their discretion, as discussed earlier in the chapters. One form of clemency is a **commutation** which a reduced sentence compared to that which was imposed during the trial. The governor may also grant a reprieve, which is a delay in the death sentence for the person convicted of capital punishment. Decisions related to the governor's reelection and other choices made by the governor in regard to capital punishment resources should be considered when determining economic efficiency.

In a practical sense, cost-effective studies should also consider how the threat of capital prosecution affects criminal pleas, as well as the subsequent cost of judicial proceedings. This allows that the threat of capital punishment grants police and district attorneys the ability to leverage capital sanctions during their investigation and/or plea bargaining processes. Certainly, persons pleading guilty to lesser charges of murder, in lieu of possible capital consequences, eliminate significant trial costs. Justice Marshall (1972) clearly did not support this consideration, stating, "If the death penalty is used to encourage guilty pleas and thus to deter suspects from exercising their rights under the Sixth Amendment to jury trials, it is unconstitutional" (*Furman v. Georgia*, 408 U.S. 238). However, it should be noted that of the 7,887 capital convictions between 1973 and 2008, "only 1.6 percent of those were exonerated by way of actual innocence, as opposed to mere due process errors" (Ward Campbell, 2008).

Some issues that have not been considered in this chapter are capital punishment in response to betrayal of one's country and the costs and benefits to the defendant's family members and the family members of the murdered person.

The management of the criminal justice system is split up between public (government) agencies and private entities. It may be of interest to determine how much of what happens in regard to capital crimes and other crimes in some way benefits private or public entities. Economic efficiency requires that all benefits and costs be considered in the analysis, so hidden benefits and costs may lead to inefficient decisions.

The case study provided a cross-sectional analysis of capital punishment and concluded that the analysis does not provide sufficient information to determine the effects of capital prosecutions over time. To truly understand the bureaucratic effects of funding capital trials, future research could include longitudinal data.

CHECK YOURSELF BOX: CHANGES IN PERSONAL BIASES ABOUT CAPITAL PUNISHMENT

This chapter has taken you through the system of capital punishment, U.S. and international laws and agreements, the history of capital punishment in Texas, experts, and the economic structure of capital punishment. What are your thoughts about the efficiency of the capital punishment system? What do you think about the motives and actions of the decision-makers? Look again at the personal biases you listed in the first check yourself box. Has the additional information in this chapter strengthened, weakened, or changed any of your thoughts about capital punishment? Have you gained any new biases about this topic? What was the most influential thing you learned? Keep writing down the changes in your biases and the reasons behind the changes. A firm knowledge of how your biases develop and change will help you become an expert known for quality research.

Section 9: Bibliography

Acker, James. (2003). The death penalty: An American history. *Contemporary Justice Review*, 6(2), 169–86.

Acker, James. (2008). Be careful what you ask for: Lessons from New York's recent experience with capital punishment. *Vermont Law Review*, 32(4), 683–763.

Adler, Roy. (2008). Saving innocent lives through capital punishment: The evidence for deterrence. *The Journal of the Institute for the Advancement of Criminal Justice*, 2, 67–72.

Alarcon, Arthur and Mitchell, Paula. (2011). Executing the will of the voters? A roadmap to mend or end the California legislature's multi-billion-dollar death penalty debacle. *Loyola of Los Angeles Law Review*, 44(0), 41–224.

Altindag, Duha. (2012). Crime and unemployment: Evidence from Europe. *International Review of Law and Economics*, 32(1), 145–57.

American Civil Liberties Union (2012). The case against the death penalty. Unpublished article. Retrieved from https://www.aclu.org/print/capital-punishment/case-against-death-penalty

Andresen, Martin. (2012). Unemployment and crime: A neighborhood level panel data approach. *Social Science Research*, 41(6), 1615–28.

Ardaiz, James. (2008). Prosecutor, judge, witness: My perspective on the death penalty. *The Journal of the Institute for the Advancement of Criminal Justice*, 2, 73–78.

Baicker, Katherine. (2004). The budgetary repercussions of capital convictions. *Advances in Economic Analysis & Policy*, 4(1), 1311–37.

Baldus, David C., Pulaski, Charles, and Woodworth, George. (1983). Comparative review of death sentences: An empirical study of the Georgia experience. *The Journal of Criminal Law and Criminology*, 74(3), 661–753.

Banner, Stuart. (2002). *The death penalty: an American history*. Boston: Harvard University Press.

Baumgartner, Frank and Dietrich, Anna. (2015, March 17). Most death penalty sentences are overturned. Here's why that matters. *The Washington Post*. Retrieved from https://www.washingtonpost.com/news/monkey-cage/wp/2015/03/17/most-death-penalty-sentences-are-overturned-heres-why-that-matters/?utm_term=.691cf74067fe

Berk, Richard. (2005). New claims about executions and general deterrence. *Journal of Empirical Legal Studies*, 2(2), 303–30.

Berry, William and Feldman, Stanley. (1985). *Multiple regression in practice*. London: Sage Publications.

Black's Law Dictionary (8th ed.). (2004). St. Paul, MN: Thomson & West.

Black's Law Dictionary (9th ed.). (2009). St. Paul, MN: Thomson & West.

Bright, Stephen. (2000). Elected judges and the death penalty in Texas: Why full habeas corpus review by independent federal judges is indispensable to protecting constitutional rights. *Texas Law Review*, 78, 1805–32.

Campbell, Ward. (2008). Exoneration inflation: Justice Scalia's concurrence in *Kansas v. Marsh. The Journal of the Institute for the Advancement of Criminal Justice*, 2, 49–63. Retrieved from https://www.cjlf.org/files/CampbellExonerationInflation2008.pdf

Civic Federation, The. (1997). *Evaluating local government financial heath: Financial indicators for Cook, DuPage, Kane, Lake, McHenry, & Will counties*. Executive Summary. Retrieved from http://civicfed.org/sites/default/files/civicfed_165.pdf

Cook, Phillip. (2009). Potential savings from abolition of the death penalty in North Carolina. *American Law and Economics Review*. Retrieved from http://www.deathpenalty-info.org/documents/CookCostRpt.pdf

Cook, Phillip; Slawson, Donna; and Gries, Lori. (1993). *The costs of processing murder cases in North Carolina*. Terry Sanford Institute of Public Policy Paper. Duke University, Raleigh, NC. Retrieved from http://www.deathpenaltyinfo.org/northcarolina.pdf

Cordner, Gary. (1989). Police agency size and investigative effectiveness. *Journal of Criminal Justice*, *17*(3), 145–55.

Death Penalty Information Center (DPIC). (2012). *The death penalty in 2012: Year-end report*. Retrieved from http://www.deathpenaltyinfo.org

Death Penalty Information Center (DPIC). (2017). *Facts about the death penalty*. Retrieved from http://www.deathpenaltyinfo.org

Dezhbakhsh, Hashem & Shepherd, Joanna. (2003). The deterrent effect of capital punishment: Evidence from a "judicial experiment." *American Law & Economics Review*, *5*(2), 344–76.

Dieter, Richard. (1994). What politicians don't say about the high cost of the death penalty. *Feminist & Nonviolent Studies*. Retrieved from http://www.fnsa.org/v1n1/dieter.html

Dieter, Richard. (2009). Smart on crime: Reconsidering the death penalty in a time of economic crisis. *Death Penalty Information Center*. Retrieved from www.deathpenaltyinfo. org

Farnworth, Margaret; Longmire, Dennis; and West, Vincent. (1998). College students' views on criminal justice. *Journal of Criminal Justice Education*, *9*(1), 39–57.

Flavin, Patrick. (2012). Income inequality and policy representation in the American states. *American Politics Research*, *40*(29), 29–59.

Forsberg, Mary. (2005). *Money for nothing? The financial cost of New Jersey's death penalty*. New Jersey Policy Perspective. Unpublished paper. Retrieved from http://www.njpp. org/rpt_moneyfornothing.html

Fuhrman, Mark. (2003). *Death and justice: an exposé of Oklahoma's death row machine*. New York: HarperCollins.

Garland, David. (2007). The peculiar forms of American capital punishment. *Social Research*, *74*(2), 435–64.

Garland, David. (2010). *Peculiar institution: America's death penalty in an age of abolition*. Cambridge, MA: The Belknap Press of Harvard University Press.

Gershowitz, Adam. (2009). *Statewide capital punishment: The case for eliminating counties' role in the death penalty*. Unpublished manuscript. Retrieved from http://works.bepress. com/adam_gershowitz/5

Goldberg, Guy and Bunn, Gena. (2000). Balancing fairness and finality: A comprehensive review of the Texas death penalty. *Texas Review of Law & Politics*, *5*(1), 49–148.

Gradess, Jonathan. (2008). *Testimony before the Maryland commission on capital punishment*. Paper presented to the Maryland Criminal Jurisprudence Committee, Annapolis, Maryland. Retrieved from http://www.deathpenaltyinfo.org/MDCommission FinalReport. pdf

Innocence Project, The. (2009). *The innocent and the death penalty*. Retrieved from https:// www.innocenceproject.org/the-innocent-and-the-death-penalty

Johnson, David. (2011). American capital punishment in comparative perspective. *Law & Society Inquiry*, *36*(4), 1033–61.

Kansas Judicial Council. (2014). *Report of the Judicial Council Death Penalty Advisory Committee*. Retrieved from https://deathpenaltyinfo.org/documents/KSCost2014.pdf

Larranaga, Mark. (2004). Washington's death penalty system: A review of the costs, length and results of capital cases in Washington State. Seattle, WA: *Washington Death Penalty Assistance Center*. Retrieved from http://www.abolishdeathpenalty.org/ PDF/WAStateDeathPenaltyCosts.pdf

Lentol, Joseph; Weinstein, Helene; and Aubry, Jeffrion. (2005). *The death penalty in New York: A report on five public hearings on the death penalty in New York conducted by the Assembly Standing Committees on Codes, Judiciary and Correction*, December 15, 2004-February 11, 2005. New York State Assembly.

Marshall, Justice Thurgood. (1972). *Thurgood Marshall concurrence in* Furman v. Georgia. Retrieved from http://documents.routledge-interactive.s3.amazonaws.com/9780415506434/document9.pdf

Mello, Michael. (2008). Certain blood for uncertain reasons: A love letter to the Vermont legislator on not reinstating capital punishment. *Vermont Law Review, 32*(4), 765–876.

Nagin, Daniel and Pepper, John. (2012). *Deterrence and the death penalty*. Committee on Law and Justice at the National Research Council.

Nasaw, Daniel. (2012, March 8). Texas execution: How much is death worth? *BBC News Magazine*. Retrieved from http://www.bbc.co.uk/news/magazine-17210285

National Research Council. (2004). *Fairness and effectiveness in policing: The evidence*. Washington, D.C.: The National Academies Press.

Nutt, Paul. (2005). Comparing public and private decision-making factors. *Journal of Public Administration Research and Theory, 16*(2), 289–318.

Oka, Tosihiro. (2003). Effectiveness and limitations of cost-benefit analysis in policy. Appraisal. *Government Auditing Review, 10*, 17–28.

Oregon Health Authority. (2017). *Death with Dignity Act: Frequently asked questions*. Retrieved from https://www.oregon.gov/oha/PH/PROVIDERPARTNERRESOURCES/EVALUATIONRESEARCH/DEATHWITHDIGNITYACT/Pages/faqs.aspx#whatis

Paternoster, Raymond. (1984). Prosecutorial discretion in requesting the death penalty: A case of victim-based racial discrimination. *Law & Society Review, 18*(3), 437–78.

Phillips, Julie Anne and Land, Kenneth. (2012). The link between unemployment and crime rate fluctuations: An analysis at the county, state, and national levels. *Social Science Research, 41*(3), 681–94.

Portney, Paul. (2008). Benefit-cost analysis: The concise encyclopedia of economics. Retrieved from http://www.econlib.org/library/Enc/BenefitCostAnalysis.html

Ren, Ling; Zhao, Jihong; and Lovrich, Nicholas. (2008). Liberal verses conservative public policies on crime: What was the comparative track record during the 1990s? *Journal of Criminal Justice, 36*(4), 316–25.

Roman, John. (2004). Can cost-benefit analysis answer criminal justice policy questions, and if so, how? *Journal of Contemporary Criminal Justice, 20*(3), 257–75.

Saubermann, Jennifer and Spangenberg, Robert. (2006). *State and county expenditures for indigent defense services in fiscal year 2005*. West Newton, MA: Spangenberg Group. Retrieved from http://www.americanbar.org/content/dam/aba/administrative/ legal_aid_indigent_defendants/ls_sclaid_def_final_reportfy_2005_expenditure_report.auth-checkdam.pdf

Sharp, Susan. (2005). *Hidden victims: The effects of the death penalty on families of the accused.* New Jersey: Rutgers University Press.

Shoesmith, Ben. (2011). An examination of the impact of police expenditures on arrest rates. *Explorations, 7*, 106–17.

Sorenson, Jonathan and Pilgrim, Rocky. (2006). *Lethal injection: Capital punishment in Texas during the modern era.* Austin: University of Texas Press.

Spangenberg, Robert and Walsh, Elizabeth. (1989). Capital punishment of life in prison: Some cost considerations. *Loyola of Los Angeles Law Review, 23*(1), 45–58.

Spangenberg Group. (1993, March). *A study of representation in capital cases in Texas.* Report to the Texas Bar Foundation. Retrieved from https://capitalpunishmentincontext.org/files/resources/representation/Spangenberg%20Group%202.pdf

Texas Appleseed Fair Defense Project. (2000). *Fair defense report: Analysis of indigent defense practices in Texas. Austin, TX:* Texas Appleseed. Retrieved from www.appleseeds.net/tx

Texas Department of Criminal Justice (TDCJ). (2014). Death row information. Retrieved from http://www.tdcj.state.tx.us/death_row/index.html

Texas Task Force on Indigent Defense. (2008). *Upholding the Constitution: 2008 Annual Report.* Retrieved from http://www.txcourts.gov/tfid/pdf/FY08 AnnualReport TFID.pdf

Thomson, Ernie. (1999). Effects of an execution on homicides in California. *Homicide Studies, 3*(2), 129–50.

Totten, Gregory. (2008). The solemnity of the district attorney's decision to seek death. *The Journal of the Institute for the Advancement of Criminal Justice, 2*, 45–8.

Tucker, William. (2002, June 21). Yes, the death penalty deters. *Wall Street Journal.* Retrieved from https://www.wsj.com/articles/SB1024617817464476960

Uelmen, Gerald. (1998). The fattest crocodile: Why elected judges can't ignore public opinion. *Criminal Justice, 13*, 5–10.

United Nations. (2006). *Social justice in an open world: The role of the United Nations.* United Nations Publication, New York, NY. Retrieved from http://www.un.org/ esa/socdev/documents/ifsd/SocialJustice.pdf

United States Department of Justice. (2011, October). *The impact of the economic downturn on American police agencies.* A report of the U.S. Department of Justice Office of Community Oriented Policing Services. Retrieved from http://www.ncdsv.org/images/COPS_ImpactOfTheEconomicDownturnOnAmericanPoliceAgencies_10-2011.pdf

United States General Accounting Office. (1989). Limited data available on costs of death sentences. GAO/GGD-89-122. Retrieved from http://www.aclu-md.org/uploaded_files/0000/0378/gao_death_penalty_cost_study.pdf

Vartkessian, Elizabeth. (2012). What one hand giveth, the other taketh away: How future dangerousness corrupts guilty verdicts and produces premature punishment decisions in capital cases. *Pace Law Review, 32*(2), 447–87.

Venetoklis, Takis. (2002). *Public policy evaluation: Introduction to quantitative methodologies.* Government Institute for Economic Research. Retrieved from http://www.vatt.fi/file/vatt_publication_pdf/t90.pdf

Vining, Aidan and Weimer, David. (2009). General issues concerning the application of benefit-cost analysis to social policy. *Journal of Cost Benefit Analysis, 1*(1), 1–38.

Woodward, Rich. (2009). *Testimony on the cost of the death penalty.* Paper presented to the Texas Criminal Jurisprudence Committee, Subcommittee on Capital Punishment, Austin, Texas.

Yearwood, Douglas and Koinis, Gerry. (2012). Revisiting property crime and economic conditions: An exploratory study to identify predictive indicators beyond unemployment rates. *The Social Science Journal, 48*(1), 145–58.

Section 10: Resources

Unit 1: Summary

Capital punishment is the trial process of a person accused of a capital crime. There are eight stages to the capital punishment process: investigation, indictment, pretrial, trial, sentencing, appeals, clemency, and execution. National and international laws and agreements are in place in relation to capital punishment. There are many controversies related to capital punishment, including whether the death penalty is a violation of human rights. The main decision-makers in the capital punishment process are policy-makers who determine capital punishment legislation, the capital murder trial defendant, the team of defense lawyers, the prosecution team, the trial judge, and the jury. Each of these groups has costs of a capital trial, while many of the groups have some benefits to the trial. The inefficiencies include multiple arguments from the opponents and defenders of capital punishment.

Unit 2: Key concepts

Aggravating circumstances: Facts that increase the accused person's blame for the criminal act.

Appeals stage: The automatic process that occurs when the defendant's trial receives a conviction (verdict of guilty) and the sentence of death.

Bond hearing: A judicial process to determine whether to allow the person charged with a crime to pay for a bond allowing the person to be free until the trial or to hold the person without a bond.

Capital: Resources used in the production of goods and services, including machinery, equipment, buildings, and vehicles.

Capital eligible: When the specific determinants are present so that the defendant may be given the death penalty.

Capital murder: A charge of murder for which the death penalty may be imposed.

Capital offense: A criminal charge punishable by the death penalty.

Capital punishment: The legal killing of a person as punishment for a capital offense.

Capital trial: The process of trying a person for a capital offense and, if convicting, administering the death penalty.

Certiorari: A document issued by an appellate court that states that they intend to review certain cases.

Clemency stage: The stage of a capital murder trial in which the governor of a state grants a temporary or permanent halt to the execution of a defendant given the death penalty.

Commutation: A form of clemency (leniency) in which a reduced sentence is imposed.

Death penalty: The punishment of execution given to a person who has been convicted of a capital offense by a court of law, although there may be reasons that the punishment is never administered.

Death row: The area in the prison system where defendants under the sentence of death live while they await the appeal trial or execution.

Death-qualifying jury: A jury made up of members in which each juror must certify that they are able to make a decision to accept a sentence of the death penalty or life without parole as possible punishments.

Defendant: A person accused of a crime in a court of law.

Due process of law (or due process): The established rules and principles in legal proceedings in order to protect and enforce private rights.

Economic efficiency: The highest value to society from resource allocation found by analyzing the costs and benefits associated with the decision.

Execution: The carrying out of the death penalty by lethal injection, gas, electrocution, hanging, or firing squad.

Extradition process: The act of law enforcement crossing into another region to bring an accused person back to stand trial in the area in which they have been charged with a capital murder.

Guilt phase: The stage of a capital murder trial when the jury must decide whether a person is guilty "beyond a reasonable doubt."

Indictment stage: The stage of a capital murder trial that encompasses the guilt phase of the bifurcated (two-stage) trial process in which the court gathers a group of citizens to be members of the jury.

Indigent: The state of lacking the funds to bear the financial burden of defense costs.

Inefficiency: When a choice is made that does not maximize net benefit (total benefit minus total cost).

Investigation stage: The stage of a capital murder trial in which law enforcement gathers evidence surrounding the crime.

Isolation or incapacitation: The act of isolating a person who has been charged with a capital murder.

Life without parole: A sentence of life imprisonment.

Marginal benefit (MB): The additional benefit from the last unit of good or service consumed or used or from the last unit of choice.

Marginal cost (MC): The additional cost of the last unit of production or choice of action.

Mitigating circumstances: Evidence that the defense provides during the sentencing phase to explain why the accused person should not receive the death penalty.

Multiple regression: The use of statistical analysis to predict the value of one dependent variable based on the values of two or more independent variables.

Opportunity cost: What must be given up to get something else.

Partial equilibrium analysis: The analysis of only a part of an economic situation.

Penalty trial: The state of a capital murder trial in which the jury reviews the evidence of aggravating and mitigating circumstances to determine whether the punishment for the capital offense will be the death penalty or life without parole.

Pre-trial stage: The stage of the capital murder trial in which the judge decides whether to dismiss the case against the accused person.

Public policy: The laws and regulations created to safeguard society.

Sentencing stage or punishment stage: The stage in the capital murder trial when the verdict of the trial is announced to the defendant.

Trial stage: The stage in the capital murder process in which the judge has decided the accused person (now called the defendant) should be tried on capital murder charges and the trial begins.

Unit 3: Review questions

1. How are capital punishment and the death penalty different?

2. What are the stages of a capital trial?

3. At what stage of a capital trial is the accused person called a defendant?

4. How have past capital trials informed later trials?

5. What laws are in place in the United States related to capital punishment?

6. What international laws and agreements are in place related to capital punishment?

7. Name some of the controversies involved in capital punishment.

8. Who are the decision-makers involved in a capital trial and what are their costs and benefits in regard to having a capital trial?

9. Name some of the inefficiencies related to capital punishment.

Unit 4: Recommended readings

Bedau, Hugo Adam. (1982). *The death penalty in America.* Oxford: Oxford University Press.

Sarat, Austin. (2001). *The killing state: Capital punishment in law, politics, and culture.* New York: Oxford University Press.

Liang, Bin and Lu, Hong. (2016). *The death penalty in China.* New York: Columbia University Press.

Mandery, Evan. (2012). *Capital punishment in America: A balanced examination.* Sudbury: Jones and Bartlett Learning.

Zimring, Franklin. (2003). *The contradictions of American capital punishment.* Oxford: Oxford University Press.

Unit 5: Web links

International Commission Against the Death Penalty: http://www.icomdp.org/links/
United States Supreme Court rulings that concern the death penalty: https://www.law.
cornell.edu/wex/death_penalty

Unit 6: Econometric analysis: The cost of capital punishment in Texas

This section is provided in online textbook supplements. The eResources can be found
at: www.routledge.com/9781138500167

3

Economics of violence against women
Contributor: Dr. Sarah Feuerbacher

■ Section 1: Introduction to the economics of violence against women

Unit 1: General introduction to violence against women

While laws prohibiting violence against women exist in most countries, there are a number of nations, mainly in Africa and the Middle East, with little or no legislation. Legal documents cannot of themselves protect women, because protection requires communication and resources at the family, neighborhood, societal, and national level. Gender-based violence manifests itself in a number of ways, including physically, emotionally, verbally, sexually, and financially. The costs of preventing violence against women are primarily monetary, and include the cost of creating legislation, providing law enforcement, educating people about violence against women, and providing social services to women who are in danger. The benefits of preventing violence against women include preventing physical injury and mental anguish, decreasing medical costs and legal fees, and protecting women's well-being, financial situations, and labor productivity. The perspectives provide a glimpse into situations that involve violence against women. Matthew Breiding et al. (2014) estimates that 27.3% of women have experienced contact sexual violence (rape, being made to penetrate, sexual coercion, or unwanted sexual contact), physical violence, or stalking by an intimate partner during their lifetimes and have experienced at least one measured negative impact related to these or other forms of violence (unwanted noncontact sexual experiences, psychological aggression, or control of reproductive or sexual health) experienced in that relationship.

Family is the most violent organization outside the police and military. The World Health Organization (WHO) (2016) estimates that 35% (one in three) women have experienced physical or sexual violence at some time in their lives. The largest portion (85%) of this violence is from husbands or boyfriends (who are referred to as intimate partners), while another 10% is perpetrated by family members and acquaintances. The first step to eliminate this threat to families and society is to gain an understanding of violence against women and its origin. The assumption is that the target is to decrease all types of violence against women by 1) identifying them, 2) eliminating factors that negatively affect them, and 3) increasing factors that protect them. With this policy, it is necessary to determine reasonable goals, current resources in place that are or are not being used, and areas lacking necessary resources.

Domestic violence, gender-based violence, and intimate partner violence are all names for violence against women. The violence may include elements of extreme and often deadly threat, emotional abuse, isolation, financial abuse and control, sexual abuse, using children to gain control, and blame. It is not only detrimental to the female victim and families, but also to local, state, and national economies, as the violence affects aspects of health care, law enforcement, social services, and legislation.

This textbook provides the theoretic foundation for an understanding of the dynamics of decisions that lead to violence against women and keep them trapped in violent situations. In addition, analytic tools are presented for economic research.

Unit 2: Survivor perspective

Hannah K. Schauer Galli, director, actor, designer

Hannah Schauer Galli is a theatre practitioner and instructor in Hawaii. She specializes in directing and costume construction. She has been fortunate to work with teachers from around the globe and travel to learn from teachers in several countries. She holds an MFA in theatre directing and a BA in communications. For the past 19 years, she has served as the costume shop manager for the University of Hawaii and directed and performed for many theatres in the area.

Once upon a time a woman made a choice to trust someone – a buddy, the brother of a friend, someone to talk to, someone in need. Then came an evening and a couple of drinks – TWO drinks – one beer and one whisky . . . then the buddy kissing, hugging, groping, grabbing in the parking lot. I am pushing him off and running to my truck, trying to get my key in the door. I start to drive home and feel funny; my brain is rattling and I can't see straight. I head to my office where I lock the door and pass out.

I wake up in the early hours in my office, head home, and go to bed. My husband kisses me goodbye as he heads to work with an odd look on his face. When I wake up again, I look in the mirror to find handprints and bruises on my neck and torso. There is a phone call to my husband and then the doctors' examination . . .

Despite my protests, the guy comes to my workplace, grabs me, kisses me in front of my co-workers, and says things: "You are mine" and "You can't throw me away." He leaves but shows up later at an event, where my co-workers block him and escort me out. Now multiple people know and it is a small town and I am scared to even write this down.

I often work late, and when our team finishes, I sit and complete my notes. As I approach the parking lot I see his truck parked beside mine. It is nearly midnight – two hours after our normal finishing time – and I know he is waiting for me. (I ask myself now why I didn't call the police?) I finally find someone to walk me to my truck and stand in front of his as I drive away. Five miles later, he pulls up next to me and yells, "I just want to talk to you." I take an illegal turn, drive fast, pull into another neighborhood, and wait in the dark for 30 minutes before driving home. He knows where I live.

Food and gifts start arriving at my office . . . and then stop for a time. I don't hear from him. Then, texts start coming in. Nasty things I won't repeat. Then phone calls and messages. I finally tell my husband how bad things have gotten and that I was scared for my husband's life. He convinces me to call the police. My voicemail is full and I can't erase the messages in case I need them in court.

I go the police station's domestic violence department where I am allowed no support beyond the assigned counselor. "I'm strong," I think to myself, "I've got this" and then end up playing with children's puzzles to keep my mind off of the problem. I have to call my colleague, the guy's sister, to get his address so that he could be served the paperwork if the judge granted my temporary restraining order request.

We go to court: First so the judge can grant my very temporary restraining order and then Family Court where I have to sit alone again in a holding area without my husband and friend who came to testify. I sit and watch mostly women crying. The advocates have their hands full and I end up reaching out my hands and arms and voice to the women who tell me, "I don't want to take his kids away from him. He loves them," and "He only hit me when the kids weren't around," and "He really only got mad when I forgot to pick up beer." The woman sitting behind us had a black eye and wouldn't talk to anyone. My problem suddenly seems so small. I move around the room assuring people as their stories pour out: "You've got this." "Be strong." "You're doing the right thing." By the time I am called in, I am a mess. I am lucky; the guy didn't show up and the judge grants my request: ten years, no contact, 300 yards from my residence, 100 yards from any of my workplaces. In hindsight, I should have gotten a lawyer. I have to tell my co-workers, the campus police, and my boss about the restraining order, then try to find a photo on Facebook to show them what he looks like.

We are moving. I call the police station to let them know my new address, but they tell me if I want to change it, I have to go back to court and have him served again. New house and new locations for the baseball bats . . .

Section 2: Fundamentals of violence against women

First, foundational definitions within the area of violence against women will be reviewed. Then the categories of violence against women will be enumerated, along with acts of violence within each category.

Unit 1: Important violence against women terms

According to the WHO (2016), **domestic violence** is "any act of gender-based violence that results in, or is likely to result in, physical, sexual or mental harm or suffering to women, including threats of such acts, coercion or arbitrary deprivation of liberty, whether occurring in public or in private life." The WHO defines **intimate partner violence** as "behavior by a partner or ex-partner that causes physical, psychological or sexual harm to women." These two definitions focus on the woman knowing the perpetrator of the violence. An **intimate partner** is a person who is in a physical, sexual, or emotional relationship with another person. For the purpose of this textbook, the term **perpetrator** means the person who has knowingly and wilfully committed an action that is harmful to another person and the term **victim** is used to designate the person who has been directly harmed by the actions of the perpetrator.

Intimate partner violence is a series of physical and nonphysical behaviors used over time to scare, harm, and ultimately control a partner. It is always progressive and can become so severe that it may lead to the death of the victim. Patricia Tjaden and Nancy Thoennes (2000) report that one in four women in the United States experience domestic violence in their lifetimes. In addition, the Centers for Disease Control (2003, April) states that two million injuries and 1,300 deaths are caused each year as a result of domestic violence in the United States. Research by Rose Fife and Sarina Schrager (2012) shows that the ". . .best estimates are that at least 20–30% of all females in the United States will be abused at some point during their lives." Matthew Breiding et al. (2014) provide that age matters, as over 70% of females who were victims of sexual violence, physical violence, or stalking by an intimate partner were below the age of 25, and 23% were below the age of 18.

Within the area of violence against women, this chapter will concentrate on three main areas: Prevalence, severity, and impact. These three characteristics will lend understanding, to some degree, of the breadth of the problems being faced and assist in ascertaining areas where economic decisions may come into play.

The National Institute of Mental Health (NIH) defines **prevalence** as "the proportion of a population who have (or had) a specific characteristic in a given time period." In terms of violence against women, the frequency of a certain type of violence or violence against a certain group of women can be assessed by age, race, or some other characteristic. In addition, violence against women is rarely a single event, but rather a series of violent acts by the perpetrator of violence over time that are used to control the victim. For example, the Center for Disease Control (CDC, 2012) in the United States reported that more than 27% of women and 11% of men have experienced contact sexual violence, physical violence, and/ or stalking by an intimate partner in their lifetime and have experienced an intimate partner violence-related impact. Prevalence asks how often violence against women happens.

In the violence against women and medical literature, **severity** is a measure of seriousness or harshness. Linda Marshall (1992) developed a 46-item scale called the Severity of Violence Against Women Scales (SVAWS) that includes the severity of physical aggression women have suffered at the hands of male partners. The scale attempts to illustrate the psychological effects of intimate partner violence. Medical professionals note that domestic violence is progressive and sometimes leads to the death of the victim. Severity asks how serious or harsh is the abuse that women suffer.

Impact refers to the effects of violence against women on quality of life. This may be the impact of violence on areas such as women's health, earning potential, and advancement. Impact could also be extended to the women's children, family members, friends, co-workers, and even employers.

Unit 2: Categories of violence against women

It is difficult, but important, to categorize the types, prevalence, severity, and impact of violence against women. Denise Hines and Kathleen Malley-Morrison (2004) state that the definitions of abuse depend upon the assumptions of "causes, effects, motivations, frequency, and intensity" and that the definitions influence whether victims of abuse "within domestic settings will receive interventions from the legal, medical, and/or social services communities." In light of this, this chapter focuses on six categories of violence against women: Physical, verbal, emotional, sexual, economic, and other categories that somehow differ. Other methods of categorizing violence against women exist. Researchers must be aware that these types of violence often happen in combination with each other and any analysis and reporting for the purpose of policy-making must therefore take care to look at the total picture and not just part of it.

Physical violence means the actions of a perpetrator inflicting injury to the victim's body. Examples include hitting with a body part or another object, kicking, grabbing, strangling, pushing, stabbing, stoning, flogging, shooting, burning, use of physical restraints, forced exposure to severe weather, murder, inappropriate use of medicine or drugs, force-feeding, prevention from seeking medical care and withholding access to resources needed to maintain health. **Physical coercion** involves the perpetrator inflicting pain or injury on the victim to reinforce the credibility of the perpetrator's threat. **Battering** is when the perpetrator repeatedly strikes the victim. **Terroristic violence** is when the perpetrator uses systematic, serious, and frequent beatings to subjugate the victim (Michael Johnson, 1995). **Battered woman syndrome** comes from the effects of severe and intermittent abuse and is similar to post-traumatic stress disorder (PTSD) (Donald Dutton and Susan Painter, 1993).

According to Matthew Breiding et al. (2014), almost a quarter of the women in their study had experienced physical violence during their lifetimes. This is in line with national estimates. Of the groups of women who reported having experienced physical violence by an intimate partner during their lifetimes, the highest prevalence was among American Indian/Alaska Native women (51.7%), multiracial women (51.3%), non-Hispanic black women (41.2%), non-Hispanic white women (30.5%), Hispanic women (29.7%), and Asian or Pacific Islander women (15.3%).

Verbal violence occurs when the perpetrator uses written or spoken words or sounds to abuse a victim by causing fear or decreasing self-esteem. Some forms of verbal abuse include shouting, arguing, interrupting, and use of words to demean or intimidate. The aggressor may bring up the person's past mistakes, express distrust, call the person names, or use abusive language.

Emotional or **psychological violence** is the perpetrator's use of verbal or nonverbal actions to inflict injury on the victim's emotional state. Threats of harm, insults, harassment, isolation, not speaking to a person, excessive possessiveness, threats of abandonment, destruction of a person's property or pets, and manipulation for control or for sex are all types of emotional abuse.

Stalking occurs when a perpetrator repeatedly harasses a person through tactics such as approaching them at home or work; following, watching, calling, writing to, texting, or emailing them; spying upon them; threatening them or implying threats of harm or murder; or a combination of these things. Research by T.K. Logan and Robert Walker (2010) on stalking by intimate partners finds a high correlation across studies between partner stalking and sexual assault. Judith McFarlane et al. (1999) finds that attempted and successful **femicide**, which is the killing of a female, is associated with intimate partner physical assault and stalking. **Spiritual violence** is included in emotional violence because it involves prohibiting a person from following their religious beliefs, belittling someone for their beliefs, or controlling a person through their beliefs.

Estimates of prevalence from Matthew Breiding et al. (2014) state that 60.8% of women in their study were stalked by current or former intimate partners, 24.9% by acquaintances, 16.2% by strangers, and 6.2% by a family member. In addition, almost half of the women in the study had experienced some type of psychological aggression by an intimate partner at some point in their lives. They estimated that 15.2% or 18.3 million women had faced a stalking situation, with 9.2% of that total involving being stalked by an intimate partner. The *National Intimate Partner and Sexual Violence Survey* (Centers for Disease Control, 2012) estimated that stalking has been experienced by one in six women at some point during their lifetimes.

Sexual violence is when a person is forced or coerced by a perpetrator to take part in sexual activity without their consent. This type of violence has components of both physical and emotional violence and may take many forms. A few examples of sexual violence include forcing a person to perform degrading sexual actions, spying on a person for sexual purposes, and purposefully infecting another person with sexually-transmitted disease. The U.S. Department of Justice's Federal Bureau of Investigations (2013) defines **rape** as "carnal knowledge of a female forcibly and against her will." Article 7 of the U.N Rome Statute of the International Criminal Court (2000) further defines rape as, ". . .penetration, however slight, of any part of the body of the victim or of the perpetrator with a sexual organ . . . committed by force, or by threat of force or coercion, or abuse of power. . ." **Acquaintance rape**

happens when a perpetrator who is known to the victim forces the victim to have sexual intercourse. **Date rape** is a type of acquaintance rape in which the victim is raped at the time the perpetrator is escorting the victim. **Marital rape** is when a husband or wife forces their spouse to have sexual intercourse. **Stranger rape** occurs when a person who is not known to the victim forces the victim to have sexual intercourse. **Sexual harassment** occurs when a person is forced or coerced to listen to or see unwanted sexual comments or invitations or to view unsolicited sexual images in a professional or social setting. Examples include vulgar comments, sexting, and attempting to undermine a person's sexuality. **Sexual coercion** is when a person pressures, deceives, or forces another person to endure undesired touch or sex. Examples include forced sexual intercourse, unwanted fondling, forced participation in pornographic photos or movies, and forced prostitution. **Sex trafficking** is the commercial sexual exploitation of the victim brought about by the perpetrator's use of force, fraud, or coercion.

According to the 2010–12 National Intimate Partner and Sexual Violence Survey, sexual violence happens to one in three women and nearly one in six men during their lifetimes. In addition, the survey reports that nearly 23 million women and 1.7 million men have experienced rape or attempted rape, while it is estimated that 6.8 million men were made to penetrate another person in their lifetime. The Breiding study (Matthew Breiding et al., 2014) reported that women overwhelmingly reported experiencing sexual violence (99.0%) and other sexual violence (94.7%) from men. It is interesting to note that men reported primarily being raped by other men (79.3%) but reported a mix of female and male perpetrators with other types of sexual violence. An estimated 19.3% of women in the study reported being raped (8.8% by intimate partners) and 43.9% reported other types of sexual violence in their lifetimes (15.8% by intimate partners). Sexual coercion was experienced by 12.5% of women in the study and more than one in four women (27.3%) experienced unwanted sexual contact. The study estimates that the highest prevalence of rape is against multiracial women (32.3%), followed by American Indian/Alaska Native women (27.5%), non-Hispanic black women (21.2%), non-Hispanic white women (20.5%), and Hispanic women (13.6%). Other sexual violence was experienced at higher rates with 64.1% of multiracial women, 55.0% of American Indian/Alaska Native women, 46.9% of non-Hispanic white women, 38.2% of non-Hispanic black women, 35.6% of Hispanic women, and 31.9% of Asian or Pacific Islander women experiencing sexual violence other than rape in their lifetimes. The majority of women in the study knew their perpetrators. An estimated 46.7% of female rape victims reported rape by an acquaintance.

Financial violence, also called **economic** or **material violence**, occurs when the perpetrator creates an economic crisis for the disadvantaged victim. The abuser uses the victim's financial situation as a method of control. This type of abuse occurs when a person uses their influence to illegally or improperly use the victim's money, property, or assets or uses the resource without the person's consent. The perpetrator may take control of the earned and unearned income of the victim, get the person fired so they do not have income, steal property or assets, forbid the victim from getting a job or going to school, or force the person to work outside the home against their will. The National Task Force to End Sexual and Domestic Violence Against Women (2005) reports that 25–50% of women lose jobs due to domestic violence, which leads to an estimated two million workdays each year (Nancy Salamone, 2010). This can be a major problem since victims of violence often report lack of income as a reason for remaining in abusive relationships. According to the U.S. Department of Justice Office on Violence Against Women (2017), economic abuse occurs across all socioeconomic levels.

There are other types of violence against women not included in the five categories listed above. Culture has a lot to do with how society values a woman, especially as it relates to the rights of the woman's family before she marries and the rights of her husband after she marries. In some cultures, wife-beating is prevalent and a woman may be killed if her family or her husband's family suspects she has had sex before marriage or outside of the marriage. Some extreme examples are when a family stones a woman to death, when a husband throws acid on a woman to make her abhorrent to another suitor, and the practice of sati, in which a woman is thrown on her husband's funeral pyre.

Interspersed among the five main types of violence against women are other abuses that are difficult to categorize. Research is needed on each abuse as careful definitions are needed for policy-making. Cultural violence occurs when a person is harmed due to the practices that are part of their culture, religion, or tradition and includes such acts as honor killings (homicide of a family member due to dishonoring family), dowry violence (violence inflicted on a bride to extort further funds from the family), forced marriage, and marry-your-rapist laws. Violence to a woman's body may include female genital mutilation, obstetric violence including forced sterilization or abortion, abuse of medicine, and coercive use of contraceptives. Neglect can be physical, medical, or emotional and occurs when the person responsible for providing physical, medical, or emotional care withholds that care.

Other types of violence against women will be discussed in later chapters. In Chapter 6, the discussion on child abuse will include female infanticide, prenatal sex selection, and child marriage. Rape as a weapon of war will be included in the discussion of hate in Chapter 8.

Section 3: Violence against women as a violation of human rights

Amartya Sen (1998) speaks of the "entitlements of every human being" to basic human rights. Human rights for women include the right to live in safety, to healthy childbearing, and to earn a living. However, not all societies believe that women have the right to be free from abuse, and certain cultures deem it the husband's right to discipline his wife. Many national and international agreements exist to promote human rights for women and an end to violence against women.

Unit 1: National agreements

The main legislation related to violence against women in the United States is the Violence Against Women Act (VAWA) of 1994. This act authorized the creation of the National Domestic Violence Hotline, which began taking calls in February, 1996. The act was modified in 2002 to include the "Rape Shield Law," with the goal of protecting female victims of violence by shielding their past sexual conduct from being used during rape trials. This act authorized the creation of the National Teen Dating Abuse Helpline in February, 2007, and the first dating abuse texting service in September, 2011.

The Family Violence Prevention and Services Act was created in 1984 to provide shelter and resources for women and children of domestic violence. This act provides funding for national, state, and community programs, which include domestic violence coalitions and the National Domestic Violence Hotline through the Domestic Violence Resource Network.

The 1990 Clery Act (the Jeanne Clery Disclosure of Campus Security Policy and Campus Crime Statistics Act) is a federal law that requires universities to report school safety policies (including educational programming, disciplinary policies, and victim rights) and crimes that occur on campus in an Annual Security Report. Under this act, educational administrations must warn their school community when there are known public safety risks on campus. The Clery Act was expanded in 2013 to include the Campus SaVE Act to clarify the colleges' requirements to report, respond, and provide education, and to address incidents of sexual violence.

The U.S. House of Representatives introduced the International Violence against Women Act of 2015 (HR 1340, 114th Congress). This act sought to establish an Office of Global Women's Issues and a senior coordinator for gender equality and women's empowerment in the U.S. Agency for International Development (USAID). The purpose of this act was to create a strategy, practices, and plans for the coordination of government efforts regarding gender initiatives in U.S. foreign policy aimed at preventing and addressing violence against women. The act was referred to the Subcommittee on Africa, Global Health, Global Human Rights and International Organizations on March 20, 2015, but was never enacted.

In 2007, the Senate introduced the Survivor's Empowerment and Economic Security Act (S.1136) and House Bill (H.R. 2395) to help victims of domestic abuse gain economic independence. The act and bill were not enacted. Many of the states in the United States have specific laws addressing non-aggravated and aggravated (with a deadly weapon or with the intent to cause bodily injury) domestic violence and assault.

The United Kingdom has two main pieces of legislation related to violence against women: Section 76 of the Serious Crime Act of 2015 makes it unlawful to use control or coercive behavior in an intimate or family relationship; the Domestic Violence, Crime and Victims Act of 2004 included provisions for the prevention of domestic violence. The Domestic Violence, Crime and Victims (Amendment) Act of 2012 crafted criminal consequences for causing or allowing the death of a child or vulnerable adult. In addition, Ireland, Scotland, and Wales have all enacted legislation related to domestic abuse and sexual violence.

The majority of countries around the world have legislation to prevent and protect women from violence. However, at the time of writing, there were a number of countries where domestic violence was legal, including Armenia, Burkina Faso, Cameroon, Congo, Ivory Coast, Egypt, Haiti, Iran, Latvia, Lebanon, Lesotho, Niger, Pakistan, Uzbekistan, and Yemen.

Unit 2: International agreements

Countries have worked together to create international agreements to end violence against women. The main treaties, agreements, and declarations come from the United Nations and focus on three areas: Right to life and security of person, right to equality, and right to freedom from torture. The 1948 U.N. Universal Declaration of Human Rights (UDHR) contains many articles related to the rights of women. These include the right to "security of persons" in Article 3, and freedom from "torture or cruel, inhuman or degrading treatment or punishment" in Article 5. The member country's signature on an international covenant is not legally binding and does not necessarily stop abuse.

Article 3 of the 1974 U.N. Declaration on the Protection of Women and Children in Emergency and Armed Conflict requires countries to end "persecution, torture, punitive measures, degrading treatment, and violence" against women and children. The declaration creates criminal penalties for "imprisonment, torture, shooting, mass arrests, collective punishment, destruction of dwellings, and forcible evictions," which would affect women and children to a greater extent.

The U.N. International Covenant on Economic, Social, and Cultural Rights (ICESCR) includes the right to "equal protection under the law and right to the highest standard of physical and mental health." This covenant was adopted in 1966 and entered into force in January 1976.

The U.N. International Covenant on Civil and Political Rights (ICCPR) reaffirms Article 3 of the UDHR, as well as Article 6 (protects the rights to life) and Article 9 (freedom from detention). It was adopted in 1966 and entered into force in 1976.

The U.N. Convention on the Elimination of All Forms of Discrimination against Women (CEDAW) condemned all discrimination against women. It was adopted in 1979 and entered into force in 1981. The CEDAW led to the adoption of U.N. CEDAW General Recommendation 19 in 1993, which declares that gender-based violence is a form of discrimination covered by CEDAW.

The U.N. Convention Against Torture and Other Cruel, Inhuman or Degrading Treatment or Punishment was adopted in 1984 and entered into force in 1987. It prohibits all forms of torture for any reason, including control, coercion, punishment, discrimination, and obtaining information.

The U.N. Commission on the Status of Women (CSW) and the U.N. Economic and Social Council (ECOSOC) succeeded in getting the U.N. Declaration on the Elimination of Violence against Women (DEVAW) adopted without vote in 1993. It does not have binding legal authority. The DEVAW definition of violence against women includes physical, sexual, and psychological violence by family, within the general community, or perpetrated by or condoned by government. It also encourages its members to create programs and training to prevent violence against women and to gather statistics.

The U.N. Optional Protocol to the Convention on the Elimination of All Forms of Discrimination Against Women (OP-CEDAW) created a system to allow women to submit claims of violations of CEDAW and the procedure whereby the CEDAW Committee can investigate "grave or systematic violations of women's rights" within member nations. It was adopted in 1999 and entered into force in 2000.

Unit 3: Controversies

Linda DeRiviere (2008) talks about the revolving door phenomenon in which abused women leave and then return to the violent relationship. Solutions must include removing the female from the abusive situation and providing wraparound support services to help her create a new life outside of the former relationship.

Robert Jenson (2004) describes the connection between pornography and violence against women. Pornography is big business and there is intense pushback when it is talked about in connection with violence against women and sex trafficking. Nancy Crowell and Ann Burgess (1996) discuss the effect of not only pornography, but also television and movies on the "objectification of women" and the "promotion of sexual aggression toward women."

There are many people who do not believe that **marital rape** is possible because they feel that being married means the two individuals have agreed to have sex with each other. There may be many reasons a woman does not want to have sex with her husband, from personal preference to avoiding disease. Marital rape happens when a woman's husband has sex with her without her consent or through coercion.

Common couple violence and women as aggressors in domestic violence are topics that create difficulty for policy-making and enforcement of laws in court. The problem comes during the determination of whether the woman is perpetuating the violence or protecting herself. Common couple violence occurs when both the husband and wife perpetuate violence against each other. Murray Straus and Richard Gelles (1990) determine that women were as likely as men to report hitting a spouse. At this time, it was concluded that the women were defending themselves. Later research found that women were as likely as men to initiate violence. There are no laws that specifically protect men or husbands. Matthew Breiding et al. (2014) finds that 14% of men in their study had experienced severe physical intimate partner violence.

Mandatory arrest laws mean that the police must arrest anyone they suspect of perpetuating the violence when they respond to a call about a domestic disturbance. Meghan Novisky and Robert Peralta (2015) find evidence that women in violent situations may hesitate to call the police because they are concerned about the consequences of that call.

There are some barriers to the prosecution of perpetrators of violence against women. For instance, crime victim laws were enacted to allow traumatized victims to avoid testifying in court. Before being overturned, these laws allowed police to convey the victim's account to a jury. A major hurdle for prosecution is the issue of getting evidence when the victim refuses to testify, testifies with a contradictory fact-pattern more favorable to the assailant, or testifies that she can no longer remember what happened.

Forced marriage occurs when a woman is forced to marry a man against her will. Sonia Frias (2017) looks at forced marriages in Mexican indigenous communities and finds that the marriage occurs due to three main situations: 1) a man is granted marriage to a woman from the family authority, usually the father, 2) the marriage occurs due to threats of physical or sexual violence, and 3) the marriage is forced due to a transgression of a community norm, such as unwed pregnancy. According to the research by Frias and the National Institute of Statistics and Geography's 2016 *National Survey on Dynamics of Household Relationships* (2017), 4.1% of indigenous women were compelled to marry, and another 4.8% were sold into marriage. There may also be the case of marriage by abduction, whereby the perpetrator kidnaps the female and forces her to marry him. In 2017, Lebanon, Jordan, and Tunisia repealed established marry-your-rapist laws which gave the rapist the right to marry the female whom he had raped. Rape as a weapon of war will be discussed in the chapter on the economics of hate.

CHECK YOURSELF BOX: PERSONAL BIASES ABOUT VIOLENCE AGAINST WOMEN

Violence against women is widespread across all socioeconomic, racial, and geographic boundaries. It is possible that this violence is a part of your personal story or the story of someone you know. On the other hand, someone you know may have been falsely accused of violence against a female. Write down your thoughts about violence against women and the background and circumstances that led to those thoughts. It is important to be honest with yourself to see where your biases lie. This is a topic for which experience generates deep-seated biases. What books have you read or what movies have you watched that depict violence against women? What was your reaction to the violence (concern, anger, fear) or did you not notice a personal reaction, or the violence itself? If you are going to study a subject, you must learn what the subject means in your own context. Then you can use this insight to move forward with your research.

Section 4: History of violence against women

Violence against women is chronicled in the some of the earliest writings. Abuse of females stems from a patriarchal cultural value system that is believed by, engaged in, and furthered by both men and women, and which has given men social permission to control women and children for centuries. Aristotle wrote, "The male is by nature superior, and the female inferior." Under Roman law, men were given the right to chastise or even kill their wives in order to hold authority over them. An old Russian Proverb said, "A wife isn't a jug, she won't crack if you hit her ten times." Pulpit advice in the Middle Ages stated, "Men should beat their wives. Wives should kiss the rod that beats them." The phrase "rule of thumb" comes from the law that specified a man could hit his wife with a rod that was the circumference of his thumb, or smaller.

Vivian Fox (2002) states that all three bodies of thought influencing the treatment of women in Western cultures (Judeo–Christianity, Greek philosophy, and Common Law legal code) assumed "patriarchy as natural: that is, male domination stemming from the view of male superiority." Fox's research focused on marital chastisement and rape prior to the eighteenth century and concludes, "In order to achieve and maintain subordination of the female, ideologies have been constructed whereby submissions to patriarchy appear in the nature of things. Ordained by the Gods, supported by the priests, implemented by the law, women came to accept and to psychologically internalize compliance as necessary."

During the eighteenth and nineteenth centuries, advocacy for human rights led to an increase in the understanding of women as citizens capable of taking care of themselves. There are however many cases of the opposite, such as wife-beating being legalized in the United States in 1824 when the Mississippi Supreme Court held that "moderate chastisement" would be allowed in "cases of an emergency" and that the husband would be exempt from prosecution.

Despite advancements in human rights and the many pieces of enacted legislation presented in this chapter, the twenty-first century is still a time of acceptance of "locker-room talk" by men in powerful positions, while one in four women will be physically abused at some point in her lifetime. Currently, between 90 and 95% of reported domestic violence cases involve a woman as the victim, and battering is the major cause of injury to women, resulting in more injuries than auto accidents, muggings, and rapes combined. Violence against women continues to thrive in all classes, races, cultures, ages, and occupations.

Research by James Balthazar (2016) focuses on current trends in the U.S. justice system, including the police, the court system, and the corrections system. Balthazar reviews new technologies for police, such as the use of Touch DNA (which allows investigators to use smaller amounts of DNA in the testing of sexual assault kits (SAKs)), electronic information from social media, and GPS tracking of phone signals. New statutes have expanded the definition and punishment of sexual assault in the court system. Some of these laws include the VAWA and two statutes related to juvenile victims of sexual assault: Audrie's Law and Megan's Law. Innovations that Balthazar notes in the corrections system are the mandatory registration of sex offenders and new approaches to their treatment, including advanced psychological and pharmacological interventions.

Section 5: Meet the violence against women experts

Research in the area of violence against women may follow several different directions. There are a wide range of experts who may assist a researcher in finding published studies and information. Table 3.1 lists some of the experts on violence against women and describes the work they do.

TABLE 3.1 Areas and fields of expertise related to violence against women

Area of expertise	Field of expertise	Description
Research and possible sources of data	Criminal justice	Criminal justice policy related to perpetrators and victims of violence against women.
	Criminology	How criminals use violence as a weapon against women.
	Cultural studies	Provides critical analysis of how power flows, operates, and manifests in cultures, cultural entities, and cultural systems that may affect the safety of women.
	Human rights	The study of national and international law to ensure women safety from violence.
	International issues	Organizations, such as U.N. Entity for Gender Equality and Empowerment (U.N. Women), provide information and resources.
	Medical	Organizations such as World Health Organization (WHO), American Academy of Family Physicians, National Institutes of Mental Health (NIMH), and Center for Disease Control (CDC) that provide statistics and policy recommendations.
	Psychology	Provide emotional assessment and treatment to perpetrators and victims of violence against women.
	Sociology	The effects of human societal norms upon violence against women.
Criminal justice institutions	Law enforcement	Local, state, and federal police who respond to incidents of violence. These provide protection to victims and reporting for legal cases.
	Legal	Law programs and lawyers who focus their practices on dealing with cases and laws regarding gender-based violence.
	Corrections	Prison officials and those with knowledge of incarcerated perpetrators of violence.
	Courts: State and federal	The judicial system responds to cases involving violence against women.
Social services	U.S. Department of Health and Human Services (DHHS)	Provide resources, referrals, and support groups for victims of violence and for perpetuators.
Expert witnesses	Experts in investigations, ballistics, psychology, etc.	Sources of evidence regarding aggravating circumstances for the prosecution.
	Experts in social work, investigations, etc.	Sources of evidence regarding mitigating circumstances for the defense.
Activism	Human rights experts	Knowledge of circumstances surrounding the violation of human rights law.
	Women who have survived domestic violence	Knowledge of the circumstances surrounding violence against women.
Medical	Medical practitioners	Provide assessment and treatment for physical and sexual violence.

TABLE 3.2   Nonprofit organizations working with violence against women

Information and programming	National Resource Center on Domestic Violence (NRCDV), National Coalition against Domestic Violence (NCADV), National Domestic Violence Hotline in Austin, Family Violence Prevention Fund, National Violence Against Women Prevention Research Center, Joyful Heart Foundation, No More, Men Can Stop Rape, National Network to End Domestic Violence, endabuse.org, Allstate Foundation Domestic Violence Program
Shelter, safe houses	Covenant House, Genesis Women's Shelter in Dallas, Texas
Survivor support groups	Victim's Circle of Support

In addition, many nonprofit organizations are involved in issues of violence against women. These organizations provide information, programming, shelter for female victims of violence and their children, and survivor support groups. Table 3.2 presents some of the nonprofit organizations involved in work regarding violence against women.

There are a number of national and international databases regarding violence against women, each with its own strengths and weaknesses. International databases include the U.N. Database on Violence against Women and the U.N. Development Fund for Women (UNIFEM). U.S. academic and nonprofit databases include the National Family Violence System (NFVS), the National Violence Against Women Survey (NVAWS), the Severity of Violence Against Women Scales (SVAWS), the National Survey of Families and Households (NSFH), and the Conflict Tactics Scale. There are a large number of U.S. government tracking systems, including the National Violence against Women Survey conducted during 1995 and 1996, the National Institute of Justice (NIJ), the Youth Risk Behavior System (YRBS), the National Crime Victimization Survey (NCVS), the National Comorbidity Survey (NCS), the National Violent Death Reporting System (NVDRS), the National Incident-Based Reporting System (NIBRS), the National Center for Injury Prevention and Control (NCIPC), the National Electronic Injury Surveillance System (NEISS), the Morbidity and Mortality Weekly Review (MMWR), the Behavioral Risk Factor Surveillance System (BRFSS), the Adoption and Foster Care Analysis and Reporting System (AFCARS), and the National Survey of Children Exposed to Violence (NatSCEV).

CHECK YOURSELF BOX: VIOLENCE AGAINST WOMEN RESEARCH AND DATA BIASES

Why would some people and organizations work toward publicizing the issues surrounding violence against women? Why might others work to keep the information secure? How do these different motivations affect the information and data that they provide to the public? Some definitions of violence against women are not well-defined. How does the lack of terms affect the research and data collection? Not all forms of violence against women are illegal in all countries. How does the culture of a nation or area affect the laws and law enforcement that seek to keep women safe from abuse? It is important to your research to take note of each of the issues that can lead to biases in the research and data.

▇ Section 6: Economic structure of violence against women

Few people would agree to live in a bubble to prevent exposure to all diseases. In a similar manner, most people are not willing to move into a bubble to prevent exposure to all forms of violence. Research begins by a defining of goals which will dictate which decision-makers, decisions, costs, and benefits will be analyzed. Different goals could be to ensure that fewer women experience violence, that each woman who has been a victim of violence escapes this violence and becomes a survivor, or something other. As seen previously in this chapter, there are many pathways to research violence against women. In order to analyze the violence through the lens of economics, this section focuses on the people making decisions and the structure of their decision-making processes in order to build the foundation for economic research. The costs and benefits involved in each of the individual choices are then considered. The focus is on a male–female relationship, although these decisions and outcomes may be present in any intimate relationship.

Female victims of violence and the perpetrators of that violence are the two main decision-makers. Secondary decision-makers are individuals and entities involved in policy-making regarding violence against women, law enforcement officials and service providers who become involved with the victims and perpetrators, and others who encounter the violence, such as family members, friends, and co-workers. In this section, the focus is on the decisions of the victims and perpetrators of violence against women.

Intimate relationship violence is a complicated process and varies based on the personal characteristics of the perpetrator and victim, legal avenues, community support, and other surrounding circumstances. Consider the situation in which women have a certain level of access to potential intimate partners based on societal, cultural, or religious aspects and have varying levels of resources to match with partners. Once a match is made, meaning that a female decides to be in a relationship with a male, the established relationship includes both satisfaction and dissatisfaction. In economics, the level of satisfaction is called **utility** and dissatisfaction is **disutility**. The female's utility from a relationship includes aspects that are psychological (love/care, being needed, status of having a partner/identity, sexual satisfaction, and loyalty/duty), financial (real and promised), material (house, clothing, and gifts), family (responsibility, children, and extended family), and economic specialization (being able to concentrate on activities that provide more income or household products and services, such as childbearing and childcare, food gathering and preparation, and domestic duties). The utility (satisfaction) that the female receives from each relationship aspect varies from individual to individual.

In addition to the decision about whether to enter a relationship, the perpetuator of violence (who, in the majority of cases, is male) makes the decision whether to abuse the female victim. The case study and graphs in Section 7 illustrate the theoretical model of household time allocation in which the female experiences violence at the hands of the male. His choices include whether to use abuse in the relationship, the type of abuse to use, the techniques to use in controlling the female victim, the severity of the abuse, and the timing of the abuse. He may also have some power to decide the timeline of the abuse – whether it is short-term, intermittent, or constant over years. The perpetrator's decision to abuse may be based upon family or community culture.

The Panel on Research on Violence against Women led by Nancy Crowell and Ann Burgess (1996) look at theories of violent offenses against women. Among the list of reasons someone might use violence, as presented by Crowell and Burgess, are evolution (the need to pass on one's genes), physiology and neurophysiology, the use of alcohol, psychopathology and personality traits, attitudes and gender schemas, sex and power motives, social learning, the dynamics of the relationship between the man and woman, institutional influences (such as family, school and religion), the influence of media, and societal influences (such as sexual scripts and cultural mores).

Dissatisfaction or disutility are evident in all relationships due to the dynamics between individuals. This is escalated when violence is added to the relationship. In this case, the female in the violent relationship may experience psychological violence (verbal, written, non-verbal, withholding of affection, denial of a problem, guilt, shame, low self-esteem), physical violence (to person, to relative, to pet, to property), sexual violence, financial violence (depriving of resources, loss of wages due to physical or psychological injuries), and deprivation of liberty (control or isolation). The decisions of the female victim may be limited by the type of control inflicted by the abuser. Some of her decisions may include whether to allow the abuse (if she has any control), to stay in a relationship with the abuser, to attempt to escape the abuse by her own means, and to ask for help from other persons or report it to legal authorities. She may be reluctant to admit the abuse because she has an emotional or financial attachment to the abuser or she fears further abuse, losing her children, or even death.

Denise Hines and Kathleen Malley-Morrison (2004) look at the four sources of vulnerability for women, including the microsystem (characteristics of victim and relationship, individual and developmental level including alcohol and drug abuse), intergenerational transmission, the macrosystem (poverty, attitudes of the family, status or power incompatibilities, stress), the exosystem (neighborhood poverty, social isolation), and other factors (mental disorders, personality characteristics of abusive men). Due to the overlapping nature of these vulnerabilities, freeing a woman from an abusive relationship can be a complex and long-term process.

Once the perpetrator has decided to use violence, the female must decide whether to stay in the relationship or leave it. The victim's disutility will change over time if violence escalates, as is often the case. Ending the relationship can lead to post-relationship violence from the previous partner. Even after an abusive relationship is ended, the psychological damage can be carried into new relationships, along with the need for physical and psychological treatment and financial hardship.

Family members, friends, and co-workers are all groups who are affected by the violence, yet they may have little or no power to interfere due to personal reasons or fear of being affected by the violence. The time, resources, and legal authority of law enforcement officials, medical providers, and social services organizations who come in contact with the victim are limited by scarcity and regulations. Taxpayers will be affected as government policies focus funding toward services to victims.

Gary Becker (1976) was one of the first researchers to use an economic cost perspective to view intimate relationships. In this type of traditional household bargaining model, the individuals know the costs and benefits of an exchange, cooperation exists between the male and female, rational efficiency (maximizing net benefits equal to benefits minus costs) is assumed, and bargaining is constrained to one time period. However, violence in intimate relationships happens over time and is non-cooperative. Violence changes the dynamics of the relationship so that the abusive partner punishes the victim and obtains desired outcomes through violence and income transfers.

Other studies assume that men include the benefits and costs of violent behavior against women in their decision-making process (Samuel Smithyman,1978; Murray Straus, Richard Gelles, and Suzanne Steinmetz, 1980; Alberto Godenzi, 1994). Rational choice models analyze the level and nature of violence in the relationship based on each person's bargaining power over marital resources and the economic alternatives available outside of the relationship. This type of model often maintains that providing financial resources to a female victim increases her chances of escaping the abuse; however, numerous studies have found that income transfers to the female can cause increased violence (Andrea Hetling, 2000; Stephanie Riger and Susan Staggs, 2004). Linda DeRiviere (2008) further warns that the existing models are limited in usefulness because there are numerous reasons women stay in a violent relationship, routes to escape, personal safety issues, and revolving door patterns in which women leave and later return into the violent relationship. The limitations on these studies should warn economists that their research in the area of violence against women must be informed by experts.

Unit 1: Costs of violence against women

There are many costs associated with violence against women. The costs have some correlation to the nature of the relationship (intimate partner, stranger), location of the violence (in the home, at work, in public), type of violence (physical, psychological, sexual, financial), as well as the prevalence and severity of the violence. This section will discuss the costs of violence against women in intimate partner violence in terms of costs to the victim, the perpetrator, and society.

Tanis Day, Katherine McKenna, and Audra Bowlus (2005) focus on four categories of costs of violence against women: Direct tangible costs, indirect tangible costs, direct intangible costs, and indirect intangible costs. A tangible cost is one that requires an outlay of money while an intangible cost is measured in terms of aspects such as emotional cost and decreases in quality of life. A direct cost is one that is directly the result of the violence used by the perpetrator against the female victim while an indirect cost is one that is influenced by the violence but is not directly attributable to an incident.

Direct tangible costs are out-of-pocket costs that must be paid due to the violence experienced by female victims. This may include payments by the female victims for hospitalization, medical or health care, and court costs. There may be additional costs due to links between domestic violence and the prevalence of disease, such as HIV/AIDS (Ifemeje Chika, 2012; Centers for Disease Control, 2012). The World Health Organization (2016) lists some of the costs to victims as medical costs due to injuries, miscarriages, depression, and limited mobility. The Centers for Disease Control (2018) estimates an annual cost of intimate partner violence of $5.8 billion, which includes medical and health care, lost productivity, and loss of earnings from those killed by intimate partner violence. Carrie Yodanis, Alberto Godenzi, and Elizabeth Stanko (2010) state that costs are low to the perpetrators of violence as long as there is a small likelihood of formal or informal sanctions due to the violence. Direct tangible costs to the perpetrator may include court costs and fines due to the violence.

Indirect tangible costs are costs that accrue to society as a result of the violence against women. This includes costs to law enforcement, criminal justice, and child welfare services systems. Medical expenses related to rape, physical assault, stalking, and homicide by intimate partner violence cost workplaces billions of dollars each year. The U.S. Conference of Mayors (December 2012) report that 16% of homelessness was due to domestic violence, with 32% of cities citing domestic violence as one of the main causes of local homelessness. In addition, indirect tangible costs are the monetary value of loss of productivity (such as decreased earnings and profits) of the victim or perpetrator due to violence. This might include cost of time lost from employment or household production or time spent creating an environment that minimizes the violence, and loss of opportunity due to impaired mental resources. A telephone survey by the Corporate Alliance to End Partner Violence (2005) indicate that of the workers who identified as domestic violence victims, 64% said the abuse significantly impacted their work. The Centers for Disease Control (April 2003) reports an annual loss of nearly eight million days of paid work (32,000 full-time jobs) due to domestic violence issues. A study in Canada by Nadine Wathen, Jennifer MacGregor, and Barbara MacQuarrie (2000) finds that 81.9% of victims of domestic violence reported that they were less productive in the workplace. The reasons for the decreased productivity were feeling tired or unwell, distractions at work, or losing work hours caused by the inability to get to work or being late for work. Medical or legal appointments, court proceedings, and incarcerations also affect work habits of victims of domestic violence.

Society has indirect tangible costs of violence for governments in terms of law enforcement, emergency, and criminal justice services. The National Center on Women & Family Law (1996) find that 33% of all police time is in response to domestic violence calls. Violence against women causes employers to lose productive workers, therefore incurring higher expenses. Costs to society increase in terms of increased needs for physical and mental health care, legal services, child care, housing, counseling, substance abuse, financial, violence prevention, and other victim-centered services.

Carrie Yodanis, et al. (2010) urge caution when using the economic perspective on violence against women. Because social services costs are so high to employers and societies, studies may cite a decrease in services leading to increased efficiency. This view takes into account indirect tangible costs, but ignores the direct tangible costs as well as both the direct and indirect intangible costs of preventing violence against women. Ignoring these costs will lead to higher future individual and societal costs. For example, Patricia Tjaden and Nancy Thoennes (2003) saw an increase in the costs of violence against women from $5.8 billion in 1995 to $8.3 billion in 2003. A study by Alberto Godenzi and Carrie Yodanis (1999) shows that it is more expensive to provide long-term incarceration for perpetrators and long-term health care for female victims than it is to provide shelters and counseling programs to get these victims out of life-threatening violent situations.

Direct intangible costs result directly from the violent act but have no monetary value. Examples are pain and suffering, and the emotional loss of a loved one through a violent death. Some of these costs include isolation, fear, concern for their own or children's safety, fear of losing children, living with threats from an abuser, and symptoms of PTSD. Perpetrators may have direct intangible costs due to physical and psychological damage from administering the violence.

Indirect intangible costs result indirectly from the violence; however, their monetary cost may be unmeasurable. These costs to the victim include lack of self-esteem, learned helplessness, health problems, drug and alcohol abuse, and depression. Past abuse can have future consequences. Victims of domestic violence have four times the rate of depression and 5.5 times the number of suicide attempts of non-battered women. Statistics from the National Institute of Mental Health (2009) indicate that between 38–75% of battered women have anxiety, 63–77% experience depression, and 54–84% suffer from PTSD. The Urban Child Institute (2014) reported lifelong costs to children who witness domestic violence within the household. Fear of arrest by legal authorities or desertion by family and friends may be indirect intangible costs of violence to the perpetrator.

Unit 2: Benefits of violence against women

Incidence of violence against women happens at all socioeconomic levels and to a staggering number of females. As seen previously, most societies accept some forms of violence against women. It is obvious that the perpetrator of the violence receives benefit from the actions in a way that causes the violence to escalate over time, and it may be the case that some women derive benefits from being in a relationship with the perpetrator.

There are many reasons, which cannot be discounted, why a female may remain in a violent situation. A female may feel strong physical ties to the male or may feel she needs him because she has a disability that precludes her from taking certain actions. Emotional reasons may include love, codependency, feelings of belonging and being needed, believing that she can help the male overcome his problems if she stays, or fear that she will be harmed or killed if she leaves the perpetrator. The female may stay for financial reasons, because she doesn't have the money and resources to move out or doesn't know how to handle financial affairs. Other reasons may be that the female is scared of losing her children in a custody battle or that others will look down on her for deserting a relationship, or cultural norms that preclude a female from leaving an intimate relationship.

Domestic violence occurs in all classes, races, cultures, age groups, and occupations. The ultimate causes of domestic violence are the core beliefs of the perpetrator. Alcohol and drug use and mental illness may be contributing factors, but they are not the causes of abuse. Violence against women is about control; thus, the aggressor would not cause violence against a woman if there were no benefits to the perpetrator. The benefits to the perpetrator include the ability to control the female's behavior and life, the retention of an unchallenged position of power (Carrie Yodanis, Alberto Godenzi, and Elizabeth Stanko, 2010), and personal satisfaction.

While studies find that violence against women by male perpetrators is strongest in patriarchal societies (Emerson Dobash,1992; Kersti Yllö and Michele Bograd, 1988), it is important to note that this is a societal value system to which men and women alike have subscribed. Many movies, television programs, video games, and music videos portray graphic violence against women. In 2017, Russia – a country with no restraining orders – changed its law so that a man who hits his wife receives only a fine for a first offense. Without changing beliefs about violence against women and behavior toward females, the costs associated with men abusing their intimate partners will continue to be measured in billions of dollars.

Unit 3: Inefficiencies in economic structure of violence against women

There is reluctance by the defenders of female victims of abuse to use a cost–benefit approach to describing the harm of violence against women. This is due in part to the complexities of interactions involved in violence against women that limit the viability of economic models. However, legislation championing women and promises of dedicated resources to fight violence against women require the ability to effectively use cost–benefit analysis to describe the decisions and incentives confronting perpetrators and victims.

There are many issues that will create ambiguity in the economic modeling and will require discussion with experts to determine whether the modeling is useable. Federal money to prevent violence against women is scarce and often decreasing, as seen in the 2017 U.S. federal funding cuts. When statistics are inflated to gain funding, the statistics will cause inaccuracy in research. Denise Hines and Kathleen Malley-Morrison (2004) find correlations between factors that indicated risk of violence to the female and outcomes, but could not determine if the risk preceded the abuse, if the abuse preceded the risk factor, or if a third variable caused both the abuse and the risk factor.

Economic models assume that the female has the choice to stay in or leave the relationship. Human trafficking, which will be discussed further in the child abuse chapter, is the use of a person's labor through force, fraud, or coercion. It does not require the transportation of the person and affects both women and men. The individual who is trafficking the person, called the human trafficker, controls the trafficked victim through threats, drugs, or emotional connections and leaves them few choices. This lack of choice negates the use of a household time allocation model to analyze the violence against women associated with human trafficking.

It is a popular belief that increasing the income of a woman in a violent relationship will improve her ability to bargain in the relationship, and thus decrease the abuse. Research, however, does not have a definitive answer. Some studies found that financial security that is not reliant on the perpetrator leads to the highest probability of a victim escaping and remaining free of domestic violence (National Network to End Domestic Violence, 2018; Deborah Anderson and Daniel Saunders, 2003; and Olaw Barnett, 2000). However, other research determined that assisting a female in earning a higher income leads to a reduction in intimate partner violence for females who have higher earnings, but causes an increase in violence for females with lower incomes (Seema Vyas and Charlotte Watts, 2009). This means that the socioeconomic status of females matters. Still other studies look at violence in a household as it relates to the absolute and relative education levels of the female and male in the household (Amartya Sen, 1998; Rachel Jewkes, Johathan Levin, and Loveday Penn-Kekana, 2002; Ruchira Naved and Lars Persson, 2005). Sidney Schuler, Syed Hashemi, and Shamsul Badal (1998) suggest that these mixed findings are related to the friction between a female's increased status and economic position in the household and the challenge to the perpetrator of the female's elevated position.

Violence against women predominates in areas where women do not have systems of female empowerment. A study of women in South Africa and Uganda (Hema Swaminathan, Cherryl Walker, and Margaret Rugadya, 2008) find that property ownership by women leads to the ability of the women to leave the violent relationship, thus reducing gender-based violence. Cultural studies expert Haley Feuerbacher (2017) studies 22 households across KwaZulu-Natal, South Africa, an area with a high incidence of gender-based violence. Feuerbacher analyzed patterns relating the Rural Women's Movement, a women-only social movement that provided resources (related to gender-based violence avoidance and land reform) to female heads of household to assist with their household survival. In most cases, the women joined the program in hopes that their procurement of land would ease their dependence on abusive men.

There are many other factors which complicate the study of violence against women. For example, the presence of codependency, alcoholism, drug addiction, gambling or pornography addiction, and poor mental health can cause dysfunction in the relationship and may lead to ongoing violence. However, despite the many ambiguities that make economic modeling difficult, the authors believe that economists have a role to play in decreasing the incidence and billion-dollar cost of violence against women.

Section 7: Case study

Household time allocation including violence against women

Economists assume that households maximize utility by jointly determining individual time allocation given the relative production abilities and preferences, absent intimate partner violence. To demonstrate this, the following household time allocation model is adapted to reflect possible results of violence from the male in the household directed against the female. The model combines the production possibility frontiers of the two members of the household – the male and the female. A **production possibility frontier** is a line or curve on a graph that illustrates the maximum amount of possible sets of two goods that a person can produce given a certain quantity of inputs. When the production possibility frontiers of two members of a household are combined, the resulting production possibility frontier is a **household production possibility frontier**. This case study focuses on the theoretical constructs of the model, but empirical research can be done following the same model.

Gary Becker (1965) introduces a model of household time allocation in which he assumed the household consisted of one male (M) and one female (F) who jointly determined their allocation of time between labor market work and household work in order to maximize household utility. Becker's model assumes that the male earns a higher wage (ω) in the labor market than the female, so $\omega_M > \omega_F$. This means the household can only maximize utility when the male's time is allocated to working full-time in the labor market before the female allocates any time to the labor market. Wages earned by the male and female enable the household to purchase market goods X, so that the wages earned by the male purchase X_{M1} market goods and the wages earned by the female purchase X_{F1} market goods. In a similar way, the model assumes that females have a higher productivity in the household. This means that the output of household goods and services (such as cooked meals, housework, and care of own children, Z) for females Z_{F1} is higher than for males Z_{M1} so that the household can only maximize utility if the male only allocates time to household work when all of the female's time is allocated to working full-time in the household. Figure 3.1 shows the production possibility frontier for the male of the household PPF$_M$. He can spend his time working full-time in the labor market to earn X_{M1}, which is the point where the production possibility frontier intersects the vertical axis. Alternately, he can work full-time in the household to earn Z_{M1}, which is the point where the production possibility frontier intersects the horizontal axis. The male can also choose some combination of labor market and household work at a point along the production possibility frontier. Figure 3.2 shows the production possibility frontier of the female PPF$_F$ earning X_{F1} if she works full-time in the labor market, Z_{F1} if she works full-time in the household, or some combination of labor market and household work that would earn some X and some Z. Notice that the male's curve is steeper because he earns a higher wage in the labor market. The female's curve is flatter because she has higher productivity in the household.

If the male and female work full-time in the labor market, they can purchase $X_{M1} + X_{F1} = X_{T1}$ market goods. If the female and male work full-time in the household, they can earn $Z_{M1} + Z_{F1} = Z_{T1}$ household goods. If the male works full-time in the labor market and the female works full-time in the household, they can purchase X_{M1} and earn Z_{F1}. This leads to the household production possibility frontier (PPF) found in Figure 3.3. If the household chooses point A, both individuals spend all of their time working in the labor market and none of their time doing household work. Point B shows both individuals spending all of their time working in the household with no labor market work. Point C represents perfect specialization dependent upon their relative productivities, so that the male works full-time in the labor market and the female works full-time in the household.

The next step is determining the preferences of the household for market goods and household goods. This model assumes that the male and female jointly choose how much time each member should allocate to the labor market and household work in order to maximize household utility, as shown by the highest utility curve (U) tangent to the household

FIGURE 3.1 Production possibilities frontier for male (PPF$_M$)

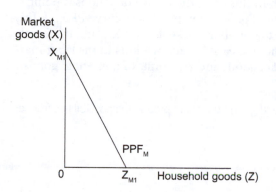

FIGURE 3.2 Production possibilities frontier for female (PPF$_F$)

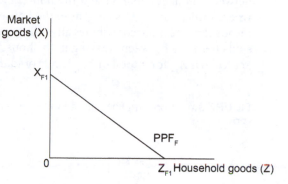

FIGURE 3.3 Production possibilities frontier for the household (PPF$_{HH1}$)

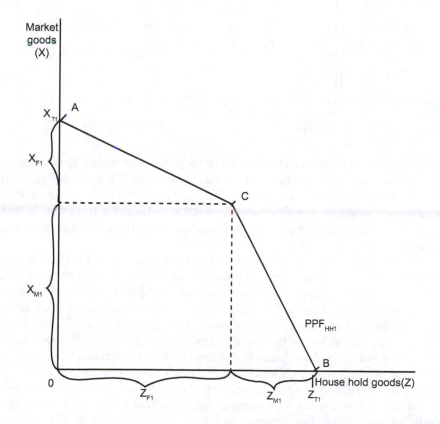

production possibility frontier (PPF_{HH1}). For this example, Figure 3.4 shows the household choice of having the male work full-time in the labor market and the female split her time between the labor market and the household. In this case, the household chooses point D where utility curve U_1 is tangent to the household production possibility curve PPF_{HH1}. This means that the male contributes all of his time to the labor market to earn X_{M1} and the female splits her time between working in the household to earn Z_{F1} and working in the labor market to earn X_{F1} for a total of X_{HH1} units of market goods and Z_{HH1} units of household goods.

FIGURE 3.4 Consumption choice by the household given household production possibilities frontier (PPF_{HH1})

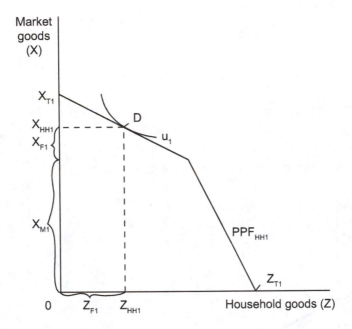

When domestic violence is introduced into the model, the assumption of mutual cooperation is violated, bargaining power is no longer equal, and the productivity (output per unit of labor) of the female may be affected. There are a number of ways the violence could affect household production as well as household consumption. It is also a possibility that the violence could affect the female and the household in multiple ways simultaneously, so that these examples are not necessarily mutually exclusive.

For the first example, the model assumes that the violence against the female member of the household reduces her productivity in the labor market. In this case, her own production possibility frontier (PPF_{F2}, Figure 3.5) would decrease, along with the household production possibility frontier (PPF_{HH2}, Figure 3.6). This means the household cannot reach utility curve (satisfaction level) U_1, but can only reach a lower utility curve, such as U_2. The lower utility curve means lower satisfaction for the household and a decrease in X or Z or both X and Z. For this example, the household has chosen X_{HH2} units of market goods and Z_{HH2} units of household goods to reach utility curve U_2, which is the highest utility curve tangent to PPF_{HH2} for this household. If the household had been consuming at the point of specialization (at the kink in PPF_{HH}) or where the male worked part-time in the household (below the kink along PPF_{HH}), the household's utility would be unchanged by the violence against the female.

FIGURE 3.5   Violence against women decreases productivity of female (PPF$_{F1}$ to PPF$_{F2}$)

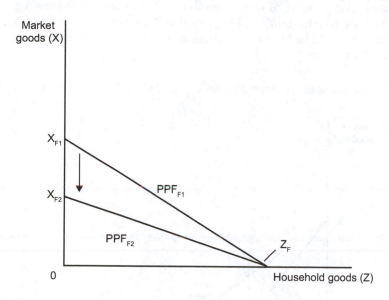

FIGURE 3.6   Violence against women decreases household production possibilities frontier (PPF$_{HH1}$ to PPF$_{HH2}$)

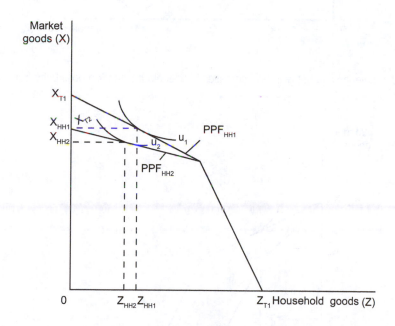

For the second example, the model assumes that violence against the female member of the household reduces her productivity in the household so that her own production possibility frontier (PPF$_{F3}$ in Figure 3.7) is decreased along with the household production possibility frontier (PPF$_{HH3}$ in Figure 3.8). Again, the household can only reach lower utility curve U$_2$, instead of higher utility curve U$_2$, leading to a lower level of satisfaction for the household and a decrease in X or Z or both X and Z. Figure 3.8 shows the case in which the household chooses X_{HH3} units of market goods and Z_{HH3} units of household goods to reach the highest utility curve tangent to PPF_{HH2} for this household (U_2). In this case, no matter what level the household had been consuming at previously, the household's utility or satisfaction level will decrease.

FIGURE 3.7   Violence against women decreases productivity of female (PPF_{F1} to PPF_{F3})

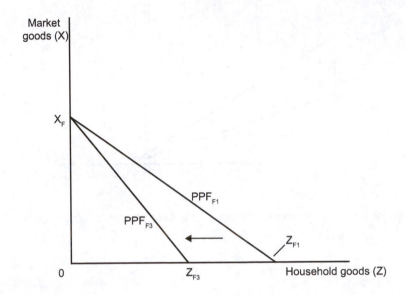

FIGURE 3.8   Violence against women decreases household production possibility frontier (PPFHH1 to PPFHH3)

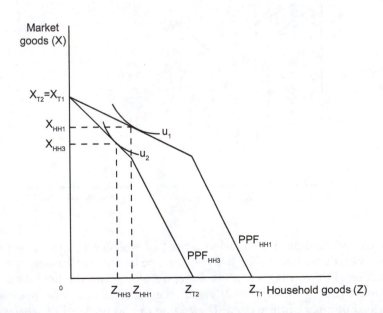

For the third example, the violence against the female member of the household may not affect her productivity, but may manifest itself in the male controlling how she allocates her time, even if it means a decrease in household utility. This could happen if the male is receiving personal utility or satisfaction from perpetuating the abuse, an aspect not included in the household time allocation model. In this case, the male may force or coerce the female to work in a suboptimal capacity, which would mean the household allocates its time at a point inside its production possibility frontier (PPF_{HH4}), as shown in Figure 3.9. For example, Point E occurs when the male forces the female to work full-time in the labor market while he does not work ($X_{HH4}=X_{F4}$ and $Z=0$). Point F arises when the male forces the female to work part-time in the labor market and part-time in the household while he is only working part-time in the labor market, such that $X_{HH5}= X_{M5}+X_{F5}$ and $Z_{HH5}= Z_{F5}$. Any choice that does not allocate time of household members on the household production possibility frontier will yield suboptimal household utility, whether the choice is made jointly or by one member of the household.

FIGURE 3.9 Sub-optimal consumption choice by the household given household production possibilities frontier (PPF_{HH1})

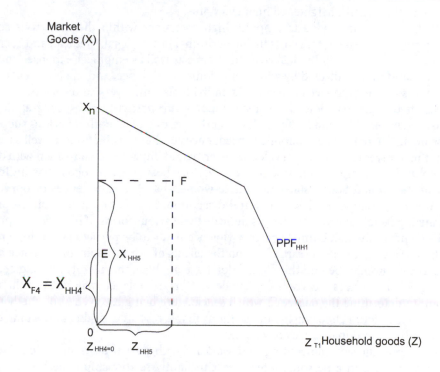

Two of the most significant limitations to this model are related to the lack of empirical evidence to support this domestic violence outcome in the household time allocation model. It is inherently difficult to acquire such data for a number of reasons, including the inability to obtain reliable data concerning households in which domestic violence is not always present across time. An organized data collection methodology would include a large number of households in which household time allocation could be analyzed at different points in time when domestic violence existed and was absent. Each household's data would need to be available over time so that patterns could be analyzed. This is important because utility is ordinal and preferences cannot be compared easily across households. Another limitation is the acquisition of data relating to the household good "Z." Market wages and prices can be analyzed to determine the productivity of a person, but there are no wages or prices for household goods and services. A possibility would be look to at the opportunity cost of a person's time in the household as time that could be spent in the labor market.

Section 8: Recommendations for future research

This chapter opens up wide avenues of economic research needed in the area of violence against women. Chapter 6 will illustrate how children are affected by many of the same factors leading to the abuse of women.

Dan Anderberg and Helmut Rainer (2013) and other researchers consider how employment status by males and females affects domestic abuse outcomes. Research in this area has not been conclusive, as some studies show a decrease in violence due to the empowerment of women while others illustrate increased violence associated with the male's outlook of losing power due to the female's heightened financial status.

Much research is needed to pinpoint high-cost areas within the numerous costs of violence against women. System costs include criminal justice, legal, medical, and social services, and there are many individual costs to victims as well as employer expenses and costs to society. Children are affected by witnessing domestic violence, and the intergenerational consequences lead to future costs to systems, individuals, employers, and society.

Despite the fact that violence against women occurs across all races, geographic areas, religions, and levels of income, different levels and types of violence affect various subcategories of women. There may be economic consequences to these distinctions as well as a foundation for incentives to decrease prevalence, severity, and impact against women with diverse backgrounds. For example, Catherine Burnett (2015), whose research focused on indigenous women in the United States, states that these women had ". . .experiences of oppression, historical and contemporary losses, cultural disruption, manifestations of oppression, and dehumanizing beliefs and values. Results indicate that various forms of historical oppression created a context in which intimate partner violence tends to be perpetuated at high rates."

There is an increasing research base on the effects of pornography on violence against women. The economics behind this connection have not been thoroughly investigated.

Even when services are available, female victims of violence may not use them. It is important to determine the degree to which services are being received and whether a gap exists due to the victim choosing to not use the available resources or due to the unavailability, inaccessibility, and inadequacy of services.

The importance of confronting and working with perpetrators of violence against women was evident in a personal interview with family relationship expert Sarah Feuerbacher (2017) when she states:

> For violence against women to end, it absolutely requires that the perpetrator of the abuse must be held accountable through professional intervention from a quality, long-standing battering intervention program. They must be in an environment that is non-violent, non-judgmental, and respectful towards partners and children. And, most importantly, they must be willing to work through a long process, being painfully honest with themselves. Plus, if you help the perpetrators change, the individual

victim is being helped, and on a larger scale, it is help towards the elimination of all violence against women!

Evidence is non-conclusive as to whether mandatory arrest in cases of domestic violence in the United States help the victim or cause increased abuse of the victim upon the release of the perpetrator from custody. Research is needed in this area.

Media continues to play a role in violence against women, whether through the depictions of violence on television, movies, and magazines or through the way reporting is done on cases of domestic violence, sexual harassment and assault, and rape. A study by Jana Bufkin and Sarah Eschholz (2000) illustrate this point, finding that most sexual assault in the 50 top-grossing films in 1996 depicted rapists as "sadistic, disturbed, lower-class individuals who prey on children and the vulnerable," which is not the reality of most incidences of rape.

CHECK YOURSELF BOX: CHANGES TO PERSONAL BIASES ABOUT VIOLENCE AGAINST WOMEN

The material in this chapter is not only heavy, but also personal to many people. What are your thoughts after working through the chapter? What areas of the information do you question? Which ones do you disagree with? After writing down these answers, look again at the biases you listed in the first check yourself box. Have your biases changed? Did you gain new biases? Did you lose any biases? Each of these additions, subtractions, and changes affect your research. Make note of them and keep updating them for future projects to add quality to your work.

Section 9: Bibliography

Anderberg, Dan and Rainer, Helmut. (2013). Economic abuse: A theory of intrahousehold sabotage. *Journal of Public Economics, 97*(C), 282–95.

Anderson, Deborah and Saunders, Daniel. (2003). Leaving an abusive partner: An empirical review of predictors, the process of leaving, and the psychological well-being. *Trauma, Violence, and Abuse, 163*(4).

Balthazar, James. (2016). *Emergent issues in criminal justice leadership.* Unpublished manuscript. Huntsville, Texas: Sam Houston State University.

Barnett, Olaw. (2000). Why battered women do not leave, Part 1: External inhibiting factors within society. *Trauma, Violence, and Abuse, 1*(4), 343–72.

Becker, Gary. (1965). A theory of the allocation of time. *The Economic Journal, 75*(299), 493–517.

Becker, Gary. (1976). *The economic approach to human behavior.* Chicago: The University of Chicago Press.

Breiding, Matthew; Smith, Sharon; Basile, Kathleen; Walters, Mikel; Chen, Jieru; and Merrick, Melissa. (2014). Prevalence and characteristics of sexual violence, stalking, and intimate partner violence victimization – National Intimate Partner and Sexual Violence Survey, United States, 2011. Centers for Disease Control and Prevention *Morbidity and Mortality Weekly Report, 63*(8), 7.

Bufkin, Jana and Eschholz, Sarah. (2000). Images of sex and rape: a content analysis of popular film. *Violence Against Women, 6,* 1317–44.

Burnett, Catherine. (2015). Historical oppression and intimate partner violence experienced by indigenous women in the United States: Understanding connections. *Social Service Review, 89*(3).

Centers for Disease Control. (2012). *Findings from the national intimate partner and sexual violence survey 2010–2012 state report.* Retrieved from https://www.cdc.gov/violenceprevention/pdf/NISVS-StateReportFactsheet.pdf

Centers for Disease Control. (2018). *Intimate Partner Violence: Consequences.* Retrieved from https://www.cdc.gov/violenceprevention/intimatepartnerviolence/consequences.html

Centers for Disease Control and Prevention National Center for Injury Prevention and Control (2003, March). *Costs of intimate partner violence against women in the United States.* Retrieved from https://www.cdc.gov/violenceprevention/pdf/ipvbook-a.pdf

Chika, Ifemeje. (2012). Gender-based domestic violence in Nigeria: A socio-legal perspective. *Indian Journal of Gender Studies, 19*(1), 137.

Corporate Alliance to End Partner Violence (2005). Workplace statistics. Retrieved from http://www.caepv.org/getinfo/facts_stats.php?factsec=3

Crowell, Nancy and Burgess, Ann (Eds.). (1996). *Understanding violence against women.* Panel on research on violence against women. Washington: National Academy Press. 49–89. Retrieved from https://www.nap.edu/read/5127/chapter/1

Day, Tanis; McKenna, Katherine; and Bowlus, Audra. (2005). *The economic costs of violence against women: An evaluation of the literature.* Expert brief for the U.N. Secretary General. Retrieved from http://www.un.org/womenwatch/daw/vaw/expert%20brief%20costs.pdf

DeRiviere, Linda. (2008). Do economists need to rethink their approaches to modeling intimate partner violence? *Journal of Economic Issues, 42*(3), 583–606.

Dobash, Emerson. (1992). *Women, violence, and social change.* London: Routledge.

Dutton, Donald and Painter, Susan. (1993). The battered woman syndrome: Effects of severity and intermittency of abuse. *American Journal of Orthopsychiatry, 63*(4), 614–22.

Feuerbacher, Haley. (2017). *State of formation.* Retrieved from http://www.stateofformation.org/author/haley-feuerbacher

Feuerbacher, Sarah. (2017). Personal interview.

Fife, Rose and Schrager, Sarina. (2012). *Family violence: What health care providers need to know.* Boston: Cengage.

Fox, Vivian. (2002, November). Historical perspectives on violence against women. *Journal of International Women's Studies, 4*(1), 15–34.

Frias, Sonia. (2017, April). Family and partner violence against women: Forced marriage in Mexican indigenous communities. *International Journal of Law, Policy and the Family, 31*(1), 60–78.

Godenzi, Alberto. (1994). What's the big deal? We are men and they are women. In Newburn, Tim and Stanko, Elizabeth (Eds.), *Just boys doing business? Men, masculinities, and crime.* London: Routledge.

Godenzi, Alberto and Yodanis, Carrie. (1999). *Male violence: The economic costs. A methodological review.* European Council of Europe, Human Rights Section Equality between Women and Men.

Hetling, Andrea. (2000). Addressing domestic violence as a barrier to self-sufficiency: The relationship of welfare receipt and spousal abuse. *Journal of Public and International Affairs, 11,* 21–35.

Hines, Denise and Malley-Morrison, Kathleen. (2004). *Family violence in the United States: Defining, understanding, and combating abuse.* Thousand Oaks, CA: Sage.

Jewkes, Rachel; Levin, Jonathan; and Penn-Kekana, Loveday. (2002). Risk factors for domestic violence: Findings from a South African cross-sectional study. *Social Science and Medicine, 55*(9), 1603–17.

Johnson, Michael. (1995, May). Patriarchal terrorism and common couple violence. *Journal of Marriage and Family, 57*(2), 283–94.

Logan, T.K. and Walker, Robert. (2010). Toward a deeper understanding of the harms caused by partner stalking. *Violence & Victims, 25*(4): 440–55.

Marshall, Linda. (1992). Development of the severity of violence against women scales. *Journal of Family Violence, 7,* 103–21.

McFarlane, Judith; Campbell, Jacquelyn; Wilt, Susan; Sachs, Carolyn; Ulrich, Yvonne; and Xu, Xiao. (1999). Stalking and intimate partner femicide. *Homicide Studies, 3*(4), 300–16.

National Institute of Mental Health. (2009). Statistics. Retrieved from https://www.nimh.nih.gov/health/statistics/index.shtml

National Institute of Statistics and Geography. (2017). *2016 National survey on dynamics of household relationships.* Retrieved from http://en.www.inegi.org.mx/proyectos/enchogares/especiales/endireh/2016/

National Network to End Domestic Violence. (2018). *Financial abuse and empowerment.* Retrieved from https://nnedv.org/spotlight_on/financial-abuse-empowerment

Naved, Ruchira and Persson, Lars. (2005, December). Factors associated with spousal physical violence against women in Bangladesh. *Studies in Family Planning, 36*(4), 289–300.

Novisky, Meghan and Peralta, Robert. (2015, January). When women tell: Intimate partner violence and the factors related to police notification. *Violence Against Women, 21*(1), 65–86.

Riger, Stephanie and Staggs, Susan. (2004, September). Welfare reform, domestic violence, and employment. *Violence Against Women, 10*(9), 961–90.

Salamone, Nancy. (2010). *Victory over violence.* Bloomington: Authorhouse.

Schuler, Sidney; Hashemi, Syed; and Badal, Shamsul. (1998). Men's violence against women in rural Bangladesh: Undermined or exacerbated by microcredit programmes? *Development in Practice, 8*(2):148–156.

Sen, Amartya. (1998). Universal truths: Human rights and the westernizing illusion. *Harvard International Review, 20*(3), 40–3.

Smithyman, Samuel. (1978). *The undetected rapist.* Claremont: Claremont Graduate School.

Straus, Murray and Gelles, Richard. (1990). *Physical violence in American families: Risk factors and adaptations to violence in 8,145 families.* Piscataway: Transaction Publishers.

Straus, Murray; Gelles, Richard; and Steinmetz, Suzanne. (1980). *Behind closed doors: Violence in the American family.* Piscataway: Transaction Publishers.

Swaminathan, Hema; Walker, Cherryl; and Rugadya, Margaret (Eds). (2008). *Women's property rights: HIV and AIDS and domestic violence: Research findings from two districts in South Africa and Uganda.* Cape Town: HSRC Press.

Tjaden, Patricia and Thoennes, Nancy. (2000). *Extent, nature, and consequences of intimate partner violence: findings from the national violence against women survey.* (NIJ Publication No. 181867). Washington, DC: US Department of Justice.

United Nations. *Rome statute of the International Criminal Court.* (2000). Article 7(1) (g)-1, July 6, 2000.

United States Conference of Mayors. (2012, December). *Hunger and homelessness survey.* Retrieved from https://www.wcspittsburgh.org/wp-content/uploads/1219-report-HH.pdf

United States Department of Justice, Federal Bureau of Investigation, Criminal Justice Information Services Division. (2013). *Crime in the United States 2013.* Retrieved from https://ucr.fbi.gov/crime-in-the-u.s/2013/crime-in-the-u.s.-2013/violent-crime/rape.

United States Department of Justice, Office on Violence Against Women. (2017). *Domestic violence.* Retrieved from http://www.usdoj.gov/ovw/domviolence.htm

The Urban Child Institute. (2014, October 17). *Domestic violence: An unwanted family legacy.* Retrieved from http://www.urbanchildinstitute.org/articles/features/domestic-violence-an-unwanted-family-legacy

Vyas, Seema and Watts, Charlotte. (2009, July). How does economic empowerment affect women's risk of intimate partner violence in low and middle income countries? A systematic review of published evidence. *Journal of International Development, 21*(5): 577–602.

Wathen, Nadine; MacGregor, Jennifer; and MacQuarrie, Barbara. (2016, July). The impact of domestic violence in the workplace. *Journal of Occupational and Environmental Medicine, 57*(7), 53–71.

World Health Organization. (2016, November). *Violence against women fact sheet.* Retrieved from http://www.who.int/mediacentre/factsheets/fs239/en/

Yllö, Kersti and Bograd, Michele (Eds). (1988). *Feminist perspectives on wife abuse: An introduction.* Thousand Oaks: Sage Publications Inc.

Yodanis, Carrie; Godenzi, Alberto, and Stanko, Elizabeth. (2010). The benefits of studying costs: A review and agenda for studies on the economic costs of violence against women. *Policy Studies, 21*(3), 263–76.

Section 10: Resources

Unit 1: Summary

Violence against women comes in many forms and is distinctive because of its prevalence, severity, and impact on the victims. There are five main categories of violence against women: physical, emotional, verbal, sexual, and financial. Most countries have national laws in place to protect women from some types of abuse. International agreements have been enacted for the direct protection of females and to guide national policy-making. There are a number of controversies regarding violence against women, many stemming from differences in culture and religion. There is a long history of violence perpetuated against women, and the violence continues today. Experts on this topic can be found in a variety of fields.

The economic decision-makers related to violence against women include the perpetrators of the abuse, the victims of the violence, society and the media; and the family, friends, and co-workers of the victim. Each of these decision-makers has costs of the violence perpetrated against women and, it can be argued, some have benefits from the abuse.

Unit 2: Key concepts

Battered Woman Syndrome: The effects of severe, irregularly-occurring abuse that is similar to post-traumatic stress disorder (Dutton, 1993).

Battering: The repeated striking of the victim by the perpetrator.

Acquaintance rape: The forced sexual intercourse with the victim by a perpetrator who is known to the victim.

Date rape: The forced sexual intercourse with the victim by a perpetrator who is known by the victim and is at the time escorting the victim.

Direct intangible costs: Costs resulting directly from the violent act that have no monetary value.

Direct tangible costs: Out-of-pocket costs that must be paid due to the violence experienced by female victims.

Disutility: The dissatisfaction or negative effect of an adverse action.

Domestic violence: As defined by the World Health Organization (2016), domestic violence is "any act of gender-based violence that results in, or is likely to result in, physical, sexual or mental harm or suffering to women, including threats of such acts, coercion or arbitrary deprivation of liberty, whether occurring in public or in private life."

Emotional violence or psychological violence: The use of verbal or nonverbal actions by the perpetrator to inflict injury to the victim's emotional state.

Femicide: The killing of a female.

Financial violence, economic violence, or material violence: The perpetrator's control of the victim through the creation of an economic crisis.

Forced marriage: The forcing of a woman to marry a man against her will.

Household production possibility frontier: A line or curve on a graph that illustrates the combined production possibility frontiers of two members of a household.

Impact: The effects of violence against women on quality of life.

Indirect intangible costs: Costs resulting indirectly from the violent act that cannot be monetarily measured.

Indirect tangible costs: Costs that accrue to society as a result of the violence against women.

Intimate partner: A person who is in a physical, sexual, or emotional relationship with another person.

Intimate partner violence: As defined by the World Health Organization (2016), intimate partner violence is "behavior by a partner or ex-partner that causes physical, psychological or sexual harm to women."

Marital rape: The forced sexual intercourse with a wife by her husband or with one spouse by the other spouse.

Perpetrator: The person who knowingly and wilfully commits an action that is harmful to another person.

Physical coercion: The inflicting of pain or injury by the perpetrator on the victim to reinforce the credibility of the perpetrator's threat.

Physical violence: The inflicting of injury on the victim's body by the perpetrator.

Prevalence: The frequency of a certain type of violence or violence against a certain group of women. As defined by the National Institutes of Mental Health (NIH), prevalence is "the proportion of a population who have (or had) a specific characteristic in a given time period."

Production possibility frontier: A line or curve on a graph that illustrates the maximum amount of possible sets of two goods that a person can produce given a certain quantity of inputs.

Productivity: Output per unit of labor input.

Rape: Non-consensual sexual intercourse or other sexual penetration occurring when the victim is forced or threatened with injury by the perpetrator.

Severity: A measure of the seriousness or harshness of abuse inflicted upon the victim.

Sex trafficking: The commercial sexual exploitation of the victim brought about by the perpetrator's use of force, fraud, or coercion.

Sexual coercion: The perpetrator's pressuring, deceiving, or forcing of the victim to endure undesired touch or sex.

Sexual harassment: The perpetrator's forcing or coercing the victim to hear or read unwanted sexual comments or invitations or to view unsolicited sexual images in a professional or social setting.

Sexual violence: The perpetrator's forcing or coercing the victim to take part in sexual activity without their consent.

Spiritual violence: The prohibition or belittling of a person for following the person's religious beliefs or the control of a person through the person's beliefs.

Stalking: The repeated harassment by a perpetrator through inflicting unwanted attention on the victim.

Stranger rape: The forced sexual intercourse with a victim by a person who is not known by the victim.

Terroristic violence: The use of systematic, serious, and frequent beatings by the perpetrator to subjugate the victim (Johnson, 1995).

Utility: The satisfaction or positive effect of a favorable action.

Verbal violence: The use of written or spoken words or sounds by the perpetrator to instigate fear or decrease self-esteem in the victim.

Victim: The person who has been directly harmed by the actions of the perpetrator.

Violence against women: According to the U.N. Declaration on the Elimination of Violence Against Women (1993), violence against women is "any act of gender-based violence that results in, or is likely to result in, physical, sexual, or psychological harm or suffering to women, including threats of such acts, coercion or arbitrary deprivation of liberty, whether occurring in public or private life."

Unit 3: Review questions

1.   How is domestic violence different than intimate partner violence?

2.   What are the three characteristics that can help us understand violence against women?

3.   What are some of the possible relationships between the perpetrator and the victim of domestic violence?

4. What are the five main categories of violence against women as described in this chapter?

5. What are two of the U.S. agreements that were created to protect women from violence?

6. What are two of the international agreements that were created to protect women from violence?

7. Who are some of the experts in the area of violence against women?

8. Who are the two main decision-makers in violence against women and what are their costs and benefits of the violence?

9. What is the media's role in violence against women?

10. How can a household time allocation model be used to better understand the effects of violence against women?

Unit 4: Recommended reading

Abusharaf, Rogaia Mustafa (Ed.). (2006). *Female circumcision*. Philadelphia: University of Pennsylvania Press.

Cook, Rebecca (Ed.). (1993). *Human rights of women: National and international perspectives*. Philadelphia: University of Pennsylvania Press.

DiGeorgio-Lutz, JoAnn and Gosbee, Donna. (2016). *Women and genocide: Gendered experiences of violence, survival, and resistance*. Toronto: Women's Press.

Edwards, Alice. (2011). *Violence against women under international human rights law*. Cambridge: Cambridge University Press.

Heineman, Elizabeth. (2011). *Sexual violence in conflict zones: From the ancient world to the era of human rights*. Philadelphia: University of Pennsylvania Press.

Sen, Mala. (2001). *Death by fire: Sati, dowry death and female infanticide in modern India*. New Delhi: Penguin Books.

Storkey, Elaine. (2015). *Scars across humanity: Understanding and overcoming violence against women*. London: Society for Promoting Christian Knowledge.

4 Economics of seeking asylum

◼ Section 1: Introduction to the economics of seeking asylum

Unit 1: General introduction to seeking asylum

Fleeing from one's home in order to avoid persecution, serious injury, or death is the basis of seeking asylum. **Asylum** is the protection granted by a nation to people who have left their country of origin in order to escape persecution. The path to asylum involves multi-stage decision-making to avoid danger and reach safety. Granting asylum is a complex, quota-based legal process. The decisions made by seekers and granters of asylum can lead to different outcomes for the asylum seeker as well as the host community in which the person is seeking asylum.

Seeking asylum is an emotion-charged topic and there are varied viewpoints on the issue. On the one hand there are supporters, who are empathetic to those who must flee the dangers they face in their home regions even though voicing concern for those people can lead to political and social recriminations. On the other hand there are opponents, who raise red flags about the threats of illegal immigrants "stealing" domestic jobs, increasing crime rates, threatening economic security and national safety, and drowning the country's welfare, schooling, and housing systems.

Economics is at the heart of this issue because many aspects of seeking asylum are affected by scarcity in the forms of lack of safety and legal status, inadequate housing, ignorance of rights, lack of official agents to process asylum seekers and to provide effective law enforcement, and poor access to interpreters. An asylum seeker may experience human rights violations prior to leaving home, during the journey toward asylum, during incarceration while asylum is being considered, and, if the plea for asylum is rejected, upon arrival in the home country after deportation. This chapter will focus on the human rights problems asylum seekers experience prior to leaving home, but will consider the issues that arise during the process of seeking asylum.

Unit 2: Asylum seeker perspective

Eleazar Javier Saldivia Flores

Eleazar Javier Saldivia Flores is a former federal criminal judge in Barcelona, Venezuela. At age 33, he was the youngest person to be appointed a judge in Venezuela's history. Over his 15-year tenure, he presided over more than 4,500 cases and has handed down over 800 sentences. In addition, Eleazar was a professor of law with a focus on criminal law at the University of Central Plains Romulo Gallegos. His master's degree is in criminal law and procedure and indigenous law of South America. Eleazar became a political asylum seeker in 2014 and now resides in California. He is pursuing a master's in law degree with a focus on international commercial law and dispute resolution. He also collaborates with some justices of the Supreme Court of Venezuela who are currently in exile, working on liberation efforts from the modern dictatorship in Venezuela.

My forced departure from Venezuela was a direct result of my defense of Venezuelan law and my home country's constitution. Under my supervision, I could not allow my courthouse to shirk its responsibilities to the Venezuelan people, despite sinister orders mandated by the most nefarious dictatorship in the contemporary history of our country. I would not partake in the plans of a group of criminal politicians who had kidnapped my country and committed the most serious violations of human rights, including inhuman torture, genocide, and the forced disappearance of opposition leaders.

In November 2013, I prosecuted a group of high-ranking police officers who had grossly violated the human rights of their prisoners. These men were executing the orders of Aristobulo Isturiz, who was state governor of Anzoátegui and would later serve under President Chavez as the vice president of Venezuela.

Over the next year, I received scathing phone calls from the vice president and from various law-makers demanding that I overturn my decision. After receiving numerous death threats from the collectives (Venezuelan civilians with police training that support the United Socialist Party of Venezuela and the Venezuelan government), I made the decision to flee from my homeland under political asylum. My colleagues and I knew all too well of the imprisonment and torture of Venezuelan Federal Judge Maria Afuini, who was attacked because she granted parole to a political prisoner based upon resolutions provided by the U.N. Working Group on Arbitrary Detention.

In 2014, I arrived in California disturbed, anguished, and full of fear. My only objective was to file for political asylum to the U.S. immigration authorities. Due to a spike in asylum cases at that time, I was informed that there was a long delay in grants for political asylum.

I met with three different immigration attorneys, but none was willing to accept my case because they said my story seemed unrealistic. What they didn't realize was that Venezuela, though one of the richest countries in the South American territory with the largest reserves of oil on the planet, was in a humanitarian crisis. After hours of interviews and translations, I had exhausted my life savings and was emotionally spent. I couldn't get a social security number or work without a temporary employment authorization document from the U.S. Citizenship and Immigration Services. I didn't have a legal identity or a credit history; therefore, I was unable to open a check account, get a credit card, or purchase medical insurance.

It took almost two years to receive my work permit and temporary social security number. I then had to navigate the U.S. employment system. My whole career existed in the Venezuelan courthouse so I never had to create a resume or a LinkedIn profile, much less learn the nuances of applying, interviewing, and obtaining references for employment. I then had to pass the California driver's exam. I could not receive driving privileges under the 2013 California law, AB 60, because Venezuela was not on the list of accepted countries.

My first U.S. job was in a home supplies company, but the schedule did not allow me to continue my English language classes, which I desperately needed. I then drove for Uber and Lyft. I am now on a path that will allow me to obtain a professional career in the United States. My goal is to practice law in the United States and I am working toward meeting the requirements to take the Bar exam and practice law in the United States of America.

Section 2: Fundamentals of seeking asylum

Unit 1: Important asylum-seeking terms

The U.N. High Commissioner for Refugees (UNHCR) describes three types of emergency situations that may cause people to flee from their homes. **Man-made** (or **human-made**) **emergencies** that threaten people's lives and livelihoods are caused primarily or directly from the actions of human beings and take the form of regional violence, civil war, and international conflict. Individuals, families, and communities around the world experience violence due to their race, religion, nationality, membership in a particular social group, or political opinion. **Natural disasters** that destroy resources and cause displacement of people from their homes are the effect of the Earth's natural processes, such as earthquakes, hurricanes, typhoons, flooding, and drought. **Health emergencies** in the form of the outbreak of infectious disease or bioterrorism cripple households and regions and can lead to migration in order to prevent serious health outcomes.

As stated before, **asylum** is the protection granted by a nation to a person who has left their country of origin in order to escape violence or persecution. Definitions regarding seeking asylum differ and are written to conform to international, national, and regional policies. This textbook incorporates definitions from the top international and national agencies, including UNHCR and the U.S. Citizenship and Immigration Services (USCIS).

UNHCR was created to protect the lives and human rights of refugees, asylum seekers, and internally displaced and stateless people. This agency works with people who have fled from their homes due to violence, persecution, war, or disaster. They provide items for emergency assistance, transportation, and income-generating projects. The goal is to provide each displaced person with the opportunity to return home or resettle in a safe place. Below are some of the definitions from this international agency that are relevant to seeking asylum.

According to UNHCR, a **refugee** is someone forced to flee their country due to violence, persecution, or war. The term refugee is defined under international and regional law. A refugee may move from one host country to another host country and is afforded the same legal protection. An **asylum seeker** is a person who is inside or outside the borders of a nation and appeals to the nation for asylum, but who has not yet been granted asylum. The goal of seeking asylum is to gain protection and material support from the asylum-granting nation. The asylum seeker must provide specific evidence as to why they fear persecution in the home country.

Persons who are caught in a country illegally can be expelled from the country in a process called **refoulement**. International law provides for **non-refoulement** for asylum seekers, meaning that a person who applies for asylum cannot be forcibly returned to their home country without a determination of need for asylum.

The term **migrant** has an international, standardized definition. It is understood that a migrant is someone who voluntarily crosses a border to seek better economic, educational, and social conditions or to join family. For example, an **economic migrant** is a person who seeks employment in another country. This does not include seeking asylum. The media often uses the term **international migration** to include the actions of voluntary migration, refugees, and asylum seekers. Many types of international migration are protected under human rights law. Due to the vulnerability of moving across international borders, displaced persons may experience the human rights violations of persecution, discrimination, arbitrary arrest and detention, rape, forced labor, and/or human trafficking. The United Nations discourages the use of the term "forced migration," stating that it is not a legal term.

Internally displaced persons (IDPs) are people who have been forced to flee their homes but have not crossed international borders. Internally displaced persons are not protected by international law or are not eligible to receive international aid, although UNHCR works to protect people who are internally displaced due to national armed conflict.

Returned refugees are people who return to their country of origin but have not yet been integrated back into their communities.

Persons are considered stateless when not identified as citizens of any country under international law.

Unit 2: The process of seeking asylum in the United States

USCIS is a governmental agency in charge of legal immigration into the United States. The task of this agency is to grant immigration and citizenship. Two of the agency's strategic goals are 1) to identify, address, and mitigate national security and fraud risks to the immigration system and 2) to promote the importance, rights, and responsibilities of citizenship.

In the United States, an application for asylum may only be sought if the person is physically in the United States or is at a U.S. port of entry, whether a U.S. airport, international highway crossing, or seaport. A person who is outside of the United States may apply for refugee status. U.S. immigration officials are authorized to use **expedited removal** to immediately deport persons who are illegally in the country. **Due process** means that each person has the right to fair treatment within the judicial system, although the rights of asylum seekers are different than the rights of the citizens of a nation. A compelling argument must be made to an immigration judge that the person asking for asylum fears death, torture, or persecution upon return to their country of origin. A person who has recently come to the United States without permission for the first time may claim **credible fear** of persecution should they be forced to return to the country of origin. If the person has 1) been previously deported, had a previous order of deportation, or was convicted of an aggravated felony (as defined by the Congress), 2) is not a lawful permanent resident of the United States, and 3) is afraid to return to their home country, the person may claim **reasonable fear** as the reason for asking for asylum. This means that the person has a reasonable possibility of being killed, attacked, or persecuted upon return to the home country.

The **affirmative asylum process** of USCIS requires seven steps. In the first step, the person who wishes to seek asylum must physically arrive in the United States or must seek entry at a U.S. port of entry. In the second step, the person must apply for asylum using a Form I-589 (Application for Asylum and for Withholding of Removal) within one year of arriving in the United States. A person may not be eligible to apply for asylum if they applies after the one-year deadline for arrival in the United States, has been previously denied asylum in the United States by an immigration judge or the Board of Immigration Appeals, or can be removed to a third country under an international agreement. In the third step, fingerprinting must be done at an application support center so that background and security checks on the asylum seeker may be completed.

The fourth step is the receipt of a notice of interview to be held at a USCIS office. In the fifth step, an asylum officer interviews the asylum seeker, as well as a spouse and children if they are also seeking asylum. The asylum seeker may bring an attorney or another accredited representative to the interview. In the sixth step, the asylum officer determines the eligibility for asylum and the decision is reviewed by a supervisory officer. The asylum seekers must provide an interpreter for this meeting, if one is necessary. The asylum officer determines whether the asylum seeker is eligible to apply for asylum, meets the definition of a refugee in section 101(a)(42)(A) of the Immigration and Nationality Act (INA), or is barred from being granted asylum under section 208(b)(2) of the INA. The final, seventh step is receipt of the decision from the asylum office, generally within two weeks of the interview. The decision will either be that the person has been granted asylum or that the person is being processed for removal from the country.

Under the U.S. **defensive asylum process,** persons can apply for asylum while they are being processed by the immigration court for expedited removal. This occurs when an affirmative asylum application has been rejected, the person has been placed in removal proceedings because they were apprehended in the United States without legal documentation to be in the United States, or the person was caught by U.S. Customs and Border Protection (CBP) while trying to illegally enter the country. If the asylum seeker has this status, the case will be heard in a courtroom setting by an immigration judge from the U.S. Department of Justice (DOJ) Executive Office for Immigration Review. Both the asylum seeker (possibly represented by an attorney) and an attorney from U.S. Immigration and Customs Enforcement (ICE) will present arguments. The court provides an interpreter; the presiding judge makes the final asylum decision.

Section 3: Issues of human rights violations associated with seeking asylum

An asylum seeker is differentially defined within both national and international legislation. In the United States, for example, seeking asylum means that a person is illegally in the country and has made a formal request to be allowed to reside within the United States because of threats of death, injury, or persecution in the person's home country.

The authors have chosen to specify this particular group of refugees due to the fact that the majority of the human rights violations appear to happen within this group. Asylum seekers are not able to safely return to their home countries. Transit countries are often overwhelmed with the multitude of people seeking asylum at any one time due to civil or territorial disputes, genocides, or other means of persecution of a person or group. Federal, regional, and local regulations on the designation of asylum seeker vary depending upon the host country.

Unit 1: National agreements

There are three federal agencies involved in operating the response to people seeking asylum in the United States: The Bureau of Population, Refugees, and Migration (PRM) in the Department of State, the Office of Refugee Resettlement (ORR) in the Department of Health and Human Services (HHS), and the asylum division of USCIS in the Department of Homeland Security (DHS). The responsibilities and activities of each organization have a certain amount of influence on the other organizations. There is some inter-agency cooperation.

PRM is charged with creating policy related to population, refugees, and migration. In addition, this bureau administers two funds related to seeking asylum. The first of these is the Migration and Refugee Assistance Act (MRA) of 1962. This fund is designated for the U.S. Government's refugee admissions and overseas refugee assistance programs and to provide for initial refugee resettlement in the United States. The second fund is the Emergency Refugee and Migration Assistance (ERMA), which provides funding to ensure that the

U.S. Government has sufficient resources for refugee assistance in unanticipated and urgent humanitarian crises. The president of the United States can draw from this fund to respond to emergencies related to refugees. The PRM works closely with the DHS, international organizations, and nongovernmental organizations.

ORR is in charge of the resettlement and integration of refugees and other vulnerable populations into the United States. The office's five divisions cover refugee assistance, refugee health, resettlement services, children's services (including unaccompanied minors), and the office of the director. This office provides social services for refugees and works to link refugee needs to available resources.

USCIS deals with administrative tasks related to migration, including handling petitions, applications, employment authorization documents, and immigrant benefits; determining whether claims of persecution are consistent with U.S. federal law; and granting permanent resident status and U.S. citizenship.

The two main legal instruments in the United States regarding the seeking of asylum are the Immigration and Nationality Act of 1965 and Code of Federal Regulations title 8, chapter I, subchapter B, part 208 of the Code of Federal Regulations (8 CFR Part 208). The Immigration and Nationality Act of 1965 (H.R. 2580; Pub.L. 89–236, 79 Stat. 911), also called the Hart-Celler Act, amended the Immigration and Nationality Act of 1952, also called the McCarran-Walter Act. Both acts were revisions of the Emergency Quota Act of 1921 which used the National Origin Formula as the basis for allocation of migrant status.

The Hart-Celler Act continued to use migrant allocation by country, but changed the way the United States allocated immigration quotas in terms of focus on immigrant skills and family relationships. National origin, race, or ancestry are no longer the basis for immigration numbers. The number of migrants was set at 170,000 per year, but this does not include immediate relatives of U.S. citizens and "special immigrants," including ministers, former U.S. government employees, foreign medical students, and other special categories.

U.S. federal law related to the procedures for seeking asylum is found in title 8, chapter I, subchapter B, part 208 of the Code of Federal Regulations (8 CFR Part 208). Subpart A relates to asylum and withholding of removal and subpart B relates to credible fear of persecution. Part 241 provides the procedures for the apprehension and detention of aliens ordered removed. Particulars of these rulings follow.

An asylum seeker must apply for asylum within one year of arriving in the United States by submitting a Form I-589 (Application for Asylum and for the Withholding of Removal) to USCIS. The application must give evidence of credible fear of persecution or torture if the applicant is returned to the home country. If the application is rejected by USCIS, the asylum seeker is issued a Form I-862 (Notice to Appear). This means the asylum seeker must appear before an immigration judge, who provides a new hearing of the case and issues a judgment about asylum that is independent of the decision by USCIS.

In the United States, an asylum seeker may apply for employment authorization using a Form I-765 (Application for Employment Authorization). The person will receive Employment Authorization Documents (EADs) to begin work 1) if asylum has been granted or 2) if the asylum application was filed 150 days in the past, no delays were caused by the applicant, and no decision has been made on the asylum application.

If the asylum seeker has been granted asylum in the United States, they may apply for a green card (Permanent Resident Card) by filing a Form I-485 (Application to Register Permanent Residence or Adjust Status) and an immigration petition with USCIS. There are a number of immigration petitions and most require that someone else sponsor the applicant.

This may be done by a relative who is a permanent resident in the United States or a company who is sponsoring a worker.

A person who has been granted asylum in the United States may petition to bring their spouse and children to the United States by filing a Form I-730 (Refugee/Asylee Relative Petition). The petition must be filed within two years of being granted asylum, except in the case of humanitarian reasons which extend this date.

According to U.S. federal law, there are a number of situations that prevent a person from being granted asylum, and these may result in removal from the country. This can happen if there are reasons to believe that the person has persecuted other people, been convicted of a serious crime, or has been firmly resettled in another country. The person may also be disqualified from asylum if there is evidence or likelihood of engagement in terrorist activity, if the person is a member or representative of a terrorist organization, or if there is reasonable proof that the person is a danger to the security of the United States.

The Immigration and Nationality Act of 1965 and the Migration and Refugee Assistance Act of 1962 were amended by the U.S. Refugee Act of 1980 (Public Law 96–212). This Act adopted the definition for refugees found in the U.N. Refugee Convention on the Status of Refugees of 1951 and the Protocol of 1967, which is discussed below. This act created a systematic procedure which 1) allows people to seek asylum regardless of their legal status in the United States, and 2) makes provisions for resettlement of refugees. In addition, the act makes provision for the U.S. attorney general to grant asylum.

Unit 2: International agreements

Article 14 of the Universal Declaration of Human Rights (UDHR) of 1948 states that all persons without restriction have the right to seek asylum and enjoy safety from persecution. Article 15 adds that each person has the right to a nationality and the right to change nationality. In addition, no person should be deprived of their nationality.

The three main international policy instruments governing the rights and obligations of seeking asylum are 1) the 1951 U.N. Refugee Convention, 2) the U.N. Protocol Relating to the Status of Refugees of 1967, and 3) the Organisation of African Unity (OAU) Convention Governing the Specific Aspects of Refugee Problems in Africa of 1969. In addition, the 1954 UNHCR Convention relating to the Status of Stateless Persons and the 1961 UNHCR Convention on the Reduction of Statelessness focus on reducing the incidence of statelessness, a subject not included in the Convention of 1951. This was followed by the 1985 U.N. Declaration on the Human Rights of Individuals who are not Nationals of the Country in which They Live, with the purpose of protecting the human rights of foreign nationals living outside their countries of origin.

The U.N. Refugee Convention on the Status of Refugees of 1951 sets the international standards for protection and treatment of refugees. UNHCR supervises the implementation of the convention among member states. When a person applies for asylum (due to fear of persecution related to nationality, race, religion, political belief, or social membership in a particular group) under the U.N. Refugee Convention on the Status of Refugees of 1951, that person officially becomes an asylum seeker. The person remains an asylum seeker until the application is approved or the refusal of the application is finalized. (Further, if the asylum seeker application is successful, the person becomes a refugee.)

Article 33 of the convention provides for non-refoulement, so that an asylum seeker cannot be forced to return to the country of origin and into situations that threaten life or freedom. Individual nations are charged with protecting asylum seekers from refoulement, except in the case where the asylum seeker has committed serious crimes in the country of origin or is a threat to national security. UNHCR advises and supports nations in carrying out the provisions of the convention. The 1967 U.N. Protocol Relating to the Status of Refugees amends the time-sensitive deadlines and geographic limitations found in the convention of 1951.

The 1954 U.N. Convention relating to the Status of Stateless Persons adds provisions for persons who are stateless, meaning that they are not recognized as a citizen of any country. Statelessness may result from leaving a non-state territory (for example, American Samoa), renouncing one's own citizenship, being a citizen of a state that has seceded from a recognized nation, being female (in some countries), and being subject to a conflict of law or administrative obstacles. Member nations that sign the U.N. Convention on the Reduction of Statelessness of 1961 agree to reduce the incidence of statelessness within their borders. The convention created rules for the provision of nationality and benefits to stateless persons.

The OAU Convention Governing the Specific Aspects of Refugee Problems in Africa of 1969 expanded on the Convention of 1951. The definition of refugee was broadened to include elements which caused the flight, including environmental catastrophes, foreign domination, and traumatic public events. In addition, the convention uses place of habitation rather than country of nationality. This convention prohibited discrimination; it also includes provisions for resettlement and financial support between member states. The convention declares that seeking asylum could not be considered by member nations to be a negative act. However, the convention accepts individual states' discretion in choosing to grant asylum. The convention prohibits refoulement in any form and was the first codification into law of voluntary repatriation, in which a refugee chooses to return to the country of origin.

The U.N. Declaration on the Human Rights of Individuals who are not Nationals of the Country in which They Live of 1985 guarantees civil, political, and working condition rights to aliens living in a country. It further prohibits expulsion of a person or group due to discriminating factors.

Unit 3: Controversies

There are a number of controversies related to seeking asylum, including issues with immigration law, officials, and detention; enforcement of immigration law; and validity of asylum claims. For example, each sovereign nation has the right to determine the number and composition of asylum seekers to which it will grant asylum. Over the years, countries have faced criticism, and even lawsuits, for legislation, processes, and procedure that were challenged as discriminatory and disregarding international law.

Expedited removal has been challenged as an unfair practice which does not allow asylum seekers the protection of presenting their cases before an immigration judge. Due process under the law means the non-refoulement process protects persons who likely would face dangerous or deadly situations if returned to their home countries. There are claims related to due process alleging that asylum seekers have been targeted for expedited removal before they can be interviewed by immigration officials or appear before an immigration judge. Due to the mass movement of people in the world today, it is difficult for countries' administrations to keep up with the need for individual asylum interviews and reviews. In 1995, several reforms by the U.S. Congress increased the number of both asylum officers and judges to help clear the backlog of asylum cases. It also made provision for an expedited removal process for anyone trying to enter the United States without proper documentation and anyone who did not claim asylum within the first year of illegally being in the country. If a person claims asylum during the expedited removal process, that person is placed into custody and held in a detention center.

Detention has been contested as a tool to deter asylum seeking. Detention procedures have been called inhumane and unfair as men, women, children, and the elderly have been detained for long periods of time in sparse or dangerous conditions with no access to due process. There are claims that governments have targeted certain groups for detention, such as those from countries where terrorist organizations are active. Conditions in detention centers have led to deaths, suicides, injuries, incidents of brutality, rape, inadequate medical and psychological care, lack of nutrition and foods that are unsatisfactory due to religious beliefs, and lack of access to immigration counselors and lawyers.

Despite the extensive asylum-seeking process, some cases of seeking asylum have been questioned as trying to bypass the normal immigration process. Incidences of this type have been associated with the circumstances of arrival into the host country. For instance, a person may claim asylum at the time of arrest by U.S. Border Patrol, even if the person has gained illegal entry through the paid services of a human smuggler.

CHECK YOURSELF BOX: PERSONAL BIASES ABOUT SEEKING ASYLUM

Write down your first thoughts when you hear the words refugee and asylum seeker. Do the terms elicit any emotions – anger, sympathy, wariness – or no emotion at all? Have you had a personal experience with a refugee or asylum seeker, or been one yourself? How do your friends and your family talk about refugees or asylum seekers? Do you tend to agree or disagree with them? Now that you know the difference between refugees and asylum seekers, do you have different opinions on the two groups? Remember that there are no right or wrong answers to these questions. Answering each can help you determine your biases in the area of asylum seeking. Having these biases in mind when you do research and stating them when needed makes your research more scientific and useable for policy-making.

◼ Section 4: History of seeking asylum

History relates that people have been migrating across the world for around 60,000 years. Migration occurred across land masses and ancient land bridges, and by water. Since the beginning of recorded history, people have fled war, slaughter, social unrest, and natural catastrophe and have sought asylum in other territories and countries. There seems to have been no beginning to this movement of endangered people, and there is no end in sight. A look through international and national legislation presents a picture of the issues faced when dealing with seeking asylum and the integration of refugees into society once asylum is granted.

In the book *The making of the modern refugee*, Peter Gatrell (2013) states, "Twentieth-century displacement was unprecedented by virtue of being linked to the collapse of multi-national empires, the emergence of the modern state with a bounded citizenship, the spread of totalizing ideologies that hounded internal enemies, and the internationalization of responses to refugee crises." The most severe refugee crises today include the displacement of over 23 million people from Syria, Afghanistan, the Lake Chad Basin, South Sudan, and Somalia (Mercy Corps, 2017), with half of the total due to conflict in Syria. Violence is the main cause of this displacement and other contributors are political instability, flooding, drought, famine, and natural disasters.

According to Eurostat (2017), there were around 2.3 million applications for asylum into the European Union in 2016, including 53,000 first-time asylum applicants. Martin Armstrong (2017) reports Organisation for Economic Co-operation and Development (OECD) statistics showing that the countries receiving the most asylum applications in 2016 were Germany (over 700,000), the United States (nearly 300,000), and Italy (over 100,000), followed by France and Turkey (around 78,000 applications to each country). Applicants to Germany were mainly from Syria, Afghanistan, and Iraq, while applicants to the United States were primarily from El Salvador, Mexico, and Guatemala.

Jens Krogstad, Jeffrey Passel, and D'Vera Cohn of Pew Research Center (2017) estimate there were eight million unauthorized immigrants in the U.S. civilian labor force (5% of the total labor force) out of the 11 million unauthorized immigrants in the United States in 2015. They further point out that 60% of these immigrants worked in California, Texas, Florida, New York, and New Jersey and two-thirds had lived in the United States for at least ten years.

Section 5: Meet the experts on asylum seeking

Three agencies within the U.S. Department of Homeland Security (DHS) control immigration into the United States: 1) U.S. Citizenship and Immigration Services (USCIS), 2) U.S. Immigration and Customs Enforcement (ICE), and 3) U.S. Customs and Border Protection (CBP). As previously discussed, USCIS handles administrative tasks related to migration: this includes handling petitions, applications, employment authorization documents, and immigrant benefits, and the granting of permanent resident status and U.S. citizenship. The other two agencies are in charge of federal law enforcement. ICE has two law enforcement directorates: Homeland Security Investigations (HSI), which deals with national security and intelligence, and Enforcement and Removal Operations (ERO), which enforces U.S. immigration laws and facilitates deportation of illegal immigrants. CBP's primary focus is the regulations of trade, customs, and immigration to provide safety at the borders of the United States.

Immigration experts and research centers can be found in many countries around the world. There are so many varieties and aspects of asylum seeking that the range of experts is wide. It includes, but is not limited to, the fields of law, politics, public policy, border security, law enforcement, international studies, economics, human rights, ethics, anthropology, and religion. Knowledge about asylum seeking can be found in studies on asylum or refugee law, human smuggling, human trafficking, and torture.

Many journals include articles that discuss asylum seeking and immigration issues. Some of these include *Journal of Refugee Studies*, *Refugee Survey Quarterly*, *Forced Migration Review*, *International Journal of Refugee Law*, *Journal of Immigrant and Minority Health*, and *Refuge*.

There are hundreds of international and regional nonprofit organizations or nongovernment organizations which work with asylum seekers. International and national nonprofit organizations include the International Rescue Committee (IRC), Refugees International, Islamic Relief, UNHCR, World Relief, Doctors Without Borders (Médecins Sans Frontières), Mercy Corps, International Medical Corps, War Child, Amnesty International, Human Rights First, the Asylum Seeker Assistance Project and the U.S. Committee for Refugees and Immigrants in Washington, D.C., the Asylum Seeker Advocacy Project in New York, the Refugee Council in the U.K., Asylum Access, the Asylum Seeker Resource Centre (ASRC) and the Asylum Seekers Centre in Australia, and the Organization for Refuge, Asylum, and Migration (ORAM). Other organizations that work in some capacity with issues of seeking asylum include Human Rights Watch, the International Committee of the Red Cross, the U.N. International Organization for Migration (IOM), Oxfam International, World Relief, Church World Service, and the Detention Watch Network. The European Council on Refugees and Exiles (ECRE) is an alliance of European non-governmental organizations that works to establish asylum policies and practices.

Within the wide range of databases related to asylum seeking are the Asylum Information Database (AIDA), the Brookings-Bern Project on International Displacement, the Internal Displacement Monitoring Centre (IDMC), and the Migration Policy Institute's Migration Data Hub. There are a number of legal databases related to asylum seeking, including the European Database of Asylum Law, HeinOnline Foreign & International Law Resources Database, and the International Association of Refugee Law Judges (IARLJ). The UNHCR has databases that include the Statistical Online Population Database as well as RefWorld, which helps to determine refugee status and contains documentation of international and national law. The OECD has the International Migration Database.

A wealth of knowledge may be gleaned from people who have been asylum seekers, including reasons for and barriers to seeking asylum, support systems, and procedures and hindrances to gaining asylum. Refugee Congress is one organization that unites asylum seekers, refugees, and stateless persons to work on national and international issues that affect their lives. This organization has a map of resettlement agencies that support refugees in the United States.

CHECK YOURSELF BOX: SEEKING ASYLUM RESEARCH AND DATA BIASES

Topics that are controversial can lead to bias in research and data collection. Seeking asylum is certainly a controversial topic, with opinions dependent upon personal experience, the opinions of friends and family, and economic and political situations. What are the "sides" of the issue? Look again at the experts on seeking asylum. What might their biases be? You can gain valuable information by looking at the biographical information on researchers and other decision-makers to see how their backgrounds play a role in their decisions. Who created the databases? Are there political, financial, or personal reasons why the data may be biased in some way? The point of this exercise is to clarify how scientific the research and data are and how they may contain bias or be misleading.

Section 6: Economic structure of seeking asylum

As long as there are wars, terrorism, torture, and social unrest, people will flee their homes to other territories for protection. The journey to safety involves decisions made by the seekers of asylum, and by the people and organizations with whom they come into contact along the journey. More decisions will be made at the end of the journey when asylum is officially sought, and when asylum is granted. The discussion now turns to the decision-makers, their decisions, and the economic structure of seeking asylum.

There are four main decision-making groups associated with asylum seeking. The first are people who seek asylum in a foreign territory when they cannot go back to their home country for fear of persecution. A person determines to undertake the quest for asylum for many reasons. The person may have spoken out about injustice in the home country or may have spoken against powerful people in the government or people in other positions of dominance, such as drug lords. In this case, individuals have chosen to follow their consciences and to speak out, knowing that there are consequences that may endanger themselves and possibly their families. Civil war, terrorism, environmental catastrophe, or other events could have been the impetus for the journey. The person could be experiencing persecution in the home country due to their race, religion, nationality, membership of a social group, or political opinion. This persecution might have involved torture or death threats against the asylum seeker or family, loss of employment, and limited freedom of speech, representation, and movement. The decision to flee is made for personal, and often family, safety. Determining to seek asylum means getting to an international border crossing or crossing an international border. At an international border, a person may state that they want to seek asylum. Whether a person legally enters or illegally crosses the border, they may then apply for asylum once inside the country.

The second group includes those in power in the home country, including the home-country government and others in positions of power. The political and social situation in a country determines how the government protects its citizens. Government officials have differing agendas and may choose to provide safety to groups who support them while persecuting groups and individuals who oppose them. If there is civil war or other types of social unrest, the government may have little power to protect anyone. The lack of protection and possibly persecution by the home government puts individuals at risk and may lead to those persons seeking asylum in another country.

An asylum seeker may move through a transit country before reaching the country where they will apply for asylum. As an example, Peter Kenyon (2015) of NPR reports that in 2015 Turkey accepted two million refugees from Syria and Iraq, paying around $7.5 billion for their shelter and food. However, Turkey will not offer these refugees asylum. Most of the refugees are dispersed throughout cities in Turkey. Those who are seeking asylum through the United Nations must wait – sometimes for years – to be resettled in other countries. Jessica Schulberg (2015) reports that a relatively small percentage (11%) of the total number of Syrian refugees in Turkey live in refugee camps. These refugees have access to medical care, but are restricted from some housing and social services.

When the asylum seekers leave home, they cross paths with many people along the journey. These include people who are sympathetic to asylum seekers; people who are opposed to immigration through or into their countries; people who are predatory in terms of taking advantage of asylum seekers; law enforcement officials; migrants; and other asylum seekers. Together, these people make up the third group of decision-makers.

Just as a homeless person on the streets may be overlooked by the citizens of that city, asylum seekers and refugees are rarely at the forefront of people's concerns and therefore are often ignored. Few people in a city know how many refugees and asylum seekers live within their city's boundaries. Some groups and individuals exploit the vulnerabilities of asylum seekers. These could be individuals who want to steal from asylum seekers or trick them into giving away useful information. Gangs or other organizations may be organized to exploit vulnerabilities of persons outside of their home territories. Human trafficking fits into this category, as asylum seekers are placed in vulnerable positions in which they may be forced to work for the people controlling them, or they may be held for ransom by the human traffickers. In this third group, however, there are many individuals and groups who genuinely care about the well-being of asylum seekers, such as the international and international nonprofit and nongovernmental organizations that work on asylum seeking and refugee issues.

The fourth group appears at the end of the journey in the form of government officials who come into contact with the asylum seekers and have made choices related to asylum-seeking procedures and outcomes. National laws may be in place to allow asylum seekers to ask for asylum once they reach a national border. If the asylum seeker has reached the border of the United States, they will engage with officials from the U.S. CBP. If the asylum seeker does not have a visa to be legally in the United States, they will be detained for an asylum hearing, as described before. Alternately, the asylum seeker may have crossed over illegally into the country intending to apply for asylum later. If the asylum seeker applies for asylum within one year of entering the country, they will go through the asylum determination process. It is also possible that ICE will catch the person illegally in the United States. The person is then held for deportation, unless they apply for asylum, as discussed previously. Only upon the granting of asylum does the asylum seeker officially become a refugee with certain rights and responsibilities in the host country.

Public opinion plays a powerful role in the determination of the characteristics and number of people who are granted asylum. The labor of immigrants as a substitute or complement to the labor of country natives plays a role in the opinions that push for smaller numbers of refugees.

The **labor market** is the place where the labor of workers is matched with the demand of firms for labor input for production. **Supply of labor** or **labor supply** (S_L) can be either the sum of the number of workers or the hours of work provided by the workers, depending upon the data used. Labor supply is upward sloping because an increase in wages leads to an increased quantity of labor supplied. **Demand for labor** or **labor demand** (D_L) is the number of workers the firm intends to hire or the number of hours of work the firm plans to use in production, which is dependent upon the market wage. Since wage is a cost to firms, an increase in wage leads to a decrease in the quantity of labor demanded by firms and thus labor demand is downward sloping. Labor demand is based on the **productivity** (output per worker hour) and the price at which the firm can sell the output produced by the worker. The labor supply and labor demand in a labor market determine the market wage and quantity of labor employed.

Some political groups and the media proclaim that international immigrants are "stealing native jobs." This claim is feasible if the migrant workers and native workers are substitutes. A **substitute** is used in place of something else. One worker's skills and talents may be the same as another worker's. This means that the labor of either worker could be equally used as an input into production without losing productivity. When migrant workers' labor input is equal to native workers' labor input, firms can choose to hire either set of workers without losing productivity. Migrant workers may be willing to work for lower wages than native workers, who are then forced to look for alternate employment. It important to note that this same situation can occur as groups of native workers (labor supply) or companies (who create labor demand) move from one area to another.

The initial labor market is shown in Figure 4.1, with native (N) labor supply S_{LN} and labor demand D_{L1}. The labor market equilibrium is at labor quantity Q_{L1} and wage w_1 and all of the labor supplied (Q_{LSN1}) and demanded (Q_{LD1}) is the labor hours of native workers.

Figure 4.2 illustrates the case in which migrant (M) labor moves into the market. The labor supply increases, as shown by the rightward movement of the labor supply curve from S_{LN} to S_{LN+M}. The graph shows that the quantity of workers finding labor increases to Q_{L2}, but at lower wages (w_2). Now, the total amount of labor supplied (Q_{LS2}) is supplied by both native workers (Q_{LSN2}) and migrant workers (Q_{LSM2}) while the total amount of labor demanded by firms is Q_{LD2} and $Q_{L2} = Q_{LD2} = Q_{LS2} = Q_{LSN2} + Q_{LSM2}$.

FIGURE 4.1 Labor market equilibrium

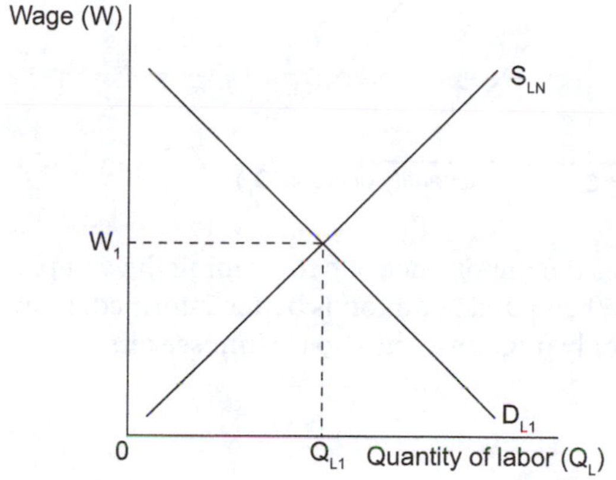

FIGURE 4.2 Movement of labor supply into a labor market

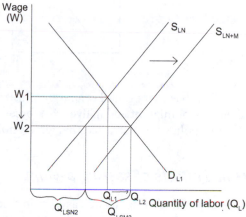

It may be the case that the skills, talents, and experiences of workers from a foreign country are quite different than those of native workers. This difference in human capital could make the foreign workers (migrants) complements to native workers. A **complement** enhances something else. In the case of labor, one worker's skills and talents may complement or enhance another worker's skills and talents, thus leading to increased productivity (output per worker hour) for one or both workers. This means that the company and thus the economy benefit from the combination of the two workers. Due to the fact that the labor of the migrant population is not the same as the labor of the native population, an increase in the labor supply of the migrant population does not increase the total labor supply of a particular market as in Figure 4.2. Instead, the increase in the migrant population leads to an increase in native workers' productivity. Since labor demand is based partially upon worker productivity (as discussed above), an increase in native worker productivity due to the increase in complementary migrant labor leads to an increase in the demand for native labor. This is shown in Figure 4.3 as a rightward shift in the labor demand curve D_{L1} to D_{L2} and the subsequent increase in the quantity of labor employed (Q_{L1} to Q_{L2}) with an accompanying increase in the native workers' wages (w_1 to w_2), due to the increased demand for native labor.

FIGURE 4.3 Increase in labor demand in a market

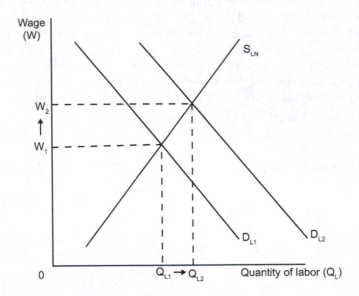

This basic labor market analysis illustrates the importance of determining the complementarity of migrant and native workforces. When public opinion is better informed, more effective policy is constructed that affects not only migrants, but also asylum seekers.

Unit 1: Costs of seeking asylum

A person who chooses to seek asylum in a new country has decided that the costs of staying at home outweigh the benefits. These costs could include loss of family property, personal possessions, and assets; and also personal or family danger from gangs, political or religious zealots, or government persecution.

The decision to seek asylum in another area or country is not a decision lightly taken. When the person chooses to seek asylum from persecution or disaster, the costs are often monetary, physical, and psychological and occur at home, along the journey, upon entry into the host country, and while integrating into the new country. Monetary costs include loss of previously-owned physical property, moving expenses if personal items can be taken along, loss of income from former employment, the difficulty of accessing personal funds in accounts in foreign countries, and funds that must be used for all aspects of international travel, to secure visas and other documentation, to pay possible bribes, and to begin a new life.

Physical costs occur when the travel is physically debilitating or dangerous. Travel circumstances that are physically costly may involve walking long distances, incurring injuries during travel, spending long periods in confined spaces, and lacking medical attention, medicines, and sanitary conditions. Danger may come when crossing hostile terrain or during incarceration, and may be in the form of physical attack, sexual assault or rape, or from travel circumstances, such as ocean travel by small boat or riding unsecured on trains or trucks.

Possible psychological costs may include loss of the security of being able to return to one's home; temporary or permanent separation from family, friends, pets, and familiar surroundings; possible loss of identity; living with fear and unknown risks; loss of culture and a familiar language; and having to rely upon strangers for support in the host country. The asylum seeker must live with the uncertainty of whether the separation will be temporary or permanent, depending upon how circumstances change in the home country. In addition, the person must learn to live in a different culture, create new social networks, find employment and schooling, and deal with many other issues associated with moving to a new country.

The asylum seekers may face detention at some point along their physical journeys. Detention means being taken in official custody and being unable to leave. Beyond the losses of the right of freedom of movement, costs of detention to the asylum seeker may include facing unsanitary and inhumane conditions, danger of injury from other detainees and from guards, loss of privacy due to severe overcrowding, and loss of time (because the detention may persist for a long time). Also, the detainee may need to learn the new culture within the detention center; lose personal possessions due to theft or confiscation by the detention center authorities or other detainees; or have to work or pay bribes in order to get better treatment, food, or consideration for removal from detention.

Losses to the home country may also be significant. Losing asylum seekers to another country may create a brain drain for the home country as educated, highly-skilled persons leave the country. The country may face political pressure and economic barriers from other nations and the international community due to the circumstances under which people fled. In addition, the asylum seeker may work to build resistance, resources, and funds in the host country to fight against injustice in the home country.

A number of costs also accrue to the country to which the asylum seeker is applying for asylum. These include the administrative costs of the asylum process, the costs of incarceration, the opportunity cost of choosing to permit one person's application while denying another's, political costs if the asylum seeker's home country retaliates for the granting of asylum, and law enforcement costs if the violence pursues the asylum seeker. There are tremendous costs to the home country in terms of the court system, law enforcement, and corrections. In addition, the host country bears the stress on local resources of supporting and integrating the asylum seeker into the new country in a process which may include housing, job and language training, employment, medical care, counseling, schooling, transportation, and further documentation. Host countries must also work to strengthen local and national security regulations, which may be a concern to both the existing population and to the people who are granted asylum. This apprehension may be due to the difficulties of integrating different cultures, the possibility of increased crime rates, pressure on bureaucracies to track asylum seekers, or fear of terrorists entering the country. A study by Tesfaye Gebremedhin and Astghik Mavisakalyan (2013) finds that political stability may be affected if the population in the receiving country is averse to the immigrant population. There may be an increased destabilizing effect in places with laws that give migrant populations citizenship.

Many countries have a limit to the number of asylum applications they approve each year, and the demand for asylum far outweighs the supply of asylum grants. When one person is granted asylum status, another person may lose the opportunity to do so.

Unit 2: Benefits of seeking asylum

The benefits of receiving asylum are evident for the seekers of asylum and subtle for decision-makers. When asylum seekers flee, they are escaping the immediate violence, persecution, or destruction in their home countries. This does not negate the possibility of confronting other volatile situations along the journey to asylum. If asylum is granted, the asylum seeker has the possibility of better employment and economic opportunities, joining family and friends in the host country, living in a stable society, and the ability to send financial assistance (called remittance payments) to those left in desperate situations in the countries of origin.

The home country that the asylum seeker left may benefit from the decreased opposition to the decisions of the government or other persons in power. Hedley Bull (2011) reports the many benefits the home country receives from migration. These include the benefit of remittances to those who stay in the home country (which bolster the local economy), the decreased governmental burden of welfare for those who migrate, decreased unemployment as people leave the country, and the use of a "safety value for the release of social tensions."

The Humanitarian Innovation Project is a venture of the Oxford's Refugee Studies Centre. The project focuses on refugee economies and highlights how economies can flourish in areas where refugees are given opportunities and resources to create businesses. Host countries who grant asylum will often benefit from the education, skills, talent, and innovative ideas brought by those fleeing persecution and disaster in their home countries. Those who migrate to new countries are looking for financial and social opportunities and have personal contributions to make to the economy and society as a whole. Once work documents are received, asylum seekers make purchases in the host economy and pay taxes on their wages. Asylum seekers are often intolerant of injustice and bring this perspective and strength into the host country.

When a person who has been granted asylum uses their opportunities well, it creates a positive outlook for other asylum seekers. New people are more likely to be welcomed into a country because of the tangible evidence of positive contributions from the original persons who sought asylum in the country.

Unit 3: Inefficiencies in economic structure of seeking asylum

Research by Jaya Ramji-Nogales, Andrew Schoenholtz, and Philip Schrag (2011) finds that multiple factors influence whether a person is granted asylum – including the personality of the immigration official. The report includes research at all four levels of the asylum decision, including the DHS, the immigration courts, the Board of Immigration Appeals, and the U.S. Court of Appeals. This finding of arbitrariness in asylum decisions is reinforced by the Transactional Records Access Clearinghouse report (2017) which states that the outcome of the asylum decision is strongly correlated to the immigration judge assigned to the case. The burden of proof is with asylum seekers, who must show that they cannot return to their countries of origin due to fear of persecution on account of race, religion, nationality, membership of a particular social group, or political opinion. It may be difficult for asylum seekers who had to leave their homes quickly with few personal items to provide the necessary evidence.

Historically, it has been difficult to do quality research on asylum seeking due to the lack of data. Christian Dustmann and Joseph-Simon Görlach (2016), however, report that better surveys and linkages between government data sources are creating more comprehensive, useable datasets.

The rules governing asylum decisions at one point in time can be changed quickly depending upon the public opinion and politics of the day. In addition, due to the mass movement of people, there is an insufficient number of immigration officers and asylum judges to cover each asylum case in a thorough and timely manner.

Section 7: Case study

Seeking asylum country choice

At any given point in time, there are multitudes of individuals undergoing the process of seeking asylum in order to gain refugee status. Most migration data, however, would predict that if safety were the only reason for seeking asylum, then between two countries, the asylum seeker would choose the country with the closest proximity to the origin country given the relative cost of traveling further distances. Furthermore, closer countries are more likely to have a similar culture to the origin country compared to further countries, which is generally appealing to migrants. However, this case study seeks to show that by using an adapted version of the Roy Model, one can demonstrate why an asylum seeker may rationally choose a country that is in farther away from their home country despite increased travel costs and less cultural similarity.

The Roy Model was first introduced in the 1950s by Professor Andrew Roy (1951). The model was then recast in mathematical terms by Dr. George Borjas (1987) and applied to self-selection in migration. Roy hypothesizes that wages are not arbitrarily distributed but rather are determined by skill level and production technology. Borjas then applies this notion to migration decisions. The theory, which was then supported empirically, is that relative wage differentials and income inequalities between the two countries motivate the migration of workers who possess skill levels in the lower and upper tails of the skill distribution. Borjas extends this to explain why the wages of migrants who self-select to settle in the receiving country for a number of years typically exceed the wages of natives.

Unlike refugees leaving a country for economic gain, asylum seekers leave primarily for safety reasons. However, by implementing a number of assumptions, it can be theoretically shown why asylum seekers may choose to seek asylum in a more distant country even if there is a closer country with a more similar culture. This model assumes that a migrant from the origin country ("O") can only choose between two destination countries, A and B. Countries A and B have relatively similar cultures, although both differ greatly from country O. Additionally, this model assumes that country A and B are equally safe and have equal likelihood that the asylum seeker will acquire refugee status in the same amount of time. Country B is further from O than A, leading to a higher cost of migrating to B relative to migrating to A. Finally, the model assumes that each asylum seeker has full decision-making ability over which country will be their destination. Given these assumptions and a cost–benefit analysis made under rational choice, asylum seekers should choose country A over country B if wages are similar in both countries. The analysis changes, however, when workers can expect to receive differing relative wages for similar skill levels in the two countries.

Assume first that asylum seekers do not consider distance to each destination country in their asylum-seeking choice. Additionally, assume country A is a transitional country that is developing its market economy yet is not considered fully developed, while country B is a developed country. Wages in country A will be relatively lower than wages in country B for low-skilled jobs for several reasons, including that developed countries like country B regularly have a legal minimum wage. Country A will have relatively higher wages for middle-skilled jobs because middle-skilled jobs make up the bulk of the professional jobs in transitional countries. High-skilled jobs will tend to earn relatively higher wages in developed Country B where high levels of technology require high-skill labor input. These distinctions, which are an adapted version of the Roy Model, are shown in Figures 4.4 and 4.5 in terms of the relative wage distributions for asylum seekers' skill levels for countries A and B. The Roy Model "negative selection" is illustrated in Figure 4.4, which shows the wage distribution for workers with low-to-middle skill levels. Figure 4.5 shows the wage distribution for middle-to-high skill levels for countries A and B, which is called "positive selection" in the Roy Model.

FIGURE 4.4   Roy Model "negative selection"   **FIGURE 4.5**   Roy Model "positive selection"

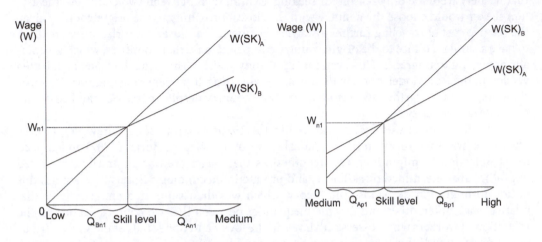

Figure 4.6 illustrates the frequency distribution of skill levels (F(s)) of the asylum seekers from country O. The asylum seekers' decisions regarding destination country come from the negative selection graph (Figure 4.4) and the positive selection graph (Figure 4.5). Asylum seekers with the lowest-skill (Q_{Bn1}) and highest-skill levels (Q_{Bp1}) will tend to choose country B while those with middle-skill levels ($Q_{An1}+Q_{Ap1}$) choose country A.

FIGURE 4.6   Frequency distribution of skill levels (F(s)) of asylum seekers

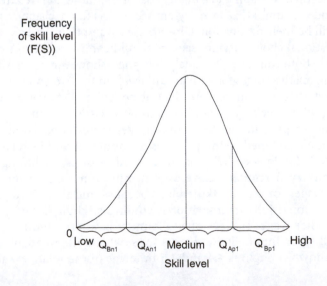

Now assume that distance to destination country is part of the asylum seeker's choice. Since country B is further from country A, the wage distribution is now discounted (decreased) for country B by subtracting the cost of distance (C_D). Figures 4.7 and 4.8 show the new relative wage distributions for asylum seekers' skill levels in the two countries. The number of middle-skill level asylum seekers to country A has increased ($Q_{An1} < Q_{An2}$ and $Q_{Ap1} < Q_{Ap2}$) while fewer people will seek asylum in country B, causing a decrease in the number of both the low-skilled ($Q_{Bn1} > Q_{Bn2}$) and high-skilled ($Q_{Bp1} > Q_{Bp2}$) asylum seekers.

FIGURE 4.7 Roy Model "negative selection" with distance discount

FIGURE 4.8 Roy Model "positive selection" with distance discount

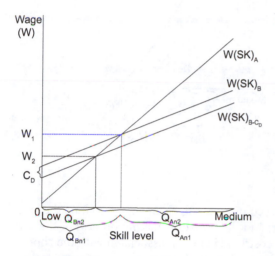
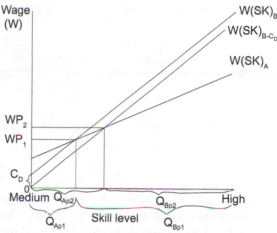

The new frequency distribution of skills is show in Figure 4.9. Not only are there fewer asylum seekers to country B, but those applying for asylum in country B are relatively lower-skilled (Q_{Bn2}) and relatively higher-skilled (Q_{Bp2}), while a wider distribution of asylum seekers with middle-skill levels will apply for asylum in country A ($Q_{An2} + Q_{Ap2}$).

The most important limitation to this theory is the lack of supporting empirical evidence. It is not the case that existing evidence rebuts the theory, but rather that there is little dependable, existing data at this point. This is partially due to the difficulties in differentiating between asylum seekers and refugees. This theory would tend to forecast that asylum seekers from the Syrian refugee crisis would choose to move to a transition country as opposed to a developed country due to relative wage differentials and distance between the destination countries. The Roy Model illustrates the importance of these two variables in the asylum-seeking decision and can be extended to include other variables.

Section 8: Recommendations for future research

The paths to seeking asylum are numerous and, in large part, unknown. It will be impossible to understand the structure of seeking asylum without knowing the ways in which people

FIGURE 4.9   Frequency distribution of skill levels (F(s)) of asylum seekers with distance discount

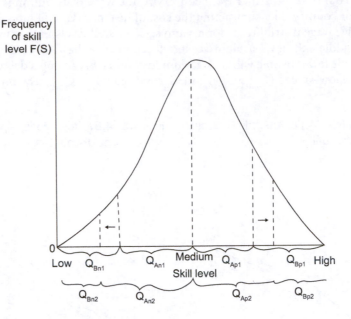

flee a country; details of the journey to the host country; the decision-makers along the journey whose decisions affect the asylum seeker; and the decision-making process of the asylum seeker. It is important to understand the costs and benefits (associated with the choices of different types of asylum seekers, human smugglers, and gangs as well as immigration officials, judges, and other individuals and groups) that may affect the journey to asylum. Determining these variables would allow the researcher to establish the markets that exist behind the process of seeking asylum. It would also illuminate the areas where human rights violations are free to flourish.

There is controversy over the fact that an asylum seeker to the United States may be denied asylum because an action by the person has been labeled an aggravated felony. In this case, the term aggravated simply means that the action has serious consequences. A felony is typically a crime involving violence that is punishable by a sentence ranging from imprisonment of more than a year to the death penalty. However, the American Immigration Council (2016) reports that the term can be used to describe non-violent misdemeanors that disqualify an applicant for asylum. This means that an asylum seeker may be denied asylum even if they have not committed an act that is truly an aggravated felony.

This chapter has focused on the human rights violations that lead to a person fleeing to seek asylum in another country or area. There are three areas that require extensive research: The human rights violations experienced in the home country (which caused the asylum seeker to flee); the human rights violations experienced along the journey to asylum; and the human rights violations experienced in the host country.

Many asylum seekers arrive in the host country after being persecuted or tortured in their home countries. Persecution may come from officials of the home government, members of an opposing political party, religious communities, or even neighbors. Torture may have been inflicted at the hands of a clandestine organization or by the home government. Article 5 of the UDHR states that "No one shall be subjected to torture or to cruel, inhuman or degrading treatment or punishment." Multiple international conventions and national laws support this conclusion. Many nations, including the United States, have been accused of using torture to extract information, punish an action, intimidate a person, gain a confession, or for other reasons.

As mentioned, there is danger of human rights violations along the journey to asylum. This is an important area of research that touches on many of the other topics covered in this textbook, including violence against women and children, terrorist and genocidal activities, and acts of hate.

In recent years, many children have fled gang violence and other dangers in the home country to seek asylum in developed countries. In order to be granted asylum, they must prove that they are personally in danger from these threats.

When asylum seekers are detained, they may be held in a prison-like setting. A congressional mandate stipulates that ICE must maintain 34,000 beds each night for those awaiting legal procedures related to seeking asylum and immigration (Ted Robbins, 2013). Many of the detention facilities are privately-run institutions that are profiting from the detention of immigrants and asylum seekers (Garance Burke and Laura Wides-Munozapmiami, 2012). In addition, a report by the U.S. Government Accountability Office (2013) reports on sexual abuse and assault in detention facilities, finding that there were numerous allegations, many of which were not reported by ICE. Another U.S. Government Accountability Office report (2016) identified insufficiencies in medical care and other provisions for detainees. It is important to determine the influence that these private businesses have on the immigration process in order to safeguard the rights of the individual as well as to ensure the efficient use of U.S. federal funding.

There is little research done on what happens to asylum seekers who are denied asylum and deported to their countries of origin. Upon arriving in the home country, the asylum seeker may be arrested, face imprisonment, and even be killed – the very threats they were intent upon escaping.

CHECK YOURSELF BOX: CHANGES TO YOUR PERSONAL BIASES ABOUT SEEKING ASYLUM

Write down your current thoughts about seeking asylum. What have you learned in this chapter that you didn't know before? Now look at the information you wrote about your personal biases about seeking asylum in the first check yourself box in this chapter. Do you have exactly the same opinions you had when you wrote them? Are any of those biases stronger or weaker? If any of your biases changed, how did they change? You are simply trying to discern how the information presented in this chapter has informed, and possibly, shaped your biases. Each time you read or watch new information there is a possibility of it affecting your personal bias. Awareness of this fact can make you a stronger researcher.

Section 9: Bibliography

American Immigration Council. (2016, December 16). *Aggravated felonies: An overview*. Retrieved from https://www.americanimmigrationcouncil.org/research/aggravated-felonies-overview

Armstrong, Martin. (2017, June 29). *The countries receiving the most asylum applications*. OECD: Statista. Retrieved from www.statista.com/chart/10061/the-countries-receiving-the-most-asylum-applications

Borjas, George. (1987). Self-selection and the earning of immigrants. *National Bureau of Economic Research*, Working Paper #2248.

Burke, Garance and Wides-Munozapmiami, Laura. (2012, August 2). *Immigrants prove big business for prison companies*. MSNBC. Retrieved from www.msnbc.com/msnbc/immigrants-prove-big-business-prison

Dustmann, Christian and Görlach, Joseph-Simon. (2016, March). The economics of temporary migrations. *Journal of Economic Literature, 54*(1): 98–136.

Eurostat. (2017, March 13). *Asylum statistics. Eurostat: Statistics explained*. Retrieved from http://ec.europa.eu/eurostat/statistics-explained/index.php/Asylum_statistics

Gatrell, Peter. (2013). *The making of the modern refugee*. New York: Oxford University Press.

Gebremedhin, Tesfaye and Mavisakalyan, Astghik. (2013). Immigration and political stability. *Kyklos: International Review for Social Sciences, 66*:3. 317–41.

Kenyon, Peter. (2015, September 24). *Turkey absorbs 2 million refugees, but won't offer asylum*. NPR report. Retrieved from http://www.npr.org/sections/parallels/2015/09/24/442880025/turkey-absorbs-2-million-refugees-but-says-they-cant-stay

Krogstad, Jens; Passel, Jeffrey; and Cohn, D'Vera. (2017, April 27). *5 facts about illegal immigration in the U.S.* Fact Tank: News in the Numbers. Pew Research Center. Retrieved from http://www.pewresearch.org/fact-tank/2017/04/27/5-facts-about-illegal-immigration-in-the-u-s

Mercy Corps. (2017). *The world's 5 biggest refugee crises*. Retrieved from https://www.mercycorps.org/articles/afghanistan-nigeria-somalia-south-sudan-syria/worlds-5-biggest-refugee-crises

Ramji-Nogales, Jaya; Schoenholtz, Andrew; and Schrag, Philip. (2011). *Refugee roulette*. New York: NYU Press.

Robbins, Ted. (2013, November 19). *Little-known immigration mandate keeps detention beds full*. National Public Radio (NPR). Retrieved from https://www.npr.org/2013/11/19/245968601/little-known-immigration-mandate-keeps-detention-beds-full

Roy, Andrew. (1951). Some thoughts on the distribution of earnings. *Oxford Economic Papers, 3*(2), 135–46.

Schulberg, Jessica. (November 20, 2015). Turkey won't turn away Syrians after terror attacks. *Huffington Post*. Retrieved from http://www.huffingtonpost.com/entry/turkey-open-door-syrian-refugee_564f4506e4b0258edb311aa9

Transactional Records Access Clearinghouse. (2017). *Asylum outcome continues to depend on the judge assigned*. Retrieved from http://trac.syr.edu/immigration/reports/490

United States Government Accountability Office. (2013, November 20). *Immigration detention: Additional actions could strengthen DHS efforts to address sexual abuse*. Report GAO-14–38. Retrieved from https://www.gao.gov/products/GAO-14-38

United States Government Accountability Office. (2016, February). *Immigration detention: Additional actions could strengthen management and oversight of detainee medical care*. Report GAO-16–231. Retrieved from https://www.gao.gov/assets/680/675484.pdf

Section 10: Resources

Unit 1: Summary

People flee seek asylum in other countries when they have faced persecution in their countries of origin or when man-made, natural, or health emergencies have caused them to flee without hope of return. Seeking asylum is a legal process wherein a person must apply for asylum and go through a process to prove credible fear or reasonable fear of persecution if returned to their home country. In order to apply for asylum, the person must either have crossed the border illegally or be at the border of the country. The person goes through an affirmative asylum process or a defensive asylum process, depending upon whether the application for asylum is being processed within the legal asylum procedures or the country is processing the person for expedited removal for being illegally in the country.

The main decision-makers in the determination of asylum are the asylum seeker; the people in power in the home country who make decisions affecting the safety and security of the person who has decided to seek asylum; the people who the asylum seeker meets in transit countries along the path to the host country; and the national officials who make the asylum decision in the host country. Each of these groups has costs and benefits in relation to the asylum seeker's process. The controversies in the national and international agreements and the inefficiencies in the asylum-seeking process create an atmosphere of uncertainty for people fleeing persecution.

Unit 2: Key concepts

Affirmative asylum process: The legal process whereby an asylum seeker may apply for asylum in the United States, provided the person is not currently being processed for expedited removal.

Asylum: The protection granted by a nation to a person who has left their country of origin in order to escape violence or persecution.

Asylum seeker: A person who is inside or outside the borders of a nation and appeals to the nation for asylum, but who has not yet been granted asylum.

Complement: In the labor market, a complement is when the characteristics of one group of workers enhance the productivity of another group of workers.

Credible fear: A legal provision that allows a person to seek asylum when they have a convincing reason to fear persecution if returned to the origin country.

Defensive asylum process: The legal process whereby an asylum seeker may apply for asylum in the United States when the person is currently being processed for expedited removal.

Demand for labor or labor demand: The number of workers or number of hours of work the firm intends to hire dependent upon the market wage.

Due process: The legal provision that each person has the right to fair treatment within the judicial system, although the rights of asylum seekers are different than the rights of the citizens of a nation.

Economic migrant: A person who seeks employment in another country.

Expedited removal: The immediate deportation of persons who are illegally in a country.

Health emergencies: Emergency situations that are the direct outcome of the outbreak of infectious disease or bioterrorism.

Internally displaced person (IDP): A person who was forced to flee their home but has not crossed an international border.

International migration: The movement of people from their countries of origin across international borders into other countries.

Labor market: The place where the labor of workers is matched with the demand of firms for labor input for production.

Man-made or human-made emergencies: Emergency situations that are the direct or primary result of events created the actions of people.

Migrant: A person who voluntarily crosses a border to seek better economic, educational, and social conditions or to join family.

Natural disasters: Emergency situations that are the direct effect of natural processes of the Earth.

Non-refoulement: The provision in international law that a nation will not forcibly return a person who has applied for asylum to their country of origin without the official determination of the need for asylum.

Productivity: Output per worker hour.

Reasonable fear: A legal provision that allows a person to seek asylum when they have not only a history of persecution in the origin country, but also have reason to fear future persecution if returned to the origin country.

Refoulement: The expulsion of a person from a country by the officials of that country.

Refugee: According to the UNHCR, a refugee is someone who is forced to flee their country due to violence, persecution, or war.

Returned refugee: A person who has returned to their country of origin after seeking refuge in another country, but has not yet been integrated back into their communities.

Substitute: In the labor market, a substitute is when the characteristics of one group of workers are similar to the characteristics of another group of workers, so that the labor of the workers may be interchangeable.

Supply of labor or labor supply: The sum of the number of workers or the hours of work provided by the workers in the labor market.

Unit 3: Review questions

1. What does it mean for a person to seek asylum?

2. What are three emergency situations that could be the cause of a person fleeing their home country to seek asylum?

3. What is the difference between an asylum seeker, a refugee, and a migrant?

4. What is the difference between the affirmative asylum process and the defensive asylum process?

5. What are the three federal agencies in the United States in charge of asylum seekers and what are their respective roles?

6. What are the main international agreements regarding asylum seekers?

7. What are some of the main controversies regarding seeking asylum?

8. Who are the experts on asylum seeking?

9. What are the major decisions that the decision-makers involved in asylum seeking must make, and what are the costs and benefits involved in those decisions?

10. What are some of the inefficiencies involved in the asylum-seeking process?

11. How can the Roy Model be used to predict the destination country where a person fleeing persecution may apply for asylum?

Unit 4: Recommended readings

Betts, Alexander and Loescher, Gil. (2011). *Refugees in international relations*. Oxford: Oxford University Press.

Hollenbach, David (Ed.). (2008). *Refugee rights: Ethics, advocacy, and Africa*. Washington: Georgetown University Press.

Mayotte, Judy. (1992). *Disposable people? The plight of refugees*. New York: Orbis Books.

Moorehead, Caroline. (2006). *Human cargo: A journey among refugees*. New York: Picador.

Powell, Benjamin (Ed.). (2015). *The economics of immigration: Market-based approaches, social science, and public policy*. New York: Oxford University Press.

Rabben, Linda. (2016). *Sanctuary and asylum: A social and political history*. Seattle: University of Washington Press.

5 Economics of terrorism

◼ Section 1: Introduction to the economics of terrorism

Unit 1: General introduction to terrorism

A nation's four sources of power – diplomacy, information, military, and the economy – are all targets of terrorism. Terrorist organizations have limited funds and resources and will pick a target that gives them the biggest payoff for their expenditure. The payoff may be in terms of gains in political, social, or economic arenas. Economic decision-making plays a significant part in each aspect of terrorism.

The Institute for Economics and Peace's Global Terrorism Index (2017) reports that the direct cost of terrorism to the global economy was $84 billion in 2016 and that 94% of the deaths were in the Middle East, North and sub-Saharan Africa, and South Asia. Terrorism tactics had changed to use simpler attacks against non-traditional and softer civilian targets in Organisation of Economic Cooperation and Development (OECD) countries. Factors that determined the presence of terrorism continued to be armed conflict, governmental political violence, political exclusion, and group grievances. The majority of terrorism was used during armed conflict or while countering repressive political regimes. Due to these two main causes, the Institute for Economics and Peace warns that counterterrorism may increase the aspects that drive terrorism. Terrorism is driven by many unknown factors, and it may therefore be impossible to know why a terrorist organization is carrying out certain acts.

After the 2001 bombing of the New York City World Trade Center and the Pentagon, the United States declared a "war on terror." This war included money being moved to finance counterterrorism operations, new legislation to increase national security, and both overt and covert actions by the U.S. military. The United States Department of Homeland Security (DHS) was founded in 2002 in response to the increased terroristic activities.

Terroristic activities are carried out for the purpose of terrorism, whose goal is the furtherance of political or social agendas through the disruption of lives and governments, destruction of property and opportunities, and increase in fear and uncertainty. Terrorism has the potential to pull down existing power structures and to supplant them with new leadership, to freeze productivity, and to discourage investment in the marketplace. Due to the fact that the means of committing terrorist acts are numerous, terrorists are able to switch between different methods of terror as they respond to counterterrorism efforts by well-equipped governments with superior technology (Eli Berman, 2009).

Putting a label on terrorists is more difficult, and the term terrorism itself is problematic. Richard Falk (2017) asks the question, "Does the term terrorism signify the identity of the actor or the nature of the violence?" There are many research topics that may be explored when analyzing terrorism, such as the characteristics of terrorist groups, the individual characteristics of terrorists, methods of terrorism, terroristic targets, and counterterrorism. This chapter builds upon existing research and expertise to create a foundation for the study of the economics of terrorism.

Unit 2: Counterterrorism perspective

Mike Fullilove SOCS (SEAL), USN, Ret.

USN SCPO (SEAL), Ret. Michael "Fulli" Fullilove holds an undergraduate degree in liberal arts from Excelsior College and a masters of professional studies (MPS) from Penn State. He has 20 years of experience operating as a SEAL across multiple SEAL teams. Mr. Fullilove began his career serving at SEAL Team 4, enhancing security by working with partner forces in South America. He then served with Naval Special Warfare Group 4,where he worked as a Navy SEAL medic providing assessments of medical risk for personnel traveling to developing countries and planning incident response for varied scenarios. Serving at SEAL Team EIGHT, Mr. Fullilove was responsible for leading teams in maritime interdiction. While at SEAL Team TEN in 2004, Mr. Fullilove conducted cultural engagement and coordinated exercises with Greek maritime counterterrorism units to enhance security during the 2004 Summer Olympics.

Mr. Fullilove led crossfunctional teams conducting complex special operations throughout the Middle East. He has worked in a variety of project and program management positions working across cultures to achieve operational goals. He spent five years at a Naval Special Warfare command where he was responsible for combining multi-intelligence disciplines with special operations expertise to defeat hostile networks.

Over the course of his career Mr. Fullilove was also deployed three times to Iraq, twice to Afghanistan, and once to Kosovo. He is the recipient of the Bronze Star Medal with Valor, the Defense Meritorious Service Medal, and numerous specific commendation medals. He has experience and expert qualifications in risk assessments (personnel and facilities), threat assessments, vulnerability assessments, counterterrorism and antiterrorism, surveillance and countersurveillance, methods of entry, and personal defense. During his deployments, he worked with senior-level foreign government leadership and focused on countering violent extremist organizations, human and physical infrastructure development for operational purposes, and personnel recovery.

Following retirement, Mr. Fullilove provided operational consultant services to military, government, and faith-based clients. He was most recently the managing director, security services for Barrister Global Solutions.

Coronado, California, 1993. As I arrived at the U.S. Navy SEAL training course, I saw a news report about someone trying to blow up the Twin Towers in New York City. Whereas before I had visions of war as conducted in Vietnam or Panama, this was my first introduction to terrorism. I remembered wondering what using cruise missiles was going to accomplish as the U.S. responded to the U.S. embassies bombings in Kenya and Tanzania in 1998. Next came the attack on the USS *Cole,* followed by the attacks of 9/11 when it seemed we were finally going to engage the terrorists and "hit back."

Eastern Afghanistan, 2003. Living in a world of rocket fire from Al Qaeda and other extremist organizations and roadside improvised explosive devices (IEDs), I discovered the tactical and operational methodology we would develop to fight terrorists. It opened my eyes to the nature of the problem: The environment facilitates terrorism and, because it was a failed state, there was nobody to defend the vulnerable. Lack of education, services, and security allowed the terrorists to create the choice of "join us or die" for much of the populace. It was obvious that the United States was going to have to make a multi-generational commitment in Afghanistan and needed a multi-pronged strategy. The question in my mind then and now is "How does one defeat an ideology?" While the United States exercises the military component of a counterterrorism strategy very well, I don't see it as being particularly successful in countering the ideology. Because the United States fails to understand the mindset of terrorists, we need to partner with other nations whose cultures provide the ability to understand how to better counter the ideological aspect.

Baghdad, Iraq, 2007. I became fully immersed in the find, fix, finish, exploit, analyze, disseminate (F3EAD) methodology and how to apply it against violent extremist organizations. This methodology fused operations and intelligence and created mutually supporting relationships to target terrorists. It is impossible to negotiate with terrorists charged with religious fervor, no desire to negotiate, and the desire to destroy Western civilization and the institutions that are not compatible with their world view.

The phrase "one man's terrorist is another man's freedom fighter" doesn't hold because the tactics of exploiting the vulnerable parts of society don't match my view of a freedom fighter. At the risk of oversimplifying, I now believe that terrorism is an extreme version of bullying. The overall tactics may be more severe, but fundamentally terrorists exploit the vulnerabilities of people who cannot defend themselves.

The F3EAD process proved extremely beneficial in locating, tracking, and capturing terrorists. The methodology also has applicability to other human rights crimes, such as human trafficking. Human trafficking, another form of bullying, is fundamentally about the exploitation of those who cannot defend themselves. Working within the public–private partnership model, I currently use the F3EAD methodology at the nonprofit organization DeliverFund to target human traffickers in the United States. Without human traffickers, there can be no human trafficking.

Section 2: Fundamentals of terrorism

Unit 1: Important terrorism terms

Along with over 100 definitions of terrorism in the international arena, there are thousands of organizations involved in terrorism and counterterrorism efforts. The definition of **terrorism** which will be used in this textbook is the use of clandestine, fear-provoking violence or threatened violence against governments, noncombatant civilian populations, or property that is designed to advance political or social agendas beyond the immediate target as a means of creating change or resisting change. Table 5.1 will provide a listing of the types of terrorism and many of the weapons used in terrorism. A **terrorist organization** is an extreme social or political faction that plans and enacts terroristic acts. A **terrorist** is a member of a terrorist organization who is involved in terroristic acts or the planning of these acts. An **insurgency** is an organized action aimed at overthrowing a government. **Fundamentalism** is the belief in and strict obedience to religious laws.

In relation to terrorism, the **international community** is an international coalition of governments and nongovernment actors who work together in various capacities to eliminate terrorist threats. **Intelligence** is the collection of information useful for defense and policy-making.

The determination of the relationship between the terrorists and the location of terroristic acts is essential to national and international policy development. When the terrorists commit these acts within their home country, the acts are considered **domestic** or **national terrorism**. **International terrorism** occurs when the terrorist organizations focus their acts of terrorism outside their home country. These organizations often operate in multiple countries, but have a geographic focus to their activities. **Transnational terrorism** occurs when terrorist organizations are based out of multiple countries, have members from many nationalities, and conduct operations around the world. Their targets may differ based on the transnational organization's varied objectives.

A **soft target** of terrorism is an individual, group of individuals, or object with little or no protection, such as civilians, commuter transportation, shopping areas, centers of tourism, and certain parts of the financial and energy sectors. A **hard target** is an individual, group of individuals, or thing that is guarded and relatively secure. Examples of targets with relatively high levels of security include protected government officials, military bases, chemical plants, and biological research labs (Joshua Sinai, 2016).

Counterterrorism (also spelled **counter-terrorism**) is the strategy and action by governments, military entities, intelligence agencies, law enforcement, and businesses to protect against the actions and financing of terrorism and to defeat or destroy terrorist organizations. The purposes of counterterrorism are to protect civilians and to reduce the risks associated with terroristic threats. Some of this process includes command and control by centralized decision-makers, target hardening (making soft targets into hard targets), damage mitigation (first responders and those who deal with the physical consequences of terrorist attacks), and provision of local security and medical services.

Unit 2: Types of terrorism and means of terroristic activity

A terrorist organization is defined by its goals. **Criminal terrorism** is terrorism used for criminal activity and for criminal profit. **Religious terrorism** is motivated by religious ideology. Politics may be at the forefront of the terrorist organization's agenda, such as in the cases of "the left," which denotes liberal thought, and "the right," which signifies conservative beliefs. **Dissent terrorism** occurs when groups rebel against their governments. This rebellion against authority is called an **insurgency**. In a similar way, **separatist terrorism** involves groups with an agenda involving separation from an existing structure through autonomy, independence, or religious freedom. **Ethnocentric terrorism** occurs when groups view their own race as superior to other races and perpetuate terroristic acts based on these racial differences. **Revolutionary terrorism** means that the group is focused on using terrorism to overthrow an existing governing body or social structure. **Political terrorism** focuses specifically on opposing persons and groups with different political ideologies. **Social terrorism** is extremist behavior based on a specific topic of interest, such as the environment or abortion, and is also called **single issue terrorism** or **special interest terrorism**. Violent terroristic acts committed for the purpose of gaining political, cultural, or ethnic freedom have alternately been called **nationalistic terrorism** and **freedom fighting**.

TABLE 5.1 Methods of terrorist activity

Methods	Description
Agricultural warfare	**Agro-terrorism** is the intentional delivery of bacteria, viruses, or other microorganisms for the purpose of disrupting a food supply system.
Animals	Animals used as vehicles to deliver explosives.
Biological warfare	**Bioterrorism** is the use of biological agents to cause mass harm.
Computers	**Cyberterrorism** is the use of computers and information technology to provoke widespread fear and uncertainty.
Explosives	Dirty bomb, letter bomb, improvised explosive device (IED), rockets, mortars, and suicide bomb.
Narcotics	**Narco-terrorism** is terrorism that is related to trade in illegal drugs, usually as a means of funding terrorism.
People	**Suicide bombing** (volunteer delivery by a person), **proxy bombing** (forcing a person to deliver bomb), use of human shields, kidnapping, and hostage-taking.
Personal contact	Murder, assassination, beheading, piracy, stabbing, rape.
Paper	**Paper terrorism** is the use of false or unnecessary legal documents as a method of harassment.
Radioactive materials	**Nuclear terrorism** is the use of radioactive materials to cause damage (Andrei Kokoshin, 2006).
Vehicles	Car bombing, vehicle ramming, hijacking of aircraft, boat, or other vehicles.

Section 3: Issues of human rights violations associated with terrorism

Terrorism is illegal in all respects on both national and international levels. Terrorism, by itself, is not a human rights violation, but the violations occur due to the outcomes of specific actions by terrorists as well as during counterterrorism activity. Terroristic acts are meant to be public in order to instill fear not only in those directly affected by the event, but also in those who hear about the death and destruction and feel that there is no hope of containing the violence.

Unit 1: National agreements

Prior to 2001, the U.S. counterterrorism focus was the protect-and-destroy style doctrine that focused on damaging terrorist organizations by killing lead operatives. This is a micro-perspective in that it focuses on targeting individual organizations and key personnel within these organizations. The deaths of almost 3,000 people and the loss of millions of dollars in property damage on September 11, 2001 (9/11) changed U.S. counterterrorism strategy to one of eliminating the drivers of violent extremism by destroying the need for terrorism. In this macro-perspective, radical views are accepted as long as the views do not lead to violence.

Under the U.S. Code of Federal Regulations, terrorism is "the unlawful use of force and violence against persons or property to intimidate or coerce a government, a civilian population, or any segment thereof, in furtherance of political or social objectives" (28 C.F.R.

section 0.85). Title 22 Chapter 38 Section 2656f defines terrorism as "premeditated, politically motivated violence perpetrated against noncombatant targets by subnational groups or clandestine agents." Title 18 Part I Chapter 113B of the federal law defines acts of terrorism, means of committing terroristic acts, and penalties for these acts. Section 2331 defines terrorism as an activity that endangers human life, is considered a criminal violation within the territorial jurisdiction of the United States, and "appears to be intended to intimidate or coerce a civilian population; to influence the policy of a government by intimidation or coercion; or to affect the conduct of a government by mass destruction, assassination, or kidnapping." Section 2332a describes a weapon of mass destruction as any weapon that uses a toxin, poisonous chemical, biological agent, or radiation to cause death or injury. Under Section 2332b, terrorism is a federal crime that violates any of the sections related to specific areas, people, property, or facilities; to the use of specific types of terrorist methods or weapons; and to the support of terrorist activities.

The USA PATRIOT (Providing Appropriate Tools Required to Interfere and Obstruct Terrorism) Act was passed in October 2001 following the 9/11 terrorist attacks in the United States. This act gave power to several U.S. Government branches to work against individuals, groups, and ideas that promote terrorism. The Homeland Security Act of 2002 created the Department of Homeland Security to coordinate U.S. national homeland security efforts.

The United Kingdom describes its counterterrorism policy using four Ps: Pursue (create ways to stop national and international terrorist threats); Prevent (track threats of terrorist attacks); Protect (implement policies and procedures that strengthen the infrastructure of the United Kingdom against terrorist attacks); and Prepare (mitigation of the likelihood of successful terrorist attacks). Before U.K. terrorism laws are passed, they are reviewed by an independent reviewer whose reports are submitted to Parliament.

The Terrorism Act of 2000 was the first of several antiterrorism acts created to fight terrorism in the United Kingdom. The Counter-Terrorism Act of 2008 increased police power to work against terrorism. The Counter-Terrorism and Security Act of 2015 amended the Terrorism Act of 2000 and focused on travel related to identified terror suspects or suspected persons. It makes provision for seizure of passports, exclusion from entering the United Kingdom, and punishment for violation of the order.

Canada's 2015 Anti-Terrorist Act (Bill C-51) created new terrorism-related criminal offenses, such as penalties for sharing physical or online terrorist propaganda and for promoting terrorism, regardless of whether a terrorist act has been carried out. The act allows arrest without a warrant if police believe someone may carry out a terrorist act, and there is increased sharing of information between government departments if someone is considered a threat to national security. In addition, the Canadian Security Intelligence Service was given the power to disrupt travel plans, bank accounts, websites, and social media accounts.

In March 2017, the European Union put into effect a directive that created a list of crimes considered terrorist activities, including "attempt to travel for the purpose of terrorism, to provide training for terrorism and to recruit for terrorism." The directive authorizes the use of covert surveillance even in private vehicles.

Vigipirate is the national security alert system in France. It focuses on protecting citizens, rather than on preventing the drivers of terrorism. The system includes checkpoints at borders, new security and policing jobs, enhancing cyber security, and efforts to integrate the Muslim populations.

The 2004 Anti-terrorism Act was passed to strengthen Australia's counterterrorism laws. The Australian Anti-Terrorism Act of 2005 increased the powers of police, including allowing them to detain suspects for two weeks without charge; to use tracking equipment to watch suspects for up to a year; and to use a shoot-to-kill approach if police believe the situation life-threatening.

Saudi Arabia has adopted a counterterror policy of prevention, rehabilitation, and after-care (PRAC). Prevention includes monitoring those considered radicals, providing alternative activities, working on radicalization within the Saudi prison system, and creating a public awareness campaign against terrorism. Islamic education and counseling is used for rehabilitation efforts. In addition, the Saudi government provides for the care of the families of prisoners. During after-care, prisoners are monitored and assisted in the construction of new lives, habits, and contacts, including helping prisoners to get apartments and jobs (since experience shows that family men are less likely to become violent extremists).

In 2015, China instituted antiterrorism laws that create a single agency to identify and act against terror suspects. One of the agency's roles is to covertly listen to private conversations.

Israel's 2016 Terror Bill was passed after six years of negotiations. It increases the punishment for terror-related crimes and broadens the power of security forces in monitoring terrorist activities, setting severe punishments for terrorists. Israel maintains a list of terrorist organizations and has laws in place forbidding membership, funding, or assistance to these organizations.

Many other countries have antiterrorism legislation. Some of the extensive powers provided to government and law enforcement agencies raise human rights concerns.

Unit 2: International agreements

As we have stated, terrorism is not in itself a human rights violation. However, terroristic acts create violations as stated in the U.N. Universal Declaration of Human Rights (UDHR). The articles that may be violated due to terroristic activity include Article 1 (denial of dignity); Article 2 (denial of rights and freedoms based on personal attributes as terrorists target specific groups); Article 3 (destruction of life, liberty, and security); Article 4 (enslavement of people); Article 5 (torture and other cruel treatment of victims of terrorism); Article 9 (kidnapping as a tool of terrorism); Article 12 (interference with privacy, family, home, and correspondence); Article 13 (restriction of freedom of movement and residence due to terrorism); Article 14 (persecution by terrorist groups); Article 16 (prevention or force of marriage of those of full age or minors); Article 17 (seizure of property by terrorists); Article 18 (force of religion and beliefs); Article 19 (restriction of freedom of opinion and expression); Article 20 (destruction of peaceful assembly and associations); Article 26 (restrictions on who can receive an education); and Article 27 (destruction of culture and history of certain groups). **Human rights law** applies during peacetime, but armed conflict may lead to a suspension of many of its provisions.

International humanitarian law is the set of rules that seek to limit the effects of armed conflict for humanitarian reasons, to protect persons who are not involved in the hostilities, and to restrict the types of warfare used. Table 5.2 provides many of the conventions related to terrorist activity.

Unit 3: Controversies

Among the definitional and policy issues, perhaps the biggest controversy stems from the question "What constitutes terrorism?" A researcher of terrorism must determine which

TABLE 5.2   International humanitarian law

Year	Agreement
1949	Geneva Convention I on Wounded and Sick in the Armed Forces in the Field
1949	Geneva Convention II on Wounded, Sick and Shipwrecked of Armed Forces at Sea
1949	Geneva Convention III on Prisoners of War
1949	Geneva Convention IV on Civilians
1972	Convention on the Prohibition of the Development, Production and Stockpiling of Bacteriological and Toxin Weapons and on their Destruction (Biological Weapons Convention)
1977	Additional Protocols of the Geneva Convention of 1949: Protection of Victims of International Armed Conflict and Protection of Victims of Non-International Armed Conflict
1980	Convention on Conventional Weapons (CCW)
1980	Convention on Conventional Weapons (CCW) Protocol I on Non-Detectable Fragments; Amendment in 2001
1980	Convention on Conventional Weapons (CCW) Protocol II on Prohibitions or Restrictions on the Use of Mines, Booby-Traps, and other devices; Amendment in 1996
1980	Convention on Conventional Weapons (CCW) Protocol III on Prohibitions and Restrictions on the Use of Incendiary Weapons
1980	Convention on Prohibitions or Restriction on the Use of Certain Conventional Weapons which may be Deemed to be exclusively injurious or to have indiscriminate Effects (Chemical Weapons Convention)
1993	Convention on the Prohibition of the Development, Production, Stockpiling and Use of Chemical Weapons and on their Destruction
1995	Convention on Conventional Weapons Protocol (IV) on Blinding Laser Weapons
1997	Convention on the Prohibition of the Use, Stockpiling, Production and Transfer of Anti-Personnel Mines and on their Destruction (Ottawa Convention or the Mine Ban Treaty)
2000	Convention on the Rights of the Child Optional Protocol on Children in Armed Conflict
2003	Convention on Conventional Weapons Protocol (V) on Explosive Remnants of War
2008	Convention on Cluster Munitions

definitions to use and the refinement of those definitions. As noted, official definitions of terrorism differ between countries and government, research, or business entities. Richard Falk (2017) warns, "Particular attention should be given to how transnational political violence and terrorist labels are being used by a variety of political actors to demonize their adversaries while validating their own violent behavior."

Differences in ideology also lead to variations in definition. For example, one group may be called freedom fighters by certain groups of people, but terrorists by opposing factions. Terrorism has a negative perspective and sees the world as "us versus them." Some definitions use vague wording that precludes a clear-cut definition for a terrorist or a terrorist organization. **Lone-wolf terrorism** occurs when an individual commits violent acts of mass murder, but not all policy-making entities include this category as a part of terrorism.

In 2016, a man, who pledged allegiance to ISIS, killed 49 people and wounded 58 in an Orlando, Florida nightclub shooting. Las Vegas country music festival attendees were targeted by a man, whose use of high-powered rifles led to the deaths of 58 people with 515 wounded from the thirty-second floor of the Mandalay Bay Hotel. Between November 2011 and July 2016, France was the target of 11 violent Islamic lone-wolf terrorist attacks: the weapons used in the attacks included firebombs, knives, gas, a machete, a large truck, and guns. It is important to determine whether these acts should be considered in counterterrorism strategy.

Some definitions of terrorism include the possibility of government involvement in terrorist activities. Walter Enders and Eric Olsen (2012) use the term **state terrorism** to mean the "planning, funding, and execution" of terrorist action by governments and reserve the term terrorism for subnational groups. There have been reports that some nations are funding or otherwise supporting terrorist organizations. Successful extradition of suspected terrorists depends on international relations between the countries.

The use of force to combat terrorism has always been controversial. During times of armed conflict, human rights laws may be suspended and nations may instead use international humanitarian law, which can place populations around suspected terrorists in jeopardy. Counterterrorism efforts encourage the use of military action at the same time as they discourage diplomatic means of decreasing terrorist threats.

Counterterrorism measures often lead to loss of life and infrastructure in the target area. The 2006 U.S. National Strategy for Combating Terrorism released by the White House states, "Not only do we employ military power, we use diplomatic, financial, intelligence, and law enforcement activities to protect the Homeland and extend our defenses, disrupt terrorist operations, and deprive our enemies of what they need to operate and survive" (U.S. Department of State Archives, 2006).

Media sources around the world are quick to report suspected terrorism and are at times slow to make sure the facts are correct before relaying the information (Erin Kearns, Allison Betus, and Anthony Lemieux, 2017). Several entities have called for a reduction in the sensationalism of terrorism by the media. Two questions remain: Does the media promote fear of terrorism, and what are the outcomes of this media-induced fear? Former FBI agent Michael German (2016) calls for four changes in counterterrorism policy. First, he recommends an end to the sensationalizing of terrorism, which he says amplifies fear and encourages terrorist attacks. Second, he says that increased surveillance does not lead to fewer terrorist attacks. Third, there is no single profile of a terrorist, so ideological radicalism is not a good predictor. Finally, Mr. German states that "lone-wolf terrorists" should not be treated as terrorists

CHECK YOURSELF BOX: PERSONAL BIASES ABOUT TERRORISM

When did you first learn about terrorism? Were you aware of counterterrorism efforts? Did you know about terrorism beyond what you see on television in movies? How did you gain this knowledge? Do you view some groups as terrorists and others as freedom fighters? If so, what is the difference to you? Have you or a close friend had a personal experience with terrorism or counterterrorism? Your personal biases determine the course of your research, in good and bad ways. Make a list of your thoughts about terrorism. Think about how you would decide how much money, use of military, and policy-making to allocate to counterterrorism.

Section 4: History of terrorism

Terror has origins in the earliest recorded history. The ancient Romans used *terror cimbricus* to describe the panic caused by being attacked by an enemy tribe. The Latin word *terrere* means to frighten. The term became *terrour* and then *terrorisme* in Old French and later developed into the late Middle English word *terror*.

The term terrorism may have originated after the French Revolution in the years 1793–4 in a time called the Reign of Terror. After the execution of Louis XVI, the political party leader of the Society of the Jacobins, Maximilien Robespierre, attacked his political enemies, sending many to be killed by the guillotine. It was a time of immense panic, with people in opposition to the Jacobins living in fear of retribution from past actions or due to political expediency. Since that time, the term terrorist has referred to a person who uses the threat of force to gain and retain power. Today, the term terrorism is still used to describe actions leading to the death or harm of citizens for the purpose of intimidating others.

The Ancient Egyptians and Romans made a practice of granting peace to nations who gave them hostages – often royal sons of defeated nations. In March 1871, a short-lived government called the Paris Commune took power for ten days. Part of the Paris Commune's strategy was to take hostages as political bargaining chips.

In 1937, the League of Nations received a proposal from France calling for a convention on terrorism. The proposal was not passed due to disputes regarding extradition of accused terrorists. The United Nations, which was formed in 1945, has not been able to create an internationally agreed-upon definition of terrorism due to the "profiling and linking problem with any religious faith" (U.N. Sixth Committee, 2005). The United Nations has created 12 conventions and two protocols describing individual acts of terrorism. The main argument about the definition of terrorism centers around when the use of violence is legitimate. Since governments are in charge of creating the legal definitions, governmental actions are usually excluded from the definition of terrorism.

The United States did not have a national intelligence service before World War II. The Office of Strategic Services (OSS) was created in 1942 to coordinate espionage activities for the U.S. military. In 1945, the OSS ceased operations and was replaced by the Central Intelligence Agency (CIA) in 1946.

The following years were witness to the rise of many terrorist groups. The number of organizations, founding dates, official names, leadership, and terrorist activities are difficult to verify due to the clandestine nature of these organizations, but here are some examples. In the 1950s, Euskadi Ta Askatasuna (ETA, the main group within the Basque National Liberation Movement) and Fatah (the Palestinian National Liberation Movement) were established. The 1960s saw the development of the Palestine Liberation Organization (PLO), the Popular Front for the Liberation of Palestine-General Command (PFLP-GC, including "Carlos the Jackal"), the Provisional Irish Republican Army (PIRA or IRA), and the Revolutionary Armed Forces of Columbia (FARC). Terrorist groups that formed during the 1970s included Black September, 17 November, the Secret Army for the Liberation of Armenia, the Red Brigades, the Red Army Faction, the Abu Nidal Organization (ANO), the Japanese Red Army, the Revolutionary People's Struggle (ELA), al-Jama'a al-Islamiyya, First of October Anti-Fascist Resistance Groups (GRAPO), the Kurdistan Workers' Party (PKK), Revolutionary Cells, and the Liberation Tigers of Tamil Eelam (Tamil Tigers). The 1980s saw the beginning of terroristic activity by the Shining Path (Sendero Luminoso), M-19, the Islamic Jihad Organization, the Islamic Jihad Movement in Palestine (PIJ), Harakat-ul-Ansar, Harakat-ul-Jihadal-Islami, the Lebanese Armed Revolutionary Brigades, the Túpac Amaru Revolutionary

Movement (MRTA), Hizballah, Aum Shinrikyo, the Egyptian Islamic Jihad (al-Jihad), Islamic Resistance Movement (HAMAS), and Al-Qaeda. During the 1990s, the terrorist groups that formed included the Armed Islamic Group of Algeria (GIA), Abu Sayyaf, the Revolutionary People's Front Liberation Party/Front (DHKP-C), the Islamic Army of Aden-Abyan, Lashkar-e-Tayyiba (the Army of the Righteous or LT), Jaish-e-Mohammed, the Taliban, and the Islamic State of Iraq and the Levant (ISIL or ISIS). The year 2000 saw the inception of groups such as the Al-Aqsa Martyrs Brigade and Avengers of the Infants.

The areas of Central Asia, the Middle East, and North Africa comprise a population that is 80% Islamic. During colonialism, these areas were largely divided between European nations. After World War II, most of these nations gained independence but adopted European or American governmental systems rather than following their Islamic roots. The Muslim Brotherhood, founded in Egypt in 1928, is one group credited with the present-day spread of Islamic fundamentalism. Various events caused the Muslim Brotherhood to split into factions, with some factions advocating the use of terrorist acts to promote fundamental Islam. The Islamic State in Iraq and Syria (ISIS, also called the Islamic State in Iraq and the Levant (ISIL)) came to power between 2010 and 2012. ISIS seeks to reestablish seventh-century Islam and destroy the enemies of Islam, using many forms of terrorist activities.

The September 11, 2001 attacks on the New York City World Trade Center and the Pentagon, which is the headquarters of the U.S. Department of Defense, led to changes in counterterrorism organizational structure and policy-making. Richard Falk (2017) makes a clear statement of the transition by stating, "The most innovative and consequential aspect of the post-9/11 discourse and approach was to break the earlier connection between terrorism and 'crime,' and insist on treating the counter-terrorist undertaking as a type of 'war' rather than as a form of law enforcement undertaken in relation to a particularly disruptive form of criminality."

The official count of terrorist organizations depends upon definitions and national laws. The U.S. Department of State Bureau of Counterterrorism lists 61 terrorist organizations in section 219 of the Immigration and Nationality Act (INA, as amended). The U.K. home secretary facilitates the Terrorist Act of 2000 to create a list of proscribed international terrorist groups that includes 71 international organizations and 14 organizations in Northern Ireland. In both of these countries and in many others, terrorist organizations may be added to or removed from the list as determined by counterterrorism authorities in that country and in regard to existing counterterrorism legislation.

Section 5: Meet the terrorism experts

Reading peer-reviewed articles and articles in major journals and watching documentaries can provide information on who could be consulted about their expertise on terrorism. Table 5.3 provides a look at some of these different fields of expertise. Each field of information can supplement the researcher's understanding of terrorism.

Table 5.4 is a list of the some of the types of intelligence gathered. The intelligence gathered depends upon a particular organization's mission.

Part of the focus of the United Nations is on eliminating the foundations of radicalization in order to prevent the spread of violent extremism by focusing on socioeconomic opportunities, helping marginalized and discriminated-against peoples, creating

TABLE 5.3   Areas and fields of expertise related to terrorism

Area of expertise	Field of expertise	Description
Research and possible sources of data	Anthropology	The study of human societies and cultures across time.
	Criminal justice	The study of systems that provide criminal justice policy.
	Criminology	The study of crime and criminals.
	Economics	The study of the choices people make when dealing with scarcity. Eli Berman, Jacob Shapiro, and Alan Krueger, Institute for Economics and Peace – www.economicsandpeace.org.
	History	The study of past events.
	Psychology	The study of human behavior.
	Political science	The study of government and political behavior.
	Research centers	Government, private, and nonprofit terrorism research centers with different focuses throughout the world.
	Sociology	The study of the development and structure of society.
Human rights	Nonprofit Organizations	An organization that uses its excess revenue to pursue a mission or social cause. For example, Campaign Against Terrorism Foundation (CATF) in Pakistan and the Simon Wiesenthal Center in Los Angeles.
Expert witnesses	Experts in investigations, ballistics (projectiles and firearms), explosives	Knowledge of evidence regarding the means by which terrorist attacks are accomplished. For example, government counterterrorism experts or companies that specialize in protecting diplomats or facilities.
	Experts in political dynamics	Knowledge of the interplay between political groups.
	Current or former members of terrorist organizations	Primary source, but questions regarding safety of person giving information and reliability of the information.
	Survivors of terrorist attacks	Primary source, but question regarding whether person has the big picture regarding attacks or whether they are influenced by media or other sources of information.

better governance and rule of law, and working to resolve conflicts. The U.N. Index of International Counterterrorism Efforts lists 11 U.N. multi-regional efforts, 31 non-U.N. multi-regional efforts, eight African efforts, six American efforts, eight Asian and Pacific region efforts, and eight European efforts. There are 70 international institutions, bodies, and networks that focus on different, but overlapping, areas of intelligence and information sharing. Table 5.5 presents some of the major counterterrorism organizations in the United States, but other organizations not on this list are partners in this effort.

TABLE 5.4 Types of intelligence gathering

Type of intelligence	Acronym	Organizational focus
Human intelligence	HUMINT	Information gathered from a person.
Geospatial intelligence	GEOINT	Information gathered from a satellite, aerial photography, and mapping.
Measurement and signature intelligence	MASINT	Information gathered from different sources on information such as weather, radiation levels, radar, seismic activity, and chemical materials.
Open-source intelligence	OSINT	General information from open sources such as the internet, interviews, and meetings.
Signals intelligence	SIGING	Information gathered from intercepting signals.
Technical intelligence	TECHINT	Information from analysis of the environmental or of weapons and equipment used by militaries.
Cyber intelligence/digital network intelligence	CYBINT/ DNINT	Information gathered from cyberspace.
Financial intelligence	FININT	Information on monetary transaction.

TABLE 5.5 U.S. counterterrorism organizations

Organization	Organizational focus
Department of Defense (DOD)	Headed by the Secretary of Defense. Includes 1) the U.S. Departments of Army, Navy, and Air Force; 2) the Defense Intelligence Agency (DIA); 3) the National Security Agency (NSA), the National Geospatial-Intelligence Agency (NGA), and the National Reconnaissance Office (NRO), the Defense Advanced Research Projects Agency (DARPA), the Defense Logistics Agency (DLA), the Missile Defense Agency (MDA), the Defense Health Agency (DHA), the Defense Threat Reduction Agency (DTRA), the Defense Security Service (DSS), and the Pentagon Force Protection Agency (PFPA).
1) Counterintelligence Force Protection Source Operations (CFSO)	Counterintelligence agencies under the Department of Defense (DOD) to protect military forces, report to military chains of command for direct support, and coordinate offensive activities include the Air Force Office of Special Investigations (AFOSI), United States Army Counterintelligence, and the Naval Criminal Investigative Service (NCIS, serving the U.S. Navy and the U.S. Marines Corps).

Organization	Organizational focus
2) Defense Intelligence Agency (DIA)	An intelligence service that is external to the U.S. federal government, but is a component of the DOD. It specializes in defense and military intelligence assistance, integration, and coordination. Includes the Defense Clandestine Service (DCS), which conducts clandestine espionage activities around the world to answer national-level defense objectives for U.S. policy-makers and military leaders.
Department of Justice (DOJ)	The focus is law enforcement and defense of the United States. Among the multiple organizations and missions under the DOJ, the main agencies dealing with terrorism are 1) the Drug Enforcement Administration (DEA); 2) the Federal Bureau of Investigations (FBI); and 3) the National Security Division (NSD). The Bureau of Alcohol, Tobacco, Firearms, and Explosives (ATF) works closely with these groups.
1) Drug Enforcement Administration (DEA)	The agency in charge of domestic and foreign U.S. drug investigations.
2) Federal Bureau of Investigation (FBI)	Lead agency for domestic counterterrorism law enforcement. Reports to the Department of Justice (DOJ).
3) National Security Division (NSD)	Focus is protecting the United States from threats to national security through prosecution, law enforcement, and intelligence. Oversees the Department of Justice's (DOJ) national security operations, including the sections and offices of Counterterrorism, Counterintelligence and Export Control, Foreign Investment Review, Intelligence, Operations, Oversight, Litigation, Law and Policy, and Executive.
4) Bureau of Alcohol, Tobacco, Firearms, and Explosives (ATF)	Law enforcement agency with the mission to provide protection in the United States from violent criminals and organizations, terrorist acts, arson and bombings, and illegal firearms, explosives, alcohol, and tobacco products.
National Intelligence Program Director of National Intelligence (DNI)	Headed by the Director of National Intelligence, who serves as an advisor to the President, the National Security Council, and the Homeland Security Council. Oversees 1) the Central Intelligence Agency (CIA); 2) Central Security Services (CSS); 3) the Office of the National Counterintelligence Executive (ONCIX); 4) the National Security Agency (NSA), and the National Counterproliferation Center (NCPC).
1) Central Intelligence Agency's (CIA) National Clandestine Service	Lead agency for international counterespionage, counterterrorism, cyber intelligence, and nonproliferation of weapons of mass destruction.
2) Central Security Service (CSS)	Responsible for signals intelligence (SIGINT), cryptology, and risk mitigation of information for the U.S. Armed Forces and the NSA.
3) Office of the National Counterintelligence Executive (ONCIX)	Responsible for facilitating, enhancing, and integrating U.S. counterintelligence efforts and awareness by enabling the counterintelligence community to better understand and handle intelligence threats.

(Continued)

TABLE 5.5 (Continued)

Organization	Organizational focus
4) National Security Agency (NSA)	Responsible for international monitoring, collecting, and processing of information and data for foreign intelligence and counterintelligence and for protecting U.S. communications networks and information systems.
5) National Counterproliferation Center (NCPC)	Provides information on weapons of mass destruction to the intelligence community.
Department of Homeland Security (DHS)	DHS contains a number of organizations for terrorism mitigation that work with state and local organizations, including the U.S. Citizenship and Immigration Services (USCIS), U.S. Customs and Border Protection (CBP): 1) the U.S. Coast Guard, Federal Emergency Management Agency (FEMA), Federal Law Enforcement Training Center (FLETC); 2) U.S. Immigration and Customs Enforcement (ICE), Transportation Security Administration (TSA), the U.S. Secret Service (USSS), the Directorate of Management, the National Protection and Programs Directorate, the Science and Technology Directorate, the Countering Weapons of Mass Destruction Office; 3) the Office of Intelligence and Analysis, and the Office of Operations Coordination.
1) Coast Guard Intelligence	The mission includes handling the proliferation of weapons of mass destruction, drug and gun smuggling, and illegal immigration in relation to U.S. maritime areas.
2) U.S. Immigration and Customs Enforcement (ICE)	The mission includes homeland security investigations and immigration enforcement and removal.
3) Office of Intelligence and Analysis	The mission is to deliver intelligence information to U.S. domestic partners and to develop intelligence from those partners to the Department of Homeland Security.
Department of the Treasury	Responsible for maintaining a strong economy and creating economic and job opportunities by promoting the conditions that enable economic growth and stability at home and abroad, strengthen national security by combating threats and protecting the integrity of the financial system, and manage the U.S. Government's finances and resources effectively.
1) Financial Crimes Enforcement Network (FinCEN)	In the Department of Treasury, clearinghouse for banks and other institutions reporting suspected money laundering, terrorist financing, etc. In general, if there is a matter to be prosecuted, the FBI will take the case.
2) Office of Terrorism and Financial Intelligence (TFI)	Responsible for the Treasury's intelligence and enforcement functions by protecting the financial system against illicit use and combating national financial security threats.

Table 5.6 provides a list of some of the major counterterrorism organizations outside of the United States along with the organizational focus. Table 5.7 presents some of the major terrorism databases and the collected information.

TABLE 5.6   International counterterrorism organizations

Area	Organization	Organizational focus
France	INTERPOL	The largest international policing organization, with 192 member countries. INTERPOL works to facilitate international police cooperation.
United Kingdom	National Counter Terrorism Security Office	A police unit that supports the "protect and prepare" strands of the government's counterterrorism strategy.
	Office for Security and Counter-Terrorism (OSCT)	An executive directorate of the U.K. Government's Home Office, created in 2007, responsible for leading the work on counter-terrorism in the United Kingdom, working closely with the police and security services. The office reports to the home secretary and the minister of state for security and counterterrorism.
	Counter Terrorism Command (CTC) or SO15	A specialist operations branch within London's Metropolitan Police Service, resulting from the merging of the Anti-Terrorist Branch (SO13), and the Special Branch (SO12).
United Nations	United Nations Office on Drugs and Crime (UNODC)	Focuses on fighting drugs, crime, and terrorism.

TABLE 5.7   Terrorism databases

Database	Managing organization	Location	Focus
Country Reports on Terrorism	United States Department of States	https://www.state.gov/j/ct/rls/crt/	Strategic assessment, 2000–2016.
Global Terrorism Database	National Consortium for the Study of Terrorism and Responses to Terrorism (START)	www.start.umd.edu/gtd	140,000 terrorist attacks with 45–120 variables for each, 1970–2014.
Integrated Network for Societal Conflict Research (INSCR)	Center for Systemic Peace	www.systemicpeace.org/inscrdata.html	High casualty terrorist bombings, 1989–2014.
International Terrorism: Attributes of Terrorist Events (ITERATE)	Duke University	http://library.duke.edu/data/collections/iterate	International terrorist incidents, 1978–2011.

CHECK YOURSELF BOX: TERRORISM RESEARCH AND DATA BIASES

Who are the individuals and groups in charge of collecting and disseminating information and data about terrorism and counterterrorism? How do each benefit from being part of the terrorism discussion? How could their individual goals affect the information and data they collect and distribute? Are there reasons that a group or individual may want to keep certain pieces of information off the record? Biases in the information and data that you use will affect the viability of your research. Try to make a note of individual biases that may affect the data you are using so that you can try to counteract the biases before they bias your terrorism and counterterrorism research.

Section 6: Economic structure of terrorism

The terrorist attacks on the United States on September 11, 2001 led to a closure of the U.S. stock market for four days. The decision was made by the New York Stock Exchange (NYSE) and the Nasdaq as they anticipated panic selling which would lead to a loss of stock value. After the stock market reopened on September 17, there was a $1.4 trillion loss in value from the week's trading. Some of the biggest stock losses accrued to the two airline carriers whose planes had been hijacked for the assault. Almost 3,000 people lost their lives due to the terror attacks and over 6,000 were wounded. Although estimates vary, it is thought that the total cost of the attacks to the terrorists was around $500,000, while the cost to the United States was around $2 trillion. The costs of terrorism are incurred at both the macroeconomic level (affecting an economy via outcomes such as investment uncertainty and industry failure) and at the microeconomic level (affecting individuals and populations via outcomes such as loss of life, income, and freedom of movement).

The first step in understanding the economic structure of terrorism is to determine the decision-makers who are involved in the choices surrounding terrorism. Terrorism is an activity that an organized group of people choose in order to gain power and resources to influence society and policy. This section reviews the costs and benefits of terrorism to the individuals and groups who are voluntarily and involuntarily involved and looks at the choices of terrorist organizations, individual terrorists, government agencies and non-government organizations concerned with counterterrorism, and noncombatant citizens.

Terrorist organizations are organized in a number of different ways. Each terrorist organization has a group of leaders and possibly a main leader. These leaders make the top-down decisions of the terrorist organization. They have a wider view (Jacob Shapiro, 2013) of the political situation and understand the structure needed to accomplish the organization's overall mission. Terrorist leaders will include both central leadership (the highest-ranking members of the terrorist organization) as well as local leadership (specific to certain terrorist activities in that region). Local leadership will be in charge of local recruiting, fundraising, and other regional activities.

There are many reasons why individuals are leaders in the terrorist organization. Alan Krueger (2007) advocates for a multidisciplinary approach to studying the causes and effects of terrorism to best understand what motivates terrorists. He looks at the characteristics of individual participants in terrorism; economic and political conditions; and the consequences of terrorism. Leaders are often the most militant terrorists and fiercely dedicated to the specific terrorist cause. They have the most to gain and lose in terms of power, resources, safety, and freedom.

Krueger and Jitka Maleckova's research (2003) find that the majority of terrorists are from the middle and upper classes and educated, which contradicts the developed world's views of terrorists: That is, that they arise from poverty and lack both education and opportunity. Krueger and Maleckova discuss the fact that when a person who has a higher level of education agrees to join a terrorist organization, it may signal commitment and ability to the terrorist organization leaders. Interviews by Ariel Merari (2004) indicate that hate and revenge are not the primary motivators of suicide attackers, and Ariel Merari, Ilan Diamant, Arie Bibi, Yaov Broshi, and Giora Zakin (2010) indicate that separate personality styles are attributed to suicide- and non-suicide-type terrorists.

Eli Berman and David Laitin (2008) use the model of a social club to describe successful religious terrorist organizations. Membership in these terrorist organizations allows the individual to be part of the "club" to access local public goods which are provided by the terrorist organization. Eli Berman (2009) finds that suicide attacks are carried out because the individual believes the action will bring great benefit to the community or country. Terrorist organizations rely on a large number of moderates – those who believe in the cause but are not willing to do terrorist acts. These people may include informants, donors, and specialists, such as engineers, doctors, and teachers who run the social services set up by terrorist organizations. They voluntarily or involuntarily play a supportive role in terroristic activities. Terrorist organizations also rely on a larger number of external organizations such as businesses that supply resources to the terrorists in exchange for money and other in-kind trades. These businesses may be terrorist-owned or non-terrorist owned.

It is important to notice that although governments are most often in opposition to terrorists, some governments may be complicit with the terrorists' activities. Those governments may act as the main terrorists against their own citizens. This area of research is outside the scope of this textbook.

Terrorist organization leaders will look for ways to recruit militant followers who will be used in a number of ways within the organization. These militants have the desire to wield power and destroy. There are different reasons behind a militants' willingness to work for the organization. Radically pure militants who are working for the terrorist cause are motivated by their personal belief in the terrorist organization's cause. They may accept low wages and harsh conditions for the greater good of the cause. These militants will be used in the terrorist organization to recruit and train other militants, for extreme fighting and suicide missions, to create and disseminate propaganda, for fundraising, and as foreign terrorist fighters. In contrast, militants are primarily motivated by mercenary desires for wages, weapons, equipment, and personal gain. They will be used to carry out the terrorist organization's local operations.

As seen earlier, counterterrorism activities are part of the duties of governments and some nongovernment agencies. These organizations have many decisions to make. The government must decide its goals in dealing with terrorism. Reducing the threat of terrorist violence to zero is unachievable. Therefore, the first decision is what combination of offensive measures (such as arrests and use of military force) or defensive measures (such as security regarding individuals, buildings, and resources) to use to combat terrorism. These decisions will be made based on the government's available resources and capabilities. Jacob Shapiro (2013) finds this debate most intense around high-value potential targets of terrorism. Another decision will involve whether to seek national and international partners in order to mount a joint defense in the face of a terroristic threat. Once the choices have been made, the government must decide which government branches and resources to dedicate to each antiterrorism and counterterrorism goal. This may include moving resources within and between departments and changing priorities. Jack Snyder (2011) states that "One irony of humanitarian military intervention is that the actions to deter the opportunistic atrocities typically threaten the relative power and security of the perpetrator and therefore increase his motivation to use atrocities to shore up his position."

It is important to think about not only the primary effects of terrorism, but also the secondary and tertiary effects. Some of the primary effects of a terrorist act are the loss of life, the destruction of property, and disruptions to income and revenue generation. Loss of future income, changes to business and society, and fear-induced repression of choice are included in secondary effects. Tertiary effects incorporate long-term changes, such as to cultural norms and to the path of government and international policies.

Here, the economics of terrorism is modeled by analyzing the costs and benefits of terrorism for individuals and groups who are voluntarily or involuntarily involved in the terrorism. The groups considered are the terrorist organizations, the persons who perform terrorist acts, the direct victims of terrorism, the persons indirectly affected by terrorism, and the media (which chooses which information to broadcast and the method of reporting the information).

Many professional organizations have the mission of providing risk modeling for terroristic attacks. The models are often linked to models of insurance, such as Gordon Woo's (2002) research on quantifying insurance terrorism risk to estimate probable maximum loss. Characteristics of individuals, groups, and countries are all possible variables in the studies. Much of this analysis is associated with **game theory**, which models situations of conflict and cooperation using mathematical modeling. It assumes **rationality**, which means the person uses all the information they possess in order make the decision that maximizes their **economic utility** (satisfaction). In game theory, two decision-makers or decision-making groups make choices that provide the best outcome (highest utility or profit) taking into account the other decision-maker's or group's choices. For example, Daniel Jacobson and Edward Kaplan (2007) analyze the choices made by terrorists and the governments using counterterrorism methods to combat terrorism through sequential game models. Each game happens during one time period and the outcomes of the subsequent games are based partially on the outcomes of completed games. Another innovation in game theory related to terrorism is Katherine Boyd's (2016) multiple membership random effects modeling (MMREM) of the cases when terrorist organizations simultaneously target several countries.

Unit 1: Costs of terrorism

Just as there are many ways to organize a business, so terrorists use a variety of organizational structures. These dissimilarities account for differences in costs to terrorist organizations. Financial costs may be one of the highest costs to these groups as items such as weapons and other equipment, training facilities, and services must be purchased and payments must be made to terrorist members and others who are in some way associated with the terrorists' activities. Time is needed for recruitment, training, finding resources, raising funds, activities to gauge counterterrorism activity, negotiations, and planning terroristic events. Time, money, and specific training may be needed to operate successfully with existing government, legal, law enforcement, and other officials. Psychological costs include being in danger from counterterrorism organizations and possibly from inside the terrorism group, or due to the dissent of the communities in which the group operates. In addition, the media could turn public opinion against the terrorist group, which could increase a variety of costs.

Jacob Shapiro (2013) describes the terrorist's dilemma as follows: "Leaders need to control how violence is executed and how finances are managed, but the tools to do so create some measure of operational vulnerabilities and therefore increase the likelihood of operatives being caught and a group compromised." Terrorist organizations face personnel issues from differing views of members about the methods, targets, and intensity of terrorist attacks. Shapiro sees the terrorists' challenges as those of security versus control, use of money and tactics, and member discipline and punishment.

Terrorist organizations are made up of individuals. Sometimes a common purpose unites them, but other times individuals join the terrorist group for money or under duress. Each person who works with a terrorist organization is at risk of losing their life. Training to be a terrorist takes time and may be physically exhausting or damaging. The individual may lose their identity apart from the terrorist organization, which could drive away family and friends. Being a terrorist may put that individual's own family at risk of reprisal by counterterrorism groups or by the terrorist group if the individual does not comply with the group's demands or fails in a terrorist attempt. Intense training and initiation may be used on a new terrorist recruit, so that the individual is always in danger of physical or psychological injury. A known terrorist attracts a criminal record and loses the ability to travel freely. Finally, the violence involved in working with a terrorist organization may affect the terrorist long after leaving the group.

Direct costs to the victims of terrorism depend upon the type of terrorist action. These costs may be loss of life or physical property; injury and the effects of rape; loss of safety and security from harm; loss of freedom of speech for fear of retribution by terrorists; fear-induced repression of opportunities (for example, investments, travel, and business transactions) and opportunities (such as travel, education, and freedom of movement). It may be difficult to get exact estimates on direct costs. The U.S. Department of State's Patterns of Global Terrorism report (2013) only takes into account property damage that exceeds $10,000. Terrorism may lead to fear of the unknown and a loss of faith in the government. This uncertainty and anxiety may be compounded due to extensive forecasting by various media channels (Anouk Rigterink and Mareike Schomerus, 2017).

Indirect costs of terrorism include loss of use of structures, areas, or regions; fear-induced repression of choices by those who have not been directly impacted by terrorism; restrictions on movement and personal rights; increased time and expense to negotiate security checkpoints; fear of being attacked; loss of income in frequently attacked areas; and ordinary citizens having to face the bigoted views of people who judge them simply because they bear similarities to stereotypes associated with a terrorist group (e.g. nervousness around a Muslim man due to the actions of radical Islam). The $84 billion global cost of terrorism reported by the Institute for Economics and Peace (2017) does not include the indirect impact on business and investment and the costs associated with security agencies in countering terrorism. The Institute states, ". . .terrorism is one of the few categories of violence where the costs associated with containment likely exceed its consequential costs. However, while the economic impact of terrorism is small it is still critical to contain it as it has the potential to spread quickly and with major social ramifications."

Governments and private security organizations are involved in counterterrorism efforts. Counterterrorism costs are associated with information-gathering by satellite, wire taps, bugging, etc., physically tracking down terrorists, concessions made to terrorists in the negotiation process, time, loss of life of counterterrorism agents, and countering the criticism and loss of faith of constituents if the terrorist movement persists. Counterterrorism, by necessity, funnels resources away from production and national service into homeland security, which adds further to already increased expenses.

As long as groups of people feel that terroristic actions are the means to their political and social ends, terrorism will exist due to the scarcity of resources available for counterterrorism. Terrorism and counterterrorism decisions are based upon the knowledge, materials, and methods available. For example, governments must weigh the costs of terroristic actions with the cost of counterterrorism measures. Pew Research Center (2013) reports that each year the United States spends around $16.6 billion to fight terrorism. As more terroristic events occur, society and the economy are increasingly damaged. This strains the capacity of existing counterterrorism organizations and requires the commitment of more scarce resources to fighting terrorism. The marginal cost of damage to a country from terrorism (MC_T) increases as the quantity of terrorism increases (Q_T), as shown in Figure 5.1.

FIGURE 5.1   Marginal cost of damage from terrorism   **FIGURE 5.2**   Marginal cost of counterterrorism

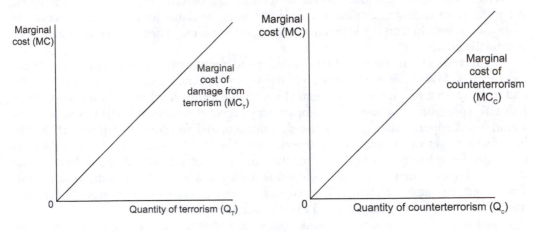

The marginal cost of counterterrorism (MC_C), the cost of the last unit of the counterterrorism effort, is illustrated in Figure 5.2. While keeping a watchful eye out for possible terrorist threats may be part of law enforcement's day-to-day role, creating agencies and laws and gathering finances and resources to commit to fight terrorism is costly. Launching a counterterrorism structure has an extremely high marginal cost during the setup phase. Those costs should decrease once the operation is underway.

One of the choices of a nation is determining the breadth of resources to commit to counterterrorism efforts and the amount of terroristic activity to "allow" (due to unknown variables and limited resources). This model assumes that the quantity of counterterrorism effort (Q_C) means a decrease in the amount of damage from terrorism activity (Q_T). This choice, as illustrated in Figure 5.3, takes into account the marginal cost of damage from terrorism (as shown in Figure 5.1) and the marginal cost of counterterrorism efforts (as shown in Figure 5.2), where the quantity of counterterrorism effort is the inverse of the quantity of terrorism activity. The most efficient choice of counterterrorism measures is found at point Q_1 where the marginal cost of damage from terrorism (MC_T) is equal to the marginal cost of counterterrorism (MC_C). This choice of counterterrorism measures provides the lowest cost of obtaining the optimal level of national security. Area TC_{T1} is the total cost of damage from terrorism and is found by adding up the marginal costs of each unit of terrorism that is not met with counterterrorism efforts. Similarly, area TC_{C1} shows the total cost of the counterterrorism efforts, which is a summing of the marginal costs of each unit of counterterrorism. The total cost for this nation is equal to TC_{T1} plus TC_{C1}.

FIGURE 5.3   Efficient counterterrorism choice

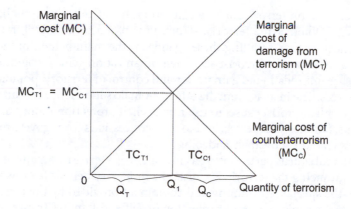

Political opinion may cause the nation to choose a quantity of counterterrorism activity that is not equal to the efficient quantity Q_1. An example is shown in Figure 5.4 when the nation chooses to increase counterterrorism efforts to Q_{C2}. In this case, the total cost of counterterrorism efforts has increased (TC_{C2}) and the cost of damage from counterterrorism has decreased (TC_{T2}), but the total cost of terrorism and counterterrorism to this nation has increased to TC_{T2} plus TC_{C2}.

FIGURE 5.4   Inefficient counterterrorism choice

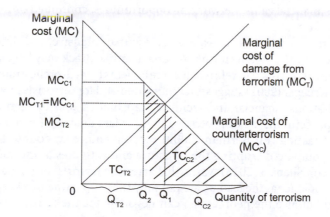

A technological or policy innovation may change the marginal cost of damage from terrorism or the marginal cost of damage. A decrease in the marginal cost of damage from terrorism would be shown by a leftward shift in MC_D, while a leftward shift in MC_C would illustrate a decrease in the marginal cost of counterterrorism.

Efficiency and inefficiency are not equal to right and wrong. The policy implication of an efficient choice is that economic utility or profit is maximized and total cost is minimized. A right or wrong choice is based upon personal, social, and political opinion and may not depend upon economic efficiency.

Unit 2: Benefits of terrorism

Neither the U.S. "war on terror" nor strategic programs of other nations have eliminated terroristic activity. Whether the terrorist structure is based on criminal, religious, revolutionary, or political reasons, fulfilling these agendas is the main benefit of terrorism. When terrorists can claim successful terrorist acts, their organization gains recognition and reputation. Terrorists use intimidation to gain power and control of territory, populations, political areas, and resources. The increased media attention makes it easier to recruit new terrorists, to gain donors for the terrorist cause, to use fear to elicit protection money and cooperation from individuals, families, businesses, and to gain concessions from governments. The publicity works to spread the movement's ideology.

Benefits to individuals participating as members of a terrorist organization include the satisfaction of advancing the terroristic cause, the monetary benefit from working with the terrorist group, the specialized training and equipment provided by the organization, gains in rank within the organization, and protection of self and families from the enemy or the retribution of the terrorist organization. Social psychologist Arie Kruglanski (Tom Jacobs, 2010) lists three elements that trigger a tendency in a person to become a suicide bomber or terrorist. First, the person seeks the society of a group (similar to Eli Berman's club good theory, 2009). Second, the individual has an ideology that accepts violent actions to benefit the group. Third, there is an emotional element that "triggers both the acceptance and personalization of the ideology." Some research suggests that personal reasons for terrorism are frustration, deprivation, negative identity, narcissistic rage, and moral disengagement (Manzio Barbagli, 2015).

There are many individuals, businesses, and political officials that work with terrorists, either voluntarily or under duress, but are not part of the terrorism organizations. Their benefits may include financial gains, networking opportunities, continued or increased political power, and safety from attack.

Counterterrorism activities are expensive, resource-intensive, and aimed at the moving targets of organic terrorist organizations. Yet one terrorist attack may cost a nation multiple times the cost to the terrorists. Therefore, there are benefits to well-orchestrated counterterrorism efforts. Alan Krueger (2007) suggests targeting demand for terrorists in ways that degrade "terrorist organizations' financial and technical capabilities, and by vigorously protecting and promoting peaceful means of protest so there is less demand for pursuing grievances through terrorist tactics." Eli Berman (2009) recommends that counterterrorism should focus on figuring out and disrupting the structure and activities of the successful terrorist organizations. Jacob Shapiro (2013) warns that arresting terrorist organization leaders may lead to increased violence as the leaders are not only the people who can keep terrorist activities in check and but also the people who can negotiate for the terrorist organization. The

Global Terrorism Index 2017 reports that terrorist organizations have three leading causes of termination: Achievement of political goals; internally splintering due to differences between team members; and defeat by military or police forces.

The Corporation for Public Broadcasting (2017) in the United States states, "The purpose of public media is to provide programs and services that inform, educate, enlighten, and enrich the public and help inform civil discourse essential to American society." Successful media organizations bring the most relevant information to their audiences. Terrorism has always grabbed viewers' attention and the media organizations capitalize on this interest to increase their revenue streams. The words, pictures, and videos used to depict the violent extremist activity can be used to disseminate fear or as an objective grounding for the public facing these threats.

Unit 3: Inefficiencies in economic structure of terrorism

The international intelligence community is represented by thousands of government and non-government agencies and individuals across the world. The U.S. intelligence community itself is expansive, with three main federal agencies and a host of nongovernment agencies collecting intelligence and doing activities related to counterterrorism. Both political issues and the coordination of the many activities and overlapping responsibilities lend themselves to some inefficiency in resource and work allocation. This can both increase costs and decrease the effectiveness of counterterrorism efforts.

Whether an individual is labeled terrorist or freedom fighter depends upon public opinion and the current political atmosphere. The detailed knowledge of terrorism experts is required to understand the intricacies of a particular organization. The researcher brings both expert knowledge and bias, and the latter can lead to inefficiencies in future terrorism research.

Section 7: Case study

Effect of terrorism by Tamil Tigers on Sri Lanka economy

Intuitively, one would likely predict that terrorism would have a substantial effect on macroeconomic indicators such as gross domestic product (GDP), inflation rates, literacy rates, foreign investment and in a country. The logic is that terrorism would destabilize a country, leading to decreased investment by foreign actors and decreased trust in the protection of the government by the citizenry of both the country itself and other countries leading to sundry negative impacts. In theory, citizens would likely isolate themselves as they see the government as no longer providing security. Such isolation would lead to an abandonment of education and participation in the economy. Empirically, however, these effects are not as obvious as one would predict. In fact, most of the predicted negative impacts cannot be seen at all.

This case study focuses on Sri Lanka and its economy from 1960 until 2017, and how its macroeconomic indicators relate to the terrorist attacks of the Tamil Tigers (or LTTE) and other factions from 1983 to 2009. As will be demonstrated, most of the relationships between the macro economy and terrorism mentioned thus far cannot be easily found; however, one strong relationship that can be found is the negative relationship between terrorism and tourism, and further economic inferences can be made from this relationship.

Sri Lanka was chosen for this case study because of the peculiar terrorism situation. Unlike a country with an infrequent terrorist attack every few years or a country with frequent terrorist attacks that have occurred for 50+ years, Sri Lanka had a concentration of terrorist attacks almost every year during its civil war from 1983 to 2009 with almost no attacks prior to or after those dates. Because of this, one can look at macroeconomic indicators before 1983, during the civil war, and after the civil war in order to better differentiate between things that are caused by the terrorist attacks and things that are caused by lurking variables.

Macroeconomic data was acquired via the World Bank (WB) and Sri Lanka's tourism development website (SLTDA). WB acquires a multitude of data from various countries. However, oftentimes the data is fragmented or missing altogether. For example, one dependent variable under examination was alcohol consumption and how it is affected by terrorism; although WB has such a category, the data is unavailable. For tourism, the focus of this analysis, WB and the SLTDA differed on the amount of revenue gained from tourism. WB gives the following definition of what it classifies as tourism receipts:

> International tourism receipts are expenditures by international inbound visitors, including payments to national carriers for international transport. These receipts include any other prepayment made for goods or services received in the destination country. They also may include receipts from same-day visitors, except when these are important enough to justify separate classification. For some countries, they do not include receipts for passenger transport items. Data are in current U.S. dollars.

While these numbers are in current U.S. dollars, SLTDA tracks tourism receipts in nominal numbers. Furthermore, SLTDA does not define what is classified as tourism receipts. Lastly, most GDP data acquired concerning Sri Lanka is real GDP. This means that an analysis with nominal tourism data would involve either converting the real GDP to a nominal number or converting the tourism data (nominal data in current prices) to the inflation-adjusted numbers (real data that is adjusted for prices).

It follows that WB data would be best to use for analysis because no numerical manipulation is required, thus minimizing human error in the analysis. However, WB is missing data concerning tourism for the years prior to 1995, whereas the Sri Lanka website has data as far back as 1970. Therefore, due to the benefits and downsides of the two datasets, each is analyzed independently.

Dummy variables are used to represent terrorism in the analysis. Specifically, the dummy variable is equal to 1 if there was a fatal non-state terrorist attack in Sri Lanka that year and 0 otherwise. The reason for choosing a dummy variable approach is that intuitively, the marginal effect of an additional death from one terrorist attack would have little or no effect compared to the attack itself. Furthermore, **non-state terrorist attacks**, which are attacks by terrorist organizations that are not associated with a nation state, were chosen specifically because to lump state and non-state attacks together would only muddle the intuition behind the results.

Before discussing the conclusions concerning tourism and terrorism, it should be noted that multiple dependent variables were analyzed in relation to terrorism but no significant relationships were found. Those dependent variables were as follows: GDP, GDP per capita growth, GDP growth, population, inflation, foreign direct investment, and gross national expenditures.

Using the WB dataset, a time-series regression analysis in STATA is utilized with tourism as a percentage of GDP as the dependent variable and the terrorism dummy variable as an explanatory variable. In addition, the best lag of the dependent variable is added as an explanatory variable to control for the influence of past values of tourism as a percentage

TABLE 5.8   Time-series regression: Tourism as a percentage of GDP (World Bank)

| Time allotment | *School and part-time household work* | | | |
	Coefficient	p-Value	95% C.I.	Adj. R^2 = 0.2365
Constant	0.0285*	–	–	–
Lag3	0.1631	0.62	-0.53–0.85	–
Terrorism dummy	-0.0107*	0.02	0.01–0.05	–

*Denotes significance at 5% significance level.

TABLE 5.9   Time-series regression: Tourism as a percentage of GDP (Sri Lanka website)

| Time allotment | *School and part-time household work* | | | |
	Coefficient	p-value	95% C.I.	Adj. R^2 = 0.4794
Constant	0.0228*	–	–	–
Lag3	0.6019*	0.00	0.38–0.82	–
Terrorism dummy	-0.0183*	0.00	-0.03–0.01	–

*Denotes significance at 5% significance level.

of GDP. The best lag was chosen based on the lowest SAIC and BIC criteria and HQIC as a tiebreaker. Under such criteria, the third lag was chosen. The regression then indicates that for every year that a fatal non-state terrorist attack occurred, tourism as a percentage of GDP fell by 1.07%.

For the SLTDA data, the best lag was also the third. By performing the same regression then but with the differing data, it was determined that for every year that a fatal non-state terrorist attack occurred, tourism as a percentage of GDP fell by 1.83%.

Comparing the two datasets, the Sri Lanka website data, although more prone to human error due to conversion from real to nominal GDP, appears to be the better regression since the adjusted R^2 is significantly higher than for WB regression. Furthermore, the SLTDA regression has 43 observations as opposed to 18 for WB, making it a more reliable sample size. Ultimately, the effect of terrorism is likely to result in an average 1.07–1.83% decrease in tourism as a percentage of GDP, but the average is likely much closer to 1.83% than 1.07%.

It should be noted that since tourism is viewed as a percentage of GDP, it is important to verify that tourism is in fact being affected, as opposed to GDP independent of tourism being affected. First, as has been mentioned, there is no observable relationship between GDP or GDP growth with terrorism. Second, there is a significant relationship between the number of tourists visiting Sri Lanka in a given year and fatal non-state terrorist attacks in the same year. Using tourism arrivals as a dependent variable and the second lag of that variable based on the same lag selection criteria, years with at least one fatal non-state terrorist attack experience about 16,000 fewer tourists than years without such an attack. This regression uses data from the SLTDA because the data dates back to 1970

TABLE 5.10   Time-series regression: Tourist arrivals

Time allotment	Coefficient	p-value	School and part-time household work 95% C.I.	Adj. R² = 0.9167
Constant	18116	–	–	–
Lag2	1.3620*	0.00	1.23–1.49	–
Terrorism dummy	-16109*	0.00	22411–-98069	–

*Denotes significance at 5% significance level.

as opposed to the matching data from WB dating back to 1995. On average, the number of tourist arrivals in Sri Lanka from 1970 to 2015 was 422,000, but the number grew to over 1,000,000 beginning in 2012.

Therefore, there is a clear effect on tourism arrivals, which leads to the conclusion that the effect of terrorism on tourism (as a percentage of GDP) is affecting the tourism part of the equation.

The most significant limitations for this study are the reliability and existence of data and the developing nature of Sri Lanka. As has been mentioned, the data for seemingly identical metrics can differ based on precise definitions for categorizations of data. Additionally, many datapoints that could be acquired – such as alcohol rates and literacy rates – are missing for Sri Lanka, which prevents analysis of possible relationships between terrorism and the macro economy. Most importantly, however, is the developing nature of Sri Lanka from the 1960s to the early 2000s. With an average annual GDP growth rate of 4.9% in that time period, changes in GDP based on terrorism are difficult to isolate because as one sector (such as tourism) may be adversely affected, another sector may be independently flourishing, offsetting any cognizable change.

Terrorism indisputably hurt the tourism industry in Sri Lanka, causing foregone GDP of 1.07–1.83%. Although such a devastating effect cannot be seen in the raw GDP or GDP growth as an effect of terrorism, the effect is no less relevant to the overall GDP of Sri Lanka. Without tourism, one could imagine that Sri Lanka would have been a developing country for a much shorter time and would have quickly reached the point of being developed. Furthermore, the GDP foregone in one year could cause a ripple effect of lower GDP in the next year, hurting sectors in unforeseen yet crucial ways. The best response, then, to a terrorist attack in terms of tourism is for a government to immediately enact policies reinforcing stability and increasing local security and policing in order to make foreigners feel as safe as they would have felt prior to the attack.

The government of Sri Lanka's military campaign to exterminate the Tamil Tigers began in 2009. Since that time, an estimated 40,000 civilians have been killed in the clashes between the two groups. War crimes and crimes against humanity (described in the chapter on genocide) were committed by both sides. Demands from the United Nations for an end to the violence have been dismissed by the Sri Lankan Government.

▋ Section 8: Recommendations for future research

Without understanding the fundamental causes of terrorism, economic analysis and modeling is limited. Research into one terrorist organization cannot be extended to cover all of these organizations because of the intricacies of the ideology, structure, and means of terrorist acts. While some terrorist organizations spring out of a resistance to the suppression of civil liberties and political rights, others develop due to gains from criminal activities.

There is a limited understanding of the effects of terrorism on human rights, local populations, travel, saving and investment, national economics, and policy-making. Equally, there is incomplete information on how counterterrorism efforts affect these areas of influence. Wider research is needed to understand the positive and negative incentives faced by terrorist organizations and individual terrorists. For example, how do oil prices affect ISIS, and what incentives cause a person to join a terrorist organization? In conjunction with knowledge of organizations and individuals involved in terrorist acts, economics can be used to determine the incentive structure that would lead to increased efficiency in counterterrorism efforts.

It is also important to determine the media's role in terrorism. Terrorist organizations and counterterrorism agencies are both helped and hurt by the media. The media has the power to incite hysteria or provide informative coverage to help a population understand what is happening and where to go for help.

CHECK YOURSELF BOX: CHANGES TO PERSONAL BIASES ABOUT TERRORISM

Have you learned any new information during the reading of this chapter? What topics made an impact on your understanding of the economics of terrorism? What areas do you disagree with? What are your current thoughts about terrorism and counterterrorism? Look back at the first check yourself box to see the list of initial thoughts you had about terrorism. Do you see adaptations to your way of thinking? What information do you still feel you are missing? Each piece of information can create a greater depth of information for you, but can also create new or changed biases. Keeping track of these changes and the reasons for these changes will help you discern how your personal biases might be skewing your research.

▋ Section 9: Bibliography

Barbagli, Marzio. (2015). *Farewell to the world: A history of suicide.* Hoboken: Wiley.

Berman, Eli. (2009). *Radical, religious, and violent: The new economics of terrorism.* Cambridge: MIT.

Berman, Eli and Laitin, David. (2008). Religion, terrorism, and public goods: Testing the club model. *Journal of Public Economics: 92*(10–11), 1,942–67.

Boyd, Katherine. (2016). Modeling terrorist attacks: Assessing statistical models to evaluate domestic and ideologically international attacks. *Studies in Conflict and Terrorism, 39*(7–8), 712–48.

Corporation for Public Broadcasting. (June 12, 2017). *Goals and objectives as adopted by the Board of Directors.* Retrieved from https://www.cpb.org/aboutcpb/goals/goalsandobjectives

Enders, Walter and Olson, Eric. (2012). Measuring the economic costs of terrorism. In Michelle Garfinkel and Stergios Skaperdas (Eds.), *The Oxford handbook of the economics of peace and conflict.* Oxford: Oxford University Press.

Falk, Richard. (2017). Contradictions in the terrorist discourse and constraints on the political imagination of violence. In Michael Stohl; Richard Burchill; and Scott Englund (Eds.), *Constructions of terrorism: An interdisciplinary approach to research and policy.* Oakland: University of California Press.

German, Michael. (2016, October 26). Counter terror smarter. *U.S. News and World Report.* Retrieved from https://www.usnews.com/opinion/world-report/articles/2016-10-26/4-counterterrorism-strategies-the-us-must-abandon

Institute for Economics and Peace (2017). *Global terrorism index 2017: Measuring and understanding the impact of terrorism.* (2017). Institute for Economics & Peace. Retrieved from http://visionofhumanity.org/app/uploads/2017/11/Global-Terrorism-Index-2017.pdf

Jacobs, Tom. (March-April 2010). The mind of a terrorist. *The Miller-McCune Interview.* Santa Barbara: The Miller-McCune Center for Research. Retrieved from https://psmag.com/social-justice/the-mind-of-a-terrorist-8638

Jacobson, Daniel and Kaplan, Edward. (2007). Suicide bombings and targeted killings in (counter-) terror games. *Journal of Conflict Resolution, 51*(5).

Kearns, Erin; Betus, Allison; and Lemieux, Anthony. (2017, March 13). Yes, the media does underreport some terrorist attacks. Just not the ones most people think of. *The Washington Post.* Retrieved from https://www.washingtonpost.com/news/monkey-cage/wp/2017/03/13/yes-the-media-do-underreport-some-terrorist-attacks-just-not-the-ones-most-people-think-of/?noredirect=on&utm_term=.251084c732cc

Kokoshin, Andrei. (2006). *A nuclear response to nuclear terror: Reflections of nuclear preemption.* The Annals of the American Academy of Political and Social Science, 607(1).

Krueger, Alan. (2007). *What makes a terrorist: Economics and the roots of terrorism.* Princeton: Princeton University Press.

Krueger, Alan and Maleckova, Jitka. (2003). Education, poverty and terrorism: Is there a causal connection? *Journal of Economic Perspectives, 17*(4), 119–44.

Merari, Ariel. (2004). *Suicide terrorism in the context of the Israeli–Palestinian conflict.* National Institute of Justice Suicide Terrorism Conference, October 25–6, Washington, DC.

Merari, Ariel; Diamant, Ilan; Bibi, Arie; Broshi, Yoav; and Zakin, Giora. (2010). Personality characteristics of "self martyrs"/"suicide bombers" and organizers of suicide attacks. *Terrorism and Political Violence, 22*(1), 87–101.

Pew Research Center. (2013, September 11). *U.S. spends over $16 billion annually on counter-terrorism.* Retrieved from http://www.pewresearch.org/fact-tank/2013/09/11/u-s-spends-over-16-billion-annually-on-counter-terrorism/

Rigterink, Anouk and Schomerus, Mareike. (2017). The fear factor is a main thing: How radio influences anxiety and political attitudes. *Journal of Development Studies. 53*(8), 1123–46.

Shapiro, Jacob. (2013). *The terrorist's dilemma: Managing violent covert organizations.* Princeton: Princeton University Press.

Sinai, Joshua. (2016). *New trends of terrorism's targeting of the business sector.* The MacKenzie Institute. Retrieved from http://mackenzieinstitute.com/new-trends-in-terrorisms-targeting-of-the-business-sector

Snyder, Jack. (2011). Realism, refugees, and strategies of humanitarianism. In Alexander Betts and Gill Loescher (Eds.), *Review of refugees in international relations.* Oxford: Oxford University Press.

Sri Lanka Tourism Development Authority (SLTDA). *Tourism growth trends – 1970 to 2016.* Retrieved from http://www.sltda.gov.lk/sites/default/files/tourism-growth-and-trends-1970-2016.pdf

U.S. Department of State Archives. (2009). *National strategy for combatting terrorism.* Retrieved from https://2001-2009.state.gov/s/ct/rls/wh/71803.htm

U.S. Department of State Bureau of Counterterrorism. (2013). *National Consortium for the Study of Terrorism and Responses to Terrorism: Annex of statistical information.* Retrieved from https://www.state.gov/j/ct/rls/crt/2013/224831.htm

Woo, Gordon. (2002). *Quantifying insurance terrorism risk.* Paper presented at the National Bureau of Economic Research meeting on February 1, 2002. Retrieved from http://citeseerx.ist.psu.edu/viewdoc/download?doi=10.1.1.406.8897&rep=rep1&type=pdf

World Bank IBRD-IDA. Data on Sri Lanka. Retrieved from http://data.worldbank.org/country/sri-lanka

Section 10: Resources

Unit 1: Summary

Terrorism involves a complicated web of decision-makers with multiple, sometimes overlapping objectives. Terrorist organizations form around one or a few central ideas involving political or social change through violent means. Individuals join these organizations for a number of reasons, weighing the costs and benefits to self and family of becoming a terrorist associated with a particular organization. These individuals are used in varying capacities within the terrorist organization. The success of terroristic activity depends in part upon the available human and material resources, the main goal of the attacks, the difficulty of the target, and the external support of donors and businesses, whether voluntarily or under duress. National governments and international organizations are at the forefront of counterterrorism efforts to protect citizens and decrease the power of the terrorist organizations. Counterterrorism measures depend partially upon the available human and material resources, the counterterrorism goal being pursued, knowledge of the terrorist organization and its operatives, and the cooperation of external sources in the area or under the influence of the terrorist organization.

Unit 2: Key concepts

Agro-terrorism: The intentional delivery of bacteria, viruses, or other micro-organisms for the purpose of disrupting a food supply system.

Bioterrorism: The use of biological agents to cause mass harm.

Counterterrorism: The strategy and action by governments, military entities, intelligence agencies, law enforcement, and businesses to protect against the actions and financing of terrorism and to defeat or destroy terrorist organizations for the purpose of protecting civilians and to reduce the risks associated with terroristic threats.

Criminal terrorism: Terroristic activity that is used for criminal activity and for criminal profit.

Cyberterrorism: The use of computers and information technology to provoke widespread fear and uncertainty.

Dissent terrorism: Terrorist acts committed by groups rebelling against their governments.

Domestic or national terrorism: Terroristic acts commit within the individual's or organization's home country.

Economic utility: The satisfaction a person derives from the use or consumption of a good or service.

Ethnocentric terrorism: Terroristic activity by a group that views its own race as superior to other races and perpetuates terroristic acts based on these racial differences.

Freedom fighter: A person who takes part in a violent resistance movement to achieve a political or social goal.

Fundamentalism: The belief in and strict obedience to religious laws.

Game theory: The mathematical modeling of situations of conflict and cooperation.

Hard target: An individual, group of individuals, or thing that is guarded and relatively secure.

Insurgency: An organized action aimed at overthrowing a government.

Intelligence: The collection of information useful for defense and policy-making.

International community: The international coalition of governments and nongovernment actors who work together in various capacities to eliminate terrorist threats.

International terrorism: Terrorism focused outside of the individual's or organization's home country.

Lone-wolf terrorism: When an individual commits violent acts of mass murder.

Narco-terrorism: Terrorism related to trade in illegal drugs, usually as a means of funding terrorist acts.

Nationalistic terrorism: Terrorist acts committed for the purpose of gaining political, cultural, or ethnic freedom.

Non-state terrorist attacks: Terrorist attacks by terrorist organizations that are not associated with a nation state.

Nuclear terrorism: The use of radioactive materials to cause damage (Kokoshin, 2006).

Paper terrorism: The use of false or unnecessary documents as a method of harassment.

Political terrorism: Terroristic actions by that oppose persons or groups with different political ideologies.

Proxy bombing: Involuntary delivery of an explosive device to a target by a person who is forced to carry the bomb.

Rationality (being economically rational): When the decision-maker uses all of the information they personally possesses in order to make the decision that maximizes their economic utility.

Religious terrorism: Terrorism that is motivated by religious ideology.

Revolutionary terrorism: Terrorism by a group focused on using terrorism to overthrow an existing governing body or social structure.

Separatist terrorism: Terrorism involving groups with the agenda to separate from an existing structure through autonomy, independence, or religious freedom.

Social terrorism/single issue terrorism/special interest terrorism: Extremist behavior based on a specific topic of interest.

Soft target: An individual, group of individuals, or object with little or no protection.

State terrorism: According to Walter Enders and Eric Olsen (2012), state terrorism is the "planning, funding, and execution" of terrorist action by governments.

Suicide bombing: Voluntary delivery of an explosive device to a target by a member of the terrorist organization who dies during the delivery.

Terrorism: The use of clandestine, fear-provoking violence or threatened violence against governments, noncombatant civilian populations, or property that is designed to advance political or social agendas beyond the immediate target as a means of creating change or resisting change.

Terrorist: A member of a terrorist organization who is involved in terroristic acts or the planning of these acts.

Terrorist organization: An extreme social or political faction that plans and enacts terroristic acts.

Transnational terrorism: The actions of terrorist organizations that are based out of multiple countries with members of multiple nationalities conducting operations around the world.

Unit 3: Review questions

1. In your own words, describe a terrorist organization, a terrorist, and a terroristic act.

2. What are some of the types of terrorism?

3. What are some of the methods of terroristic acts?

4. Name some of the U.S. laws regarding terrorism.

5. What are the major international agreements regarding terrorism?

6. How do politics create controversies regarding terrorism?

7. What is the media's role in terrorism and counterterrorism?

8. What are some reasons that it is difficult to determine how many terrorist organizations exist and are active at a given time?

9. In your own words, describe what intelligence is (as it relates to terrorism) and name some of the types of intelligence that are gathered.

10. Who are some of the experts on terrorism? How would you choose whom to contact regarding research on terrorism?

11. Who are the group and individual decision-makers involved in terrorism and counterterrorism? What are their costs and benefits related to terrorism?

12. How can you use a dynamic economic model to determine how much counterterrorism activity should be controlled by one of two agencies?

13. What are some ways terrorism may affect the macroeconomics of a country?

Unit 4: Recommended readings

Berman, Eli. (2009). *Radical, religious, and violent: The new economics of terrorism*. Cambridge: MIT Press.

Burleigh, Michael. (2008). *Blood & rage: A cultural history of terrorism*. New York: Harper Perenniel.

De Londras, Fiona. (2011). *Detention in the "War on Terror": Can human rights fight back?* Cambridge: Cambridge University Press.

Krueger, Alan. (2007). *What makes a terrorist: Economics and the roots of terrorism*. Princeton: Princeton University Press.

Mayer, Jane. (2009). *The dark side: The inside story of how the war on terror turned into a war on American ideals*. New York: Anchor Books.

Phillips, Peter. (2016). *The economics of terrorism*. New York: Routledge.

Schultz, William. (2003). *Tainted legacy: 9/11 and the ruin of human rights*. New York: Thunder's Mouth Press.

Shapiro, Jacob. (2013). *The terrorist's dilemma: Managing violent covert organizations*. Princeton: Princeton University Press.

Stohl, Michael; Burchill, Richard; and Englund, Scott (Eds.). (2017). *Constructions of terrorism: An interdisciplinary approach to research and policy*. Oakland: University of California Press.

Wright, Lawrence. (2016). *The terror years: From Al-Qaeda to the Islamic State*. London: Constable.

Unit 5: Econometric analysis: Effect of terrorism by Tamil Tigers on Sri Lanka economy

This section is provided in online textbook supplements. The eResources can be found at: www.routledge.com/9781138500167

6

Economics of child abuse

Contributor: Megan Parker-Hoffman, Doctor of Management (Homeland Security)

■ Section 1: Introduction to the economics of child abuse

The National Data Archive on Child Abuse and Neglect (NDACAN) at Cornell University, which collects data on child abuse and neglect from the 50 states of America, Washington D.C., and Puerto Rico through the National Child Abuse and Neglect Data System (NCANDS), reports nearly 700,000 victims of child abuse and neglect in 2015. Most of these children were under the age of one and either White (43.2%), Hispanic (23.6%), or African-American (21.4%). Neglect was the highest factor (75.3%) followed by physical abuse (17.2%), although a child may have suffered from several forms of abuse. There were an estimated 1,670 child fatalities due to abuse or neglect. Three-quarters (74.8%) of these children were below three years old and four-fifths (77.7%) of the abuse cases involved a parent.

Many of the definitions covered in this chapter will be similar to those used in the chapter on violence against women. A major difference will be that children have a higher vulnerability and have fewer choices in terms of how to escape abusive situations. A child is rarely the principle decision-maker in the social unit so when family violence occurs, the child's limited choices are to endure the abuse, to try to mitigate or avoid the abuse, to run away, or to engage in self-destructive behavior.

Unit 1: Child abuse perspective

Al "Jeep" Castorena

Al "Jeep" Castorena is a personal trainer with eight years of experience in Oregon and Texas. He attended American River College in California where he majored in music and nutrition. He has managed gyms and other facilities for 14 years and was a sous chef for a number of years. Jeep's hobbies include writing, playing music, cooking, painting, drawing, hiking, and camping. He was a member of a Red Hot Chili Peppers cover band for six years. Jeep believes that faith and hope are the keys to a happy and successful life and that change is possible if you want it.

I remember a short, normal life as a kid: going to the beach, camping. The abuse that started on my mother and drifted to me happened when my stepfather drank. He beat me many times with a wet belt, a strong hand, and a broomstick. My mom said he beat me because he hated me. The physical and verbal abuse made me feel awkward and confused. I was only a child, but I spent a lot of time outside to avoid him and the beatings. I would stare out my bedroom window looking up at the stars and count them to forget for a few minutes.

My mom and stepfather eventually split up. He kidnapped my brothers and me and took us to stay at the sheep ranch of one of his friends. He left us there and I got to roam around the fields to pet the friendly sheep, see nature, and forget. I fantasized about running away and becoming a sheep when my stepfather came back.

We left the ranch and lived in the station wagon in the parking lot of a public park. I felt abandoned and alone. My brothers were older so they could go places and do things that I couldn't. My stepfather would leave for weeks and we would have to fend for ourselves. My brothers would go to small grocery stores to steal bread and sandwich meat. Some of the homeless living in the park would feed us. I missed my mom and cried for her every day, but she was out of my reach.

We moved to live with my stepfather's cousin, but they didn't want to get in trouble with the police so we lived in an abandoned building. My stepfather would go off for weeks, get temporary work, and spend his money on anything except his sons. The police eventually caught up with him. When the cops took us into custody and put me in the police car, I felt I had done something wrong. We were taken to an orphanage holding center and my brothers and I were separated. I was four years old at this time. My brothers and I were placed in foster homes in different cities and no one would tell me where my brothers were. I needed to know I still had a family; that they were okay. I felt robbed of a lot of things. To the adults, I was just a foster kid.

Over the years I was placed in many, many foster homes, each one promising that it would be a place to call home. As a foster kid being placed in these new families, I would get new things such as clothes and bedding. These families already had children and their children would get jealous and pick on me and I would be packed off to yet another foster home. Sometimes I was locked in. Sometimes I was fed very little food. Sometimes I was made to do chores, such as clean the crevices of a brick patio full of dog hairs with a toothbrush. I wanted to run, but I was just holding on for something that was so far gone. Why am I being treated this way? The best foster home I got to live at for two and a half years, but one day, without notice, I was taken away from only place I felt safe and called home. My foster mother, another foster kid, and I cried as they had to drag me out of the home and into the car. I felt betrayed. I didn't want to go back home after eight years in the foster-care system. Why would I want to go back where I was unwanted?

Once again another stepfather beat and told me that I was nothing, worthless, and a fag. I went to school with bruises and black eyes and many times I thought I wouldn't survive. My stepfather said if I said anything, they would come and take me away again. I was not allowed to eat with my family when he was there. I stayed in my room to draw and read, or at school so I wouldn't have to be home.

When I was 13, I worked stocking groceries, cutting lawns, and delivering newspapers, so my stepfather said I had to pay rent. At 17, I was buying my own food, clothes, school supplies, everything so I decided to leave the house. A few months later, I tried committing suicide.

I'm a survivor, no doubt about it. I have seen life from many sides and I am determined to take all of it and make it positive. I have peace and strength.

Unit 2: Child trafficking perspective

Sandy Storm

Sandy Storm is a sex-trafficking survivor who experienced a powerful transformation and now lives what can only be described as a brand-new life. She is an author and public speaker on the subjects of domestic minor sex trafficking and she shares her own experiences while trapped as a child sex slave, in the commercial sex industry as a young adult, and on the subject of the effects of pornography upon our culture. Sandy is development director for the nonprofit organization New Life Refuge Ministries and also sits on the steering committee of the Texas Coastal Bend Border Region Human Trafficking Task Force. Sandy's life has been redeemed from victim to survivor and now she is truly thriving.

As a child, I became the victim of sex trafficking as the result of depraved choices my despairing mother made in a desperate struggle to remove herself from the grips of poverty. Circumstances played out to create the perfect storm of poverty, abuse, drug addiction, and exploitation.

My mother grew up in a small town as a member of a large, dysfunctional family, experiencing dire poverty from a one-person income. To escape, she dropped out of school at 17 to marry a man recently enlisted in the military. Desperate to switch off the constant barrage of thoughts telling her she would never achieve a healthy, functional life, and caught in the drug culture of the 1970s, she spent much of her time strung out on drugs. The fractured marriage was laced with domestic assault from a maniacal husband who committed suicide when I was five years old, leaving behind a vulnerable widow with two young daughters.

Quickly, my mother became the target of a smooth-talking businessman. He persuaded her to leave her safety network and move across the country. His perfidy became apparent as he found every opportunity to bring me into his bedroom and teach me how to be sexual and perform to satisfy his sick desires. At only six years old I was completely unaware of what was happening and relished the attention of the male father figure in our home. The abuse became a daily cycle of sexualized activities and regular exposure to pornographic images and videos. As the lecherous routine evolved, the limits of my psyche and my tiny body were pushed to adapt to behaviors meant for only mature adults. I formed a deep, albeit traumatic bond with the abuser which strengthened as he carefully groomed me to allow access to more of myself, whether through a camera lens as he produced child pornography or by the introduction of new people, locations, and devices.

As the exploitation increased, new furniture, cars, and clothes seemed to appear daily. Many men my abuser associated with came to our house, or we went to parties at country clubs and in luxurious homes on waterfront properties. I would be expected to have sex with men in upstairs bedrooms or sitting areas behind locker-room showers. I was taught to recruit and train other girls my age to perform acts for the men or for the camera.

After six years, the predator who had preyed upon me daily failed an attempt to molest one girl who had been trained by her parents to resist a sexual offender and to report the violation. My mother's provision source vanished and our poverty returned. To cope with the confusion and stress, I became addicted to drugs and alcohol. There were no resources established to serve a child with severe trauma and the local law enforcement and court systems had no training in how to assist me. I bounced from juvenile detention to mental health facilities and foster homes, and ultimately returned to the care of my mother, who took us back to her poverty-stricken, dysfunctional family. Now vulnerable myself, I was quickly exploited by predatory men, leading to my trading sex for drugs or money and dancing in strip clubs. Each financial reward or other benefit I received chipped away at my ability to resist the chains of servility.

Central to every instance of my exploitation was the element of coercion. Whether through the real exchange of finances (money or my cell-phone bill paid) or the implied trade of protection from loss of resources (a hotel room for the night), the common thread was always the expectation of exchange: The commodity of my humanity exchanged for a temporary provision.

Unit 3: Child advocate perspective

Molly Arnold, Ph.D. and Ardis Lo

Molly Arnold, Ph.D. is a licensed marriage and family therapist, a licensed professional counselor, and a registered play therapist. She holds a doctor of philosophy in family therapy and a master of science in counseling and development from Texas Woman's University. She has worked with families and children in counseling and casework capacities since 1993 and holds a strong systemic view of individuals and families, believing that individuals are best understood within the contexts of their lives. Through CASA of Denton County, Dr. Arnold is a volunteer court-appointed special advocate for abused and neglected children.

Ardis Lo, M.Sc. is a licensed professional counselor and a registered play therapist. She holds a master of science degree in counseling from Southern Methodist University and has special training in play therapy, activity therapy, child-parent relationship training, group therapy, and geriatrics therapy. She volunteered as a court-appointed special advocate for seven years then transitioned into mental health therapy. Now Ms. Lo works with various age groups (from children to geriatrics) seeking support for life and mental-health challenges. Ardis is currently working in private practice. She believes counseling is a component of overall health care, and that each person has their own unique story and level of resilience.

I lie in bed unable to move. I know he is coming. The house is so quiet. I wonder why I am the only one who hears his footsteps. I am frozen in fear. Attempting escape, I somehow leave while my body remains in this bed. I go away: Away from the scratchiness of his hands, the itch of his beard, the smell of his mouth, and the weight of his body on top of mine. If I sleep, it all happens again in my dreams. I have no escape. I cannot remember a time when it was not happening. First mom's boyfriend, then my cousin. Maybe this is my fate? I am helpless, scared, lonely, and confused.

At school, my brother and I are called to the office. Someone I do not know knows our names and asks us a lot of questions. I am crying, screaming, kicking, and clawing to get to my brother. Why is she taking him away from me? Where am I going? How did they find out? She takes me to a stranger's home without my brother, or my mom. I am again helpless, scared, lonely, and confused. My brother and mom and I only see each other at a place where we sit in a small room with toys and coloring books while someone watches us from the doorway. It is so uncomfortable. He always said to keep it a secret "or else." Is this the "or else?" This is my fault; everyone is mad at me. My stomachache has not stopped since that night. (CASA, 2017)

This is the horrible reality for many children, and it is a truth that many of us wish to ignore or avoid as the solutions are complex and often uncomfortable. Children's advocates hear this type of statement on a regular basis. When children are at risk to the point that the authorities need to get involved, the solutions are often unclear. Children need both safety and family connections.

CASA, Inc., the national social agency that utilizes volunteer court-appointed special advocates, reports that the number of children in foster care grew by 3.5% in 2016 and total expenses for CASA were over $9 million. Children in foster care have a lower than average high school graduation rate, are more likely to be trafficked, and experience higher rates of incarceration and homelessness as they enter adulthood. Children can avoid these poor outcomes with help from CASA's nationwide advocacy network.

As a volunteer court-appointed special advocate, I act as the child's guardian for the trial and make recommendations about what I believe is in the child's best interest. To make informed recommendations, I must know as many facts about the child and the family as possible. I visit the child's home, placement, and school; observe family visits; attend meetings and court hearings; visit with other professionals involved with the child; and visit with family members. I am often the most consistent person in the child's life.

As an advocate, I am shocked and humbled by the stories I hear. It is disheartening to hear about the horrors that children experience. The protective part in me wants to swaddle them up and prevent them from having access to anyone who has hurt them. However, cutting children off from family connections can create other problems and the children need me to be balanced and open-minded in my recommendations. That is how I can truly act responsibly in my role as the child's advocate. The CASA investment I make is emotionally involved, and I have to ensure that I care for my own needs so I can serve the children well.

Section 2: Fundamentals of child abuse

Unit 1: Important child-abuse terms

In the United States, a **child** is someone who is under 18 years of age and has not been emancipated as an adult. A child is legally under the guardianship of an adult, whether a parent, relative, non-related caregiver, or the government. A guardian has legal authority over the child and the child's property and makes decisions for the child. A child's parents are the legal guardians at the child's birth. However, the parents may relinquish guardianship of the child to another person or to the government on a temporary or permanent basis. **Child abuse** is defined by the Federal Child Abuse Prevention and Treatment Act (2010) as "at a minimum, any recent act or failure to act on the part of a parent or caretaker which results in death, serious physical or emotional harm, sexual abuse or exploitation; or an act or failure to act which presents an imminent risk of serious harm."

The government may remove the child from the parents' home under circumstances of child endangerment. When this happens, the child is either returned to the parents when the situation of endangerment is resolved, placed with a foster family or in a treatment center, or adopted by someone else.

This chapter adds to the foundational information provided in the chapter on violence against women. As before, the term **perpetrator** means the person who purposefully does an action to harm another person and the **victim** is the person who is harmed by the actions of the perpetrator.

The main distinction relating to violence against women and child abuse is that children have much lower levels of self-determination due to being under the legal guardianship of other persons. In addition, there are more factors that lead to child endangerment. The terms prevalence, severity, and impact are also important when discussing child abuse. **Prevalence** asks how often a situation occurs. In the case of child abuse, prevalence is the percentage of the population of children who have specific characteristics or are experiencing certain types of abuse during a specific period of time. It is important to study the prevalence of child abuse and neglect based on characteristics such as the child's gender, age, socioeconomic background, race, religious background, and level of physical and mental functionality. It is also important to consider the child's situation – such as whether they are in the home, in foster care, in residential treatment centers, on the streets as runaways, or in legal custody.

Severity is the degree of harshness or seriousness. This is important when discussing the difference between discipline and abuse. **Discipline** is using punishment to correct disobedience to the rules of the household. **Corporal punishment**, such as spanking, is used to cause physical pain as a form of discipline, although it is considered abuse by some. **Abuse** is the cruel or violent treatment of the victim by a perpetrator. Forms of child abuse are discussed in the next section. According the U.S. Penal Code (Sec. 11165.6. [Cr.]), abuse "includes physical injury to a child inflicted by other than accidental means as well as unlawful corporal punishment or injury," severe child abuse "includes the knowing use of force on a child that is likely to cause great bodily harm or death," and unlawful corporal punishment is when a person knowingly inflicts "cruel or inhuman corporal punishment or injury resulting in a traumatic condition." In many cultures, it is not acceptable for an intimate partner to either discipline or abuse the female in the relationship. However, in most cultures it is customary for the parent or caretaker of a child to discipline a child. Abuse is less culturally accepted and often illegal.

Impact is the current and future effects of the abuse on the children. **Reasonable force** is the level of physical force that is appropriate and legally justified to correct a child. **Unreasonable force** or **cruel discipline** is the use of excess or unnecessary force in correction.

Unit 2: Forms of child abuse

The chapter on violence against women identified five main types of violence: Physical, verbal, emotional, sexual, and other (such as neglect). Research by Alexandra Cook et al. (2005) finds that children's exposure to complex trauma leads to difficulties in self-control and interpersonal skills and increases their risk of lifelong illness, emotional disorders, addictions, and handling day-to-day situations. The death of a child is often the result of multiple types of child abuse. The Child Welfare Information Gateway (2017) reported the main causes (with some of the deaths the result of more than one cause) of child death in 2015 as neglect (73%), physical abuse (44%), medical abuse (7%), psychological abuse (1%), and sexual abuse (1%).

Child neglect is the failure of the child's guardian to provide the child's essential needs, i.e. adequate nutrition, shelter, clothing, supervision, safety, nurturing attention, health and medical care, and education. As stated before, neglect is the main cause in almost two-third of cases of child death. For example, an unattended infant may drown as a result of child neglect by the guardian. A young person who is not given adequate food by their guardian may starve to death or become physically handicapped as a result of the lack of nutrients.

Physical abuse is when perpetrators wilfully inflict pain and injury on a child. There are numerous types of physical abuse used against a child, such as beatings with a hand or object, choking, tying a child down, locking a child up, intentionally burning a child, deliberately starving a child, and not giving the child the nutrition needed for healthy growth.

One form of physical child abuse that has received much attention in recent years is child trafficking or the human trafficking of children. **Human trafficking** is defined by the U.S. Department of State in the Trafficking Victims Protection Act of 2000 as the "recruitment, harboring, transportation, provision, or obtaining of a person for labor or services, through the use of force, fraud, or coercion for the purpose of subjection to involuntary servitude, peonage, debt bondage, or slavery." It is modern-day slavery and does not require the transport of the person from one area to another. **Child trafficking** is the use of force, fraud, or coercion to exert pressure on a child to do a particular type of work. Children are less developed physically and mentally than adults, which makes them vulnerable and the targets of child traffickers. There are three types of child trafficking: **Labor trafficking** is the forcible use of a child's labor in commercial areas such as agriculture, textiles, weaving, or housework, or as child soldiers or child brides. **Organ trafficking** is using children's bodies as sources of human organs, tissues, or body parts. **Sex trafficking** (which will be studied in the sexual abuse section) is any use of the child in the creation of pornography or the performance of sex acts. With increases in the number of economically and socially vulnerable people in the world, children become more vulnerable to all forms of human trafficking.

Medical child abuse is when the child is given medical treatment that is unnecessary and harmful or potentially harmful because of the information provided by the caregiver of the child. An example of this is when a small child has been shaken but the caregiver reports the child was injured from a fall. If the medical professional takes the caregiver's word as truth, incorrect and possibly injurious treatment may be given to the child.

Extreme cases of neglect, physical abuse and medical abuse of a child can lead to the death of the child. NCANDS defines **child fatality** in the context of child abuse as "the death of a child caused by an injury resulting from abuse or neglect or where abuse or neglect was a contributing factor."

Verbal and emotional child abuse are closely related. **Verbal abuse** is used by the perpetrator as a means of controlling and demeaning the victim. This type of abuse may be used against a child by an adult, youth, or another child. Verbal abuse may be spoken to the victim or to another person about the victim, or the abusive words may be written in a note or text message.

Berit Brogaard (2015) lists 15 types of verbal abuse: Withholding (information or feelings); countering (being argumentative); discounting (denying relevance of victim); verbal abuse disguised as jokes, blocking or diverting (denying victim's participation in conversation); accusing or blaming (of things outside victim's control); judging or criticizing (negative evaluation); trivializing (stating insignificance of what victim says); undermining (making victim question own opinions); threatening, name calling, forgetting, ordering or demanding, denial (of perpetrator's bad behavior or abuse); and abusive anger. The perpetrator may use several forms of verbal abuse, from calling the child names to telling others that the child is incorrectly at fault for an action. Other adults are more likely to believe the words of an adult or older child than the child being victimized. The perpetrator may use verbal abuse to threaten the child if the child tells someone else about the physical or sexual abuse used by the perpetrator.

Research by Martin Teicher et al. (2003) finds that the brains of children who experience severe stress and mistreatment develop differently from children who grow up in safe, nurturing environments. The child's mind adapts to the environment and if the setting is hostile or lacks support, parts of the brain that control motor, sensory, emotion, cognition, and decision-making are negatively affected. The researchers believe that this process may lead to psychiatric disorders during the child's development.

Emotional abuse (or **psychological abuse**) occurs when the perpetrator knowingly tries to control or demean the victim by decreasing the child's identity, dignity, and self-worth. The perpetrator may emotionally abuse the child through the use of confinement (imprisonment) or isolation from other people, by ignoring or withholding affection, and by making threats to hurt self, the child, or the child's personal possessions (such as a doll or a puppy) based on the child's actions or responses. Emotional abuse may result from words spoken to the child, which is also called **verbal abuse**. Studies by Naomi Eisenberger (2012) and Ethan Kross, Marc Berman, Walter Mischel, Edward Smith, and Tor Wager (2011) find that social rejection creates the same negative neurological effects as physical pain. The child may experience emotional abuse as rejection by the perpetrator. The perpetrator may also use **spiritual violence** against the child by playing upon the child's beliefs, such as believing in Santa Claus or ghosts.

Article 26 of the Universal Declaration of Human Rights (UDHR) states that everyone has the right to at least elementary education. Barriers to education cause a decrease in a child's potential as a productive member of society. Institutional barriers may include general school fees, matriculation (graduation) and exam fees, requirements for documentation, and restrictions on the number, gender, or race of children who are allowed to attend classes. When a guardian of a child prohibits the child from gaining a primary education, it is a violation of human rights.

A study by Amy Silverman, Helen Reinherz, and Rose Giaconia (1996) finds that over two-thirds of 21-year-olds who had been abused as children showed characteristics of at least one type of emotional disorder. In a report by the U.S. Department of Justice (1999), 14% of men and 36% of women prisoners reported being abused as children.

Because a child is too young to give consent, any form of sexual activity with a child is **child sexual abuse**. Forms of sexual abuse with a child include exposure of an adult's genitalia to a child; masturbating in front of a child; fondling (erotically stroking or caressing); sexual intercourse (penetration of the child's vagina, anus, or mouth with a body part or object); sexual communication through text messages, emails, phone calls, or other forms of social media; exploiting a child through the production of pornographic material; sex trafficking a child; and all other forms of sexual contact with a child. All forms of sexual intercourse with a child are **rape**. Federal and state laws specify sexual intercourse by an adult with a minor as **statutory rape**, because the child cannot give consent. When an adult has sex with or seeks sex with a child or creates, owns, or trades child pornography, it is called **pedophilia** (also spelled **paedophilia**), which is illegal in the United States and many other countries.

Organized sexual abuse is when the child is victimized by more than one predator. This includes sex trafficking, child pornography, and **ritual abuse** (when a group of people participate in a ritual that involves the abuse of children). These types of abuse can lead to increased harm to the child, such as through sadistic practices.

Forced abortion is another example of sexual abuse in which the perpetrator forces the child to undergo a medical procedure to have an abortion. The guardian of a child or someone else who has control of the child may attempt to coerce a child who has become pregnant into having an abortion. In *Roe v. Wade*, the Supreme Court determined that it is legal for a pregnant female to make the decision to abort a fetus. However, forced abortion through coercion or physical force is illegal. Forced abortions are often seen in incidents of sex trafficking of female youth.

Female genital mutilation (FGM) or female circumcision is the cutting, piercing, or removing of part or all the external female genitalia or sewing the genitalia closed for non-medical reasons (Jasmine Abdulcadir et al., 2016). Female genital mutilation is a cultural practice and practitioners hold to beliefs that the circumcision will 1) ensure virginity until marriage and fidelity after marriage, 2) increase sexual pleasure for the male, and 3) control female sexuality. The procedure is often done by persons with no medical training who may use unsterilized instruments, thus increasing the risk of infection and HIV infection.

Child sex trafficking (or commercial sexual exploitation of children) occurs when a perpetrator uses force, fraud, or coercion to influence a child to perform a sexual act or allow pornographic images to be taken. A child is too young to give consent for sex acts so the child cannot be called a child prostitute, but is rather a child victim of prostitution or a sex-trafficked child. Victims of child trafficking are from all nationalities, races, socioeconomic statuses, and religions. The trafficker may be a friend of the family, a teacher or coach, a stranger, or even a parent or sibling. Child traffickers gain financial or material income from using the child to perform sexual acts.

The buying and selling of humans is one of the most profitable illegal businesses in the world, ranking with and often accompanying drug and weapon trafficking. Human trafficking is a low-risk, high-yield investment. Traffickers' annual profit from each trafficking victim range from a few thousand to multiple thousands of dollars, depending upon the market and the type of abuse to the child (Elizabeth Wheaton, Edward Schauer, and Thomas Galli, 2010; Alexis Aronowitz, Gerda Theuermann, and Elena Tyurykanova, 2010). Trafficking victims rarely receive any of the money earned by their exploitation. The International Labour Organization (2017) estimates that worldwide there are over ten million child victims of modern slavery.

Some types of child abuse are perpetuated by other children or youth. **Bullying** is aggressive behavior by one child or multiple children against another child, and often occurs in an educational setting. **Cyberbullying** is when the perpetrators use the internet to bully their victims, often because the internet allows the perpetrators to remain anonymous. Both types of bullying will be discussed in the chapter on hate.

Unit 3: The process of removing a child into protective custody

The child welfare agency in each state contracts with the U.S. Federal Government to provide Child Protection Services (CPS) when there is a report of child abuse or neglect. The state's child welfare agency will investigate reports of abuse or neglect; provide services such as family counseling to children and their families; place, monitor, and support children in foster care and residential treatment centers; and help with child adoptions. When the child welfare office receives a report of child abuse, a Child Protection Services caseworker investigates the report and makes the determination of the child's safety. If the caseworker finds significant risk factors, they recommend or assign services to address the problem, or file a petition for civil court action to protect the child. This protection may include removing the child from the home and ending the rights of the parent over the child. The process of investigation and removal of a child from a household may differ by state. The goal is to assure the best interests of the child.

The U.S. Department of Health and Human Services reports that there were over 400,000 children in foster care at the end of September 2016 with an average placement of 31.2 weeks, or over two and a half years. This includes 100,000 children who were waiting to be adopted. The highest number of children removed from their homes (21,495 or 18% of children) are in foster homes for three to four years. The average age of a child in foster care is eight and a half years. Most children are placed into foster care due to neglect (61%), drug abuse by a parent (34%), inability of the caregiver to care for the child (14%), physical abuse (12%), child behavioral problems (11%), housing issues (10%), parent incarceration (8%), alcohol abuse by the parent (6%), abandonment of the child (5%), sexual abuse (4%), drug abuse by the child (2%), child disability (2%), relinquishment of the child by the parent or caregiver (1%), and parent death (1%). Annually, over 1,000 cases of foster placement are due solely to the abusive use of alcohol by the child. As is clear from the percentages, there may be multiple reasons why a child is placed in foster care.

Section 3: Child abuse as a human rights violation

Most nations have some provisions for the protection of a child. Each of the states makes provisions for a parent or guardian to use reasonable physical force when necessary and appropriate to maintain the discipline of a minor. Abuse takes place when the discipline (or neglect) presents substantial risk of harm to the child. The purpose of laws against child abuse are to safeguard and promote the welfare of children.

Unit 1: National agreements

The main federal law related to child abuse and neglect is the 1974 Child Abuse Prevention and Treatment Act (CAPTA, Public 93–247: S. 1191, 42 U.S.C.§5101, § 5106g). The act triggered the creation of the National Center on Child Abuse and Neglect and provided funding through 1977. In addition, this law established a federal definition of child abuse as "Any recent act or failure to act on the part of a parent or caretaker which results in death, serious physical or emotional harm, sexual abuse or exploitation; or an act or failure to act, which presents an imminent risk of serious harm." Under this law, a child is anyone under the age of 18 or who is not an emancipated minor. The act was amended and reauthorized in 1978 as the Child Abuse Prevention and Treatment and Adoption Reform Act of 1978 (Public Law 95–266: H.R. 6693). The Children's Justice and Assistance Act of 1986 (Public Law 99–401: S. 140) again amended the act to provide incentives for states to create child protection legislation and administration for the prosecution of child abuse cases and to provide emergency child care for infants and handicapped children. The Child Abuse Prevention, Adoption and Family Services Act of 1988 (Public Law 100–294: H.R. 1900) simultaneously reauthorized several acts and gave direction for the U.S. Department of Health and Human Services to create the National Child Abuse and Neglect Data System (NCANDS) to collect and analyze data on child abuse and neglect. This system is maintained by the Children's Bureau – Administration for Children and Families, which publishes child maltreatment reports based on data voluntarily reported from the United States and its territories.

The definitions first used in the 1974 Child Abuse Prevention and Treatment Act were upheld in the CAPTA Reauthorization Act of 2010 (Public Law 111–320. 111 P.L. 320; 124 Stat. 3459; 2010 Enacted S. 3817; 111 Enacted S. 3817) which amended the Child Abuse Prevention and Treatment Act, as well as the Family Violence Prevention and Services Act, the Child Abuse Prevention and Treatment and Adoption Reform Act of 1978, and the Abandoned Infants Assistance Act of 1988. This act defines sexual abuse and specific cases of abuse related to medical treatment, but does not specifically define physical abuse, neglect, or emotional abuse. States that receive funding under this act must meet minimum standards but define their own civil and criminal statutes for abuse and neglect of children.

The 50 states, the District of Columbia, and the U.S. Territories of American Samoa, Guam, Northern Mariana Islands, Puerto Rico, and the U.S. Virgin Islands have laws related to child abuse and neglect. All of these areas have child protective services (CPS) agencies and professionals to whom child abuse and neglect cases are to be referred. Most state laws

TABLE 6.1   Exemptions to the state child abuse and neglect laws

States	Exemption
Arizona, Connecticut, Washington	Christian Scientists.
Arkansas, Colorado, Florida, Georgia, Indiana, Mississippi, Oklahoma, Washington	Corporal punishment.
Colorado	Cultural practices.
California	Informed medical decision.
Washington	Physical disability.
Illinois	Plan of care.
Indiana	Prescription drugs.
Arkansas, District of Columbia, Florida, Pennsylvania	Poverty.
California, Colorado	Reasonable force.
California, Colorado, Delaware, District of Columbia, Florida, Georgia, Idaho, Illinois, Indiana, Kentucky, Michigan, Mississippi, New Mexico, Oklahoma, Pennsylvania	Religion.
Alabama, Alaska	Religious reasons for failure to obtain medical help for child.
Illinois	School attendance.
Arizona	Unavailability of reasonable resources for a parent's failure to obtain medical help for the child.

Source: FindLaw.com, 2017.

recognize neglect, physical abuse, psychological abuse, and sexual abuse. The laws differ based on what acts or omissions constitute child abuse and neglect, who is responsible for mandatory reporting of child abuse, the basis for reporting the abuse or neglect of a child, the agency to whom the abuse is to be reported, and the penalty for failure to report or false reporting. Some states have exceptions to their state child abuse and neglect law requirements. Table 6.1 gives some examples of these exemptions.

The Child Abuse Prevention and Treatment and Adoption Reform Act of 1978 helped facilitate the adoption of children with special needs. The 1978 Indian Child Welfare Act (Public Law 95–608: S. 1214) sought to prevent the separation of Indian children from their families and to establish standards for foster care and adoption. The Adoption Assistance and Child Welfare Act of 1980 (Public Law 96–272) set up state assistance for foster care and adoption. The 1975 Education for All Handicapped Children Act of 1975 (Public Law 94–142: S. 6) was reauthorized by the Education of the Handicapped Amendments of 1986 (Public Law 99–457: S. 2294), which also set up special provisions for situations involving handicapped infants. Every Student Succeeds Act of 2015 worked specifically to ensure educational stability for children in foster care. The Comprehensive Addiction and Recovery Act of 2016 (Public Law 114–198: S. 524) set standards and procedures specifically for infants born with Fetal Alcohol Spectrum Disorder due to alcohol intake by mothers.

The Victims of Trafficking and Violence Protection Act of 2000 (TVPA, Public Law 106–386: H.R. 3244) set procedures and federal statutes for preventing human trafficking, protecting victims and survivors, and prosecuting human traffickers. The act created the Office to Monitor and Combat Trafficking in Persons, which publishes the annual Trafficking in Persons (TIP) report, and the Interagency Task Force to Monitor and Combat Trafficking. The Trafficking Victims Protection Reauthorization Act of 2003 (Public Law 108–193: H.R. 2620) established provisions for trafficking victims to sue their traffickers and for the protection of victims and their families from deportation, and made human trafficking a crime listed on the Racketeering Influenced Corrupt Organizations (RICO) statute.

The Adam Walsh Child Protection and Safety Act of 2006 (Public Law 109–248: H.R. 4472) sought the protection of children from sexual exploitation (including child pornography and internet safety) and violent crime. It included requirements for checks of national criminal background and the child abuse registry before foster parents were approved for foster care or adoption placement. The William Wilberforce Trafficking Victims Protection Reauthorization Act of 2008 (Public Law 110–457: H.R. 7311) required screening of alien children traveling unaccompanied as potential human-trafficking victims, new penalties for traffickers, and expanded human-trafficking definitions.

The PROTECT Our Children Act of 2008 (Public Law 110–401, S. 1738) created requirements for the U.S. Department of Justice to "develop and implement a National Strategy Child Exploitation Prevention and Interdiction, to improve the Internet Crimes Against Children Task Force, to increase resources for regional computer forensic labs, and to make other improvements to increase the ability of law enforcement agencies to investigate and prosecute child predators." The Child Protection Act of 2012 (Public Law 112–206, H.R. 6063) reauthorized the 2008 act, established further penalties for child pornography and child exploitation, and created a National Coordinator for Child Exploitation Prevention and Interdiction. The Protect Our Kids Act of 2012 (Public Law 112–275, H.R. 6655) provided for the creation of "a commission to develop a national strategy and recommendations for reducing fatalities resulting from child abuse and neglect."

The Preventing Sex Trafficking and Strengthening Families Act of 2014 (Public Law 113–183: H.R. 4980) focused on the prevention of child sex trafficking in foster care. The Justice for Victims of Trafficking Act of 2015 (Public Law 114–22: S. 178) provided grants to states "to combat trafficking, child abuse investigation and prosecution programs, services for victims of child pornography, and domestic child human trafficking deterrence programs." It also authorized training programs for the identification, response to, and rescue of child-trafficking victims. The International Megan's Law to Prevent Child Exploitation and other sexual crimes through Advanced Notification of Traveling Sex Offenders of 2016 (Public Law 114–119: H.R. 515) concentrated on protecting children from sex trafficking and sex tourism by creating a notification system for U.S. registered sex offenders traveling abroad or foreign sex offenders traveling to the United States.

The U.S. Code of Federal Regulations addresses runaways and homeless youth and defines a missing child as "any individual less than 18 years of age whose whereabouts are unknown to such individual's legal custodian" (42 U.S.C. § 5772). This federal law requires law enforcement agencies to immediately accept a missing child report (42 U.S.C. § 5780) and to enter the information into the Federal Bureau of Investigation's National Crime Information Center database and state law enforcement databases within two hours of receiving the missing child report. Laws regarding runaway children differ by state. In Washington, a runaway child who has been reported as missing to a law enforcement agency may be taken into custody by a police officer. The U.S. Court of Appeals, Fifth Circuit finding *Gates v. Texas Department of Protection and Regulatory Services* made it increasingly difficult to remove a child from the home without a court order.

Unit 2: International agreements

The rights of a child have been widely debated. International agreements take years to create and are often not ratified by all members because of the cultural differences. Children's rights include identity as a human being, the right to association with both parents, age-appropriate criminal laws, freedom from discrimination and abuse, and provision of basic needs such as food, shelter, education, and health care. Table 6.2 lists a number of international agreements relating to the rights of the child.

TABLE 6.2   International agreements on the rights of the child

Year	International agreement	Focus
1924	Geneva Declaration on the Rights of the Child	Adopted by the League of Nations; recognizes specific rights of children.
1946	United Nations International Children's Emergency Fund (UNICEF)	Aid and medical care to children affected by World War II.
1948	United Nations Universal Declaration of Human Rights (UNUDHR), Article 25 and 26	Recognized rights to special assistance and universal education for children.
1950	European Convention for the Protection of Human Rights and Fundamental Freedoms	Sets legal procedures for children to bring lawsuits in court.
1953	UNICEF	Becomes a permanent United Nations' agency.
1959	United Nations Declaration of the Rights of the Child	Extended form of the Geneva Declaration on the Rights of the Child; defines universal children's rights to protection, education, health care, shelter, and nutrition.
1966	United Nations International Covenant on Economic, Social and Cultural Rights	Sets standards for care and education of children.
1966	United Nations International Covenant on Civil and Political Rights	Sets standards for juvenile justice for children.
1967	European Convention on the Adoption of Children	Sets standards for the adoption of minors.
1969	American Convention on Human Rights	Sets provisions for protection of children.
1973	International Labour Organization Convention 138: Minimum Age Convention	Sets labor standards and minimum age for children in labor.

(Continued)

TABLE 6.2   (Continued)

Year	International agreement	Focus
1974	Declaration on the Protection of Women and Children in Emergency and Armed Conflict	Sets provisions for children in emergency and armed conflict situations.
1979	Convention on the Elimination of all Forms of Discrimination against Women	Sets standards for guardian and state protection of children and for child marriage.
1980	Hague Convention on the Civil Aspects of International Child Abduction	Sets standards for abduction of children under the age of 18 by parents or others.
1980	European Convention on the Recognition and Enforcement of Decisions Concerning the Custody of Children	Sets international standards for child custody and access to children.
1981	African Charter on Human and People's Rights (Banjul Charter)	Sets rights of the family and the child's duties toward the family.
1984	Inter-American Convention on Conflict of Laws Concerning the Adoption of Minors	Sets standards for the adoption of minors.
1989	United Nations Convention on the Rights of the Child	Sets universal provisions for children in peacetime and during armed conflict.
1990	World Declaration on the Survival, Protection and Development of Children	Adopted at the first World Summit for Children.
1993	Hague Convention on the Protection of Children and Cooperation in Respect of Intercountry Adoption	Sets standards for international adoption of minors.
1996	Hague Convention on Jurisdiction Applicable Law, Recognition, Enforcement and Co-operation in Respect of Parental Responsibility and Measures for the Protection of Children	Establishes civil child protection measures, including disputes, protection for unaccompanied minors, and foster care.
1996	Change to UNICEF organizational mission statement	Adoption of child rights perspective for organizational mission statement.
1999	International Labour Organization Convention 182: Worst Forms of Child Labour Convention	Set definitions, standards, and provision for children working in worst forms of child labor.
2000	Optional Protocol to the Convention on the Rights of the Child on the Sale of Children, Child Prostitution, and Child Pornography	Addresses topic of sex trafficking and sexual exploitation of children.
2000	Optional Protocol to the Convention on the Rights of the Child on Involvement of Children in Armed Conflict	Addresses topic of child soldiers.
2014	Optional Protocol to the Convention on the Rights of the Child on a Communications Procedure	Allows children to complain directly to the U.N. Committee on the Rights of the Child about allegations of rights violations.

The implementation of the U.N. Convention on the Rights of the Child (UNCRC) is monitored by the U.N. Committee on the Rights of the Child (CRC), which also monitors the Convention's three optional protocols on child soldiers, child sexual exploitation, and communication. The United States is a signatory of the U.N. Convention on the Rights of the Child and the first two optional protocols; however, the United States has not ratified the U.N. Convention on the Rights of the Child or the protocol on the rights of a child to communicate alleged rights violations to the United Nations.

Unit 3: Controversies

Cultural differences make up many of the controversies on the rights of children. It is important for the researcher to look at whether a country has signed an international agreement and what provisions have been made or rejected. The international agreement that is accepted may be very different to the original agreement that was proposed. A few controversial issues are the age at which a child is considered an adult, child marriage, corporal punishment, immunization of minors, immigration detention for child asylum seekers, when discipline becomes abuse, capital punishment of children, and criminal treatment and punishment of a child. For example, the Becca Bill in Washington State requires the school and juvenile justice system to take action against a child who repeatedly skips school. If the truancy is considered a serious violation of the law, a judge may order that the child spend time in juvenile detention.

CHECK YOURSELF BOX: PERSONAL BIASES ABOUT CHILD ABUSE

Child abuse hits close to the heart, whether it is from personal experience or witnessing the abuse of a child first-hand or in movies and literature. You may not consider some of the topics discussed to be child abuse, or you may have other topics that you consider child abuse that are not included in this textbook. Write down your thoughts about child abuse. What does child abuse mean to you? Have you personally experienced child abuse? Were you a witness to the abuse of a child? If someone is at fault, who is that person? Is there too much emphasis on child abuse today or does there need to be more? Which topics of child abuse are more important than others? Honest answers to this type of question will help you see where you are biased in the area of child abuse. Although your bias may be from wanting to champion the protection of children, the bias will stand out in your writing and may change your interpretation of information and data. If you have a strong bias in this area, you may want to ask another disinterested person to review your writing and edit for bias. This process will strengthen the way in which you do scientific research and make your research viable for policy-making.

Section 4: History of child abuse

Children have always been in danger of abuse, exploitation, and neglect. In 1096, Pope Urban II complied with the request of Emperor Alexius I to send troops (including the Knights Templar and the Teutonic Knights) to fight against the Muslims who had captured the Holy

Lands in the Crusades, which resulted in 8 major Crusades expeditions. In 1212, caught up in the fervor of the Crusades, a 12-year-old shepherd boy named Stephen mobilized many thousands of children to become the Children's Crusade and march to the Holy Lands to fight. Few details are available about the journey to Marseilles in southern France, but there the expedition split into two parties. One group made an arduous journey across the Alps in which two-thirds of the children were killed. Many of the surviving children settled in Genoa, Italy, while others continued to Pisa, where some of the children were allowed to get on ships to Palestine but were never heard from again. The remaining children from this group went to Rome for an audience with Pope Innocent, who sent them home. The second group of children were given passage on five ships at Marseilles. Two of the ships were shipwrecked with no survivors. The other three ships took the children to the Algerian coast where they were sold into slavery, an arrangement that had been made by the Marseilles merchants who provided for the children's ship passage. The Children's Crusade was a failure that resulted in child fatalities, child exploitation, and many other forms of child endangerment.

Since the dawn of history, children have been considered property to be used, bought, or sold at the discretion of the child's caretaker. In the mid-1800s, laws were created in Europe to protect child workers in mining and factory work and to provide the right for children to be educated. The list of international agreements shows that social, medical, and legal rights for children formed during the twentieth century. Developments in the twenty-first century have addressed protection for children in certain exploitative circumstances, such as forcing children to be soldiers, and child trafficking.

As the story of the Children's Crusaders shows, child trafficking has existed for a very long time. Today, it not only exists but has developed into a multifaceted, transnational business. Child exploitation exists in all countries and industries and evolves as business and communication methods change.

Section 5: Meet the child abuse experts

Experts on child abuse are found in a variety of backgrounds. Reading published research in journals and publications on government, national, and nonprofit organization websites will lead to experts on specific areas of child abuse. Table 6.3 contains a list of some of the areas where experts may be identified relating to research topics of interest.

TABLE 6.3 Experts on child abuse

Field of expertise	Description
Child protection	Organizations like National Center for Missing & Exploited Children (NCMEC) provide assistance on missing and runaway children.
Cultural studies	Provides a background of how a distinct society views children and child rights.
Education and special education	Teachers, administrators, and other school officials.
Juvenile justice	Judges, legal officials, detention center officials, and Court Appointed Special Advocates (CASA).
Law enforcement	Child victims units.

Field of expertise	Description
Legal	Lawyers specializing in child abuse and juvenile justice cases.
Human rights	Government, international (such as UNICEF), nonprofit organizations.
Medical	Pediatric physicians, nurse practitioners, and medical assistants trained for child abuse evaluation and work and forensic pediatrics consultants.
Parents	Information on daily life with children.
Psychology	Child psychiatrists and counselors.
Sociology	Social workers.
U.S. Department of Health and Human Services (DHHS)	Provides resources, referrals, and help groups for victims of child abuse and for perpetrators of abuse.
Child protection	Organizations like the National Center for Missing & Exploited Children (NCMEC) provide assistance on missing and runaway children.
Nonprofit organization	National and state child advocacy centers, shelters such as Covenant House, anti-bullying organizations.

There are a number of national and international databases regarding child abuse. As with the databases for violence against women, each child abuse database has strengths and weaknesses. Researchers need to determine the level and complexity of data needed for analysis and then sort through the databases to find out if sufficient data is available to supply research needs. Government tracking systems include the Center for Disease Control (CDC), the National Institute of Justice (NIJ), the Youth Risk Behavior System (YRBS), the FBI's Violent Crimes Against Children Program (VCAC), the National Crime Victimization Survey (NCVS), the Department of Justice (DOJ), the National Comorbidity Survey (NCS), the National Violent Death Reporting System (NVDRS), the National Incident-Based Reporting System (NIBRS), the National Child Abuse and Neglect Data System (NCANDS), the National Center for Injury Prevention and Control (NCIPC), the National Electronic Injury Surveillance System (NEISS), the U.S. Department of Health and Human Services (DHHS), *Morbidity and Mortality Weekly Report* (*MMWR*), the Behavioral Risk Factor Surveillance System (BRFSS), the Adoption and Foster Care Analysis and Reporting System (AFCARS), and the National Survey of Children Exposed to Violence (NatSCEV).

CHECK YOURSELF BOX: CHILD ABUSE RESEARCH AND DATA BIASES

What are the backgrounds of people who do child abuse research? Which groups control the child abuse databases? Who champions child abuse legislation? What are the primary goals of the government organizations that deal with child abuse? How is the funding of a nonprofit organization affected by the type or prevalence of child abuse it addresses? As we have seen in the previous sections, there are many reasons why children need champions. It is important to determine the biases of the different individuals and groups involved in child abuse work, research, and policy-making. Their biases can create intended or unintended changes in the information disseminated and the data gathered and will affect your research effectiveness.

Section 6: Economic structure of child abuse

Child abuse is the result of decision-making by adults or other children who have some power over the child. Within the economic structure of child abuse, five individuals or groups who make decisions about a child are considered: The child's guardian or guardians; the perpetrator of abuse who has access to the child; bystanders (neighbors, teachers, other parents); the government (law enforcement, child protective services, the juvenile justice system); and the child. Their choices contribute to the safety or endangerment of the child.

The guardian of a child has several overlapping choices to make regarding the child. There are a number of crucial decisions the guardian makes, including whether to actively protect the child, passively neglect the child, or abuse the child. Protecting a child means the guardian supervises the child and provides shelter, clothing, food, medical care, and nurturing for the child. Alternatively, protecting a child may mean trusting someone else to supervise and provide for the child. Guardians often have less oversight over older children. Neglecting a child means the guardian is not concerned with the supervision of the child and may not supply some or all of the child's basic needs. If the guardian neglects the child, the child is at risk of being abused by other persons.

When an adult or older child has contact with a child, that person chooses to protect, neglect, or abuse the child. Protecting the child means doing everything within the person's power to make sure the child is safe from danger and has basic provisions for a healthy life. It is commonly accepted that an adult who has supervision over a child will protect the child from self-harm or harm by others and will provide necessities for the child. The adult may be the child's guardian (such as a parent or foster parent) or another adult or older child who has temporary oversight (such as a relative, teacher, coach, or neighbor).

The perpetrators of child sexual abuse may be one or both parents or foster parents; siblings; other children or adult relatives; persons who are given temporary supervision of a child, such as babysitters, teachers, doctors, and coaches; other acquaintances who gain access to the child; or strangers. According to research by Howard Snyder (2000), the majority of child sexual abuse victims (90%) know the perpetrator. In addition, almost 70% of the perpetrators of child sexual assault are members of the child's family.

If a perpetrator of abuse has been allowed access to the child, there are often extenuating circumstances around why the guardian of the child is not there as a protector. This could be as simple as trusting that coaches will protect their players or needing to rely upon a babysitter due to long work hours. It may be that the perpetrator has groomed the family to believe they are a responsible and trustworthy individual who should be trusted alone with the child. It is also possible, and unfortunately common, that the child's guardian is the perpetrator of the abuse.

Child abusers take many forms. The child abuser may be the child's parent, guardian, or someone else who has supervisory control of the child. As with violence against women, perpetrators of child abuse decide what forms of abuse to use, how often to abuse the child (prevalence), how severe the abuse will be (severity), and the location of the abuse. The abuse may be physical, verbal, emotional, or sexual, or a combination of these. Child abuse may occur while the child is in the home, in the protective care of someone else, in foster care, or in public. When the abuser is the guardian of the child, the child may live in an atmosphere of constant abuse or neglect. In 2015, the National Data Archive on Child Abuse and Neglect (NDACAN) at Cornell University reported over 500,000 child abuse and neglect perpetrators in the United States. One-third of perpetrators abused two or more children.

When bystanders notice that abuse or neglect is happening with a child, they have to decide whether to ignore what is happening or get involved. Adults within a household may not report the abuse because they do not consider the actions to be abuse; consider the abuser to have the right to abuse the child; are also abusers; or are also being abused. Adults outside the household may not report the abuse if they do not know *how* to report it, feel it will personally affect them, or fear that reporting the abuse will cause further injury to the child. Many companies that work with children in some capacity have child abuse training courses. Neighbors may not say anything because they are afraid of being caught in the violence or afraid that the children will be taken away from their homes. There is an added danger to a child when a bystander becomes an abuser. This is seen in child trafficking when a child confides abuse to a person who then further abuses and exploits the child.

Government officials working in law enforcement, child protective services, and the juvenile justice system are restricted by law on what they can do to protect a child. In addition, they have limited resources to use in investigating and intervening in child abuse. Law enforcement may be the first to become aware of child abuse as they respond to family violence situations. Law enforcement works within a legal framework which sets out when they can intervene in a suspected child abuse case.

Child Protective Services (CPS) in each of the states is responsible for responding to reports of child abuse and neglect. When a report is entered, they must determine whether to investigate or ignore the report of abuse. If the abuse is investigated, the officials decide whether to close the case, monitor the situation, or remove the child from the situation. If a determination is made that a child is to be removed from a situation, the courts will take into account the best interests of the child and where to place the child for guardianship. This may be with one of the child's relatives or in a non-relative foster home. The child is removed temporarily until the dangers to the child are removed. If the dangers are not removed, the child may be removed permanently and placed in foster care or adopted.

Because they are under the legal guardianship of others and due to their lesser physical and psychological development, children have fewer choices than adults. Children may experience abuse in the household from a parent, sibling, other relative, family acquaintance, or stranger. The child has a number of options when faced with abuse, but none of them is good. The child may 1) remain silent and stay in the abusive situation, 2) tell someone about the situation in an attempt to escape the abuse, 3) fight back against the abuser, 4) run away short-term to mitigate the abuse or long-term to escape the situation, or 5) commit suicide. Younger children have few ways to escape abusive situations.

Child trafficking occurs when the legal guardian of the child – or someone who has illegally taken over supervision of a child – exploits the child by forcing the child to do labor, perform sex acts, or participate in the creation of pornography. In this case, the person who has supervision of the child is not the only abuser, but so is every perpetrator who uses the services of that child, whether by buying the services or products produced by the child, molesting the child, or using pornographic images of the child. Because the child trafficker uses the child as a good to be bought and sold, the economic model of human trafficking developed by Elizabeth Wheaton, Edward Schauer, and Thomas Galli (2010) expresses the trade of human beings as the trade for goods sold on a market rather than as a transfer of labor hours. The model for child trafficking is represented as a monopolistic competition in which the child trafficker acts as an intermediary between the forced supply of the child's labor and the demand by consumers of child-produced products and services. In the case of child sex trafficking, the demand is from pedophiles. **Monopolistic competition** occurs when there are many suppliers of a product or service and suppliers attempt to increase sales by differentiating their product or service from their competitors' products or services.

Unit 1: Costs of child abuse

The costs of child abuse to the child's guardian are extensive. Depending upon the type, prevalence, severity, and impact of the abuse, the household faces expenses for medical visits; short- or long-term counseling and psychiatric services; medications; adverse behavior and attempted suicide by the child due to the abuse; the time and energy involved in handling interactions with law enforcement, child protective services, and schools; and legal fees involved in fighting to keep a child within the household. These expenses can be long-term and affect other family members and the family's position in society due to the stigma of child abuse.

There are many national and international laws and procedures set up to punish perpetrators of child abuse. The perpetrator faces risk of imprisonment, fines, parole, and social humiliation from even one event of abuse – a danger that increases with the prevalence and severity of the abuse. If the perpetrator is the child's guardian, there are the potential additional costs of losing the right to be the guardian of a child and having a broken household.

There are costs to society of abuse to children. The effects of child abuse are long-term and may prevent the child from becoming an independent, productive adult. The abuse may keep the person in a cycle of abuse in which they are abused by others or further the abuse by abusing their own or other children. Research by Vincent Fellitti et al. (1998) and Robert Anda et al. (2006) points to adverse health effects in adults who experienced traumatic living situations during childhood. Shanta Dube et al. (2001 and 2003) add that a person who has experienced child abuse has an increased risk of illegal drug use and suicide as an adult. Society pays many of the costs for child welfare and protection in addition to the law enforcement, legal, and incarceration costs for perpetrators.

Expenses from law enforcement, child protective services, courts, child advocates, foster care and group home care, and adoptions are all costs of child abuse and neglect to the government. The U.S. Department of Health and Human Services (HHS) reported spending of $300 million in 2013 for crisis intervention, prevention and support services, time-limited family reunification, adoption promotion, and administrative costs related to child welfare. The National Council for Adoption (2011) states that the state and federal administration costs of placing and monitoring almost 700,000 children in foster care were $4.3 billion. This made the average cost per child per year almost $7,000.

It is clear, however, that the main costs are to the child who experiences abuse or neglect. The impact on the child depends upon the type of abuse used, the prevalence and severity of the abuse, the relationship with the abuser, and the personal characteristics and resilience of the child. The Centers for Disease Control (2016) reports that the suicide rate in the United States for teenage males and females increased between 2007 and 2015 by 30% and 50% respectively, while the suicide rate in 2015 for teenage males (14.2 per 100,000) was almost three times that for teenage females (5.1 per 100,000). The rate of suicide is higher for youth who have been in the juvenile justice system or the foster care system; are lesbian, gay, bisexual, or transgender; are American Indian or Alaska Native; or are military service members (Erin Sullivan, Joseph Annes, Simon Thomas, Feijun Luo, and Linda Dahlberg, 2015).

Research by Matthew Bramlett and Laura Radel (2014) finds that children who were placed in foster care away from at least one parent were between two and three times as likely to have at least one experience of abuse or neglect. Further, they report that over half of the children in foster care experienced abuse from the caregiver or lived with someone who had been incarcerated or had issues with drugs or alcohol. Children in group homes settings experienced fewer incidents of abuse and neglect, but more than when living with biological parents.

Unit 2: Benefits of child abuse

To fully analyze the economic structure of child abuse, it is important to consider the benefits of child abuse to each of the decision-makers. Violence within the household is detrimental to the family structure. To decrease this stressful situation, the parent or guardian of a child will work to protect children and alleviate circumstances that could potentially harm the family. There can be no benefits of child abuse unless 1) the guardian is the perpetrator of abuse, 2) the guardian benefits monetarily, materially, or emotionally from the abuse of the child at the hands of the perpetrator, or 3) the child abuse mitigates the violence that the guardian experiences at the hands of the perpetrator. When a child is placed in foster care, the benefit in terms of reimbursement to the foster parent is around $25 per day for the child's care, although it varies based on the age of the child.

There are many reasons a perpetrator abuses or neglects a child. The internal (psychological) and external (norms) barriers that would normally prevent the perpetrator from hurting a child have been removed. Culture, beliefs or the use of alcohol, drugs, or pornography may make the child abuse acceptable to the perpetrator. The guardian may have unrealistic expectations of the child or be overwhelmed by the stress of raising the child without support. The perpetrator may have been abused as a child or later in life and then transfers that abuse to the child victim who is helpless to resist. Perpetrators may have emotional disorders that manifest themselves in abuse or neglect of the child.

Bystanders may feel that they benefit from staying out of the situation in which the child is being abused. Remaining neutral means the bystander is not faced with the need to fill out paperwork, report to law enforcement, or appear in court. It also decreases the danger of the perpetrator striking out at the bystander for supporting the child.

Child welfare administration, child protection, and juvenile justice costs range in the millions of dollars each year. Decreasing child abuse and neglect frees up the money for other purposes.

There is no benefit to a child of experiencing abuse. Removal from an abusive home may help the child's emotional and physical development.

Unit 3: Inefficiencies in economic structure of child abuse

Many pediatric medical professionals, officers of law enforcement, and legal professionals do not have specific training to identify and handle child abuse cases. Child protective services may not have the capacity to fully handle the child abuse and neglect caseload. This may manifest as a lack of urgency in investigating child abuse cases, inefficiency in receiving and processing child abuse reports, and not pursuing child abuse cases. National laws and international treaties may be inadequate or contain loopholes that allow perpetrators to get away with limited punishment or continued control over their child victims. Statistics are often inadequate to make informed decisions and enact public policy regarding child endangerment. There is little research on the sexual abuse of children in residential centers and foster care, although Saskia Euser et al. (2016) found the prevalence of sexual abuse in out-of-home care to be highest for children who have a mild intellectual disability.

◼ Section 7: Case study

Household time allocation for children in Kenya

Child labor presents itself in various forms based on region and regulations. Because of this, it can be difficult to generalize from a particular occurrence of child labor in a given country to child labor broadly. However, this difficulty is greatly lessened when the catalyst necessitating the labor as well as the household characteristics are similar across countries. Here, the focus is on the basic need for family sustenance manifested by income derived from child labor as the catalyst, and the intra-family relationship between a fostered child and the head of the household as the general characteristic. Although the extent of poverty and the prevalence of fostering vary across countries, the interaction between the two should theoretically still hold even if the occurrence of either is slight in a given country.

By 2000, there were 3.0 million deaths from HIV/AIDS and 13.1 million children in sub-Saharan Africa who were orphaned by AIDS (Mohammed Abdullah, 2000). Because of this epidemic, it became common in Kenya for families to consist of children who were related to the head of the household and non-relatives, some of who had been orphaned by AIDS. In order for the child to live within a household, it is assumed that the head of the household has some control over the allocation of the child's time between schooling, work in the household, and work in the labor market. The Kenyan Central Bureau of Statistics (2001) reported that 18% of children in Kenya between the ages of five and 17 were working outside the household in 2000.

This model comes from the dissertation by the author of this textbook, Elizabeth Wheaton (2007). It looks for a disparity between the activities of a child related to the head of the household and those of an unrelated child, all governed by the head of the household. There are a number of assumptions for this model. The first assumption is that there are two children in the household: The head of the household's own child (H) and a child who is unrelated to the head (U). Second, the head of the household's choice is for the child to either go to school or to work (in the household or in the labor market). Third, each child has an equal benefit from schooling, which means that the children have equal marginal benefit curves. Fourth, the marginal cost of schooling is constant and equal for both children. Fifth, it is assumed that the head of the household is equally altruistic between the two children. Figures 6.1 and 6.2 show the determination of net benefit (equal to benefit minus cost) curves for each of the children. The net benefit for each child is the area under the marginal benefit curve above the marginal cost curve. If the marginal cost of schooling was the only constraint, each child would maximize net benefit at Q_1 units of schooling. This means that the own child's schooling is Q_{O1} units and the unrelated child's schooling is Q_{U1} with a total amount of amount of schooling for the household (Q_{T1}) equal to $Q_{O1}+Q_{U1}$.

Figure 6.3 uses each child's net benefit to determine the optimal allocation of schooling between the two children when there is no scarcity of resources that prevents both children from attending school. Each child gains an equal amount of schooling ($Q_{O1}=Q_{U1}$). Net benefit for each child is shown as the area under the child's individual net benefit curve up to the quantity of schooling allocated to the child. Here, total net benefit ($NB_{O1}+NB_{U1}$) is maximized because both children get their maximum net benefit from schooling.

FIGURE 6.1   Net benefit of schooling for own child

FIGURE 6.2   Net benefit of schooling for unrelated child

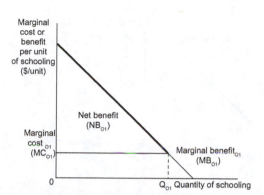

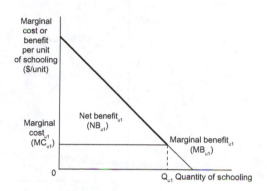

FIGURE 6.3   Household time allocation to schooling with no scarcity

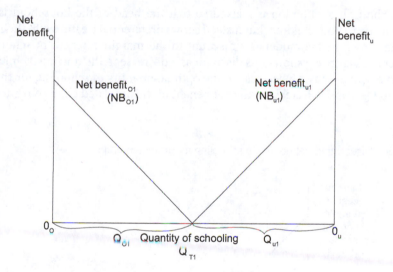

Next, the sixth assumption is introduced: The household can only afford to dedicate a limited number of the children's hours to schooling due to scarcity of household resources and institutional constraints. This means that the total amount of schooling for the household (Q_{T2}) is less than $Q_{O2}+Q_{U2}$. Figure 6.4 illustrates the case where scarcity affects the allocation of schooling time for each child. The net benefit for the head of the household's own child is the area until the own child's net benefit curve from O_0 to Q_{02} and the net benefit for the unrelated child is the area under the unrelated child's net benefit curve between 0_U and Q_{U2}. It is clear that neither child gets as much schooling as they would prefer, so each individual child's net benefit has decreased and the total net benefit ($NB_{02}+NB_{U2}$) is smaller than in Figure 6.3.

FIGURE 6.4   Household time allocation to schooling with scarcity

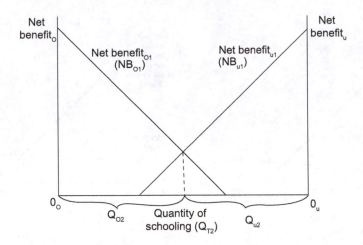

Now, the fifth assumption is relaxed so that the head of the household is no longer equally altruistic to both children, but instead shows preferential treatment to their own child. This can be shown in the model as a discount to the marginal benefit of schooling to the unrelated child. Figure 6.5 shows this discount as a decrease to the unrelated child's marginal benefit curve, which causes a decrease in the optimal quantity of schooling for the unrelated child (Q_{U1} to Q_{U2}) and a decrease in the net benefit of the unrelated child (NB_{U1} to NB_{U2}).

FIGURE 6.5   Discounted net benefit to schooling for unrelated child

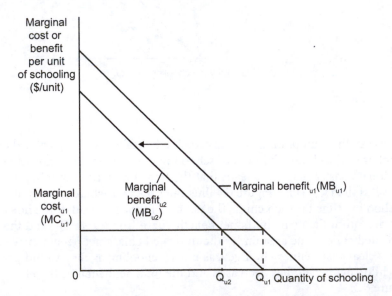

Continuing the assumption that scarcity leads to a limited number of schooling hours (Q_{T2}) for the household, Figure 6.5 now illustrates that the discount to the unrelated child leads to an unequal allocation of the total schooling hours to the head of the household's own child and the unrelated child ($Q_{O3} > Q_{U3}$). In addition, the unrelated child's net benefit is decreased (NB_{U3}), while the head's own child receives increased net benefit (NB_{O3}).

FIGURE 6.6 Household time allocation to schooling with scarcity and discount

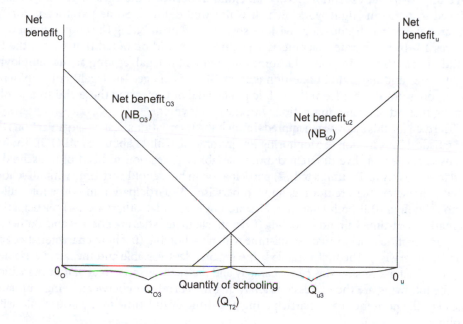

The model assumes that the head of the household allocates each child's time to schooling or work. If the head of the household is biased between their own child and the unrelated child, the unrelated child will be allocated more work hours than the head's own child. This model was tested with data relating to child time allocation in Kenya between December 1998 and January 1999 from the International Labour Organisation's Statistical Information and Monitoring Programme on Child Labor (SIMPOC).

The data in this model shows that there may be a correlation between being unrelated to the head of the household and working in the household part-time or full-time while not being in school. The study then looked at the correlation between being unrelated to the head of the household and working in the labor market part-time or full-time while not being in school. As will be shown, there is no statistically significant relationship between being unrelated to the head of the household and working part-time or full-time in the household at a 95% confidence interval; however, there is a positive statistically significant relationship between being unrelated to the head and working part-time or full-time in the labor market at a 99% confidence interval. Therefore, foster children with no relation to the head of the household are more likely to be placed in the labor market without schooling than related children, presumably due to lack of altruism shown towards unrelated children.

Kenya had a particularly large number of foster children due to the HIV/AIDS pandemic which had been ongoing since the early 1980s. The focus of the aforementioned disparity is the relation to families with restricted resources. Approximately 40% of families were below the poverty line in 2003, causing resource restriction so that the head of the household had to find a way to increase income and theoretically would choose to develop an unrelated child into a non-schooling income source before choosing to do so with a related child. The focus is on children aged six to 14 in this study even though it may be reasonable to consider some older children in other situations.

Kenya's Employment Act of 2007 § 56(1) prohibits the employment of children below the age of 13 without exception. However, children between the ages of 13 and 16 may be employed to perform "light work," which is not well-defined. Some parameters for "light work" are set out in subsequent provisions such as § 58 prohibiting the employment of children ages 13–16 to operate machinery. Therefore, it should be noted that within the focus on children from six to 14 years old, some employment is legal, as long as that employment is "light work" and the child in question is 13 or 14 years of age. The legality of employment, however, does not detract from the public policy goal of preferring these children to obtain schooling instead of or in conjunction with the employment.

The data for this study was acquired through the International Labor Organization's (ILO) 1999 Statistical Information & Monitoring Programme on Child Labour (SIMPOC). The analysis focused entirely on five different dummy variables: 1) relation to head of household (0 if related in some way or 1 if unrelated), 2) participation in household part-time with no schooling (0 if both characteristics are not met and 1 otherwise), 3) participation in household full-time with no schooling (0 if both characteristics are not met and 1 otherwise), 4) participation in labor market part-time with no schooling (0 if both characteristics are not met and 1 otherwise), and 5) participation in labor market full-time with no schooling (0 if both characteristics are not met and 1 otherwise). The first variable is the independent variable and the latter variables are dependent. Each regression was run separately and the analysis ran a total of four regressions.

The following are the regressions analyzing the correlation between being unrelated to the head of the household and participating part-time or full-time in the household with no schooling:

TABLE 6.4 Relation to head of household and part-time household participation

	Part-time household participation			
Part-time household participation	Coefficient	p-value	95% C.I.	$r^2 = 0.0000$
Constant	0.0208*	–	–	–
Relationship dummy	–0.0083	0.60	-0.04–0.02	–

*Denotes significance at 5% significance level.

TABLE 6.5 Relation to head of household and full-time household participation

	Full-time household participation			
Full-time household participation	Coefficient	p-value	95% C.I.	$r^2 = 0.0003$
Constant	0.0130*	–	–	–
Relationship dummy	0.0245	0.06	-0.001–0.050	–

*Denotes significance at 5% significance level.

The notable takeaway from both regressions is that based on the p-values of 0.60 and 0.06 and r^2 of 0.0000 and 0.0003 respectively, the relationship between the child and the head of the household has almost no bearing on whether the non-schooling child will work in the household part-time or full-time. Further, there is little to no difference in analyzing the part-time work and the full-time work. Thus, the head of the household shows no additional altruism toward relatives as opposed to fostered children when allocating household work if neither of the two children receive any schooling. The story changes greatly when instead of the household labor allocation, labor market participation is considered.

The following are the regressions analyzing the correlation between being unrelated to the head of the household and participating part-time or full-time in the labor market with no schooling:

TABLE 6.6   Relation to head of household and part-time labor market participation

Part-time labor market work	Part-time labor market work			
	Coefficient	p-value	95% C.I.	$r^2 = 0.0111$
Constant	0.0012*	–	–	–
Relationship dummy	0.0488*	0.00	0.0005–0.0019	–

*Denotes significance at 5% significance level.

TABLE 6.7   Relation to head of household and full-time labor market participation

Full-time labor market work	Full-time labor market work			
	Coefficient	p-value	95% C.I.	$r^2 = 0.4692$
Constant	0.0028*	–	–	–
Relationship dummy	0.7222*	0.00	0.708–0.737	–

*Denotes significance at 5% significance level.

Both regressions show a statistically significant positive correlation between being unrelated to the head of the household and working in the labor market with no schooling based on the p-values of 0.00 and 0.00 respectively. However, the r^2 of the two regressions, showing how much of the variability in the dependent variable is explained by the independent variable, differs greatly between the part-time and full-time analysis. For part-time work, the relationship dummy variable, although statistically significant, only explains 1.11% of the variability in part-time labor market participation for non-schooled children. In contrast, the relationship dummy variable in the full-time analysis explains 46.9% of the variability in full-time labor market participation for non-schooled children. Therefore, the relationship between the child and the head of the household is a more relevant and controlling characteristic when allocation is being made between part-time and full-time labor market participation for non-schooled children.

The seemingly greatest limitation on the Kenyan child labor analysis is the accuracy and dependability of the data. For legally employed children, data is reliable and easily obtainable due to § 61 of the Kenya Employment Act of 2007 requiring registration of employed children. However, there is a strong incentive to hide the employment status of illegally-employed children.

Unrelated children are most susceptible to disparate treatment when the head of the household is allocating a child's time to full-time labor market participation without schooling. Because of this conclusion, policy to prevent such child labor should be based at least in part on the relationship characteristics of the children. Without such policy tailoring, there is an incentive to foster children so as to increase family income so long as the benefit of the income is not outweighed by the cost of fostering. Lastly, the case of Kenya can be generalized to support the notion that these same time allocation dynamics likely exist in countries with greatly weakened social safety nets and resource restrictions for fostering families.

Section 8: Recommendations for future research

It is rare to find economic research on issues of child abuse and neglect, but it is clear there are numerous areas that could benefit from economics research. For example, it is crucial to discover how economic or financial stress affects child endangerment. In addition, it is important to determine how monetary punishments or rewards affect the prevalence of child abuse. Understanding and creating technology will continue to have a large impact on child trafficking.

Matthew Bramlett and Laura Radel (2014) call for further research on the adverse experiences of children in foster care and group homes settings. They cite evidence from Paula Fomby and Andrew Cherlin (2007) that points to decreased child well-being when the child cannot live with at least one parent, and from the Robert Wood Johnson Foundation (2013) pointing to increased risk to health from multiple traumas caused by being removed from the family and moved between foster care situations.

Research by Michael Newcomb and Thomas Locke (2001) looks at the intergenerational transmission of abuse and neglect – i.e. how abuse and neglect as a child affect an adult and whether the person abuses other children. They cite both definition and measurement irregularities and access to only reported cases of child abuse and neglect as factors affecting the reliability of the research.

CHECK YOURSELF BOX: CHANGES TO PERSONAL BIASES ABOUT CHILD ABUSE

What knowledge did you gain as you read through this chapter? Were there any relevant issues about which you were unaware? Does a part of you wish you had not learned about some of the topics? Research on child abuse can be emotionally difficult and it is an important step for you to journal the research experience, take time away to rest your mind, and to talk with someone who can understand the difficulties you are facing. Read over the personal biases you listed in the first check yourself box. How have your biases changed? Are there specific topics you now want to pursue? Do you simply want to move on to other "lighter" topics? Being honest with yourself in answering these questions will allow you to deal with the information and determine your biases about child abuse. Although this is a hard process, it will improve your ability to perform research on emotionally-charged topics and address the needs of policy-makers.

Section 9: Bibliography

Abdulcadir, Jasmine; Catania, Lucrezia; Hindin, Michelle; Say, Lale; Petignat, Patrick; and Abdul-cadir, Omar. (2016). Female genital mutilation. *Obstetrics & Gynecology, 128*(5), 958–63.

Abdullah, Mohammed. (2000). *HIV/AIDS in Kenya: Impact of the epidemic.* Kenyan National AIDS Committee. Report to Joint United Nations Programme on HIV/AIDS (UNAIDS). Retrieved from https://www.slideshare.net/jwthacher/impact-of-aids

Anda, Robert; Felitti, Vincent; Bremner, Douglas; Walker, John; Whitfield, Charles; Perry, Bruce; Dube, Shanta; and Giles, Wayne. (2006). The enduring effects of abuse and related adverse experiences in childhood. A convergence of evidence from neurobiology and epidemiology. *European Archives of Psychiatry and Clinical Neuroscience, 256*(3), 174–86.

Aronowitz, Alexis; Theuermann, Gerda; and Tyurykanova, Elena. (2010). *Analysing the business model of trafficking in human beings to better prevent the crime.* Office of the Special Representative and Coordinator for Combating Trafficking in Human Beings. Retrieved from http://www.osce.org/cthb/69028?download=true

Bramlett, Matthew and Radel, Laura. (2014). Adverse family experiences among children in nonparental care, 2011–2012. *National Health Statistics Report 74.* Hyattsville, MD: National Center for Health Statistics.

Brogaard, Berit. (2015). *On romantic love: Simple truths about a complex emotion.* New York: Oxford University Press.

CASA. *National CASA Association annual reports.* (2017). Retrieved from http://casaforchildren.org/site/c.myJSJ7MPIsE/b.5574309/k.9511/Annual_Report.htm

Centers for Disease Control (CDC). (2017). QuickStats: Suicide rates for teens aged 15–19 years, by sex in the United States, 1975–2015. *Morbidity and Mortality Weekly Report, 66*(816). Retrieved from DOI: http://dx.doi.org/10.15585/mmwr.mm6630a6

Child Welfare Information Gateway. (2017). *Child abuse and neglect fatalities 2015: Statistics and interventions.* Washington, DC: U.S. Department of Health and Human Services, Children's Bureau.

Cook, Alexandra; Spinazzola, Joseph; Ford, Julian; Lanktree, Cheryl; Blaustein, Margaret; Cloitre, Marylene; DeRosa, Ruth; Hubbard, Rebecca; Kagan, Richard; Liautaud, Joan; Mallah, Karen; Olafson, Erna; and van der Kolk, Bessel. (2005). Complex trauma in children and adolescents. *Psychiatric Annals, 35*(5).

Dube, Shanta; Anda, Robert; Felitti, Vincent; Chapman, Daniel; Williamson, David; and Giles, Wayne. (2001). Childhood abuse, household dysfunction, and the risk of attempted suicide throughout the life span: Findings from the Adverse Childhood Experiences Study. *The Journal of the American Medical Association, 286*(24), 3089–96.

Dube, Shanta; Felitti, Vincent; Dong, Maxia; Chapman, Daniel; Giles, Wayne; and Anda, Robert. (2003). Childhood abuse, neglect, and household dysfunction and the risk of illicit drug use: The Adverse Childhood Experiences Study. *Pediatrics, 111*(3), 564–72.

Eisenberger, Naomi. (2012). The pain of social disconnection: examining the shared neural underpinnings of physical and social pain. *Nature Reviews Neuroscience, 13*(6), 421–34.

Euser, Saskia; Alink, Lenneke; Tharner, Anne; van IJzendoorn, Marinus; and Bakermans-Kranenburg, Marian. (2016). The prevalence of child sexual abuse in out-of-home care: Increased risk for children with a mild intellectual disability. *Journal of Applied Research in Intellectual Disabilities, 29*(1), 83–92.

FindLaw.com. *State child abuse laws*. Retrieved from http://statelaws.findlaw.com/family-laws/child-abuse.html

Fomby, Paula and Cherlin, Andrew. (2007). Family instability and child well-being. *American Sociological Review, 72*(2), 181–204.

International Labor Organization's (ILO) 1999 *Statistical information & monitoring programme on child labour (SIMPOC)*. Retrieved from http://www.ilo.org/ipec/ChildlabourstatisticsSIMPOC/Questionnairessurveysandreports/lang--en/index.htm

International Labour Organization and Walk Free. (2017). *Global estimates of modern slavery: Forced labour and forced marriage*. Geneva: International Labour Organization. Retrieved from http://www.ilo.org/wcmsp5/groups/public/---dgreports/---dcomm/documents/publication/wcms_575479.pdf

Kenyan Central Bureau of Statistics. (2001, May). *ILO-IPEC, Kenya country program 1992–2001: Brief profile of activities*. Retrieved from http://www.ilo.org/ipec/Regionsandcountries/Africa/Kenya/lang--en/index.htm.

Kross, Ethan; Berman, Marc; Mischel, Walter; Smith, Edward; and Wager, Tor. (2011). Social rejection shares somatosensory representations with physical pain. *Proceedings of the National Academy of Sciences of the United States of America,108*(5), 6270–5.

National Council for Law Reporting. (2012). *Laws of Kenya, Employment Act*, Chapter 226. Retrieved from http://www.kenyalaw.org/kl/fileadmin/pdfdownloads/Acts/EmploymentAct_Cap226-No11of2007_01.pdf

National Data Archive on Child Abuse and Neglect (NDACAN) at Cornell University. (2015). National Child Abuse and Neglect Data System (NCANDS) Agency File FFY 2015. Retrieved from https://www.ndacan.cornell.edu/datasets/dataset-details.cfm?ID=206

Newcomb, Michael and Locke, Thomas. (2001). Intergenerational cycle of maltreatment: A popular concept obscured by methodological limitations. *Child Abuse & Neglect, 25*, 1219–40.

Robert Wood Johnson Foundation. (2013). *The truth about ACEs*. [Infographic.] Retrieved from http://www.rwjf.org/en/about-rwjf/ newsroom/newsroom-content/2013/05/Infographic-The-Truth-AboutACEs.html

Silverman, Amy; Reinherz, Helen; and Giaconia, Rose. (1996). The long-term sequelae of child and adolescent abuse: A longitudinal community study. *Child Abuse & Neglect, 20*(8), 709–23.

Snyder, Howard. (2000). *Sexual assault of young children as reported to law enforcement: Victim, incident, and offender characteristics*. Bureau of Justice Statics. Retrieved from http://www.bjs.gov/content/pub/pdf/saycrle.pdf

Sullivan, Erin; Annest, Joseph; Simon, Thomas; Luo, Feijun; and Dahlberg, Linda. (2017). Suicide trends among persons aged 10–24 years, 1994–2012. *Morbidity and Mortality Weekly Report, 64*, 201–32. Retrieved from https://www.cdc.gov/mmwr/pdf/wk/mm6408.pdf

Teicher, Martin; Anderson, Susan; Polcari, Ann; Anderson, Carl; Navalta, Carryl; and Kim, Dennis. (2003). The neurobiological consequences of early stress and childhood maltreatment. *Neuroscience and Biobehavioral Reviews, 27*(1–2), 33–44.

U.S. Department of Health and Human Services, Administration for Children and Families, Administration on Children, Youth and Families, Children's Bureau. *Report to Congress on state child welfare expenditures* (Title IV-B, Subpart 2 of the Social Security Act), Promoting Safe and Stable Families Programs (attachment E). Retrieved from https://www.acf.hhs.gov/sites/default/files/cb/cfs101_report_congress_2016_attach_e.pdf

U.S. Department of Health and Human Services, Administration for Children and Families, Administration on Children, Youth and Families, Children's Bureau, www.acf.hhs.gov/cb *Preliminary estimates on adoption and foster care analysis and reporting system (AFCARS) 2016 data as of Oct 20, 2017 (24).* Retrieved from https://www.acf.hhs.gov/sites/default/files/cb/afcarsreport24.pdf

U.S. Department of Health & Human Services, Administration for Children and Families, Administration on Children, Youth and Families, Children's Bureau. (2017). *Child maltreatment 2015.* Retrieved from http://www.acf.hhs.gov/programs/cb/research-data-technology/statistics-research/child-maltreatment.

U.S. Department of Justice. (1999). *Prior abuse reported by inmates and probationers.* Bureau of Justice Statistics, April 1999, NCJ 172879. Retrieved from www.bjs.gov/content/pub/pdf/parip.pdf

Wheaton, Elizabeth. (2007). *The effects of intra-family relationships on child labor outcomes in Kenya.* Unpublished doctoral dissertation for the Temple University Economics Department.

Wheaton, Elizabeth; Schauer, Edward; and Galli, Thomas. (2010). Economics of human trafficking. *International Migration, 48*(4), 114–41.

■ Section 10: Resources

Unit 1: Summary

Child abuse in its many forms is a human rights violation against children. There are many forms of child abuse and differences in prevalence, severity, and impact on children. Both national and international laws and agreements are in place to protect children and there is a wide range of experts working in areas related to child abuse. The costs of child abuse extend to the child victim, the child's family and other relatives, and society. The benefits of child abuse are solely to the perpetrator.

Unit 2: Key concepts

Abuse: Cruel or violent treatment of the victim by a perpetrator.

Bullying: Aggressive behavior by one child or multiple children against another child that often occurs in an educational setting.

Child: In the United States, a child is a person who is under 18 years of age and has not been emancipated as an adult.

Child abuse: The Federal Child Abuse Prevention and Treatment Act (2010) defines child abuse and neglect as "at a minimum, any recent act or failure to act on the part of a parent or caretaker which results in death, serious physical or emotional harm, sexual abuse or exploitation; or an act or failure to act which presents an imminent risk of serious harm."

Child fatality: According to the National Child Abuse and Neglect Data System (NCANDS), a child fatality in a child abuse context is "the death of a child caused by an injury resulting from abuse or neglect or where abuse or neglect was a contributing factor."

Child neglect: The failure of the child's guardian to provide the child's essential needs.

Child sex trafficking or commercial sexual exploitation of children: When a perpetrator uses force, fraud, or coercion to influence a child to perform a sexual act or allow pornographic images to be taken.

Child sexual abuse: Any form of sexual activity with a child.

Child trafficking: The use of force, fraud, or coercion to exert pressure on a child to do a particular type of work.

Corporal punishment: Physical punishment used to cause pain as a form of discipline.

Cyberbullying: The perpetrator's use of the internet to bully their victim.

Discipline: The act of using punishment to correct disobedience to the rules of the household.

Emotional abuse or **psychological abuse:** When a perpetrator knowingly tries to control or demean the victim by decreasing the child's identity, dignity, and self-worth.

Female genital mutilation (FGM) or **female circumcision:** The cutting, piercing, or removing of part or all the external female genitalia or the sewing closed of the genitalia for nonmedical reasons (Abdulcadir, et al., 2016).

Forced abortion: The perpetrator forces the victim to undergo a medical procedure to have an abortion.

Human trafficking: According to the U.S. Department of State in the Trafficking Victims Protection Act of 2000, human trafficking is the "recruitment, harboring, transportation, provision, or obtaining of a person for labor or services, through the use of force, fraud, or coercion for the purpose of subjection to involuntary servitude, peonage, debt bondage, or slavery."

Impact: The current and future effects of child abuse on a child.

Labor trafficking: The forced or coerced use of a child's labor in commercial areas.

Medical child abuse: When a child is given medical treatment that is unnecessary and harmful or potentially harmful because of the information provided by the caregiver of the child.

Monopolistic competition: An economic model in which there are many suppliers of a product or service and suppliers who attempt to increase sales by differentiating their product or service from their competitors' products or services.

Organ trafficking: The harvesting of part or all of a child's body as a source of human organs, tissues, or body parts.

Organized sexual abuse: When a child is victimized by more than one predator.

Pedophilia: When an adult has sex with or seeks sex with a child or creates, owns, or trades child pornography.

Perpetrator: A person who purposefully does an action to harm another person.

Psychological abuse or **emotional abuse:** When a perpetrator knowingly tries to control or demean the victim by decreasing the child's identity, dignity, and self-worth.

Physical abuse: When a perpetrator wilfully inflicts pain and injury on a victim with an instrument or use any part of their body.

Prevalence: The percentage of the population of children who have specific characteristics or are experiencing certain types of abuse during a specific period of time.

Rape: All forms of intercourse with a child.

Reasonable force: The level of physical force that is appropriate and legally justified to correct a child.

Ritual abuse: When a group of people participate in a ritual that involves the abuse of a child.

Severity: The degree of harshness or seriousness.

Spiritual violence: Playing upon a child's beliefs to inflict abuse upon the child.
Statutory rape: Sexual intercourse by an adult with a person under the age of 18.
Unreasonable force or cruel discipline: The use of excess or unnecessary force in correction.
Verbal abuse: The use of words or sounds as a means of controlling and demeaning the victim.
Victim: A person who is harmed by the actions of the perpetrator.

Unit 3: Review questions

1. Define child abuse.

2. What are some different types of child abuse?

3. What is the most prevalent form of child abuse?

4. What is child trafficking?

5. What laws are in place in the United States to protect children?

6. What international agreements are in place to protect children?

7. What are two ways that child abuse differs from violence against women?

8. What are some of the inefficiencies that may prevent a child from being protected from child abuse?

9. Who are the five decision-makers in the area of child abuse?

10. Why might a child in the United States be removed from their home into protective custody?

11. What are some of the costs associated with child abuse?

12. Is there any benefit to child abuse? If so, to whom?

Unit 4: Recommended readings

Amnesty International. (1997). *In the firing line: War and children's rights*. London: Amnesty International United Kingdom.

Beah, Ishmael. (2007). *A long way gone: Memoirs of a boy soldier*. New York: Sarah Crichton Books.

Bhabha, Jacqueline (Ed.) (2011). *Children without a state: A global human rights challenge*. Cambridge: MIT Press.

Bourdillon, Michael; Levinson, Deborah; Myers, William; and White, Ben. (2010). *Rights and wrongs of children's work*. New Brunswick: Rutgers University Press.

Weston, Burns H. (Ed.). (2005). *Child labor and human rights: Making children matter*. Boulder: Lynn Rienner Publishers.

7 Economics of genocide

Section 1: Introduction to the economics of genocide

Murder, mutilation, rape, kidnapping, property destruction, land seizure, economic restriction, and control of reproduction are all parts of the atrocity called genocide. International law scholar Raphael Lemkin (1944) first used the term genocide to mean "the practice of extermination of nations and ethnic groups" after World War II in the context of the Nazi atrocities against Jews. Later in this chapter, information will be presented on the many overlapping types of genocide.

The French term *genocidaires* means "those who commit genocide" and was used during the Rwandan genocide in 1994 to describe a group of people who view the killing of another group of people as eliminating "the problem," plan genocide, and initiate the ideas passed on to those who commit genocidal acts. Genocidaires and perpetrators of genocide systematically erase their victims' culture by displacing people, removing children, physically changing communities, and destroying property and cultural artifacts (Daniel Goldhagen, 2009). Genocide involves the killing and destruction of a group of people with less political and social power (referred to as the minority due to the group's relative lack of position) by those who hold power (referred to as the majority). Gaining control may involve taking political power, land, wealth, or resources; forcing conformation to one's ideals or religion; or making one's own group "safe." Hate speech, a topic covered in the next chapter, is a powerful tool of genocidaires, who create an atmosphere in which using speech and action to dehumanize their opponents is commonplace.

Unit 1: Survivor perspective

Célestin Musekura, Ph.D.

Dr. Musekura is the president and founder of African Leadership and Reconciliation Ministries (ALARM, Inc.), a nonprofit organization with the mission to develop leaders, reconcile relationship, and transform communities. He is an ordained Baptist minister, born and raised in Rwanda. He has a Ph.D. in theological studies and a master of sacred theology from Dallas Theological Seminary, a master of science in justice administration and leadership at the University of Texas at Dallas, a master of divinity at the Africa International University (AIU), formerly Nairobi Evangelical Graduate School of Theology (NEGST) in Kenya, and a bachelor of theology from Kenya Highlands Evangelical University in Kenya. He studied conflict resolution, mediation, restorative justice, and reconciliation at the Eastern Mennonite University and Southern Methodist University. As an international speaker and author, Dr. Musekura specializes in communal forgiveness, servant leadership, restorative justice, and justice administration.

Based not only on my personal experience as a victim survivor and but also on my experience as a perpetrator by association, I believe that genocide and mass murder of innocent members of a group accused of committing genocide are gross violations of human rights. Because I belong to the Hutu tribe accused of committing genocide against Tutsi in my country of Rwanda, even though I left the country six years before the genocide happened, I lost many family members and neighbors in the Tutsi revenge against Hutus that followed the Rwandan genocide.

The seed of genocide is sown in the abyss of the worst type of discrimination and differentiation that considers victims as less human; as people who do not deserve to live. In my native country of Rwanda in the years leading up to the genocide of the Tutsi, some of the human rights violations included the denial of freedom of movement, the removal of people from their properties, the alienation of Tutsis from specific professions, discrimination in education, the scapegoating of Tutsis as the driving force that caused division between Hutu politicians and military leaders, and the dehumanization of Tutsis to the level of cockroaches. At the commemoration of the twentieth anniversary of the Rwandan genocide (2014), former U.N. Secretary General Ban Ki-moon affirmed that "human rights violations must be seen as early warning signals of conflict and mass atrocities." In the aftermath of the Rwandan genocide, many Hutus were indiscriminately murdered by Tutsi soldiers who believed that all Hutus were beasts and killers who should be shot at first sight. Many acts that precede and follow genocide are violations of human rights.

Adama Dieng (2015), special adviser to the U.N. Secretary General on the Prevention of Genocide, indicates that the challenge faced today is to devise strategies to detect and deter processes and patterns of discrimination and other systematic and serious abuses of human rights that result from identity-based conflicts. Linda Woolf (n.d.) of Webster University provides a convincing and eloquent rationale for the study of genocide in her course syllabus. She says, "It is imperative that a greater understanding of the psychological, cultural, political, and societal roots of human cruelty, mass violence, ethno-political conflict, and genocide be developed. We need to continue to examine the factors which enable individuals collectively and individually to perpetrate evil/genocide and the impact of apathetic bystanders as fuel for human violence."

The international community must support research to discover how genocide develops and how to prevent it. Governments must establish and implement policies that mitigate against crimes against humanity. Governmental and nongovernmental organizations must collaborate in developing models and policies towards early warnings and the prevention of mass murder and genocide. And where such atrocities have taken place, these bodies must develop models of peaceful conflict resolution, communal forgiveness, reconciliation, and reconstruction. The international community must support more studies in the prevention of what I call "genorevenge," the indiscriminate revenge and mass murder of members of the groups accused of perpetuating genocide by the army or police forces dominated by members of the group of victims of the genocide.

Because genocide is more than an issue of human rights and security, its atrocities and impact on the world must be studied by students in most major fields of study including theology, psychology, sociology, political science, peace and security, economics, community development, public health, law, and international law. As Robert Gallately and Ben Kiernan (2003) put it, "more research is needed on the history, anthropology, economics, demography, literature, law and psychology of genocide, and its perpetuators, victims, bystanders, and survivors." Students and educators must develop a world view that they are part of humanity and therefore responsible for the solutions of humanity's problems.

The study of genocide is critical to the prevention of future crimes against humanity and to the development of attitudes that foster respect for all human rights. We must foster harmonious and communal life in which the sanctity of life and the rights of individuals and groups are protected.

Unit 2: Communications perspective

Ben Voth, Ph.D.

Dr. Voth is an associate professor and the director of debate and speech research at Southern Methodist University in Dallas, Texas. He has a Ph.D. in communication studies from the University of Kansas and both an M.A. in speech communication and a B.A. in communication and journalism from Baylor University. He is the author of three books on using communication to change the world, has collaborated with national and international institutes, and teaches courses in public speaking, argumentation and debate, persuasion theory, political communication, communication and ethno-violence, and communication and genocide. He emphasizes the role of free speech, dissent, and argument in preventing and reversing problems of human injustice.

Holocaust survivor Elie Wiesel (1986) stated, "What hurts the victim most is not the physical cruelty of the oppressor but the silence of the bystander." The communication premise of Wiesel's observation, which is derived from the agonies of the Holocaust, is the foundation of my communication teaching and research, which aims to equip individuals all over the world to have their voice.

In March 2017, I traveled with a team to Rwanda. The incredible natural beauty of the country was illuminated by bright sunlight and gorgeous greenery set upon a luscious dark soil. My colleague Dr. Betty Gilmore wrote, ". . .we visited a church in Nyamata, the site of a massacre and where 50,000 people were buried. Although we thought we were prepared for what we were about to see, we were wrong." Thousands of lives were lost in an ethnic supremacist fantasy. Broken-down brick buildings and dark Christian crosses marked the landscape for the peculiar human festivities of killing the innocent that interrupted the placid landscape in 1994. In the church, we saw the victims' clothes and belongings and dark stains where people had been murdered, and "Our guide's pain in telling the story was palpable." The essential infrastructure common to civil society – a church, a school house – were now housing thousands of human remains. The annihilation of innocence was amplified by displays of neatly ordered rows of human skulls . . . and so many of the skulls were too small to be adults. Rwanda had reminded us of the human willingness to kill the innocent.

Later we sat in the shade of a modest house while a survivor who had lost her husband and sons in the genocide stood shoulder-to-shoulder with a man who had served 20 years in prison for his participation in the genocide. As part of the reconciliation program, the man worked on reconstructing the community he helped to destroy . . . and he had built the woman's house. Somehow grace was defeating judgment in Rwanda.

We spent three days training 50 members of the Rwandan security forces in conflict resolution. These men on the lowest level of security in the state, below both the army and the police, wore bright green uniforms and smiling faces. They did not have firearms and their primary weapon was dialogue within the communities they served each day. We laughed often about our difficulties translating English to Kinyarwanda, Kinyarwanda to English.

Our activities focused on a mixture of strategy explanation and small group discussions followed by presentations from those groups on their local discernment of how these strategies would work best in Rwanda.

My offering was methodologies in conflict resolution rooted in the experiences of American civil rights hero and "great debater" James Farmer, Jr. I explained that principles like these allowed the American Civil Rights Movement in the United States to overcome ethnic violence directed at African Americans. A pivotal portion of my presentation involved a distillation of James Farmer's 13 rules for non-violent direct action in resolving conflicts, including 1) Get the facts first, 2) Do not respond with hurtful words, 3) Understand why they are hurt, and 4) Seek creative solutions.

We visited the official national memorial to the genocide in Kigali. It illustrated that the genocide was an intellectually-orchestrated crime against humanity and showed the shrewdness not only of the perpetrators but also of the international community, which deliberately stood by and did nothing while almost one million Rwandans were killed. We stood by the mass graves. We visited Hotel Rwanda. In each place, I was struck not only by incredible horror, but also by Rwanda rising and the endless possibility of humanity defeating death as a text in the agonizing reality of genocide.

Section 2: Fundamentals of genocide

Unit 1: Important genocide terms

There are multiple definitions of genocide. The United Nations (1946) defines **genocide** as "killing members of a group; causing serious bodily or mental harm to members of a group; deliberately inflicting on the group conditions of life calculated to bring about its physical destruction in whole or in part; imposing measures intended to prevent births within the group; and forcibly transferring children of the group to another group." Vahakn Dadrian (1975) states that "Genocide is the successful attempt by a dominant group, vested with formal authority and/or with preponderant access to the overall resources of power, to reduce by coercion or lethal violence the number of a minority group whose ultimate extermination is held desirable and useful and whose respective vulnerability is a major factor contributing to the decision of genocide." These definitions are similar, and Darian further defines the dimensions of genocide and the actions of decision-makers that occur in each genocide. Genocide begins with the perpetrator's intent to annihilate another group of people. This includes the ideological and practical rationalization of genocide, creating an atmosphere in which genocide is accepted, and authorizing the acts of genocide by perpetrators. Genocide is distinguished from other crimes by the level of victimization and number of victims. The United Nations set out the structure of genocide in the Convention on the Prevention and Punishment of the Crime of Genocide (1948, also called the Genocide Convention), broadly defining genocide as "any of the following acts committed with intent to destroy, in whole or in part, a national, ethnical, racial or religious group, as such: a) killing members of the group, b) causing serious bodily or mental harm to members of the group, c) deliberately inflicting on the group conditions of life calculated to bring about its physical destruction in whole or in part, d) imposing measures intended to prevent births within the groups, e) forcibly transferring children of the group to another group" (Adam Jones, 2006).

Leo Kuper (1981) points out that the U.N. definition omits political groups as potential victims of genocide while Barbara Harff (2003) states a distinction between genocide and politicide, which is the destruction of an opposing political group. Jack Porter (1982) discusses three major components of genocide as "ideology, technology, and bureaucracy/organization." Yehuda Bauer (2006) notes that **holocaust** refers to the complete annihilation of all members of a group while genocide refers to destroying part of a population. Clark McCauley and Daniel Chirot's (2006) definition contains the inclusion of combatants and noncombatants in the targeted population. Donald Bloxham (2009) states that the area of the genocide need not be limited to a certain territory.

As previously discussed, **genocidaires** are the forces behind a genocide. They are the decision-makers who are the leaders in planning genocide, preparing the propaganda, assembling necessary resources, and determining the timing of the atrocity. **Perpetrators of genocide** are the individuals who do the actions, such as murder, rape, kidnapping, and property seizure, that constitute the genocide. **Bystanders of genocide** are those persons who do not engage in the actions of the genocide but also do not actively work to prevent the genocide or to safeguard the victims of the genocide. The **international community** is the group of countries, governments, businesses, and organizations that make decisions regarding when and how to intervene in a genocide. The decisions of the international community are not necessarily made collectively.

An **atrocity** is a shockingly cruel act of violence. Genocide is often referred to as an atrocity in that it is an extremely terrible act of one group of people against fellow human beings. The U.S. Federal Bureau of Investigation (FBI) defines **mass murder** as the act of killing four or more people in a limited amount of time and in a specific geographic area. Mass murders may be committed by a group of people, as in genocide, or by a single person, as with lone-wolf terrorism.

International law related to **forced deportation** (or **forced population transfer**) includes the removal of people from one country to another and from one area within a country to another area against the will of those persons. The term **forced migration** may also be used in this context. Andrew Scholten (2016) states, "Expulsion is an act by a public authority to remove a person or persons against their will from the territory of that state. A successful expulsion of a person by a country is called a deportation." **Ethnic cleansing** (or **population cleansing**) means targeting a group of people for removal from an area through violence or the inducement of fear of removal in order to create an ethnically homogeneous population (Cherif Bassiouni and Peter Manikas, 1996).

Systematic rape is the targeting of victims for rape as a weapon of war. The perpetrators of genocide are encouraged by the genocidaires to rape women, children, and even men. The acts of rape are demeaning to the victims, cause physical and disease issues, and may lead to impregnation by the perpetrators, or even death. All of the types of physical violence discussed in the chapter on violence against women are present during genocide. **Biological subjugation** is the enslavement of people for the purpose of preventing the reproduction of biological families. This type of subjugation includes the kidnapping and removal of children from the victim's households, forced abortion, and compulsory sterilization.

Economic subjugation is the enslavement of people by restricting earning of income, involvement in economic transactions, access to markets, and avenues of savings. Plans for genocide often include taking control over the victims' finances, which restricts their activities and lives.

Unit 2: Forms of genocide

According to Daniel Goldhagen (2009), **eliminationism** – a term similar to genocide which means the belief or policy that a group should be forced out of an area or killed – has five principle forms: 1) Transformation, in which a group's identity in terms of politics, society, or culture is destroyed, 2) repression, in which a group is confined to a restricted geographical area, 3) expulsion, in which a group is forced out of an area or into holding areas, 4) prevention of reproduction, in which sterilization or rape are used to prevent pregnancy or change the biological makeup of the group, and 5) extermination, in which the group members are killed. However, Frances Stewart (2011) states that it is difficult to define a specific genocide by only one of these labels as many genocides have multiple characteristics. Table 6.1 lists the major types of genocide proposed by researchers along with a definition and examples.

TABLE 7.1   Types of genocide

Type of genocide	Definition	Example
Cultural genocide (Darian, 1975)	Mass conversions as victims are forced to become part of the majority group.	Armenian Genocide by Ottomans (1895–1896)
Despotic genocide (Fein, 1979)	Elimination of real or potential opposition.	Idi Amin in Uganda (1971–1979)
Developmental genocide (Fein, 1979)	Minority group destroyed so majority group may exploit resources.	Destruction of aboriginal groups during national expansions
Genocide of substitution, genocide of devastation, genocide of elimination (Savon, 1972)	Motives of perpetrators lead to substitution (such as one religion for another), devastation, or elimination.	
Ideological genocide (Fein, 1979, Smith, 1987)	Imposition of a specific belief on the minority group.	Holocaust, Cambodia
Institutional genocide (Smith, 1987)	Due to military conquest of a nation, mainly in the ancient and medieval worlds.	
Latent genocide (Darian, 1975)	War that leads to the unintended destruction of a civilian population.	Strategic bombing during WWII (Japan), Trail of Tears
Monopolistic genocide (Smith, 1987)	From the desire to monopolize power.	Bangladesh, Burundi
Retributive genocide (Fein, 1979, Smith, 1987)	Revenge in a local area to destroy a long-term enemy.	Pograms in Russia (late 1880s), Wounded Knee, Rwandan genocide
Utilitarian genocide (Darian, 1975, Smith, 1987)	Material gain from land or resources leads to destruction of a population.	Spanish Inquisition

Unit 3: Origins of genocide

Gregory Stanton (1996) described ten developmental stages of genocide. The events do not necessarily happen in a linear order (from Stage I to Stage X), but all happen at some time during genocide. Stage I is classification, which is creating a distinction between different groups so that there is a recognized "us and them." Stage II is symbolization and includes creating a name for the other group and associating symbols with that group. Stage III is discrimination, in which the majority group refuses the rights of the minority group through the use of political power, laws, and customs. Hate speech and other actions to make the minority group seem less-than-human or alien play a large part in the dehumanization of the minority group, which is Stage IV in the development of genocide. Stage V is the organization of genocide by the genocidaires. Stage VI is polarization, in which the genocidaires drive apart the majority and minority groups through propaganda, laws forbidding contact, and targeting moderates in the majority group who might not acquiesce to the demands of the genocidaires. Stage VII is preparation. At this stage the genocidaires are planning the genocide and mobilizing resources to be used against the minority group. Victims undergo persecution in Stage VIII as they are targeted, put on death lists, physically segregated from the majority, denied resources, have their children forcibly removed, and are tortured and illegally killed. Extermination of the minority group begins in Stage IX with brutal acts. For instance, 800,000 people were killed in the 1994 Rwandan genocide, which lasted 100 days. Denial is the inevitable Stage X as the genocidaires and perpetrators of genocide deny that they committed crimes, blame the victims, block investigations, destroy evidence, and may flee to prevent being tried for their crimes.

Using Stanton's developmental stages of genocide, the nonprofit organization Genocide Watch (2016) has listed 14 countries at Stage IX of genocide, which is extermination. The countries and groups involved in genocide are included in Table 7.2.

TABLE 7.2 Countries experiencing genocide with perpetrators and victims of the genocides

Country	Perpetrators of genocide	Victims
Afghanistan	Taliban, Al Qaeda	Government supporters
Burma/Myanmar	Army, Buddhist extremists, Rakhine	Shan, Kachin, Karen, Rohingya, democrats
Cameroon	Boko Haram	Christians, government officials, schools
Democratic Republic of Congo	Hutu militia, various rapists	Women, Banyamulenge
Iraq	ISIS	Yazidis, Christians, Kurds, Shia
Nigeria	Boko Haram	Christians in Borno, government officials, schools
North Korea	Korean army, police	Government opponents
Pakistan	Taliban, Al Qaeda	Government supporters
Somalia	Al Shabaab	Opposing clans
South Sudan	Dinka army, Nuer rebels	Civilians, women, children
Sudan	Sudan army, Arab militias	Darfurese, Abyei, Nuba

Country	Perpetrators of genocide	Victims
Syria	Assad, Alawite loyalists, Army, ISIS, Al-Nusra	Anti-Sunni rebels, Christians, Shia
Turkey	Turkish army police	Kurds
Yemen	Al Qaeda, Saudi Air force, Houthi	Elected government, Houthi

Source: Genocide Watch, 2016.

Genocide Watch also lists four countries at Stage VIII in the genocide development structure. These countries are Burundi (Hutu targeting Tutsis and Hutus), Chad (Sudanese Janjaweed targeting Zaghawas, Fur, Massaleit, and Nuba), Egypt (Egyptian army targeting Muslim Brotherhood and Copts), and Libya (ISIS and tribal militias targeting government officials, police, and army). In addition, there are 15 countries at Stage VII (persecution), 11 at Stage VI (polarization), and 13 at Stage V (organization).

Section 3: Genocide as a human rights violation

Unit 1: National agreements

Many nations have laws enabling the prosecution and extradition of perpetrators of genocide. The major laws in the United States and the United Kingdom are reviewed below.

U.S. Code Chapter 50A, Section 1091, Title 18 (18 U.S.C. 1091) defines genocide, makes genocide illegal in wartime or peacetime, and sets the penalty at death or life imprisonment on conviction of participating in genocide, and fines for the incitement of genocide. It states that genocide "includes violent attacks with the specific intent to destroy, in whole or in part, a national, ethnic, racial, or religious group." Sections 1101, 1182, and 1227 set up further provisions for the denial of entry into the United States or deportation from the United States for a person convicted of genocide. This chapter of U.S. federal law includes the U.N. Genocide Convention Implementation Act of 1987 (also called the Proxmire Act) and implements the U.N. Convention on the Prevention and Punishment of the Crime of Genocide (UNCG) in the United States.

In 2017, the U.S. Department of State Office of Global Criminal Justice, which formerly advised the U.S. Secretary of State on genocides, war crimes, and crimes against humanity, was downgraded to be housed under the Bureau of Democracy, Human Rights, and Labor which is under the U.S. Under Secretary for Civilian Defense, Democracy, and Human Rights. This office had been in charge of coordinating experts and intelligence information for international courts prosecuting persons accused of mass atrocities.

U.S. diplomats and officials continue to attend conferences and forums to state the commitment of the United States to preserving human rights. However, it has most often been the case that U.S. national interests and domestic policies have been considered higher priorities and have led to inaction in genocides. Samantha Power (2013) states the four reasons that U.S. leaders give for inaction. First, there is a long history of violence between the groups; second, fear that U.S. involvement could either not work or make the genocide worse; third, U.S. official concern about being identified as taking action based on emotional response; and finally, the word genocide is not explicitly used and therefore there is no action required. Power's research shows that an unconcerned U.S. public has led to a situation in which U.S. political leaders are hesitant to tackle genocide issues.

The United Kingdom (U.K.) International Criminal Court Act (ICC) of 2001 took the place of the Genocide Act of 1969. The ICC became part of U.K. domestic law and British citizens may be charged with genocide and with supporting genocides for actions after May 2001. The Coroners and Justice Act of 2009 changed the ICC so that persons could be prosecuted for genocide from January 1991 (in relation to the former Yugoslavia).

The United Kingdom stated in April 2017 that South Sudan is now experiencing tribal genocide, despite the fact that the United Nations has not yet recognized the actions in that nation. The U.K. failed to respond to the Rwandan genocide.

Unit 2: International agreements

Nazi leaders accused of crimes against peace and crimes against humanity during World War II were tried in all four occupied zones and in other countries between 1945 and 1949. The defendants were accused of numerous crimes, including the systematic extermination of six million European Jews and four to six million non-Jews. The trials held in Nuremburg, Germany were known as the Nuremburg Trials and led to the establishment of the International Criminal Court (ICC). The findings from the war trials were used in the creation of the United Nations Genocide Convention (1948), the Universal Declaration of Human Rights (1948), and the Geneva Convention on the Laws and Customs of War (1949).

Principle VI of International Law, which was recognized in the Charter of the Nuremberg Trial and in the Judgment of the Tribunal (1950), describes crimes of peace, war crimes, and crimes against humanity. **Crimes against peace** involve conspiring to plan, prepare, initiate, or wage a war that violates international agreements. **War crimes** are actions that violate the laws or customs of war and include a list relating to the brutal treatment of civilians and the destruction of property. **Crimes against humanity** are actions committed as part of a known, systematic attack against a civilian population. These terms are used in the U.N. Criminal Justice Standards for U.N. Police (UN DPKO, 2009).

According to the U.N. Holocaust Memorial Museum (2018), the first conviction for genocide occurred in 1998 in Tanzania when the International Criminal Tribunal for Rwanda convicted Jean-Paul Akayesu, a Hutu mayor, of crimes against humanity and genocide. Later convictions included other Hutus of Rwanda, Serbs of Bosnia and Herzegovina, members of the Macias regime in Equatorial Guinea, members of the Ethiopian government, members of the Iraqi government under Saddam Hussein, and an Italian radio presenter who incited violence in the Rwandan genocide.

There are many formal pieces of international human rights law and of international humanitarian law related to genocide. **Human rights law** is the body of law that protects a person's basic human rights. Table 7.3 lists the main international human rights laws related to genocide.

International humanitarian law (also known as the law of war or the law of armed conflict) governs behavior during war. Table 7.4 lists some of the main humanitarian laws related to genocide.

TABLE 7.3 International human rights laws related to genocide

Date	Legal instrument
1948	Convention on the Prevention and Punishment of the Crime of Genocide
1953	European Convention on Human Rights
1966	International Covenant on Civil and Political Rights (includes forced migration)
1966	International Covenant on Economic, Social, and Cultural Rights
1968	Convention on the Non-Applicability of Statutory Limitations to War Crimes and Crimes Against Humanity
1973	Principles of International Co-operation in the Detection, Arrest, Extradition and Punishment of Persons Guilty of War Crimes and Crimes Against Humanity
1984	Convention against Torture and Other Cruel, Inhumane or Degrading Treatment or Punishment
1985	Declaration of Basic Principles of Justice for Victims of Crime and Abuse of Power
1989	Indigenous and Tribal Peoples Convention
1992	Declaration on the Rights of Persons Belonging to National or Ethnic, Religious and Linguistic Minorities
1992	Declaration on the Protection of Persons from Enforced Disappearance
2005	Updated Set of Principles for the Protection and Promotion of Human Rights to Combat Impunity
2005	Basic Principles and Guidelines on the Right to a Remedy and Reparation for Victims of Gross Violations of International Human Rights Law and Serious Violations of International Humanitarian Law
2006	International Convention for the Protection of All Persons from Enforced Disappearance
2007	Declaration on the Rights of Indigenous Peoples

Source: U.N. Office on Genocide Prevention and the Responsibility to Protect.

TABLE 7.4 International humanitarian laws

Date	Presiding legal body	Legal instrument
1945	Nuremburg Tribunals	Charter on the International Military Tribunal (Nuremberg)
1946	Tokyo Tribunals	Charter on the International Military Tribunal (Tokyo)
1946	International Court of Justice	Statue of the International Court of Justice
1950	International Law Commission	International Law Commission Principles of International Law recognized in the Charter of the Nuremberg Tribunal and in the Judgment of the Tribunal
1951	International Court of Justice	Advisory Opinion – Reservations to the Convention on the Prevention of the Crime of Genocide
1993	International Criminal Tribunal for the former Yugoslavia	Statue on the International Criminal Tribunal for the former Yugoslavia

(Continued)

TABLE 7.4 (Continued)

Date	Presiding legal body	Legal instrument
1994	International Criminal Tribunal for Rwanda	Statue on the International Criminal Tribunal for Rwanda
1996	International Court of Justice	Advisor Opinion – Legality of the Threat or Use of Nuclear Weapons
1996	International Law Commission	International Law Commission Draft Code of Crimes Against the Peace and Security of Mankind
1998	International Criminal Court	Rome Statute on the International Criminal Court
2000	Courts of Kosovo	UNMIK Regulation 2000/64 Panels in the Courts of Kosovo
2000	Special Court for Sierra Leone	Statute of the Special Court for Sierra Leone
2000	District Court of Dili (Timor-Leste)	UNTAET Regulation No. 2000/15 on the Serious Crimes Panels in the District Court of Dili (Timor-Leste)
2001	Courts of Cambodia	Law on the Establishment of Extraordinary Chambers in the Courts of Cambodia
2001	International Law Commission	International Law Commission Draft Articles on the Responsibility of States for Internationally Wrongful Acts
2002	State Court of Bosnia and Herzegovina	Law No. 16/2002 on the War Crimes Chamber in the State Court of Bosnia and Herzegovina
2006	International Court of Justice	Judgment – Armed Activities on the Territory of the Congo (DRC v. Rwanda)
2007	International Court of Justice	Judgment – Application of the Convention on the Prevention and Punishment of the Crime of Genocide (Bosnia and Herzegovina v. Serbia and Montenegro)
2010	International Criminal Court	Elements of Crimes
2010	International Residual Mechanism for Criminal Tribunals	Statue on the International Residual Mechanism for Criminal Tribunals
2011	International Law Commission	International Law Commission Draft Articles on the Responsibility of International Organizations
2012	International Court of Justice	Judgment – Questions related to the Obligation to Prosecute or Extradite (Belgium v. Senegal)
2013	Courts of Senegal	Extraordinary African Chambers within the Courts of Senegal
2015	International Court of Justice	Judgment – Application of the Convention on the Prevention and Punishment of the Crime of Genocide (Croatia v. Serbia)

Source: U.N. Office on Genocide Prevention and the Responsibility to Protect.

The International Criminal Court (ICC) is located in the Netherlands. It is governed by the Rome Statute and is an independent international organization. Its authority is based on international treaties so that it can prosecute people accused of crimes that affect the international community.

The International Court of Justice (ICJ) is the U.N.'s judicial branch. It is located in New York City, New York. The ICJ's role is to provide legal advice to the United Nations and to make legal decisions about disputes between members of the United Nations.

The International Law Commission (ILC) was created by the United Nations General Assembly. The role of the ILC is to develop and codify (systematically arrange) international law.

Unit 3: Controversies

Without a unified definition of genocide, there will always be argument about the meaning of the term and a difference in the laws and regulations related to genocide. A critical question is whether genocide should be bound strictly to killing or if it should be expanded to other actions. For example, cultural genocide is the systematic destruction of the culture of a people and may include destroying language, traditions, and other things that make the group of people unique. Some activists worry that calling these "lesser" events genocides will diminish the relative seriousness of massive atrocities like the Holocaust.

Politics plays a part in defining genocide and may keep politics from being included in the definition. Governments are a part of genocide when politicide occurs. In politicide, one party attempts to systematically destroy members of a rival party, such as happened during the 1965–1966 anti-communist purges in Indonesia.

CHECK YOURSELF BOX: PERSONAL BIASES ABOUT GENOCIDE

The mass killing of people is not a topic most people dwell upon. Since genocides are going on at all times, most people are bystanders who do not get involved in the issue. What are your initial thoughts about genocide? Do you have a personal experience or do you know people who have had an experience that involved genocide? Have you read about or seen depictions of genocide? Is genocide a topic that interests you or one that challenges you? Does it concern you that a genocide is at times the historical aftermath of a past genocide by the opposing group? Your biases will partially determine how much of the information about genocide you are able to understand and use for research. Take time to write down your thoughts on the issue of genocide so that you will be aware of times when your biases are affecting your understanding, and therefore the way you use the information.

Section 4: History of genocide

A main difficulty in creating a historical timeline of genocide is that the designation of a mass atrocity as a genocide depends upon the definition used. The authors of this textbook again stress the importance for the student to first determine specific definitions before proceeding with research. In this textbook, the broadest definition of genocide is used to provide the deepest source of information.

While the first use of the term genocide was in 1948 by Raphael Lemkin, genocide has been described since the beginning of recorded history. Ben Kiernan (2004) declares Rome's destruction of Carthage in 146 B.C. to be the first genocide as the words *Delenda est Carthago*, meaning "Carthage must be destroyed," were recorded. Others state that the earliest genocide happened around 30,000 years ago as humans' earliest ancestors killed off the Neanderthals. Evidence of the brutal killing of men, women, and children 10,000 years ago was found at Nataruk, Kenya (Brian Handwerk, 2016). European expansion into North America resulted in the spread of diseases which killed an estimated 90% of the Native American population, and atrocities were also part of this history. U.S. Congress's passing of the Indian Removal Act in 1830 led to the forced relocation of approximately 100,000 Cherokee, Chickasaw, Choctaw, Creek, and Seminole Indians to the area known as Indian Territory located west of the Mississippi River. In 1838, the Trail of Tears occurred when the U.S. Army forced Cherokee Indians off of their native lands, resulting in many deaths from exposure, hunger, and disease (Cherokee National Cultural Resources Center, 2018). This is by no means an exhaustive list of the genocides that occurred. The problems of documenting genocides emanate from the inability to document intentions in the historical past. As technology and record-keeping has advanced, the ability to discern the intentions is becoming clearer.

The twentieth century began with Germany's annihilation of the Herero in south-west Africa (now Namibia) between 1904 and 1907 followed by the genocide of Armenians, Assyrians, and Greeks carried out by the Ottoman Turks between 1915 and 1923. The Nazi Holocaust between 1933 and 1945 led to the deaths of six million Jews and five million Roma, Slavs, Jehovah's Witnesses, dissidents (political and religious), and homosexuals. Within three months in 1972, the extremist Tutsi government of Burundi exterminated 200,000 educated Hutus. From 1975 until 1979, the Khmer Rouge took over the Cambodian government and killed nearly two million Cambodians through starvation and abuse in labor camps. As introduced in Dr. Musekura's perspective at the beginning of the chapter, the 1990 civil war in Rwanda turned into a genocide in 1994 after the attack on President Juvenal Habyarimana's plane which led to his death. Approximately 800,000 Tutsis and Hutus were killed during a 100-day period during the Rwandan genocide. In 1992, Bosnia and Herzegovina declared independence from Yugoslavia. The ethnic cleansing by the Serbs that followed led to the murder of around 100,000 people between 1992 and 1995, including the four-day Srebenica genocide of 8,000 Bosniaks (Bosnian Muslims) in July 1995, the second largest massacre in Europe. Conflicts in Sudan have led to approximately 300,000 deaths of citizens with three million displaced from their homes. Multiple areas of Sudan have been centers of genocidal activity since 2003 and conflict continues to the present day. Since 2015, Muslim members of ISIS have been killing, kidnapping, raping, and trafficking Iraq Yazidi Christians. There are many other instances of genocides and genocidal actions that have happened up to the present day.

Section 5: Meet the genocide experts

Genocides and genocidal activity are happening around the world in many cultures and contexts. Experts in the topic often specialize in a particular genocide or area of the world. Reading peer-reviewed journal articles provides a perspective on who is doing the research, who has the data, and where information may be obtained. Table 7.5 provides a list of a few areas and fields of expertise related to genocide.

There are many academic programs in Holocaust and genocide studies around the world. Some of these include the Ph.D. program at Clark University in Massachusetts and masters programs at Collegium Civitas in Warsaw, Freier University in Berlin, Kingston University in London, Monash University in Victoria, Australia, the University of Amsterdam,

TABLE 7.5 Areas and fields of expertise related to genocide

Area of expertise	Field of expertise	Description
Research and possible sources of data	Anthropology	The study of human societies and cultures across time, and how societies and cultures can be destroyed by genocide.
	Communications	The study of the processes of human communication.
	Criminal justice	The study of systems that provide criminal justice policy and how those systems are used in the case of genocide.
	Criminology	The study of crime and criminals as they relate to genocide.
	Economics	The study of the choices people make leading up to, during and after a genocide when dealing with scarcity.
	History	The study of past events that led up to genocides.
	Psychology	The study of human behavior during genocide.
	Political science	The study of government and political behavior during genocide.
	Research centers	Government, private, and nonprofit research centers throughout the world with different focuses on genocide.
	Sociology	The study of the development and structure of society and how genocide disrupts society.
Human rights	Nonprofit organizations	Organizations with a mission to prevent genocides, help the victims of genocide, and educate the public about genocide.
Expert witnesses	Experts in peace keeping	Knowledge of occurrences during peace-keeping missions in times of genocide.
	Experts in political or social dynamics	Knowledge of the interplay between political or social groups related to genocide.
	Current or former perpetrators of genocide	Primary source, but questions of bias.
	Survivors of genocide	Primary source, but questions of bias.

TABLE 7.6 Databases related to genocide

Database	Managing organization	Focus
Atrocity Forecasting Project	University of Sydney	Global forecasting of mass atrocities and genocide.
The Polity Project	Center for Systemic Peace	Research on political violence.
Early Warning Project	United States Holocaust Memorial Museum	Advance genocide prevention by identifying at-risk countries.

the University of Haifa, the University of Minnesota, the University of Siena, and Uppsala University in Sweden. In addition, many universities include genocide and Holocaust studies as part of other degree programs. There are also many research programs that focus on genocide, including the Auschwitz Institute for Peace and Reconciliation, Yale University's Genocide Studies Program, and the Institute on the Holocaust & Genocide in Jerusalem. Independent research groups gather groups of experts and investigators to focus on specific aspects of genocide. For example, the Sentry is a research group created by the nonprofit organizations Enough Project and Not On Our Watch (NOOW) to focus on "following the money that funds atrocities and crimes against humanity." Table 7.6 presents some of the databases related to genocide.

An internet search on genocide and nonprofit organizations will provide an extensive listing of nonprofit organizations doing work related to genocide and reconciliation. For example, textbook perspective author Celestine Musakura is the founder and president of African Leadership and Reconciliation Ministries (ALARM, Inc.) in Texas. Due to the number of organizations, a researcher will want to narrow the search by looking at nonprofit organizations that are in a certain country or geographic area, doing a certain type of work, or focused on a specific genocide. In addition, the Institute on the Holocaust & Genocide in Jerusalem provides a directory of some of the organizations working against genocide at http://www.ihgjlm.com/directory-of-organizations-for-genocide-awareness.

CHECK YOURSELF BOX: GENOCIDE RESEARCH AND DATA BIASES

The purpose of genocide is to eliminate the existence of an opposing group. How do the experts and researchers benefit from being involved in the conversation surrounding genocide? What are the primary and secondary goals of the government and nongovernment organizations involved in preventing genocide? Who is collecting the data and how might their biases be affecting the numbers collected? Do any of these groups tend to belittle certain actors in a genocide situation? While the prevention and elimination of genocide are noble goals, biases can affect the viability of research and data for policy-making. Keeping track of these biases will help you determine your own biases and improve the quality of your personal research.

◼ Section 6: Economic structure of genocide

Daniel Goldhagen (2009) writes that there is a necessary distinction between definition, explanation, and moral evaluation. Using the previously reviewed definitions, economics theory and modeling will now be used to study the decision-makers, their overlapping choices, and the outcomes of those choices. This provides the elements needed to describe the economic structure of genocide. Moral evaluation is beyond the scope of this research and, in Goldhagen's words, "requires us to judge the character of events and the culpability of the actors."

The Rwandan genocide is not only about a geographic location, but also about a country of many peoples. Because the events of a genocide are inspired and performed by human beings, emphasis must be placed on the people who make the decisions, perform the acts, and face the circumstances present during genocide. Frances Stewart (2011) finds that economic or political inequalities between groups raises the risk of conflict and the presence of both inequalities further increases the risk. Benjamin Valentino (2004) discusses social cleavages (between ethnicities, cultures, religions or beliefs, classes, political groups, or economic groups) that polarize societies and increase the likelihood of conflict between the groups as people's decisions are in opposition to each other.

There are five main actors in genocide: Genocidaires, perpetrators, bystanders, victims, and the international community. Each person's decision includes personal costs and benefits. In genocide, decisions overlap and conflict in ways that bring about destruction and generational enmity. As was previously seen with terrorist leaders, the genocidaires have a social, political, or economic agenda and may have overlapping agendas. Ben Voth (2014) describes the characteristics of the genocidaire to be 1) possessing sovereignty of ultimate decision-making power, 2) using the public sphere to promote the rightness of the genocidaires' decisions, and 3) presiding over mass killing. These leaders come to power in a society experiencing high tensions, which are used to the genocidaires' advantage. The genocidaires' interests include eliminating "the problem" of the minority group, gaining political power, seizing control of the land and resources, creating safety for the majority group from violence by the minority group, and seeking revenge for past genocides.

Fueled by the rhetoric, incentives, and resources provided by the genocidaires, the perpetrators commit the acts of genocide. Beliefs, experiences, and their own or the genocidaires' dreams for a world that does not include a particular people group fuel the person's passions to commit genocide activities. For example, Rwandan political and military leaders manipulated historical tribalism to incite the genocide. Daniel Goldhagen (2009) and Omar McDoom (2013) find that "micro space" or social influence was an important determinant of whether a person participated in the Rwandan genocide. When a person lived within a household or neighborhood with persons who were committing genocide, that person was more likely to also be involved in the genocide. Daniel Goldhagen (2009) describes some characteristics of people who participated in the Rwandan genocide, including that they were 95% men; between the ages of 25 and 44 and therefore probably having a wife and children; citizens and not government officials; having some material incentives for committing the atrocities; and not distinguishable from non-perpetuators by individual characteristics. Similar to the incentives of the genocidaires, the perpetrators of genocide are motivated by a potential gain in political and social prestige and power over their victims by murder, mutilation, rape, and terror. Genocides are about getting something that someone else has and may lead to a reallocation of resources, whether those resources are money, land, material wealth, livestock, people in general, or women and children specifically.

Holocaust survivor Elie Wiesel (1986) said, "What hurts the victim most is not the physical cruelty of the oppressor but the silence of the bystander." Fred Grunfeld (2000) defines a bystander as "the third party that will not act or that will not attempt to act in solidarity with the victims of gross human rights violations." Once it occurs to a bystander that something is happening, that person has many choices: 1) Remain ignorant or find out what is happening, 2) get involved or choose not to get involved, and 3) if choosing to get involved, decide whether to help the perpetrator of the victim. These are serious decisions and each one will be discussed below.

When bystanders choose to remain ignorant, that ignorance might allow atrocities to happen to other people. For instance, if someone screams, a bystander must choose whether to ignore the situation or go and find out what has occurred. By ignoring the scream, a bystander may be unknowingly helping the perpetrator of an atrocity. The goals of the perpetrators of genocide include keeping bystanders either ignorant of the atrocities or paralyzed by a sense of inevitability, thereby preventing them from acting to help the victims. Ervin Staub (1989) states, "By turning away or remaining passive in the face of threats to human life, the conditions for genocide are maximized."

If curiosity wins out, the bystander chooses to seek answers to questions about current events. Once the situation is made more clear, the bystander must decide if there is something that can be done and whether to engage in doing that something. If the choice is to not engage, the bystander remains a bystander. This person would again be labeled a collaborator at the conclusion of a genocide.

Once the bystander decides to act, the choice is whether to act to the benefit of one group (or person) or another. In the case of genocide, the person who has decided to stop standing by and watching must decide whether to help the perpetrators of the atrocities or the victims. None of these decisions are all-or-nothing. A person can choose at any time to change direction and help the other group or even try to become a bystander again. This will be difficult because once the person has performed actions, they will gain the label of perpetrator or opponent of the genocidaires. Each decision comes with a price.

Genocidaires create plans to limit the choices of their victims. Some of the limits put in place may be geographic (victims are only allowed to live or travel within certain areas), political (restrictions on voting rights and political appointments), material (constraints on the living quarters, vehicles, weapons, etc.), or monetary. When the genocide begins, people faced with human rights violations must make choices that are limited by time, scope, and legality. They must determine whether to flee or remain and to remain passive or fight. Decisions are made on whether to send children, women, and the elderly to a safe place. These choices become more constrained and urgent due to the adaptive plans and whims of the genocidaires and perpetuators of genocide.

Although both national and international laws exist concerning genocide, there are serious ramifications of entering into the politics of a genocide as a peacekeeping or military force. This leads to difficult decisions for the international community (comprised of sovereign nations who converse and sometimes work together on global issues) and individual nations. These groups have five initial responses: 1) Choose to do nothing and allow the event to unfold without international intervention, 2) use economic controls (such as embargoes on imports or withheld foreign aid) to decrease the power of the group committing the genocide, 3) send forces for peacekeeping missions to protect victims, 4) aid indigenous resistance forces with military aid, and 5) deploy their military power to stop the genocide by force. Each decision is multi-faceted and takes time. Once a decision is made, people and resources must be gathered, organized, and sent to vital locations. If a peacekeeping force or military force has been deployed, the authority must decide when to pull those resources out of the area due to danger, politics, or the foreseen end of a conflict.

On January 11, 1994, the commander of the U.N. peacekeeping force in Rwanda sent a fax to the U.N. headquarters in New York warning of a plan to exterminate the Tutsis. The commander was not given authorization to act and the 100-day genocide that resulted in the deaths of hundreds of thousands of Rwandans started three months later. In 2005, all members of the United Nations signed a commitment called the Responsibility to Protect that set guidelines to help sovereign states protect all populations from human rights violations such as genocide, crimes against humanity, and ethnic cleansing. Despite this, there are multiple genocides happening today with little intervention from the international community.

One theme seen over and over in genocide is the redistribution of limited wealth, including property, material goods, money, and even people (through slavery and human trafficking, for example). While this redistribution of scarce resources can be seen during the genocide atrocities, it also occurs during earlier developmental stages when the genocidaires create barriers to jobs and income (which would lower demand for resources) and to the acquisition of resources (which would increase costs).

The following model is used to analyze the distribution of the scarce resources between two groups of people prior to genocide. First, the model examines each group's **net benefit**, which is benefit minus cost, when they have equal marginal benefits and marginal costs. Second, the individual net benefit curves are drawn together in a two-vertical-axes graph, with one vertical axis for each group. This step is shown first with no resource scarcity and then with scarcity of resources. Third, the minority group's net benefit is affected as the barriers created by genocidaires decrease the ability of the minority group to buy resources (decrease marginal benefit) and increase the costs of the resources (increase marginal cost). A two-vertical-axes graph is again used to show how the change in minority group's net benefit affects distribution of resources.

The state of not having enough resources to fulfill all needs is called **scarcity**. When scarcity exists, it is necessary to allocate the scarce resources between people, groups, or time periods. **Marginal benefit** (MB) is the benefit of each additional unit of a resource and is equal to the person or groups total willingness to pay for resources. **Marginal cost** (MC) is the cost of each additional unit of a resource. **Net marginal benefit** (NMB) is the sum of marginal benefit minus marginal cost for each additional unit of the resource and is found at the top of the marginal benefit curve after marginal cost has been subtracted.

The net marginal benefit curves for the majority and minority groups are illustrated in Figure 7.1 and Figure 7.2 as the darkened portion of the marginal benefit curves, after subtracting the marginal costs. Each graph shows the traditional downward-sloping demand (marginal benefit) curve for the group. The two graphs assume that demand (shown as marginal benefit of each unit of a resource) and costs (shown as marginal cost of each unit) are equal for both groups and that marginal cost is constant (shown as horizontal line MC). Net benefit is the difference between the total benefits from the resources minus all of the costs to obtain the resources. If there is no scarcity, each group can acquire Q_1 units of the resource.

E 7.1   Net benefit of majority group

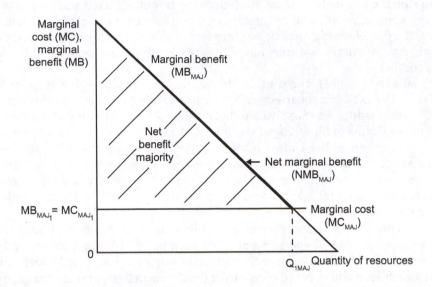

FIGURE 7.2   Net benefit of minority group

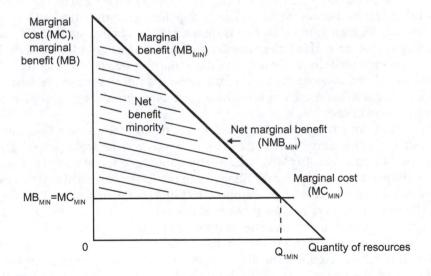

This model is also functional when benefits and costs are not equal for the two groups, such as when the majority group is larger than the minority group. In this case, the majority group's net benefit would be larger than that of the minority group.

Figure 7.3 shows the two-vertical-axes model in which there is no scarcity. In this case, both the majority and minority groups get all of the resources that they want (Q_{1MAJ} and Q_{1MIN}) so that the total quantity (Q_T) is greater than or equal to Q_{1MAJ} plus Q_{1MIN}.

FIGURE 7.3   Resource allocation with no scarcity

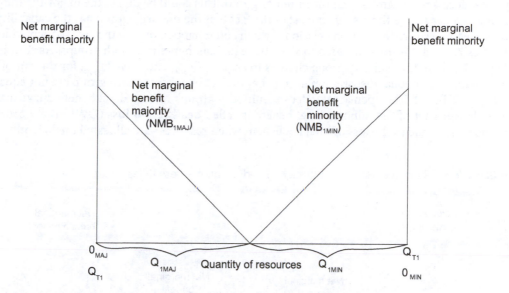

If resources are scarce, then the total quantity is less than Q_{1MAJ} plus Q_{1MIN}. This means that resources must be allocated between the two groups. The allocation of scarce resources given the net benefits in Figures 7.1 and 7.2 is shown in Figure 7.4. In this case, if the groups have equal access to resources, each group will be able to get Q_2 resources ($Q_{2MAJ} = Q_{2MIN}$) and have equal marginal net benefits of the last unit ($NB_{2MAJ} = NB_{2MIN}$). Net benefit for the majority group is the area under its net marginal benefit curve between 0_{MAJ} and Q_{2MAJ} while the net benefit for the minor group is the area under its own net marginal benefit curve between 0_{MIN} and Q_{2MIN}. Net benefit for both groups is the sum of the areas under both marginal net benefit curves.

FIGURE 7.4   Resource allocation with scarcity and equal access to resources

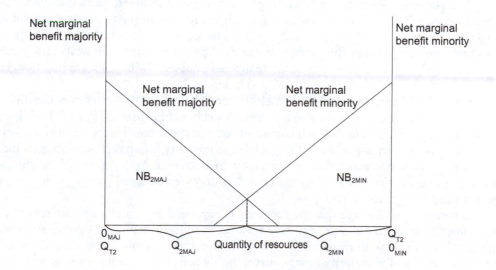

Figure 7.5 shows the allocation of the scarce resource when the majority group has greater access to resources than the minority group. This could be due to the majority group living in areas where the resources exist or the fact that the majority group has the capability to make the resource allocation decisions, which could happen during the cycle of genocide. Figures 7.1 and 7.2 are again used to show the equal net benefits of both groups. As seen in Figure 7.5, here the majority group chooses to acquire Q_{3MAJ} and leave Q_{3MIN} for the minority group. The unequal distribution means that the net benefits for each group are not equal ($NB_{3MAJ} > NB_{3MIN}$). The open area under the minority group's marginal net benefit curve that is no longer part of the minority's net benefit is called **deadweight loss** (DWL) that occurs in the market due to the loss of total net benefit when resources are allocated inefficiently.

FIGURE 7.5 Resource allocation with scarcity and unequal access to resources

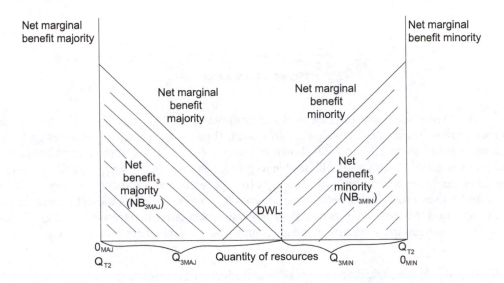

As a genocide develops, decisions by genocidaires lead to decreases in income for the minority group. This is shown in Figure 7.6 as a leftward shift in the minority group's marginal benefit curve, from MB_{1MIN} to MB_{4MIN}. In addition, genocidaires have power over the costs to the minority group. This pushes the marginal cost curve for the minority group from MC_{1MIN} to MC_{4MIN}. The resulting net marginal benefit curve (NMB_{4MIN}) is smaller than the original net marginal benefit curve (NMB_{1MIN}) in Figure 7.2.

Figure 7.7 illustrates the case in which the majority group has power over the minority group's income and costs. The majority group's net benefit is that of Figure 7.1 while the minority group's net benefit due to income and cost shocks is now Figure 7.6. The majority group now receives an allocation of Q_{4MAJ} while the minority group receives only an allocation of Q_{4MIN} due to decreased ability to pay and increased costs. As in Figure 7.5, the unequal distribution means that the net benefits of each group are not equal ($NB_{4MAJ} > NB_{4MIN}$) and there is a deadweight loss (DWL_3).

It may also be the case that the economy is experiencing scarcity of resources at the same time the genocidaires are negatively affecting the minority group's income and costs. This graph would look like Figure 7.5, but with the minority group's net marginal benefit curve smaller than the majority group's curve. In this case, the majority group would again receive a higher allocation of resources.

FIGURE 7.6   Net benefit of minority group with adverse income and cost shocks

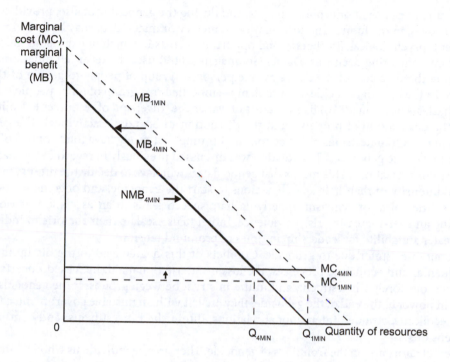

FIGURE 7.7   Resource allocation with minority group income and cost shocks

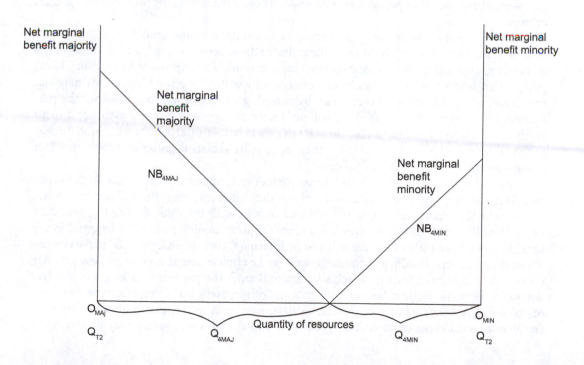

Unit 1: Costs of genocide

Each group has costs not only building up to and during the genocide but also, provided the group survives, in the future. The costs may be monetary or material, or may be freedom-of-movement, psychological, life, liberty, and opportunity costs in which one decision must be made from competing decisions. Daniel Goldhagen (2009) uses the term "eliminationism" to describe the true cost of the desire by one person or group of people to get rid of their problem. In the case of genocide, the problem is embodied in a group of other people.

Charles Anderton (2010) lists the costs of war as the "diversion of resources to military goods, the destruction of property, and the disruption of economic activities." The genocidaires make initial decisions about actions and timing, but rarely have total control of the perpetrators of the genocide. This situation was discussed previously in regard to the leaders of terrorist organizations. This means that genocidaires will have to decide the timing, methods, and intensity of their hate speech, actions to start the genocide, and ongoing genocide activities. The spiral of cynicism underlying hate speech leads to an escalation of words, producing an ever-increasing risk of violence. Individuals escalate their rhetoric to indicate their greater suitability for leadership in times of profound tension.

Economies suffer due to genocide. Conflicts of this degree lead to the disruption of governmental and economic processes, the loss of international aid, increased uncertainty that drives out foreign investment, and future mistrust between groups. If the genocidaires remain in power at the end of the genocide, they are left with an unstable government, a fluctuating economy, strained international relations, diminished investments, and continued social tensions.

Perpetrators are on the frontlines of genocide. They are the individuals who kill, injure, rape, steal from, and control the victims. The perpetrators may incur psychological costs, potential injury or death during the conflict; loss of relationships with those who oppose the genocide or certain actions of the individual; loss of their own property and freedom if the genocidaires or other perpetuators turn against them; and possible prosecution for their crimes.

Each person in the majority group may be called upon by the genocidaires and perpetrators of the genocide to join in the killing, destruction, seizures, rape, and removal of the minority group. Bystanders must make careful decisions. As is apparent in Dr. Musekura's perspective, when a person or family decides against joining the genocidaires, they may lose privileges, property, and even their lives. By choosing to do one act to help either the perpetrators or victims of genocide, they will be labeled as supporters or opponents and incur further costs. If the bystanders at some point decide to become perpetrators in the genocide, they will later be held accountable for their actions by the rival group and they may face charges in an international criminal court.

As discussed, the victims have limited choices in terms of their response to the genocide. Whether they fight back, run away, or hide, they often lose everything. They experience loss of security, health, and even life. Families may be split up while fleeing the genocide. Daniel Goldhagen (2009) describes how people's actions are determined by external forces in which they have little or no free will and by internal forces in which people make choices about their actions. Goldhagen states, "People make choices about how to act, even if they do not choose the contexts in which they make them." The perpetrators of genocide may destroy or seize the victims' houses, property, and other assets, including raw materials. Loss of culture may occur when a population is destroyed, removed from an area, or forced to conform to a different culture. Family bloodlines of the minority group may be lost when rape of women is used as a weapon of genocide. When the majority group takes power, the minority group will lose freedoms, including the freedom of movement, speech, and representation. When the genocide is over, surviving victims of a genocide must decide whether they will choose a path of peace with the majority group or further ignite intergroup hatred.

Costs to the international community of intervening in a genocide are massive. Preceding the conflict, resources often flow from the United Nations and various countries to assist in conflict resolution and humanitarian assistance. During genocide, the need for policing is added, as well as the coordination and expense of moving more people and resources to the area. John Eriksson (1996) states that the estimated cost of international assistance during the Rwandan genocide was $1.4 billion, including expenses within Rwanda and in countries in which refugees from the conflict were seeking asylum.

Unit 2: Benefits of genocide

It is difficult to imagine that there are benefits from genocide, but something must tip the scale from the cost outweighing benefit to an overall positive net benefit (benefit minus cost) in order for a genocide to happen. Much can be learned by considering 1) the possible areas of benefit related to genocide, 2) the persons who gain from instigating and committing acts of genocide, 3) the persons who benefit from not getting involved in genocide, and 4) the particular benefits received.

The Democratic Republic of the Congo (also known as the Congo or the DRC) is a nation with abundant natural resources. The Congo River is the world's second-largest river and the soil is fertile for growing crops. In addition, the land has deposits of the **conflict minerals** gold ore, coltan (used in cell phones), cassiterite (used for tin), and wolframite or tungsten (used in chemical compounds because it is strong and durable). They are called conflict minerals because it has been determined that they are being used to fund the conflict in the Congo. In addition, there are deposits of diamonds, copper, cobalt (used in aircraft engines and batteries), uranium, and oil. It is estimated that around six million people have been killed in the Congo since 1997 (Dena Montague and Frida Berrigan, 2001). The wars in the Congo have involved not only the Congolese, but also foreign armies and investors from neighboring countries. Murder, rape, and seizure of property are all being used as weapons of war to force people out of the area. The Lord's Resistance Army, a rebel group in the Congo and surrounding countries, forces children to work as soldiers and sex slaves.

There are clearly economic benefits for those who own the resources in the Congo, including the genocidaires, perpetrators of genocide, bystanders who may gain when the victims are driven out of the area, and investors with a stake in the Congo.

Genocidaires are the main beneficiaries of genocide. After the Rwandan genocide, the nation's wealth was divided among the top politicians and military leaders. Once they had control, they fought for position and possessions rather than for the rights of the people. Research by Benjamin Valentino (2004) and Sang Hoo Bae and Attiat Ott (2008) shows that the benefits leaders expect to receive motivate mass killings.

Charles Anderton (2010) researches the economic motivations behind genocide and how they are used in the decision-making processes of the perpetrators of genocide. The motives include gaining political and social power and control, eradicating the possibility of future disruption of power by the rival group, and taking territory whose ownership is being disputed by the two groups. There are four areas in which perpetrators gain benefit from committing genocide. First, they benefit financially as they gain control over money, financial systems, and commerce. Second, perpetrators gain materially as they lay hold of personal and business property, buildings, and land. Third, they gain physical power over the victims as they murder, rape, force migration, and enslave the vulnerable. Finally, the group gains psychological control over the other group by participating in activities that demean and alienate victims. Another possibility is that when the group's primary goal is to convert victims to their belief system, the genocide provides them with a way to try to force their victims to accept their beliefs and adhere to the tenets of those beliefs.

Although it may seem that being a bystander of genocide is a benign position to take, Daniel Goldhagen (2009) and Linda Wolff (n.d.) point out that the inaction of bystanders leads to increased violence and a lengthening of the genocide. Charles Anderton (2010) enumerates ways bystanders may actively or passively benefit from genocide. Bystanders may gain actively from advancement in their careers and opportunities to gain wealth from the removal or enslavement of the victims. In addition, they may benefit passively as they preserve their families' lives from violence and possibly as they see their hatred of the victims being taken out on the victims.

Unit 3: Inefficiencies in economic structure of genocide

It is still difficult to predict when a genocide will happen and how to stop an ongoing genocide. Genocides are multi-faceted and evolve as the violence continues. Linda Melvern (2005) reports, "In the three months that the genocide lasted, April–July, the killing was faster at the outset; the end of May, when the large-scale massacres were over, bore no resemblance to the coherence and systematic nature of the killings when they began."

Because genocide happens during times of civil war, it is difficult to get information and data on what is happening. The best that can be done is trying to interview people during the genocide and to taking assessments post-genocide.

Genocides are complex events that occur over time. The extend of the violence may not be known until years later, if ever. This makes it difficult to pinpoint a group of people or a geographic area to protect. In response, Jacques Semelin (2007) calls for "the creation of multidisciplinary research teams working on precise case studies."

Genocides may happen across international borders, which increases the complexity of intervention by the international community. Laws are being created post-genocide as the criminal acts of the perpetrators of genocide become known.

◼ Section 7: Case study

Rwandan genocide

There has been little theoretical research on genocide from an economic perspective and even less empirical research. However, existing research can be utilized to tie together theory and its empirical counterpart and then apply it to a particular genocide in hopes of further understanding why a genocide occurs and how it can be prevented. For the purposes of this case study, politicide (genocide instigated by a government) is included in the definition of genocide.

First, a condensed version of the game theory approach from Charles Anderton (2010) is reviewed. Second, the global empirical data from Daniel Goldsmith and his colleagues is used to analyze the data from a slightly different perspective than what was done in their published work (Daniel Goldsmith, Charles Butcher, Dimitri Semenovich, and Arcot Sowmya, 2013). Third, Anderton's game theory is applied along with Goldsmith's data to study the dynamics of the 1994 Rwandan genocide.

The purpose of analyzing the Rwandan genocide through the combined lens of Goldsmith and Anderton is to build upon the two approaches in a practical matter. Anderton's model is in the abstract and no concrete example is given of a situation in which a prescriptive route could be adopted to prevent genocide. Similarly, Goldsmith's article centers around predicting genocides a year out and contemplates preventing the genocides accordingly, but it does not establish the appropriate steps needed to achieve such prevention. This case study takes a practical look at a particular genocide event to put forth potential steps that could have been taken to prevent the genocide. The study is therefore meant to be a proxy for what steps to take when a future genocide is imminent given predictive models such as Goldsmith's.

Rwanda was chosen for this case study because of the nature of the state leading up to and igniting the genocide. Specifically, Rwanda was chosen because of the years of instability prior to the genocide, the ethnic classification of the ruling elite, and the assassination of President Juvénal Habyarimana that sparked the genocide. Furthermore, since the Rwandan genocide occurred relatively recently, the data and coverage concerning the event is easily obtainable.

Anderton's macroeconomic model lays out what conditions must be met on a macroeconomic scale for the choice of genocide by a ruling group to be a rational one. In this model, Anderton considers two risk-neutral groups (A and B) – one being the potential perpetrator (A) and one being the potential victim (B) at the outset – and takes into account their respective scarce resources (R_A and R_B) which are used in part to purchase military goods (M_A and M_B). Furthermore, the relative effectiveness of M_B compared to M_A is represented by Z. $\tilde{R}$ represents the "disputed item" at the heart of the conflict. When genocide is chosen, a portion (δ) of the disputed item is destroyed and cannot be recovered by either group. If genocide is avoided and peaceful settlement occurs, the disputed item is kept intact. If no extraneous conditions exist, peaceful settlement is likely to be the result because each group's payoff $\frac{1}{2}\delta\tilde{R}$ is greater than it would be with genocide. For the purposes of the case study, the proof behind this conclusion is not disputed and need not be repeated; however, see the cited source for the payoff schedules (Anderton, 2010).

The conditions relevant to this case study that can affect the end-game result in favor of genocide are 1) an increase in the perceived vulnerability of the perpetrating group's power due to the strength of the victim group or 2) an increase in the perception of future costs brought about by the persistence of the victim group. The first condition changes the payoffs in the model by adding the relative increase in power of the victim group (e) to the payoff of the victim group and subtracting it from the payoff of the perpetrating group when a peaceful settlement is met. The payoffs under genocide remain unchanged. Therefore, if e is either relatively large or δ is relatively small, genocide will be the rational best choice because it is chosen when $e > \dfrac{\delta}{2(1-\delta)}$ (Anderton 2010).

The second condition simply contemplates a two-period game where a choice between peaceful settlement or genocide must be made in each period. Furthermore, allocating scarce resources to military goods and the state of the disputed item are reset in the second period. Therefore, if a peaceful settlement is reached in the first period, A will still have to divert resources to M_A in the second period and will have to settle for only part of $\tilde{R}$ in both periods. On the other hand, if A chooses genocide in the first period and succeeds, then A diverts no resources to M_A in the second period and receives all of $\tilde{R}$ in the second period. However, A may fail to accomplish the genocide, at which point peaceful settlement would be best in the second period since it is the end of the game. Overall, genocide is the best option in the first period if $\delta > \dfrac{2 + Z}{2.5 + 2Z + 0.5Z^2}$. Therefore, if destructiveness from the genocide is relatively low or B's military ability is relatively quite weak, genocide is the rational best choice. Again, the proof behind this condition can be found in the article (Anderton, 2010).

Now that the framework of the theory has been laid out, real world data must be matched with it to give the theory a more practical application. Goldsmith and his colleagues utilized global genocide data from 1988 to 2003 in order to forecast the onset of future genocides. It should be noted that although they used the data predictively and were not concerned with the statistical significance of explanatory variables, the same data can be utilized for significance (Goldsmith et al., 2013). For this case study, a few significant variables are determined and then matched to Anderton's game theory. Table 7.7 represents a multiple regression with genocide as a dependent variable.

Genocide here relates only to the first instance in which a genocide episode occurs in a given state. This variable would not be affected if genocide lasted longer periods of time in one state as opposed to another. The ruling elite majority variable is a dummy variable that equals 1 if the majority ethnicity is the ruling elite in the prior year and 0 otherwise. Similarly, the ruling elite minority variable equals 1 if the minority ethnicity is the ruling elite in the prior year and 0 otherwise. Genocide is more likely to occur if the ruling elite in the year prior to the onset of genocide was of the minority ethnicity in the state. The ruling elite variables were the only variables manipulated by this case study in Goldsmith's dataset to create this study's two ruling elite variables. Instability is a dummy variable related to instability in the country in the year prior to the onset of genocide. Assassination is a dummy variable showing that the assassination of a well-known political or social figure occurred in the year of the genocide in the country.

The ruling elite variables and the assassination variable fit neatly into Anderton's first condition leading to genocide, termed here the power struggle condition. When the ruling elite is a minority, the ruling elite's power is relatively more vulnerable to opposition in the country because the opposition would likely be from the majority group. The majority group would be larger by definition and would thus be relatively strong. In contrast, when the

TABLE 7.7 Time-series regression: Genocide

Time allotment	Coefficient	p-value	95% C.I.	Adj. $R^2 = 0.016$
		Genocide		
Constant	0.0002	–	–	–
RulingEliteMajority	0.0000	0.99	-0.01–0.01	–
RulingEliteMinority	0.0196*	0.00	0.01–0.03	–
Instability	0.0170*	0.00	0.01–0.02	–
AssassinDum	0.0118*	0.00	0.004–0.020	–

*Denotes significance at 5% significance level.

ruling elite is the minority, the opposition would be smaller by definition and would then be relatively weak. The minority ruling elite then, according to Anderton, would be more likely to want to keep the majority's power at bay and retain its own power, which is achieved by choosing genocide. Similarly, assassination leads to an immediate perceived vulnerability for the group whose member has been assassinated. The variable e in Anderton's model would become much higher when an assassination occurs and therefore genocide is relatively more incentivized. Instability, on the other hand, fits into Anderton's second condition, termed here the persistence effect. The longer instability occurs consecutively, the more likely it will continue. Long-term instability leads to costs in the present and the future because instability can lead to economic downturns due to decreased investment in markets and sometimes the country's isolation from markets. Therefore, if the group that is considering genocide sees the opposing group as being the cause of long-term instability, genocide may become the rational choice as the expected time of instability increases.

This case study focuses on the 1994 genocide of the Tutsi people and Hutu sympathizers by the Hutu people. Goldsmith's data indicates that Rwanda had been in a state of instability since 1990, which was the beginning of the Rwandan Civil War between the Rwanda Defense Force (representing the government of Rwanda) and the Rwanda Patriotic Front (led by the minority group in the country). The final catalyst for the genocide was the assassination of President Habyarimana. The government at the time of the genocide was run by the Hutu, the ethnic majority. President Habyarimana had been planning to bring the Rwanda Patriotic Front into the government in accordance with a peace deal (Raymond Bonner, 1994).

Although the ruling elite at the onset of the genocide was part of the majority group, the analysis of the ruling elites' ethnicity is still relevant as a product of the peace deal. According to the peace deal, the minority group was going to be integrated into the ruling elite, leading to a clear perceived vulnerability in the power of the ruling elite majority. Therefore, according to Anderton's model, e would be relatively high here, which would incentivize the ruling elite to choose genocide as a solution in order to retain power. For this variable, genocide could have potentially been thwarted by a modified peace deal – specifically, a peace deal leaving the majority in charge but still rewarding the opposing faction in a way that did not diminish the ruling group's power could have decreased the incentive of genocide. In Anderton's model, this modified peace deal would have led to a much lower e making $e < \dfrac{\delta}{2(1-\delta)}$ and thus preventing genocide.

The assassination of Habyarimana would seem to be straightforward in that, in theory and in reality, it would threaten the power of the ruling elite, which would also lead to an increased incentive for genocide. What makes this assassination peculiar is that at the time of the attack, it was not clear which group was responsible for it. It was unclear whether the attack was perpetrated by Hutu extremists (in an attempt to provoke genocide and prevent the combining of the governments), by the Rwanda Patriotic Front, or even by a foreign group (Bonner, 1994). However, the true perpetrator is irrelevant for Anderton's model because all that matters is that the power of the ruling group be "perceived" as vulnerable. This perception is particularly hard to prevent because one does not know when an assassination will take place until it occurs, whereas it is easier to grasp that there is a ruling elite or that there has been prolonged instability in the area. However, knowing the potential genocidal consequences of an assassination, outside groups can immediately react and send in peacekeeping support in order to be proactive when an assassination occurs. This is not always a feasible solution but it may be the best solution given the potential consequences of assassinations.

Instability as a result of civil war generates the perception of increased future costs, thus incentivizing genocide in the near term to prevent destruction in the future. This variable is interesting for Rwanda because of the peace deal. One may think that the peace deal would have prevented the future costs because it would have corrected the instability. However, as Anderton's model shows, peaceful settlement can still fail and lead to a future choice between peaceful settlement and genocide. If successful, genocide can surely prevent a second round of decision-making. To avert the genocide, outside countries may need to focus more heavily on the countries that are experiencing ongoing civil war with the understanding that as the conflicts continue, genocide is more likely to occur. Specifically, the model shows that it may be in the best interest of the victimized group for outside countries to actually bolster the perpetrating party in hopes of giving the perpetrating party security from power vulnerability and increasing the perpetrating party's hope for a quick and relatively permanent resolution that does not include genocide.

The limitations of the applicability of this case study are forecasting abilities, scarce international resources to monitor and combat genocide, and the number of potential factors leading to genocide. First, while Goldsmith's model can predict genocide with a high level of accuracy, it can only forecast for one year into the future. Second, in order for outside countries to intervene and prevent atrocities such as genocide, there must be adequate resources, including military goods and manpower. Lastly, as can be seen by the adjusted R^2 of 0.016 in the multiple regression above, the variables discussed here are only a small part of the significant variables related to genocide. It is possible for these variables to be absent and genocide to still occur. The high amount of variation in genocide makes it more difficult to predict and correct than other phenomena.

There have been efforts to predict and warn about genocide. Among the most important and recent efforts is the Early Warning Project (2018) initiated by experts at the U.S. Holocaust Memorial Museum and Dartmouth College. They provide the following description of their methodology:

> Our system analyzed over 50 years of historical data and dissected the conditions present prior to mass atrocities. We use that historical base to recognize contemporary warning signs in countries around the world and to rank those most at risk.

The Early Warning Project uses two complementary methods: 1) A statistical risk assessment to calculate the tendency of a nation to commit mass atrocities "based on current measures of economic and political instability as well as forecasts of future coup attempts and civil wars" and 2) an expert opinion poll that "comprises regional and subject matter experts who respond to specific questions about dynamic events and about countries that may be identified through the statistical risk assessment." The goals of the project are to prevent atrocities and engender "early and effective response."

This project has for several years now constituted one of the most stable statistical determinations of genocide risks. As noted previously, experts currently rate 30 of the nearly 200 nations in the world as having significant genocide risks. Recent cases such as Burma and Burundi are publicized by prominent organizations such as the U.S. Holocaust Memorial Museum to help enable concerned citizens and empowered decision-makers to arrest and reverse the social processes leading to genocide. There are some substantial indicators of success with this project as genocide appears to be in decline over the past 50 years, as shown in Figure 7.8. The recent uptick seen in this data is on the decline as ISIS, one of the most genocidal organizations in the world, is losing its sovereign control over approximately seven million people living in regions of Iraq and Syria.

FIGURE 7.8   Prevalence of mass killings 1945–2013

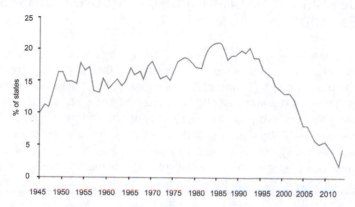

Source: Ulfelder, Jay. (2015, January 1). Trends over time in state-led mass killing through 2014. Early Warning Project. Retrieved from http://cpgearlywarning.wordpress.com. Ulfelder, Jay and Valenatino, Benjamin, "Assessing Risks of State-Sponsored Mass killing" (2008, 1 February). Available at SSRN: http://ssrn/com/abstract=1703426 or http://dx.doi.org/10.2139/ssrn. 17034426

Section 8: Recommendations for future research

Since individuals must make choices in genocide, economics (the study of choice when dealing with scarcity) provides a foundation to determine what benefits and costs are faced by each of the groups involved. Knowing this information allows for the creation of an incentives structure that can be used to decrease the frequency and severity of genocides.

There is no shortage of research that needs to be done in the area of genocides. It is important to understand the motives and actions of the genocidaires, perpetrators, bystanders, the international community, and the victims of genocide. The implications of policy-making and government actions illustrate the potency of decision-making leading to genocide and the role of policy in eliminating discrimination and persecution.

Economics always plays a role in genocide. Francis Stewart (2011) says there is evidence of economic inequalities leading to genocide, but little research has been conducted to provide the proof. There is some evidence of reallocation of resources due to genocide. Research in this area would require information relating to the reallocation of resources during genocide and during other types of conflict.

It is important to understand how a government or majority group's monopoly power plays a part in genocide. A government has control of law-making, law enforcement, the criminal justice system, and most of the resources within its border. Genocidaire governments use these resources against a minority population. The political science and sociology concept of **state monopoly on violence** means that the government "claims the monopoly of the legitimate use of physical force within a given territory" (Max Weber, 2004).

Genocidaires actively work to gain a monopoly on power so that genocides can begin and continue. However, with genocide comes a disruption to the economy and the destruction of resources (Charles Anderton, 2010). There is little research to show the actual costs of genocide to the area, the country, the targeted population, and the international community.

Genocides end, but it is unclear why they end. Determining these factors could lead to quicker ends to genocidal actions and decreased damage from genocide.

CHECK YOURSELF BOX: CHANGES TO PERSONAL BIASES ABOUT GENOCIDE

You have read about the way a genocide develops, the legal agreements surrounding the issues, and the participants and their motives for involvement. What are your current thoughts on genocide? Do you see it as an issue that cannot be solved or an issue that needs to be addressed in a number of different ways? What do you view as the primary causes of genocide? Write down your current biases on the issue of genocide and the different actors. How have your biases changed from what you initially wrote in the first check yourself box? Did you gain new biases? Because genocide involves an intricate system of benefits and costs, your research as an economist is vital to finding solutions and creating effective policy. Knowing your biases helps to remove them from the equation so that you can research and write scientifically.

■ Section 9: Bibliography

Anderton, Charles. (2010). Choosing genocide: Economic perspectives on the disturbing rationality of race murder. *Defense and Peace Economics, 21,* 459–86.

Bae, Sang Hoo and Ott, Attiat. (2008). Predatory behavior of governments: The case of mass killing. *Defense and Peace Economics, 19*(2), 107–25.

Bassiouni, Cherif and Manikas, Peter. (1996). *The law of the International Criminal Tribunal for the former Yugoslavia.* New York City, NY: Transnational Publishers.

Bauer, Yehuda. (2006). On the Holocaust and other genocides. Joseph and Rebecca Meyerhoff Annual Lecture, October 5, 2006.

Bloxham, Donald. (2009). The final solution: A genocide. *Journal of Genocide Research, 13*(1–2), March-June 2011, 107–52.

Bonner, Raymond. (November 12, 1994). Unsolved Rwanda mystery: The president's plane crash. *The New York Times.* Retrieved from http://www.nytimes.com/1994/11/12/world/unsolved-rwanda-mystery-the-president-s-plane-crash.html

Cherokee Nation Cultural Resource Center. (2018). *A brief history of the Trail of Tears.* Retrieved from http://www.cherokee.org/About-The-Nation/History/Trail-of-Tears/A-Brief-History-of-the-Trail-of-Tears

Dadrian, Vahakn. (1975). A typology of genocide. *International Review of Modern Sociology, 5,* 201–12.

Dadrian, Vahakn. (1991). Review of *The history and sociology of genocide. Contemporary Sociology, 20*(2), 218–9.

Dieng, Adama. (2015, September 14). *United Nations Special Adviser on the Prevention of Genocide welcomes the adoption of the International Day of Commemoration and Dignity of the Victims of the Crime of Genocide and of the Prevention of this Crime.* Retrieved from http://www.un.org/en/genocideprevention/documents/media/statements/2015/English/2015-09-14_International%20Day%20Victims%20of%20Genocide_English.pdf

Eriksson, John. (1996). *The international response to conflict and genocide: Lessons from the Rwanda experience: Synthesis report*. OECD Joint Evaluation of Emergency Assistance to Rwanda. Retrieved from https://www.oecd.org/countries/rwanda/50189495.pdf

Fein, Helen. (1979). *Accounting for genocide: National responses and Jewish victimization during the Holocaust*. New York City, NY: Free Press.

Fein, Helen. (1993a). Accounting for genocide after 1945: Theories and some findings. *International Journal on Group Rights, 1*(2), 79–106.

Fein, Helen. (1993b). *Genocide: A sociological perspective*. London: Sage Publications.

Fisanick, Christina (Ed.). (2004). *Rwanda genocide: At issue in history*. Farmington Hills, MI: Greenhaven Press, 12.

Gallately, Robert and Kiernan, Ben (Eds.). (2003). *The spector of genocide: Mass murder in historical perspective*. Cambridge: Cambridge University Press.

Gilmore, Betty. (April 2017). *Going to Rwanda to train security forces in dispute resolution*. Southern Methodist University website. Retrieved from https://www.smu.edu/News/2017/betty-gilmore-rwanda-18april2017

Goldhagen, Daniel. (2009). *Worse than war: Genocide, elimination-ism, and the ongoing assault on humanity*. New York City, NY: Public Affairs.

Goldsmith, Benjamin; Butcher, Charles; Semenovich, Dimitri; and Sowmya, Arcot. (2013). Forecasting the onset of genocide and politicide: Annual out-of sample forecasts on a global dataset, 1988–2003. *Journal of Peace Research, 50*(4), 437–52.

Grunfeld, Fred. (2000). The role of the bystanders in human rights violations. In Fons Coomans; Fred Grunfeld; Ingrid Westendorp; and Jan Willems (Eds.), *Rendering justice to the vulnerable: Liber Amicorum in honor of Theo van Boven*. Leiden, Netherlands: Martinus Nijhoff Publishers, 131–43.

Handwerk, Brian. (January 20, 2016). Smithsonian.com. Retrieved from https://www.smithsonianmag.com/science-nature/ancient-brutal-massacre-may-be-earliest-evidence-war-180957884

Harff, Barbara. (2003). No lessons learned from the Holocaust? Assessing risks of genocide and political mass murder since 1955. *American Political Science Review, 97*(1), February 2003, 57–73.

Jacob Blaustein Institute for the Advancement of Human Rights. (2015, December 8). *JBI calls for combating religious repression worldwide*. Retrieved from http://www.jbi-humanrights.org/jacob-blaustein-institute/religion

Jonassohn, Kurt and Chalk, Frank. (1987). A typology of genocide and some implications for the human rights agenda. In Isidor Walliman and Michael Dobkowski (Eds.), *Genocide and the modern age: Etiology and case studies of mass death*. New York City, NY: Greenwood Press, 3–20.

Jones, Adam. (2006). *Genocide: A comprehensive introduction*. London: Routledge.

Ki-moon, Ban. (2014). United Secretary-General, Remarks at the commemoration of the 20th anniversary of the Rwandan Genocide (April 7, 2014). Retrieved from https://www.un.org/sg/en/content/sg/statement/2014-04-07/remarks-commemoration-20th-anniversary-rwandan-genocide-english-and

Kiernan, Ben. (2004). The first genocide: Carthage, 146 BC. *Diogenes, 203*, 27–39.

Kuper, Leo. (1981). *Genocide: Its political use in the twentieth century*. New Haven: Yale University Press.

Leander, Sebastian. (2012). Structural violence and conflict: Vertical and horizontal inequity in post-genocide Rwanda. In Frances Stewart; Rajesh Venugopal; and Arnim Langer (Eds.), *Horizontal inequities and post-conflict development*. London: Palgrave Macmillan, 230–48.

Lemkin, Raphael. (1944). *Axis rule in occupied Europe: Laws of occupation, analysis of government, proposals for redress*. Clark, NJ: The Lawbook Exchange, Ltd.

McCauley, Clark and Chirot, Daniel. (2006). *Why not kill them all? The logic and prevention of mass political murder*. Princeton, NJ: Princeton University Press.

McDoom, Omar Shahabudin. (2013). Who killed in Rwanda's genocide? Micro-space, social influence and individual participation in intergroup violence. *Journal of Peace Research, 50*, 453–67.

Melvern, Linda. (November 2005). Review of Fisanick, Christina (Ed.), The Rwanda genocide: At issue in history. H-Genocide on H-Net Reviews. Retrieved from https://networks.h-net.org/node/3180/reviews/6280/melvern-fisanick-rwanda-genocide-issue-history

Montague, Dena and Berrigan, Frida. (2001). The business of war in the Democratic Republic of Congo: Who benefits? *Dollars and Sense*, July/August 2001.

Pillay, Navi. (2014). Opening remarks at the 25th session of the Human Rights Council: High level panel discussion dedicated to the sixty-fifth anniversary of the Convention on the Prevention and Punishment of the Crime of Genocide, March 7, 2014. Retrieved from https://www.ohchr.org/en/NewsEvents/Pages/DisplayNews.aspx?NewsID=14339&LangID=E

Pinker, Stephen. (2007). A history of violence. *Edge: The Third Culture*. Retrieved from http://www.edge.org/3rd_culture/pinker07/pinker07_index.html

Porter, Jack. (1982). *Genocide and human rights: A global anthology*. Lanham, MD: University Press of America.

Power, Samantha. (2013). *A problem from hell: America and the age of genocide*. New York City, NY: Harper Perennial.

Rosling, Hans. (2010). *200 Countries in 200 years*. BBC video. Retrieved from https://www.youtube.com/watch?v=jbkSRLYSojo

Savon, Herve. (1972). *Du cannibalisme au genocide*. Paris: Hachette Litterature.

Scholten, Andrew. (2016). *International law aspects of forced deportations and expulsions*. Malaga, Spain: Congress on Urban Issues. Retrieved from https://www.aacademica.org/andrew.scholten/9.pdf

Semelin, Jacques. (2007). *Purify and destroy: The political uses of massacre and genocide*. New York City, NY: Columbia University Press.

Smith, Roger. (1987). Human destructiveness and politics: The twentieth century as an age of genocide. In Isidor Walliman Michael Dobkowski (Eds.), *Genocide and the modern age: Etiology and case studies of mass death*. New York City, NY: Greenwood Press, 21–40.

Stanton, Gregory. (1996). *The 10 stages of genocide*. Genocide Watch. Retrieved from http://www.genocidewatch.com/ten-stages-of-genocide.

Staub, Ervin. (1989). *The roots of evil: The origins of genocide and the other group violence*. Cambridge, England: Cambridge University Press.

Stewart, Frances. (2011). Economic and political causes of genocidal violence: A comparison with findings on the causes of civil war. *MICROCON Research Working Paper, 46*, Brighton: MICROCON.

Totten, Samuel and Parsons, William. (2012). *Century of genocide: Critical essays and eyewitness accounts* (4th ed.). Abingdon, England: Routledge.

United Nations Department of Peacekeeping Operations (UN DPKO). (2009). *United Nations criminal justice standards for United Nations police.* New York: United Nations, 15. Retrieved from http://www.unodc.org/documents/justice-and-prison-reform/08-58900_Ebook.pdf

United Nations General Assembly. (1946). *The crime of genocide,* G.A. Res 96 (1), UN Doc A/RSS/96 (I) (December 11, 1946).

United States Holocaust Memorial Museum. (2018). *Early warning project.* Retrieved from https://www.ushmm.org/wlc/en/article.php?ModuleId=10007095

Valentino, Benjamin. (2004). *Final solutions: Mass killing and genocide in the 20th century.* Ithaca, NY: Cornell University Press.

Voth, Ben. (2014). *The rhetoric of genocide: Death as a text.* Lanham, Maryland: Lexington Books.

Voth, Ben. (2016). President Bush's rhetoric and policy against genocide. In M. Bose and P. Fritz (Eds.), *George W. Bush Presidency, Volume III.* New York City, NY: Nova Science Publishers, chapter 12.

Weber, Max. (2004). *The vocational lectures: Science as a vocation/politics as a vocation.* Indianapolis: Hackett Publishing Company, Inc.

Weitz, Eric. (2015). *A century of genocide: Utopias of race and nations.* Princeton, NJ: Princeton University Press.

Wiesel, Elie. (1986). Foreword. In Carol Rittmer and Sondra Myers (Eds.), *The courage to care.* New York City, NY: New York University Press.

Woolf, Linda. (n.d.). *Genocide, mass violence, and human rights: A path to internationalizing the psychology curriculum and promoting social responsibility.* Retrieved from http://faculty.webster.edu/woolflm/flohandout.html

◼ Section 10: Resources

Unit 1: Summary

Genocides are currently happening in multiple areas of the world and may be perpetrated for a number of overlapping reasons. There are behavioral characteristics that provide some forecasting capability, but it is impossible to know with full accuracy when and where genocide will occur. Genocidaires, perpetrators, bystanders, the international community, and victims of genocide all play roles in the perpetration, actions, and outcomes of genocide. There are both costs and benefits of genocide to different groups. Past qualitative and quantitative research on genocide provides the foundation for future research.

Unit 2: Key concepts

Atrocity: A shockingly cruel act of violence.

Biological subjugation: The enslavement of people for the purpose of preventing the reproduction of biological families.

Bystanders: Persons who do not engage in actions of the genocide, but also do not actively work to prevent the genocide or to safeguard the victims of genocide.

......es against humanity: Actions committed as part of a known, systematic attack against a civilian population.

Crimes against peace: Crimes involving conspiring towards, planning, preparing for, initiating, or waging a war or a war that violates international agreements.

Deadweight loss: The loss of total net benefit resulting from an allocation of a scarce resource at a point where the marginal net benefits for each group are unequal.

Economic subjugation: The enslavement of people through the restriction of earning of income, involvement in economic transaction, access to markets, and avenues of savings.

Economics: The study of choice when dealing with scarcity.

Eliminationism: The belief or policy that a group should be forced out of an area or killed (Goldhagen, 2009).

Ethnic cleansing/population cleansing: Targeting a group of people for the inducement of fear of removal or actual removal from an area through violence in order to create an ethnically homogeneous population (Bassiouni and Manikas, 1996).

Forced deportation/forced population transfer/forced migration: The removal of people from one country to another and from one area within a country to another area against the will of those persons.

Genocidaires: The decision-makers who are the leaders in planning genocide, preparing the propaganda, assembling necessary resources, and determining the timing of the atrocity.

Genocide: As stated by the United Nations (1946), genocide is "killing members of a group; causing serious bodily or mental harm to members of a group; deliberately inflicting on the group conditions of life calculated to bring about its physical destruction in whole or in part; imposing measures intended to prevent births within the group; and forcibly transferring children of the group to another group."

Holocaust: The complete annihilation of all members of a group (Bauer, 2006).

Human rights law: The body of law that protects a person's basic human rights.

International community: The group of countries, governments, businesses, and organizations that make decisions about when and how to intervene in a genocide.

International humanitarian law: Law which governs behavior during war.

Marginal benefit (MB): The benefit of each additional unit of a resource. It is equal to the person or group's total willingness to pay for resources.

Marginal cost (MC): The cost of each additional unit of a resource.

Mass murder: According to the U.S. Federal Bureau of Investigation (FBI), mass murder is the act of killing four or more people in a limited amount of time and in a specific geographic area.

Net benefit: The sum of all of benefits minus all costs. Negative net benefit is possible.

Net marginal benefit (NMB): The sum of marginal benefit minus marginal cost for each additional unit.

Perpetrators: Individuals who do the actions that constitute genocide.

Scarcity: Not having enough resources to fulfill all wants and needs.

State monopoly on violence: A public law term that means the government "claims the monopoly of the legitimate use of physical force within a given territory" (Weber, 2004).

Systematic rape: The targeting of victims for rape as a weapon of war.

War crimes: Actions that violate the laws or customs of war, including the brutal treatment of civilians and the destruction of property.

Unit 3: Review questions

1. How is genocide different from holocaust?

2. What are the different roles that people play in a genocide?

3. Name some of the actions and atrocities that are committed during a genocide.

4. What are some of the types of genocide?

5. What are the five principle forms of eliminationism according to Daniel Goldhagen (2009)?

6. Describe the ten developmental stages of genocide as described by Gregory Stanton (1996).

7. What are some of the U.S. laws related to genocide?

8. What are some of the international laws related to genocide?

9. How are crimes of humanity different than crimes of peace?

10. How is human rights law different than international humanitarian law?

11. Name some of the experts on genocide.

12. Who are the decision-makers in genocide?

13. Who benefits from genocide? How do they benefit?

14. What are the costs of genocide? To whom do these costs accrue?

Unit 4: Recommended readings

Anderton, Charles and Brauer, Jurgen (Eds.). (2016). *Economic aspects of genocides, other mass Atrocities, and their prevention.* New York: Oxford University Press.

Goldhagen, Daniel Jonah. (2009). *Worse than war: Genocide, eliminationism, and the ongoing assault on humanity.* London: Little Brown.

Kiernan, Ben. (2007). *Blood and soil: A world history of genocide and extermination from Sparta to Darfur.* New Haven: Yale University Press.

Power, Samantha. (2002). *A problem from hell: America and the age of genocide.* New York: Harper Perennial.

Schabas, William. (2009). *Genocide in international law: The crime of crimes.* Cambridge: Cambridge University Press.

Totten, Samuel and Feinberg, Stephen (Eds.). (2016). *Essentials of holocaust education: Fundamental issues and approaches.* New York: Routledge.

Voth, Ben. (2014). *The rhetoric of genocide: Death as a text.* London: Lexington Books.

8

Economics of hate

■ Section 1: Introduction to the economics of hate

In 2018, a student took a taxi to his high school in the United States and used his legally-purchased semiautomatic AR-15 rifle to kill 17 people. Tempers are flaring around the country as people blame the National Rifle Association (NRA) for lack of gun control, the U.S. Federal Bureau of Investigation (FBI) for failure to follow procedure, U.S. Congress for doing too much investigating and not enough legislating to address problems, parents for lack of discipline in the home, video game manufacturers for making violence acceptable, and society for lack of moral values and not addressing mental health problems. In 2016, at a time when the media in the United States was centered on the deaths of black men who were killed by white police officers, a black gunman showed his outrage by killing several police officers who were protecting the participants of a Black Lives Matter demonstration in downtown Dallas, Texas. Issues of hate are at the forefront of the social agenda in the United States and around the world.

The *Merriam-Webster Collegiate Dictionary* (2004) defines **hate** as "intense hostility and aversion usually derived from fear, anger, or sense of injury." Researchers Semir Zeki and John Paul Romaya (2008) find distinct activity in the brain associated with hate, which starts out as an internal mental and physical response to an outside stimulus, in such forms as thoughts and tightening of muscles. Hate can escalate into words (spoken or written, private or public, self-ascribed or anonymous) or depictions (hand signals, body language, graffiti, or pictures). When intensified past this point, hate becomes actions, such as physical attack, murder, rape, and destruction.

Each of the topics of human rights violations covered in this textbook has an element of hate, whether from fear, racism, sexism, homophobia, religious fervor, politics, or past experiences. For example, there are some people who believe that persons convicted of capital punishment are "undeserving of life" and that asylum seekers are "not worthy of help." Hate can develop into violence against women or child abuse in a number of ways, including rape and different forms of abuse and bullying, both physical and psychological. Terrorists and genocidaires use ideology and propaganda to incite feelings of hatred and the use of violence against targeted adversaries. Because hate is at the root of human rights violations, the final chapter of this textbook focuses on the economics of hate. The economic theory of discrimination is used to analyze hate-motivated words and actions.

Unit 1: Race perspective

Earl McClellan, pastor

Earl McClellan is a dynamic communicator who is passionate about developing leaders committed to making it "On Earth as it is in Heaven" inside and outside the walls of the local church. He is the founder and lead pastor of Shoreline City Church based in Dallas, Texas and with locations emerging around the world. Under his engaging leadership and "come as you are" teaching style, Shoreline City has grown from 15 people to almost 4,000 in just six short years. With a degree in theology from Oral Roberts University, Earl has been in pastoral ministry for over 20 years in areas including (but not limited to) collegiate ministry, overseas ministry, and ministry in the local church. Pastor Earl and his wife Oneka both have a heart for adoption, as two of their three children are adopted. Earl played basketball for Bill Self (current head coach at the University of Kansas) at Oral Roberts University. Earl feels called to break racial stereotypes for Sunday morning church by leading an ethnically-diverse church congregation. He speaks at conferences around the world and believes in service to others.

I've never been called nigger: At least not to my face. But my parents and grandparents and great-grandparents had this hate-filled word shouted at them on multiple occasions. I was born in the late seventies, so my generation is the one of Michael Jordan, Troy Aikman, Saved by the Bell, and the original 90210. Though I grew up in an inner city tormented by drugs, dropouts, prostitution, and alcohol, I went to a very prestigious high school on the other side of town. Though I was one of a handful of minorities, my high school peers (many Jewish and most rich, by my standards) were all incredibly welcoming. I was on student council every year and even became school president. My peers and friends celebrated me as the first black president of our school, though I believe there was one more before me. Because of my mother's prayers, my friends' acceptance, and the faith I had in God, I had dreams of being president of the United States and an astronaut.

My world was always full of color, but as I got older it became even more obvious my world was not everyone's world. It became clear to me that people tend to stay with "their own kind." It became clear to me that it was possible for some of my affluent, white friends to never have a black, Indian, or Asian doctor, leader, or professor if they stayed in a certain bubble. But for me, as a black man, if I wanted to move forward in life, I would probably have to understand, interact, work for, and learn from an Anglo at some point. How I saw the world and how many of my friends saw the world was different. I wasn't right and they weren't wrong; it was just a reality.

When you are a minority (or a majority) that feels as though you have been marginalized, looked down upon, looked over and beaten. . . When you hear from those who have gone before you of lynching, burnings, and thrown bricks, an angst can build in your soul.

The U.S. FBI (2017) defines a hate crime as a "criminal offense against a person or property motivated in whole or in part by an offender's bias against a race, religion, disability, sexual orientation, ethnicity, gender or gender identity." This branch of the federal government was tasked with handling hate crime in the sixties when it became clear people were committing this type of crime. While the motivation of some crimes is that a person is hungry or simply angry, other crimes are committed because an individual or a group of people has a disdain and hate toward another group of people: The Crusades, the Holocaust, the Rwandan genocide, and the Al-Anfal campaign against the Kurds are some examples.

It is my personal belief that hate crimes are an affront to the *Imago Dei*, that is, the image of God. Whenever a person sees another human being as less than human, a space is created for the worst possible acts. Sometimes it's just verbal assaults, but these verbal assaults can escalate into demeaning and sometimes deadly actions.

My wife and I, married for 20 years, have two African American sons and a daughter of Hispanic and Anglo descent. I don't know what people think of us as we walk through the mall or play in the park. Most times we get very kind remarks on the beauty of our family. Very rarely do we receive awkward stares. But my being a six-foot-two-inch-195-pound black man walking beside my beautiful porcelain-skinned daughter can make people look with perplexity. Their eyes say it all: "How did they end up together?" We live in a country and a world with a sad history of taking such a small question and distorting it into something very right or so very wrong. On the right side, the moral side, the love your neighbor side, we see a world full of open arms, care, compassion, kindness, and acceptance. On the wrong side, we see a world of hate, us versus them, division, and manipulation. That is why my antidote for such tendencies is never to look to the ever-changing culture. My antidote is based on an unwavering, unshakable truth found in the Eternal Creator of all things. This truth is clearly articulated in the first chapter of Genesis: "So God created man his own image, in the image of God he created him; male and female he created them." May this be the mirror into which all humanity sets its gaze. May the truth of it empower us to love our neighbor as we love ourselves. The *Imago Dei* is our hope. Hate is an evil counterfeit.

Unit 2: Law enforcement perspective

Dan Russell, North Texas police officer

Daniel Russell is a veteran law enforcement officer with over a decade of experience. He has worked as both a deputy sheriff in rural Washington State and as a police officer at a large municipal agency in north Texas. Daniel spent his career dedicated to active operations, patrol service, as a school resource officer, as a member of an anti-crime team, and as a field train-ing officer. He has instructed police officers in the United States and Africa, and frequently serves as a subject matter expert in areas such as conflict resolution, mindfulness, and writ-ten and verbal communitarian (connecting individuals and the community) at area police academies and the Caruth Police Institute. He holds two undergraduate degrees from Central Washington University and a master of arts in dispute resolution from Southern Methodist University. His passions include teaching and instructing, helping to develop best-practice programming and procedures, writing lengthy social media posts, physical fitness, and taking adventurous road trips around America with his wife, Allison, and two dogs, golden retriever Brisbane and chocolate lab Jaxon Pontchartrain.

I felt his spit land on my face. It came out as a fine mist, more incidental than inten-tional. His saliva splattered my eyelids, my cheeks, and some got in my mouth. I blinked reflexively, disgusted and disturbed at the unwanted contact with the bodily fluids of a com-plete stranger. I had to resist the impulse to reach up and wipe the spittle from my face.

"DON'T YOU FUCKING TOUCH ME, YOU FILTHY MURDERING PIG."

His anger at my physical contact was plainly displayed. His face was purple with rage, his eyes wide and furious. More spittle flew from his mouth as he continued to scream at me at the top of his lungs, shocked and offended by my physical contact as I gently touched him on the shoulder and calmly said, "Move back sir, we have to clear the freeway for your safety. Step back, please." In reply to his rage and angry shouts, I responded with a calm demeanor and firm directives. But inside, I was seething.

It was November 25, 2014. I was standing in the middle of the freeway on Interstate 35E using my body, clad in the much-hated blue uniform of a Dallas police officer, to block traffic for an angry crowd that had marched up onto the middle of the freeway to express their displeasure at the outcome of a Grand Jury hearing in a little town that until recently no one had ever heard of called Ferguson, Missouri.

In response to shielding the hundreds of protestors with my body, willingly placing my life in the hands of a bunch of anonymous drivers traveling at over 60 miles per hour in one-ton cars, I was being called a filthy murdering pig. I was standing in such close proximity to the protestors as we tried to coax them off the roadway as to have the spittle of an anonymous hipster purple with rage land upon me, shocking me with the disrespect towards not just my duties and the service I was currently performing – protecting him from himself – but also the violation of my own humanity. I didn't arrest that young man that night, but I will never forget his face.

During my decade in law enforcement, I touched and affected many lives, saved a few – and took exactly one. I held weeping mothers in my arms as I told them their children were dead. I pleaded with suspects to comply so that their lives could be saved. To protect the innocent, I chased perpetrators through open fields, across city streets, and into wooded areas so dense in vegetation that the flesh has been ripped from my arms and face. I spilled my own blood on the streets. I shed tears in the quiet of my squad car where no one could see. I woke with nightmares from lives I could not save, the sheets soaked with my sweat as my wife tried to calm me down. I raged against the injustices of the world I saw every time I cleared the station and headed out to patrol. I responded to attacks on the public, whether from jilted lovers, nefarious gangsters, domestic terrorists, or somebody who just had a really bad day and decided it was time for someone to die. I felt the fear of mortal peril running towards the sounds of gunfire, my sidearm in my hand and determination in my heart. Too many times, I heard the screams on the radio, "SHOTS FIRED, OFFICER DOWN!" That is what I signed up for.

But what I didn't expect, what I didn't sign up for, and what I could never know until the day it happened, is what it would feel like to be the subject of a crazed man with a gun's ire and focused intent: To kill as many police officers as possible. This has happened multiple times so far in my career.

On a busy street, a gunman dies after agreeing to turn himself in for beating his girlfriend to death. It was in the news for one day, then the world forgot. But I will never forget.

On a busy street, a gunman in an armored car who was angry at the world and the police for his previous arrests attacked police headquarters, shot hundreds of rounds and left behind bombs, one of which exploded in the officers' personal parking lot. The world watched for a short time, then forgot. But I will never forget.

On a busy street, a body-armored gunman with an assault rifle who was angry at the police for the recent high-profile deaths of black men elsewhere in the country murdered five of my brothers in blue and shot nine other officers, their blood staining the streets of downtown Dallas, Texas as we rushed to recover them, protect them, and end the threat to the public. The world watched as we mourned, as we buried our dead and celebrated their lives and service. But eventually, the camera trucks left and life returned to some level of normal. But I will never forget.

On the freeway, the hipster who was so angry and screamed so forcefully that night didn't know me. He had never seen me before, and likely never will again. His rage was not directed at me, the human inhabiting my uniform with the corporal stripes on the sleeve and the badge on the chest, but at the uniform itself.

Every time I put my blue uniform on, Velcro body armor to my chest, strap my duty belt to my waist, lock my pistol in its holster and go out to do the good work of serving and protecting the community, my humanity is reduced to the color of clothing I'm wearing and the black and white squad car I'm driving. I'm no longer a husband, a son, a lover of dogs, an aficionado of the outdoors or any of the other things that make me who I am. I am no longer the sum of my experiences, desires, hopes, and dreams. I am a police officer. A target. A punchline. A pig. I am subject to being assaulted, ridiculed, screamed at, spat upon, or murdered – simply because I am out there to serve. To serve *you*. And I will not quit, because you are worth it.

Section 2: Fundamentals of hate

Important hate terms

To understand, discuss, and research hate, students of economics need to agree upon the definitions of hate-related terms. These terms include descriptors of hate and the emotions and circumstances leading up to hate-induced words and actions. As stated before, **hate** is an "intense hostility and aversion usually derived from fear, anger, or sense of injury" (Merriam-Webster, 2004). Hate appears on the continuum of emotions from positive (good-will and fairness) to negative (hate and prejudice). The spectra are based on **bias**, which is a strong inclination or preconceived opinion toward or against a person, thing, idea, or feeling. A person may show bias by being fond of the color orange or disliking spaghetti. As seen in the overview of national agreements, there is no law in the United States against thinking or speaking in a biased way. In fact, the First Amendment secures the rights of individuals to freedom of speech. Law applies to bias when the bias becomes so strong that actions based upon that bias are determined to be especially harmful to others in the form of hate crimes.

Discrimination is the treatment of people, things, ideas, or feelings toward which the person is negatively biased. A person may discriminate against another person based on their specific characteristics, such as race, skin color, national origin, religious beliefs, disability, gender, age, sexual orientation, gender identity, or the status of a person in terms of things such as being married or pregnant, or being a military veteran or a police officer. **Nepotism** is treating a person or group of people more favorably than another person or group based on specific characteristics. Here, bias has turned into action. Both discrimination and nepotism are actions. As described in the national and international agreement sections, there are laws against discrimination in the workplace, place of education, medical treatment facilities, and other places in which people find themselves.

To analyze discrimination and nepotism, a point of reference is needed in which there is neither a positive or negative bias. From this point, bias can be determined by how one person or group is treated relative to the other. One person or group may be treated worse than another (discrimination), or one person or group may be treated preferentially (nepotism). It does not work to study two groups of people and consider both discrimination and nepotism at the same time as this is double-counting of the difference in treatment of the two persons or groups.

A person or group may experience discrimination through being granted lower wages, educational opportunities, promotional prospects, living arrangements, and levels of medical care. **Harassment** is discrimination in the form of distressing language or jokes or unwanted physical contact which creates a hostile environment for living and working.

A **hate crime** (or **bias-motivated crime**) is a traditional crime (such as murder, arson, or vandalism) that is usually violent and is motivated by bias due to specific characteristics of a person or group.

Hate speech is the use of spoken or written words, or physical actions that portray words, to incite violence or discrimination against a person or group due to specific characteristics. Hate speech may be used to silence criticism against a ruling party or to suppress unpalatable truths.

Bullying is aggressive behavior by one child or multiple children against another child (often in an education setting) or by adults in the workplace. Little distinction has been made between bullying among adults and workplace harassment. The aggression may be physical, verbal, emotional, or a combination of these. It may include gossip about the bullied victim, name-calling, excluding the victim from activities, and other forms of social harassment. **Cyberbullying** is when the perpetrators use the internet to bully their victims, often because the internet allows the perpetrators to remain anonymous. Research by Hyojin Koo (2007) states that bullying includes the use of power (over the victim), pain (knowingly caused by the perpetrator), persistence (of the bullying over time against the victim), and premeditation (awareness by the perpetrator of the effects of the bullying on the victim). Ken Rigby and Peter Smith (2011) find that although there was a decrease in reports of bullying between 1990 and 2009, cyberbullying increased. Historically, bullying was simply dismissed with the platitude "kids will be kids." Research by Young Shin Kim and Bennett Leventhal (2008) reports that bullying victims are more likely to consider suicide than other youth, and recent years have shown an increase in bullying-related suicides by adolescents.

▇ Section 3: Issues of human rights violations associated with hate

Unit 1: National agreements

Hate crimes, also called bias-motivated crimes, are crimes in which the perpetrator's bias against another person's personal characteristics is the reason, or one of the reasons, for the committing of the crime. As stated previously, the FBI includes the biases of actual or perceived race, national origin, religion, disability, sexual orientation, ethnicity, gender, and gender identity as factors driving the commission of hate crimes.

There are three types of federal and state laws related to hate crimes. In the first type, a hate crime may be treated as a regular crime, such as murder, with more severe penalties added due to the bias motivating the crime. In the second type, hate crime is considered to be a completely separate type of crime. In the third type, the law sets down requirements related to the collection of data on hate crimes.

The Civil Rights Act of 1968 (18 U.S.C. § 245(b)(2)) created the option of federal prosecution for a person who "willingly injures, intimidates or interferes with another person, or attempts to do so, by force because of the other person's race, color, religion or national origin." The act makes it illegal to violently interfere with six federally-protected activities, such as attending school, voting, traveling, acting as a juror, using public facilities, and applying for employment.

The Hate Crimes Statistics Act of 1990 (28 U.S.C. § 534) requires the U.S. Attorney General to collect data on crimes committed due to the victim's race, ethnicity, religion, disability, or sexual orientation. This was the first federal law that recognized homosexuality and bisexuality. The publication of hate crimes statistics is a joint project of the Department of Justice and the FBI. This data is used by Congress to create policy related to hate crimes.

The 1994 Violent Crime Control and Law Enforcement Act (28 U.S.C. § 994 note Sec. 280003) created the requirement for increased federal penalties for hate crimes. The basis of the hate-motivated crimes included actual or perceived hatred of race, color, national origin, ethnicity, gender, or religion. The Hate Crime Sentencing Enhancement Act, originally a separate act, was added as an amendment to the 1994 act. The Pattern and Practice statute

(42 U.S.C. § 14141) is a provision of the act of 1994 that prevents the use of excessive force, harassment, false arrest, coercive sexual conduct, or unlawful stops, searches, or arrests by law enforcement.

The Hate Crimes Act of 2009 (also called the Matthew Shepard and James Byrd, Jr. Act, 18 U.S.C. § 249) is a rider to the National Defense Authorization Act for 2010 (H.R. 2647). The act expanded the 1968 federal hate crime law by applying it to crimes motivated by the victim's actual or perceived gender, sexual orientation, gender identity, or disability. In addition, the act removed the requirement that the victim be engaged in a federally-protected activity, such as voting or attending school, at the time of the attack. The act also gave federal prosecutors the ability to pursue investigations into hate crimes that local authorities chose not to pursue. The act created the requirement for the FBI to add gender and gender identity to hate crime statistics.

There are a number of other federal laws that work to prevent bias-motivated crime. The Conspiracy Against Rights statute (18 U.S.C. § 241) makes it a crime to create a conspiracy between two or more people to intimidate or injure a person who is exercising their rights and privileges under the Constitution and U.S. laws. The Deprivation of Rights Under Color of Law (18 U.S.C. § 242) makes it illegal for any lawful authority to deprive a person of their rights and privileges unless there is probable cause of a violation of a law or regulation. The 1996 Damage to Religious Property, Church Arson Prevention Act (18 U.S.C. § 247) makes it a crime to damage or destroy religious property or to obstruct a person's freedom of religious expression. The Freedom of Access to Clinic Entrances (FACE) Act (18 U.S.C. § 248) provides penalties for persons who use force or threats against persons trying to access clinics or damage property or facilities of the clinic. The Criminal Interference with Right to Fair Housing statute (42 U.S.C. § 3631) criminalizes the use or threat of force to prevent housing rights based on a person's characteristics.

There are no federal hate crime laws against killing a member of law enforcement, but many states in the United States have laws or some provisions for additional penalties for killing an officer. Rulings by the U.S. Supreme Court determined that the First Amendment does not justify or make an exemption for hate speech. State laws are subject to these federal rulings.

There are no federal laws applied specifically to bullying or cyberbullying, although anti-discrimination laws may be applied in some cases when the bullying is based on gender (Educational Amendments of 1972, Title IX), race or national origin (Civil Rights Act of 1964, Title VI), religion, or disability (Rehabilitation Act of 1973, Section 504 and Americans with Disabilities Act of 1990, Title II). All 50 states have passed anti-bullying legislation in regard to schools. Bullying is defined either by individual states or by local school boards. The anti-bullying or anti-discrimination laws of some states are based on gender identity or sexual orientation. School officials of some states are required to report incidents of bullying as well as to have a procedure in place for investigating and responding to bullying. The victim or the bully may be referred to mental health services. Bullying and cyberbullying are considered criminal acts when they include physical assault, gender or racial harassment, threats of violence or death, phone calls and texts that are obscene or harassing, sexting, extortion or sexual extortion (sextortion), child pornography, stalking, hate crimes, and private photographs taken without the person's knowledge.

Unit 2: International agreements

International agreements related to hate may be non-binding or binding. Non-binding agreements are called treaties and constitute recommendations to member nations. The

Geneva Conventions and the European Convention on Human Rights are international treaties. Binding agreements are called international law, which means that the member nations agree to be subject to the statutes listed in the agreement as if they were national law. This is called **supranational**, meaning that the organization given this status has authority that transcends the power of national governments. International law comes about due to treaties that give power to supranational tribunals, called international courts of law, which include the European Court of Human Rights (ECHR) and the International Criminal Court (ICC).

The European Convention on Human Rights, also called the Convention on the Protection of Human Rights and Fundamental Freedoms, is the basis for the establishment of the supranational ECHR. The court advises and rules on concerns by individuals, groups, or member nations about human rights violations breaching the statutes or protocols of the convention. The court is governed by the Parliamentary Assembly of the Council of Europe (PACE).

The ICC, established by the United Nations in 1998 at The Hague in the Netherlands, prosecutes atrocity crimes of genocide, crimes against humanity, and war crimes. Prosecution may be pursued by the ICC when particular international situations are referred to the court or when national courts cannot or will not prosecute criminals. The ICC was founded on and is governed by the Rome Statute, a multinational treaty between member nations. The Elements of Crime elaborates on the atrocity crimes described in the Rome Statute. One example is the provision in the Rome Statute that give the court jurisdiction over cases of rape, sexual slavery, and forced prostitution (human sex trafficking), pregnancy, and sterilization when these crimes against humanity are prevalent and being practiced systematically.

Two sets of conventions created a basis for international law regarding war and war crimes. Two international peace conferences at The Hague in 1899 and 1907 led to the creation of the non-binding, multilateral treaties and declarations called The Hague Conventions, which focus on the use of weapons of war. The four treaties and three protocols making up the Geneva Conventions set the foundation for humanitarian practices during war, including the treatment of civilians in war zones. As noted by Theodor Meron (1993), the reference to sexual violence in The Hague Regulations and the Geneva Conventions and Additional Protocols limits sexual crimes to the prohibition of rape, with no express definition of what constitutes rape.

Before the establishment of the ICC, the United Nations had established the International Criminal Tribunal in Yugoslavia and in Rwanda to prosecute atrocity crimes during conflicts in those areas. For example, Article 27 of the Fourth Geneva Convention (1949) explicitly prohibits wartime rape and enforced prostitution. The 1977 Additional Protocols reinforced these prohibitions, but still made rape of female adults and children merely a crime against honor or dignity. It was not until the International Criminal Tribunals in Yugoslavia and Rwanda that rape was considered a crime against humanity involving torture and enslavement that could be investigated for prosecution. At this point, rape was considered a physical and psychological violation. Due to the tribunal in Yugoslavia, warrants were issued for the arrest of Bosnian Serb police officers, soldiers, and members of parliament for gang rape, torture, and sexual enslavement of women used as a weapon of war in the captured city of Foca in Bosnia-Herzegovina in 1992.

Members of the Organization for Security and Co-operation in Europe (OSCE) agree upon the non-binding statutes set out by the organization, including issues of human rights and national minorities. The Inter-American Court on Human Rights provides services to member nations as a supranational judicial institution. The Inter-American Commission on Human Rights monitors, reports on, and makes recommendations about human rights violations. Together, they work to protect human rights within the member nations of the Organization of American States (OAS).

Under the Organisation of African Unity (OAU), the African Commission on Human and Peoples' Rights (ACHPR) works to promote and protect human rights and collective rights of groups of people among its member nations and interpret the African Charter on Human and People's Rights (the Banjul Charter). The African Court on Human and Peoples' Rights was established in 2004 under the statutes outlined in the Protocol to the African Charter on Human and Peoples' Rights on the Establishment of an African Court on Human and Peoples' Rights, which was adopted in 1998 by member states. The court complements the activities of the ACHPR.

Several articles in the Universal Declaration of Human Rights (UDHR, 1948) provide for the right to freedom from hate- or bias-motivated words, depictions, and actions. Article 6 says that everyone is equal in legal settings. Articles 7, 8, and 10 prevent discrimination and mandate equal protection for everyone in legal settings and in national tribunals. Unjustified arrest, detention, and exile are prohibited under Article 9, while Article 11 gives the person the right to be presumed innocent until proven guilty. The U.N. International Convention on the Elimination of All Forms of Racial Discrimination (ICERD), which was put into force in 1969, works to eliminate racial discrimination among member nations.

Unit 3: Controversies

There are many controversies regarding hate. Some of these include hate in relation to freedom of thought, allegations of law enforcement targeting of certain individuals, rape as a weapon of war, bullying, and freedom of speech.

One of the main controversies regarding laws against hate is the concept of freedom of thought. Labelling a crime as bias- or hate-motivated implies that the offense is receiving additional penalties because of the thoughts and feelings behind the crime. Many contend that a crime is a crime and that the reasoning behind the crime should have no bearing on prosecution for that crime.

Law enforcement is subject to continual accusations that they allegedly target specific persons or groups for traffic stops and arrests, and that the level of force applied is based on characteristics of an individual. Multiple lawsuits have been filed against officers and law enforcement agencies for discriminatory practices.

The physical and psychological effects of rape as a weapon of war is a relatively new challenge accepted by law-makers. Currently there is insufficient legal recourse for this crime against humanity. Past laws have focused on the loss to male status due to the violation of a female (Fionnuala Aoláin, 1997). Inger Skjelsbaek (2001) points out that rape is continually being used as a weapon of war against females and males and is being used in a "systematic political campaign which has strategic military purposes."

Some contend that the right to freedom of speech includes the right to use hate speech. Some hate groups have responded to the suppression of hate speech with violence. As another example of the controversial nature of protection from words that are deemed an attack on others, a study by John Villasenor (2017) presented college- and university-level students who are U.S. citizens with the following scenario: "A public university invites a very controversial speaker to an on-campus event. The speaker is known for making offensive and hurtful statements." The students were then asked for their view on the scenario if "a student group opposed to the speaker uses violence to prevent the speaker from speaking." Almost one-fifth (19%) of the college students in this study said it was acceptable to use physical violence to silence speech. Of the respondents who agreed to the acceptability of the use of violence, 30% were male and 10% female; 21% were private school students and 19% were public school students.

CHECK YOURSELF BOX: PERSONAL BIASES ABOUT HATE

When confronted with an idea or trait that you dislike, are you able to step back, analyze the facts, and make educated decisions, or do you have an automatic and possibly quick-tempered response? No matter your race, gender, religion, politics, or creed, you have beliefs that bias your research. In order to become known as a researcher who provides valuable, unbiased research, it is important that you brainstorm and list any biases that you perceive may affect your research. Take some time to write down areas in your life where you have strong preferences for and against ideas, people, and other things. Be honest with yourself. In this way, you will be better able to analyze the decision-making process related to bias, discrimination, and hate presented in this chapter and to do relevant research in the areas related to hate.

Section 4: History of hate

Actions of hate are documented from the beginning of time. According to paleontologists at the Instituto de Salud Carlos III in Madrid, the oldest known murder was committed 430,000 years ago (Sala et al., 2015). At the Sima de los Huesos or "Pit of Bones" site in Spain, scientists found evidence of "lethal interpersonal violence" in the form of a skull with two matching holes caused by blunt force trauma from the same weapon but from two different directions. While this killing may have been the result of tribal warfare, the researchers reason that the multiple blows imply that there was an intention to kill.

The word hate, meaning an extreme dislike or strong aversion to a person or thing, comes from the Old English words *hete* (noun) and *hatian* (verb), the Dutch word *haten*, and the German words *hassen* (verb) and *Hass* (hatred). Even from the fourth century B.C., philosophers have studied hate. For example, Greek philosopher Aristotle (384–322 B.C.) defines hate as an intense, negative perception of a person or group such that the person filled with hate wants to harm the object of hatred.

Semir Zeki and John Paul Romaya (2008) examined brain activity in subjects while they looked at a photo of a person they hated. They found that two areas in the brain light up for both a loved one and someone hated, including the part of the part of the brain that prepares a person for action. The main difference is that seeing a hated person also engages the part of the brain responsible for judgment and critical thinking, while there is a marked decrease in activity in this area when viewing the photo of the loved one. Zeki and Romaya conclude that reasoning and evaluation are parts of the process of hate.

Researcher Martin Oppenheimer (2005) says that modern-day hate is incited by a person or group of people who discover and exploit the insecurities and frustrations of a larger group of people. The perpetrators of hate then feed this group of people information to convince them that another, opposing group of people is the reason for their own lack of security and opportunity. Hate speech and propaganda are used in the campaign of hate. Social media has increased the ability and ease of reaching and communicating with a much larger audience while giving the perpetrators a high level of anonymity.

Bullying was first seriously documented in the late 1970s (Dan Olweus, 1978). The topic has gained public attention in connection with mass shootings in school settings. The Center for Disease Control's Youth Risk Surveillance System Survey (2018) states that 20% of participating students are subjected to bullying and that those students are more likely to carry a weapon to school. This percentage increases as students experience other risk factors at school, such as receiving threats, feeling unsafe, having property stolen or damaged, or being in a fight.

Section 5: Meet the experts on hate

There are many national and international organizations and individuals who are experts on actions related to hate. When looking for information, it is helpful to look at the list of partners and websites provided by the organization having expertise as it might lead you to more information sources for those working against hate.

In the United States, the Southern Poverty Law Center monitors hate crime and compiles lists of specific crimes, perpetrators of hate crimes, and related statistics. In addition, it provides links to news stories about hate crimes. Other U.S. nonprofit organizations working against bias- and hate-motivated crime include the Anti-Defamation League and the Tahirih Justice Center. International nonprofits fighting against issues related to hate include the International Alliance of Women, Amnesty International, Disability Rights International, Human Rights Watch, and the International Work Group for Indigenous Affairs. The Office for Democratic Institutions and Human Rights (ODIHR) of the Organization for Security and Co-operation in Europe (OSCE) is tasked with observing elections, reviewing legislation, and advising governments in order to "uphold, promote, and monitor human rights."

There are many university programs focused on the study of hate, including the Gonzaga Institute for Hate Studies in Spokane, Washington, the Centre for the Study of Hate and Extremism at California State University, and the International Network for Hate Studies (INHS) at Cardiff University. Each program fights against hate through the exchange of scholarly knowledge, the promotion of understanding its root causes, and the determination of solutions. Organizations such as the University of Nebraska at Lincoln's Bullying Research Network focus on a particular type of hate.

Hate crimes (or bias-motived crimes) in the United States are the jurisdiction of the U.S. Department of Justice (DOJ), which has five departments that work with hate crimes: 1) Bureau of Justice Statistics, 2) Civil Rights Division, 3) Community-Oriented Policing Services, 4) Community Relations Service, and 5) Office for Victims of Crime. In addition, there are two agencies within the Department of Justice involved in hate crime-related tasks. The first is the U.S. FBI, which is tasked with investigating hate crimes and collecting data on them through the National Incidence-Based Reporting System. The second is the Bureau of Alcohol, Tobacco, Firearms and Explosives (ATF) which regulates the U.S. industry for guns and explosives that are often used in hate crimes. The Department of Justice may partner with U.S. attorneys and local and state law enforcement during the prosecution of hate crimes cases.

Due to the wide range of aspects of hate, there are experts from a variety of fields who offer valuable resources. Some of their areas of expertise include law, human rights, psychology, sociology, criminal justice, and criminology. Other persons who may be helpful to economics research are perpetrators of hate and those who have experienced bias-motivated discrimination and hate.

CHECK YOURSELF BOX: HATE RESEARCH AND DATA BIASES

Hate is an intense emotion and actions and words related to hate elicit strong personal responses. Check into the backgrounds of the activists, researchers, and organizations working in areas related to hate. Who is collecting the information and data related to hate? What are their motivations – personal experience, academic or career prestige, funding, or something else? How does the data on hate affect these individuals' and organizations' primary and secondary goals? Could their motivations bias the data they collect and the information they disseminate? Understanding the biases present in the data and literature you are reviewing and using can help you sort out the biases that affect your own understanding and the effectiveness of your research for policy-making.

Section 6: Economic structure of hate

As stated previously, sound research requires that the economist be aware of their own biases as well as the biases of others. People are biased based on things like their backgrounds, circumstances, and interactions, and when a negative bias is extreme, it can become hate. When the bias turns into action, it becomes discrimination. Intense negative bias turned into action can manifest itself in hate crimes and hate speech. The economic analysis of hate presented here is an extension of the economics of discrimination as presented by Gary Becker (1957, 1971). In addition, the four decision-making groups involved in the economics of hate and their incentives will be considered.

Becker was the first to translate **taste discrimination**, discrimination based on a person's preferences, into economic terms and create the theory of the economics of discrimination. His work focuses on taste discrimination based on a person's race by employers, employees, and customers. This means that the person's bias affects decision-making in the marketplace.

According to Becker, **employer discrimination** is when an employer is prejudiced against hiring a person based on a personal characteristic of that person. The employer must pay this person the regular market wage (w), but feels as if they are having to pay a wage greater than the market wage (w<w(1+d), where d is a discrimination coefficient that measures the amount of prejudice). A higher level of prejudice leads to a higher discrimination coefficient.

Prejudice is illustrated in Figure 8.1 using isocost and isoquant lines. An **isocost line** (equal-cost, I) is a producer's budget line, which shows the cost of hiring different quantities of two groups of workers: black (B) and white (W). Here, the model assumes that each employee is paid the same market wage (w). An **isoquant line** (equal-quantity, Q) is a curve that shows a particular quantity of output that can be produced with varying amounts of labor input from the two worker groups. This model assumes that the workers are exact substitutes for labor input, meaning that they have the same productivity (output per worker hour). Point X on the graph shows a point where cost is minimized; B_1 is the quantity of labor (number of workers) of type B hired and W_1 is the number of group W workers hired. Point Y shows discrimination in which the employer produces the same output (Q_1) but chooses to hire more white workers (W_2) and fewer black workers (B_2), which increases the cost of producing Q_1 units of output from I_1 to I_2. The employer is acting upon their bias against black workers and, in effect, changing the labor cost structure of the firm. This could happen because as the employer chooses to hire more white workers, the relative wage for W workers increases (increased demand leads to increased prices). The employer may deduce that the higher wages paid to white workers are equal to the wages they feel they are having to pay to hire the black workers ($w(1+d)$).

FIGURE 8.1 Employer discrimination

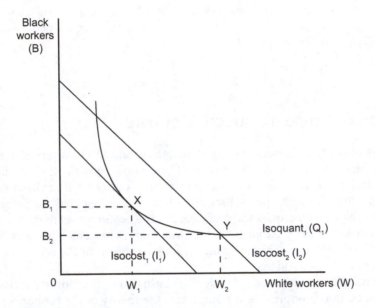

Employee (or co-worker) **discrimination** occurs when an employee must work with a person against whom he is prejudiced. In this case, the employee receives wage = w, but feels as if they are only receiving wage = $w(1-d)$ because he has to work with the person whom he dislikes. The d in the equation is the percent of prejudice the employee feels against his co-worker and wd is the amount the employee feels he is losing by having to work with the other person. The higher the discrimination, the lower the wage the employee feels he is receiving.

A labor supply curve (S_L) shows that a higher wage (w) leads to a higher quantity of labor supplied (Q_{LS}) by a worker, as illustrated in Figure 8.2. Point X on the graph shows the number of hours the person would work (Q_{LSMkt}) at the market wage (w). In contrast, point Y shows the number of hours the employee would work (Q_{LSDisc}) if he has to work with someone against who he is prejudiced. The number of hours of labor supplied decreases because the employee acts as if he is receiving $w(1-d)$, where d is the degree of discrimination he feels against his co-worker. In reality, the employee may not decrease the number of hours he works, but his productivity (output per worker hour) may decrease because of his dislike for working with the person against whom he is prejudiced. In either case, employee income would decrease due to his negative bias.

FIGURE 8.2   Employee discrimination

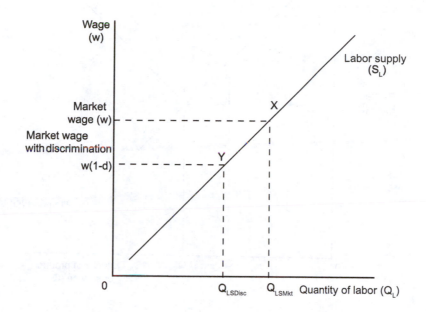

Customer discrimination is associated with prices being paid, rather than wages being received. The customer with prejudice feels she is paying a higher price when she must buy something from a person or place she doesn't like. The customer pays market price = p, but feels as if she is paying price = p(1+d), where pd is the amount of purported "markup" cost the customer feels she is paying when she has to buy the product from a person or place against whom she is prejudiced.

A **demand curve** (D) shows the relationship between the price of a market-produced product or service and the quantity of that product or service demanded by the customer, as illustrated in Figure 8.3. If there is no prejudice, the customer chooses to buy quantity (Q_{Mkt}) of the product or service at market price (P_{Mkt}), which is point X on the graph. If the customer must buy the product from a person (or place) against whom she is prejudiced, she feels she is having to pay price $P_{Mkt}(1+d)$. This is shown as point Y on the graph when the customer only buys quantity Q_{Disc}. The decreased quantity demanded (Q_{Disc}) may be due to a single decrease in purchasing the product or service or due to the customer avoiding buying the product for longer periods of time so she doesn't have to interact with the person or place against whom she is biased.

On the other side of the coin, Becker looks at nepotism as a benefit to hiring, working with, or buying from someone with whom the person has an affinity. In this case, the employer feels he is only paying wage = w(1-n) < w to hire someone whom he favors. The employee feels he is being paid wage = w(1+n) > w to work with someone whom the employee favors. The customer feels he is only paying price = p(1-n) < p because he gets to purchase the product from a certain person whom he favors.

FIGURE 8.3 Customer discrimination

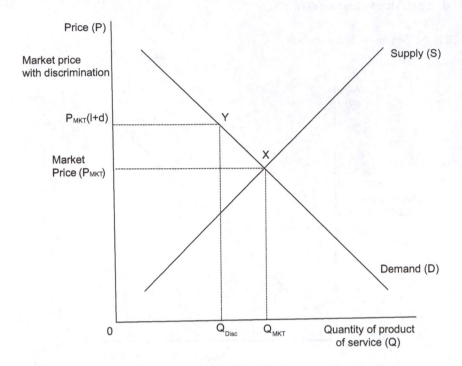

As discussed previously, discrimination and nepotism are not used simultaneously when talking about how one is biased between two people or groups. To assign a discrimination coefficient against the person the person is prejudiced against and a nepotism coefficient toward the other person is double counting. Instead, the average feeling of the person making the judgement call is determined. If a person is disliked more than the average, a discrimination cost "mark-up" is assigned. If, however, the person is liked more the average, then decisions or actions toward the favored person are assigned a nepotism cost "mark-down." If there are more than two people or groups, there may be differing levels of discrimination or nepotism present.

There are four main decision-making groups involved in the economics of hate: Perpetrators of hate, victims of hate-motivated actions, bystanders who become aware of the actions of hate, and the media, which chooses whether and how to report the hateful actions. There is a range of hate-motivated actions, so that one act of hatred may look entirely different from another: two examples are a murder based on hatred of a specific race, and bullying within schools.

Perpetrators of hate-motivated actions choose when to turn the hatred into action and choose the actions that will translate into their outward expression of their inner emotions. An act of hate may occur in one instance, during a short period of time, or may be extended over weeks, months, or years. The perpetuator may choose to use one or multiple actions to express the hatred.

Victims of hate are affected by the actions of perpetrators when they are killed or are injured physically or psychologically. Whether the act of hatred is the creation of hateful depictions or graffiti, the use of verbal or digital words that lead a person to commit suicide, rape as an action of war or hate, or a hate-motivated physical attack, the victim or victims of the attack and the bystanders plus, to some degree, society are all emotionally affected.

Awareness of hate-motivated actions and words may affect bystanders. Bystanders' biases toward a situation or person determine whether they are affected by the publicized hatred. For example, a mass shooting often causes anger, recriminations, and calls for policy change at a national level. However, hateful graffiti painted on a church or mosque may viewed as an attack on a particular group that does not affect unrelated groups of bystanders.

Part of the response of bystanders is due to the media's portrayal of the situation, the perpetrator, and the law enforcement response. At times, the media has the power to persuade the public of the seriousness of one crime while downplaying another crime's significance. When heinous acts are publicized, society must determine whether and how to deal with the hateful actions of the perpetrators.

Researchers David Finkelhor, Heather Turner, Anne Shattuck, and Sherry Hamby (2015) study juvenile hate crimes. Basing their research on police records from the National Incident-Based Reporting System (NIBRS), they determine that juveniles are more likely to experience a hate crime than an adult. Violent assault is a part of 63% of hate crimes against juveniles, but only 39% of those against adults. Hate crimes against males between the ages of 12 and 17 are more likely than hate crimes against females in this age range. Hate crimes with an anti-black motivation make up 38% of juvenile hate crimes, of which 22% had anti-white and 13% anti-Hispanic motivations. School occurrences make up one-fifth of hate crimes against juveniles. Juveniles make up 64% of perpetrators of hate crimes against other juveniles and most perpetrators of the violence know their victims.

Research by Matt Ryan and Peter Leeson (2010) shows little evidence that hate crimes are committed by hate groups or with poverty as the motivating factor. In addition, they find that demographic variables are significant in determining where hate crimes may occur. They state that hate crimes "are a result of learned attitudes and behaviors, observed violence toward strangers, being mimicked."

Hate groups promote hateful ideology and teach their members how to hate. The Southern Poverty Law Center, which monitors and reports on hate groups and their activities in the United States, states that there has been a 56% increase in active hate groups since 2000.

The FBI 2016 Hate Crime Statistics (2017) provides the hate crime statistics as reported by law enforcement agencies. This includes 7,615 victims and 5,770 perpetrators of hate crimes. Over half of the single-bias hate crimes is due to race, ethnicity, or ancestry while 21% are based on religion, almost 18% on sexual orientation, 2% on gender identity, 1.2% on disability, and 0.5% on gender. Almost 30% of the hate crimes involve intimidation, over a quarter destruction, damage, or vandalism, 23% simple assault, and 11.9% aggravated assault. The majority of the hate crimes victims are individuals (81.3%), while 5.5% were businesses, 3.1% government entities, 2.2% religious organizations, and 1.1% the public or society.

The use of rape as a weapon of war has only been legally recognized since the International Criminal Tribunals for Yugoslavia (1993–2017) and for Rwanda (1994–2015). There are continual reports of rape as a weapon of war, including the rape of females in the ongoing conflicts in South Sudan and the Rohingya crisis in Myanmar (Burma), and the rape of males to neutralize opponents in Libya and Tamil ethnic minorities in Sri Lanka.

Unit 1: Costs of hate

Hate starts out as an internal psychological and physical response. An escalation of this response may be an external response in the form of hate-motivated words, representations, and actions. The costs associated with this external response are numerous and widespread.

As noted earlier, the legal costs to the perpetrator of a hate-motivated crime depend upon national and international laws, law enforcement, and the actions of courts of law. If a person is caught committing a crime that is labeled a hate crime, they may be prosecuted for the crime and receive additional penalties due to the hate bias. People view hate crimes as particularly heinous and a person who publically uses hate speech, harasses or bullies another person, or creates a hate-motivated picture may be incarcerated, fired from employment, kicked out of school, or prevented from entering some establishments or participating in some activities. In addition, the perpetrator may be shunned from society, lose relationships, or be personally attacked in retaliation. A person who commits a hate-motivated murder or a rape as a weapon of war may be prosecuted, have to sit before a war tribunal, and endanger family and friends due to retaliatory actions by the people against whom the murder or rape was committed. This means the costs of committing a hate crime can be financial, psychological, and physical.

Victims of hate-motivated actions often experience physical, psychological, health, family- and community-related, financial, and legal costs, as well as the loss of freedom of speech and damage to personal property, with the victim's race, gender, religion, or sexual orientation being the reason for the attacks. This has an emotional effect on the victim as well as on bystanders who share or have empathy for the victim. The victims may lose their ability to work or physically function, their personal property, their sense of security (due to the hate-motivated actions of the perpetrator), and potentially their lives (due to the hate-motivated actions). Financial costs to victims of hate crimes may include physical therapy or counseling following a verbal, physical, or sexual attack; loss of employment; moving expenses to get away from the perpetrator; security equipment to deter further attacks; legal and court costs to prevent contact with the perpetrators and to bring the perpetrator to justice. Physical and sexual attacks can lead to loss of physical enjoyment and relationships. Bullying may force the victim to change schools or may induce suicide. Hate expressed as rape as a weapon of war leads to loss of dignity and health, psychological injury, loss of sense of security, loss of opportunity to participate in marriage or other activities due to the culture's views of the rape victim. There is also the cost of raising children born from rape, and the need to protect the victim's family when rape is seen as an attack on family honor. Victims may be prevented from speaking out against the injustice as they fear retribution from the perpetrators of hate.

Bystanders and society as a whole are not exempt from the costs of hate. A community loses productive citizens when hate leads to physical or psychological damage or death. Many medical, social services, law enforcement, legal, and criminal justice expenses associated with hate-motivated crime are paid for through taxes. Society may lose property or have to pay for its repair. In addition, fear may spread through and have an impact on specific groups and entire communities.

The media's portrayal of the victim of hate may lead to further damage to the victim's life, health, and livelihood. The media also chooses how to portray an alleged perpetrator of a hate-motived crime, oftentimes before the full legal investigation is complete. As the media continues to hype the event to produce more news, damage may occur to the alleged perpetrator, their family and community, and others with similar characteristics to the alleged perpetrator. The credibility of the media may be damaged if reporters incorrectly portray the hate-motived event, the victims, or the perpetrator.

Unit 2: Benefits of hate

The benefits of hate-motivated words, depictions, or actions are limited. It is possible that people use hate speech and depictions as a pressure valve; however, studies show that perpetrators of hate crimes progressed from hateful thoughts to words and physical representation of hate to the actual hate crime (Mark Walters, Rupert Brown, and Susann Wiedlitzka, 2016). Daniel Burke (2017) reports four reasons people commit hate crimes: Thrill-seeking, defending territory, retaliating against past offenses, and because of prejudice against a specific characteristic of people, such as race or religion. Hate graffiti or the destruction of property might be viewed as less negative outlets for hate than a physical attack on a person.

In the United States, the First Amendment protects the freedom of speech. The right to use hate speech provides economic benefit to those who value their use of hate speech as a form of freedom of speech, even though the hate speech itself undermines the freedom of speech of the victim. Studies of social media, which offers anonymity (and thus freedom of speech) to the perpetrators of hate speech, show that this anonymity leads to an escalation of hate speech (Rebeca Rebs and Aracy Ernst, 2017). Used in this way, the right to freedom of speech can have the unintended consequence of inciting violence.

There are no benefits to victims of hate-motivated actions. Once the perpetrator is caught and convicted, the victim may feel that the conviction gives them the chance to regain at least part of what was stolen through the hate speech, depictions, or actions. Legislation based on past hate crimes may lead to benefits for future victims of hate-motivated actions if they are more protected and have greater avenues for legal recourse.

Bystanders and society may gain from hate-motivated actions if they lead to a better understanding of the stimulus behind the hate and better ways to confront the hate to decrease future hate crimes. For example, when a person commits a mass killing, society can become empowered and safer if it does reliable research to determine the causes of the crime, creates better regulations related to the weapons used, and addresses the underlying issues surrounding the hate-motived event.

Media has the role of providing information about hate crimes, investigations, legislation, and trials. The dissemination of information in a responsible and accurate manner by media can help to increase understanding of the processes and decrease people's fears. However, the media benefits from any event that can be widely publicized and capture maximum audience attention. Hate crimes are big news, and both real and speculative information is used to draw people's attention to the event. This attention leads to increased ratings for the media platform.

Unit 3: Inefficiencies in economic structure of hate

The numerous controversies related to national and international agreements on hate illuminate the fact that there will be inefficiencies in the economic structure of hate. Inefficiencies occur due to the varying definitions and laws related to hate crimes and the differential treatment of hate-motivated actions. This makes prosecution difficult. The opportunity cost may be high in relation to law enforcement, criminal court time, and the resources needed to pursue increased penalties based on the bias motivation. Hate crime statistics and legislation can only be developed when the victims of hate-based actions come forward to report on events. Some victims may not feel safe, and those actions will remain unknown. The accuracy of interpretation and reporting by the media can influence not only society, but also the ways in which laws are created, interpreted, and enforced.

◼ Section 7: Case study

Hate by the numbers

One of the most prevalent topics in the news for the past several years has been relations between police officers and the black community. Specifically, the media has publicized multiple questionable shootings in which white police officers have shot and killed unarmed black individuals. News outlets have focused primarily on these types of shooting and subsequently research has focused on whether race is a deciding factor when officers are choosing whether or not to use lethal force. This issue can be studied from an economic vantage point insomuch as econometric modeling and analysis can be coupled with choice theory to analyze the decisions of police officers. The first step in such an analysis is to acquire the necessary data, which (as will be explained) can be difficult in this area. The second step is to analyze whether race plays a significant role in relation to varying aspects of the shooting. For this case study, the focus is whether race, as an explanatory variable, has a statistically-significant relationship with whether the shot individual is unarmed or armed. Lastly, one must determine whether there are any lurking variables and then analyze which theory best explains the relationship.

A **lurking variable** (also called a **confounder**) is a variable that affects the significance of the relationship between the explanatory and dependent variable. For example, let us assume that race C is more likely to live in lower socioeconomic areas than other races. Further, assume that police patrol lower socioeconomic areas more than others because of higher crime rates in such areas. Here, individuals of race C are more often killed by police officers than any other race and thus conclude that race is the determining factor when in fact the lurking variable is that the police interact with race C at a disproportionate rate relative to population proportions due to socioeconomic status.

It should be noted that this case study intends primarily to examine the available data and how it should be handled. Whether any existing relationships are driven by racism in particular is not analyzed here due to the inability to accurately generalize in this situation due to the extraordinary number of relevant factors.

Generally, obtaining reliable data in relation to fatal police shootings is difficult, but data has become more readily available in recent years. The reason for the difficulty is that when someone is fatally shot by a police officer, typically most information concerning the shooting is held by the police station itself. Furthermore, police stations do not store this information in a nationwide database accessible to the public. One can feasibly contact police stations directly to obtain data; however, as has been noted by some studies utilizing this method, it comes with inherent flaws. Roland Fryer, a Harvard economist, points out two particular issues in his own study which relied heavily on information from police stations. First, he admits that the stations willing to provide the data may do so because they know there is nothing negative about their particular data, as opposed to a station which may choose not to provide data because the reverse is true. Second, he points out the potential bias of police officers when providing contextual information about the incident (Fryer, 2016).

Another way to obtain data which removes at least the first concern of Dr. Fryer and in part the second concern is to use data that has been aggregated by news agencies. In particular, the focus here will be on the *Washington Post*, which has collected fatal police shooting data from news articles concerning the shootings starting at the beginning of 2015 and continuing to the present. Dr. Fryer's first concern is alleviated in that even if a particular news agency has bias, other sources with the opposite bias can be found in order to corroborate the base facts of a particular shooting. The second concern is partly corrected in that news agencies could have access to witnesses who would have the opportunity to rebut potentially incorrect facts provided by a police officer. However, this correction has its own inherent problems because if the witness is acquainted with the shot individual, they may be equally biased. One may think concerning this second concern that many of the news stories that have gained notable popularity are accompanied by body-cam footage, which should alleviate factual disputes; however, according to the *Washington Post* data, approximately 88% of the shootings that have occurred since the beginning of 2015 were not accompanied by body-cam footage. This particular concern becomes less of a problem as more departments implement body-cams and more individuals also involved in the incidents have readily accessible recording devices. Even when body cameras were not available, most shootings in recent years appear in the news, even if only a single short article is published.

While collections of data similar to and including the *Washington Post* are arguably easier than data directly obtained from police departments, there are still flaws. For one, if there is a shooting which is not accompanied by any news coverage, the shooting will likely not be included. The main concern, however, which is the focus of this case study, is the definition and coding of variables. In particular, this case study looks at the "unarmed" variable coded by the *Washington Post*, which has recently come under fire by prominent scholars such as Heather MacDonald in the Marshall Project and news agencies such as *The Daily Wire* (Aaron Bandler, 2016). Specifically, the attack focuses on the failure of the *Washington Post* to further differentiate between fatal police shootings of unarmed individuals that are purposeful and shootings that are accidental. The other criticism is that the unarmed variable should control for whether the victim is attacking the officer and is thus, in effect, armed. The critics then conclude that the statistically significant relationship between race and being unarmed or not is inappropriate when performed with the unmodified "unarmed" variable, and that the true data "paints a different picture" (Bandler, 2016). The "different picture" language then implies that the *Washington Post*'s mistake is of consequence and has a substantial effect on the outcome of the data. This case study seeks to empirically analyze this assertion and concludes that although the fatal police shootings of some "unarmed" black persons should be coded differently for clarity, the same is true for some "unarmed" non-black persons and ultimately the statistical relationship is largely unaffected, thus making the *Washington Post*'s failure to differentiate between the two types of shooting harmless.

Prior to any data modifications, the *Washington Post* estimates that from January 1, 2015, to August 8, 2017, 171 of the 2,560 persons killed by police were "unarmed." Of these 171 fatalities, 63 were black, 67 were white, 34 were Hispanic, zero were Asian, two were Native American, four were "other," and one was unknown. As a reference point, the 2,560 shootings were spread across these races with 1,203 white, 623 black, 39 Asian, 425 Hispanic, 31 Native American, and the remainder being other or unknown. It should be noted that these fatalities only include fatalities for which there is at least some related news report. The news reports of every "unarmed" fatality provided two critical variables that were not included in the *Washington Post* dataset. First, the race of the officer who fired the fatal shots is classified. The addition of this variable proves fruitless as many times there was more than one officer and it was unclear who fired; other times details about the officers were not released or the name of an officer did not lead to a clear determination of that officer's race. Second, the determination was made as to whether the killed individual was purposely shot by the police. If purpose was ambiguous, this study erred on the side of purposeful.

After extracting the aforementioned variables, the data was modified accordingly. In particular, the "0" dummy variable representing a killed individual as being "unarmed" was left as a blank if the shooting was non-purposeful. Therefore, this observation was essentially removed from the dataset. As critics of the *Washington Post*'s "unarmed" variable point out, there are a number of shootings in which a black victim was unarmed but the shooting was accidental. Clearly these should be removed, since arguably race cannot play a role in an accidental shooting. What critics failed to mention was the analogous instances in which non-black victims were also shot accidentally, which affects the ultimate relationship between race and being unarmed. In fact, while five of the shootings involved accidental shootings of unarmed black individuals, five shootings also involved the accidental shootings of unarmed non-black individuals. Examples of these instances include one in which an officer shot an adult white male and the bullet went through the male and hit his unarmed daughter. Clearly the shooting of the daughter was not purposeful.

Now that the data is modified, two regressions must be performed. First, a regression must be made in which the explanatory variable is race and the dependent variable is the unmodified "unarmed" variable. Second, the same regression must be performed with the modified "unarmed" variable as the dependent variable. Third, the regressions must be compared to see if there is any substantial change in the relationship between the variables.

Table 8.1 is the first regression. As is shown, black individuals who are fatally shot by police officers are statistically more likely to be unarmed than non-black individuals. However, the low r^2 should be noted as it demonstrates that race explains only an extremely small amount in the variation of unarmed individuals who were shot by police officers as opposed to individuals who were armed at the time they were shot. The second regression is presented in Table 8.2.

TABLE 8.1 Cross-sectional regression: Unarmed (Unmodified)

Variable	Unarmed (Unmodified)			
	Coefficient	p-value	95% C.I.	$R^2 = 0.0044$
Constant	0.0620*	–	–	–
Race	0.0391*	0.00	0.02–0.06	–

*Denotes significance at 5% significance level.

TABLE 8.2 Cross-sectional regression: Unarmed (Modified)

Variable	Unarmed (Modified)			
	Coefficient	p-value	95% C.I.	$R^2 = 0.0036$
Constant	0.0593*	–	–	–
Race	0.0346*	0.00	0.01–0.06	–

*Denotes significance at 5% significance level.

This regression also shows that black individuals fatally shot by police are statistically more likely to be unarmed than non-black individuals. When comparing the two regressions, the modification makes little difference: The coefficient for race decreases slightly (by 0.0045), and the r² also drops slightly. Most importantly, however, race continues to have a statistically-significant relationship to being unarmed as opposed to armed.

While critics of the *Washington Post*'s dataset on police shootings are correct in that some of the variables are best analyzed after some manipulation, the empirical difference in relation to the "unarmed" variable is harmless. Where the critics blundered was only looking at specific cases relating to a single race as opposed to all cases relating to the unarmed category. It should be noted that whether unarmed individuals are more likely to attack police based on the individual's race is analyzed in the accompanying econometric exercise in this chapter. Going forward, persons utilizing data from mass collection sites like the *Washington Post* would be best served by verifying variables and paying close attention to the definitions of the variables. Lastly, when handling the *Washington Post* data, there were two realizations that further emphasize the importance of personally checking the data. First, the *Washington Post*'s filter options for their data do not include Native Americans as a race filter. Instead, Native Americans (unlike most other races) are lumped into other groups. This is especially important because it should incentivize analysts to look at the underlying raw data rather than the user-friendly data presented. Second, some variables with this type of data are coded according to initial news releases and not adjusted when, say, an autopsy report changes some of the initial facts. For example, one shooting was coded as unarmed based on news reports even though later it was determined he had brass knuckles, a knife, and a handgun readily available. Although mass collection sources such as data from the *Washington Post* may be the best information available, they are far from perfect.

Section 8: Recommendations for future research

As seen in this chapter and throughout the textbook, hate is a major factor in the majority of human rights violations. Research into each particular topic is needed to understand the incentives behind the bias- or hate-motivated actions and the potential remedies for the issues. While gun laws by themselves may decrease mass shootings, the hatred may simply manifest itself in some other way. This means that it is imperative to gain an understanding of the motivations for these actions.

CHECK YOURSELF BOX: CHANGES TO PERSONAL BIASES ABOUT HATE

Within each chapter of this textbook, you saw actions that related to feelings like hate. Each of us has strong feelings for and against certain ideas, people, and things. Do you have a better understanding of how bias, especially in the extreme case of hate, plays a role in people's actions and words? What are your current thoughts about hate? Are some actions or words based on intense feelings acceptable to you? What are the situations in which this could occur? Review the information you wrote in the first check yourself box in this chapter. Has this chapter in any way changed your perception of hate? Understanding your personal biases helps you not only to sort out the issues within yourself, but also makes you more attuned to other people's biases that can have an effect on your research.

Section 9: Bibliography

Aoláin, Fionnuala Ní. (1997). Radical rules: The effects of evidential and procedural rules on the regulation of sexual violence in war. *Albany Law Review, 60*(3), 888.

Bandler, Aaron. (2016, July 7). 5 Statistics you need to know about cops killing blacks. *The Daily Wire*. Retrieved from https://www.dailywire.com/news/7264/5-statistics-you-need-know-about-cops-killing-aaron-bandler#exit-modal

Becker, Gary. (1957, 1971). *Economics of discrimination*. Chicago: The University of Chicago Press.

Burke, Daniel. (2017, June 12). *The four reasons people commit hate crimes. CNN U.S. Edition*. Retrieved from https://www.cnn.com/2017/06/02/us/who-commits-hate-crimes/index.html

Center for Disease Control and Prevention (CDC). (2018). *1991–2015 High school youth risk behavior survey data*. Retrieved from http://nccd.cdc.gov/youthonline

Federal Bureau of Investigation. (2017). *Hate crimes*. Retrieved from https://www.fbi.gov/investigate/civil-rights/hate-crimes

Finkelhor, David; Turner, Heather; Shattuck, Anne; and Hamby, Sherry. (2015). Prevalence of childhood exposure to violence, crime, and abuse. *JAMA Pediatrics, 169*(8), 746–54. doi: 10.1001/jamapediatrics.2015.0676 (CV 331). Retrieved from www.unh.edu/ccrc/general/factsheet_hatecrimes.html

Fryer, Roland. (2016, July). An empirical analysis of racial differences in police use of force. *National Bureau of Economic Research*. Working paper, No. 22399. Retrieved from http://www.nber.org/papers/w22399.pdf

Kim, Young Shin and Leventhal, Bennett. (2008, April). Bullying and suicide: A review. *International Journal of Adolescent Medicine and Health, 20*(2), 133–54.

Koo, Hyojin. (2007). A time line of the evolution of school bullying in differing social contexts. *Asia Pacific Education Review, 8*(1), 107–16.

MacDonald, Heather. (2016, March 8). Black and unarmed: Behind the numbers. *The Marshall Project*. Retrieved from https://www.themarshallproject.org/2016/02/08/black-and-unarmed-behind-the-numbers

Meron, Theodor. (1993). Rape as a crime under international humanitarian law. *The American Journal of International Law, 87*(3), 425.

Merriam-Webster Collegiate Dictionary (11th ed.). (2004). Springfield, MA: Merriam-Webster Incorporated.

Olweus, Dan. (1978). *Aggression in the schools: Bullies and whipping boys*. Oxford, England: Hemisphere.

Oppenheimer, Martin. (2005). *The hate handbook: Oppressors, victims, and fighters*. Oxford: Lexington Books.

Rebs, Rebeca and Ernst, Aracy. (2017, July-December). Haters and the hate speech: Understanding the violence in social network sites. *Diologo das Letras*. 6(2), 24–44.

Rigby, Ken and Smith, Peter. (2011). Is school bullying really on the rise? *Social Psychology of Education*, 14, 441–55.

Ryan, Matt and Leeson, Peter. (2010). Hate groups and hate crime. In Alain Marciano and Giovanni Ramello (Eds.), *Encyclopedia of law and economics*. New York, NY: Springer.

Sala, Nohemi; Arsuaga, Juan Luis; Pantoja-Pérez, Ana; Pablos, Adrián; Martínez, Ignacio; Quam, Rolf; Gómez-Olivencia, Asier; Bermúdez de Castro, José María; and Carbonell, Eudald. (2015, May 27). Lethal interpersonal violence in the Middle Pleistocene. *PLoS ONE, 10*(5), e0126589. Retrieved from http://journals.plos.org/plosone/article?id=10.1371/journal.pone.0126589

Skjelsbaek, Inger. (2001). Sexual violence and war: Mapping out a complex relationship. *European Journal of International Relations, 7*(2), 213.

United States Federal Bureau of Investigation (2017, January 9). *What we investigate – civil rights*. Retrieved from https://www.fbi.gov/investigate/civil-rights/hate-crimes

United States Federal Bureau of Investigation. (2017). *2016 hate crime statistics*. Retrieved from https://ucr.fbi.gov/hate-crime/2016/topic-pages/incidentsandoffenses

Villasenor, John. (2017, September 18). *Views among college students regarding the First Amendment: Results from a survey*. Brookings University. Retrieved from https://www.brookings.edu/blog/fixgov/2017/09/18/views-among-college-students-regarding-the-first-amendment-results-from-a-new-survey/

Walters, Mark; Brown, Rupert; and Wiedlitzka, Susann. (2016). *Causes and motivations of hate crimes*. Manchester: Equality and Human Rights Commission Research Report Series. Retrieved from https://www.equalityhumanrights.com/sites/default/files/research-report-102-causes-and-motivations-of-hate-crime.pdf

The Washington Post. *2015–2017 Police shooting data*. Retrieved from https://www.washingtonpost.com/graphics/national/police-shootings-2017

Zeki, Semir and Romaya, John Paul. (2008). Neural correlates of hate. *PLoS ONE* 3(10), e3556. Retrieved from https://doi.org/10.1371/journal.pone.0003556

Section 10: Resources

Unit 1: Summary

Hate is an intense, negative bias against a person, group, thing, or idea. When hate is put into action, the consequences affect not only the victims of the hateful actions or words, but also bystanders. National and international agreements are in place to fight against hate, but it is difficult to determine when a crime is motivated by hate. There are a variety of government and nongovernment organizations as well as individuals working on different aspects of hate. The media plays a role in the dissemination and interpretation of hate-motivated actions. Gary Becker's (1957) economic theory of taste discrimination can be used to analyze decision-making when hate is present.

Unit 2: Key concepts

Bias: A strong inclination or preconceived opinion toward or against a person, thing, idea, or feeling.

Bullying: Aggression behavior by one child or multiple children against another child (often in an education setting) or by adults in the workplace.

Customer discrimination: When a customer is prejudiced against an organization or an employee at the organization where the customer buys goods or services.

Cyberbullying: When the perpetrators use the internet to bully their victims, often because the internet allows the perpetrators to remain anonymous.

Demand curve (D): The relationship between the price of a market-produced product or service and the quantity of that product or service demanded by the customer.

Discrimination: The treatment of people, things, ideas, or feelings toward which the person is negatively biased.

Employee discrimination: When an employee must work with a person against whom he is prejudiced (Gary Becker, 1957).

Employer discrimination: When an employer is prejudiced against hiring a person based on some personal characteristic (Gary Becker, 1957).

Harassment: Discrimination in the form of distressing language or jokes or unwanted physical contact which creates a hostile environment for living and working.

Hate: According to *Merriam-Webster Collegiate Dictionary* (2004), hate is "intense hostility and aversion usually derived from fear, anger, or sense of injury."

Hate crime or bias-motivated crime: A traditional crime (such as murder, arson, or vandalism) that is usually violent and is motivated by bias due to specific characteristics of a person or group.

Hate speech: The use of spoken, written, or displayed language to incite violence or discrimination against a person or group due to specific characteristics.

Isocost (equal-cost) line: A producer's budget line showing the cost of hiring different quantities of two groups of workers.

Isoquant (equal-quantity) line: A curve showing a quantity of output that can be produced with varying amounts of labor input from the two groups.

Lurking variable (also called a **confounder**): A variable that affects the significance of the relationship between the explanatory and dependent variable.

Nepotism: The treatment of people things, ideas, or feelings toward which the person is favorably biased.

Supranational: Having authority that transcends the power of national governments.

Taste discrimination: Discrimination based on a person's preferences.

Unit 3: Review questions

1. How are hate, bias, and discrimination related to each other?

2. How can a person's perspective affect the way they view a situation?

3. What are the major U.S. laws associated with hate?

4. What are the major international agreements associated with hate?

5. Name some of the controversies related to hate.

6. Who are the experts who might help you in your research about hate?

7. What are the three types of taste discrimination discussed in Gary Becker's (1957) research?

8. How does discrimination affect the decision of an employer? An employee? A customer?

9. What are the four main decision-makers involved in the study of hate?

10. What are some of the costs of hate?

11. What are some of the possible benefits of hate?

12. How is a hate crime different than a regular crime?

Unit 4: Recommended readings

Gerstenfeld, Phyllis. (2013). *Hate crimes: Causes, controls, and controversies* (3rd ed.). Los Angeles: SAGE Publications Inc.

Jenness, Valerie and Broad, Kendal. (2007). *Hate crimes: New social movements and the politics of violence*. New Brunswick: Aldine Transaction.

Lewis, Clara. (1981). *Tough on hate? The cultural politics of hate crimes*. New Brunswick: Rutgers University Press.

McClintock, Michael and Sunderland, Judith. (2004). *Antisemitism in Europe: Challenging official indifference*. New York: Human Rights First.

Whillock, Rita Kirk and Slayden, David (Eds.). (1995). *Hate speech* (1st ed.). Los Angeles: SAGE Publications Inc.

Zeskind, Leonard. (2009). *Blood and politics: The history of the white nationalist movement from the margins to the mainstream*. New York: Farrar, Straus and Giroux.

Unit 5: Econometric analysis: Hate by the numbers

This section is provided in online textbook supplements. The eResources can be found at: www.routledge.com/9781138500167

Index